Classroom Assessment

Fourth Edition

Classroom Assessment

Concepts and Applications

Peter W. Airasian

Boston College

Boston   Burr Ridge, IL   Dubuque, IA   Madison, WI   New York   San Francisco   St. Louis
Bangkok   Bogotá   Caracas   Lisbon   London   Madrid
Mexico City   Milan   New Delhi   Seoul   Singapore   Sydney   Taipei   Toronto

McGraw-Hill Higher Education

A Division of The **McGraw-Hill** Companies

CLASSROOM ASSESSMENT: CONCEPTS AND APPLICATIONS
FOURTH EDITION

Published by McGraw-Hill, an imprint of The McGraw-Hill Companies, Inc., 1221 Avenue of the Americas, New York, NY 10020. Copyright © 2001, 1997, 1994, 1991 by The McGraw-Hill Companies, Inc. All rights reserved. No part of this publication may be reproduced or distributed in any form or by any means, or stored in a database or retrieval system, without the prior written consent of The McGraw-Hill Companies, Inc., including, but not limted to, in any network or other electronic storage or transmission, or broadcast for distance learning.

Some ancillaries, including electronic and print components, may not be available to customers outside the United States.

This book is printed on acid-free paper.

4 5 6 7 8 9 0 QPF/QPF 0 9 8 7 6 5 4 3

ISBN 0–07–232272–1

Vice president and editor-in-chief: *Thalia Dorwick*
Editorial director: *Jane E. Vaicunas*
Sponsoring editor: *Beth Kaufman*
Developmental editor: *Cara Harvey*
Marketing manager: *Daniel M. Loch*
Senior project manager: *Kay J. Brimeyer*
Production supervisor: *Kara Kudronowicz*
Coordinator of freelance design: *Michelle D. Whitaker*
Cover designer: *Annis Wai-Yi Leung*
Main cover image: *©John Henley/The Stock Market*
Cover background: *©PhotoDisc: Education, Volume 24*
Senior photo research coordinator: *Lori Hancock*
Photo research: *LouAnn K. Wilson*
Senior supplement coordinator: *David A. Welsh*
Compositor: *Shepherd, Inc.*
Typeface: *10/12 Palatino*
Printer: *Quebecor Printing Book Group/ Fairfield, PA*

Library of Congress Cataloging-in-Publication Data

Airasian Peter W.
    Classroom assessment : concepts and applications / Peter W. Airasian. — 4th ed.
        p.   cm.
    Includes bibliographical references and index.
    ISBN 0–07–232272–1 (acid-free paper)
    1. Educational tests and measurements—United States. 2. Academic achievement—United States—Testing. 3. Education—United States—Evaluation. I. Title.

LB3051 .A5627   2001
371.26'0973—dc21

                                                                        00–037994
                                                                            CIP

www.mhhe.com

About the Author

Peter W. Airasian is Professor of Education at Boston College in the Department of Educational Research, Measurement, and Evaluation. He received his AB degree in chemistry at Harvard College and his AM and Ph.D. degrees at the University of Chicago with a concentration in assessment and evaluation. He is a former high school chemistry and biology teacher. Currently, his main teaching responsibility is instructing pre- and in-service teachers in classroom assessment. He is the author or co-author of *School Effectiveness: An Assessment of the Evidence* (1980), *The Effects of Standardized Testing* (1982), *Teacher Self-Evaluation Tool Kit* (1997), *Assessment in the Classroom: A Concise Approach* (2000), and *Educational Research: Competencies for Analysis and Application* (2000). He is a past Chair of the American Educational Research Association's Special Interest Group on Classroom Assessment. Currently, with others, he is completing a revision of Bloom's Taxonomy of Educational Objectives and is participating in the development of Student Evaluation Standards.

Brief Contents

Contents

Preface

❈ A Conceptual and Applied Approach

Classroom Assessment: Concepts and Applications, fourth edition, is designed for students taking a first course in classroom assessment. Its special message is to show how assessment principles and applications encompass the full range of teacher decision making and assessment. The text is organized to follow the natural progression of teachers' decision making: from organizing the classroom as a social setting, to planning and conducting instruction, to the formal assessment of pupil learning, to grading students, and finally to interpreting standardized tests and statewide assessments. The goal is to show students that assessment is an ongoing part of teaching, not some esoteric activity that is divorced from the daily classroom routine.

The ability to construct and use classroom assessments is an essential educational skill for all teachers. Ongoing formal and informal classroom assessments provide teachers with the information they need to monitor and make decisions about their teaching and their student's learning. Increasingly, teachers must address not only their own traditional classroom assessments, but also those required by external sources of assessment such as statewide testing and standardized tests. This text covers the broad range of assessments that confront teachers in both their classrooms and beyond. Each type of assessment is presented with an emphasis on both concepts and application, so students will understand the reasons and cautions that are inherent in the assessments they construct and interpret.

❈ Proven Features and Content

This edition includes the features of prior editions such as

> *Realistic Assessment:* The focus throughout is on the realities of classrooms and how assessments can serve these realities.
>
> *Validity and Reliability:* These central assessment concepts are introduced in the first chapter and then linked in later chapters to each specific type of assessment information. The validity and reliability issues of informal assessment, planning and delivering instruction, grading, using paper-and-pencil tests, performance assessments, and standardized testing are identified. Practical strategies to improve validity and reliability of varied assessment approaches are presented in each chapter.

Practical Guidelines: A significant portion of each chapter focuses on practical guidelines to follow and common errors to avoid when using the type of assessment being presented. The implications of ignoring the recommendations are also described.

Teacher Thinking: Excerpts found throughout the text from teachers about assessment add the wisdom of day-to-day practice to assessment situations.

Student-Friendly Writing Style: The text is written with a clear, friendly, and accessible style and is well integrated with examples and tables to thoroughly engage students.

✵ New to This Edition

In addition to retaining the focus of the prior editions, the Fourth Edition contains new or expanded coverage of the following topics.

State Standards: An expanded and more thorough discussion of statewide standards and assessments with additional examples of standards, benchmarks, and strategies of teaching to standards is provided.

Objectives: Chapters 3 and 4 now provide a more focused explanation of stating objectives that combine both cognitive processes (Bloom's Taxonomy) and different types of knowledge (factual, conceptual, and procedural) to strengthen the alignment of objectives and appropriate instruction approaches as well as the alignment of instructional approaches and appropriate assessments.

Inclusion: This edition provides extended coverage of disabilities and accommodations during instruction and assessment, with a focus on both legal aspects of dealing with disabilities and accommodations for particular disabilities.

Aligning Objectives, Instruction and Assessment: The text provides an introduction of three cognitive processes and three related knowledge types (remembering factual knowledge, understanding conceptual knowledge, and applying procedural knowledge) for developing close alignment among objectives and instruction, instruction and assessment, and objectives and assessment.

Performance Assessment: The text has been expanded to include two chapters on performance assessment, one titled *Performance Assessment* and the other *Applications of Performance Assessment* (new chapter!) with a focus on the initial planning, constructing, applying, using, and scoring rubrics and portfolios.

Student Cheating: New coverage has been added on issues of cheating, with information about pupil cheating, types of cheating, varied strategies to prevent cheating, and an example of a school cheating policy.

Websites: A new appendix includes a list of thirty Websites related to educational and classroom assessment providing and describing all facets of classroom assessment.

✄ Acknowledgments

With appreciation for their efforts to improve this work, I acknowledge the following reviewers whose frank and detailed suggestions added much to this revision:

> Christopher Atang, *Texas Southern University*
> Ruth Duncan, *St. Leo College*
> Bruce Frey, *University of Kansas*
> John P. Gustafson, *Winona State University*
> Dwight Haun, *Southwest Baptist University*
> Nancy J. Kline, *Saint Francis College*
> Margaret M. Shuff, *Rowan University*

I dedicate this book to Gwen, Lynn, and Greg, who are the inspiration for all my endeavors. Their support is greatly appreciated.

Beth Kaufman and Cara Harvey at McGraw-Hill were exceptionally helpful and supportive in the preparation of this revision. Their many contributions and suggestions are acknowledged. Kay Brimeyer ably guided the manuscript through production.

A great deal of gratitude is owed to Lisa Abrams, my graduate assistant, for all her help providing both conceptual and clerical contributions to the revision. Her efforts have materially improved this revision. Finally, I acknowledge and remember Benjamin Bloom whose guidance and perspective continues to influence my thought and work. His legacy has touched innumerable teachers and researchers for the betterment of education.

Peter W. Airasian
Boston College

The Classroom as an Assessment Environment

Chapter Outline

❖ Purposes of Assessment

❖ Some Definitions: Assessment, Test, Measurement, and Evaluation

❖ Methods of Collecting Assessment Information

❖ Standardized and Nonstandardized Assessments

❖ Individual and Group Assessment

❖ Characteristics of Good Assessment: Validity and Reliability

❖ Ethical Issues and Responsibilities

Chapter Objectives

After reading this chapter, the pupil will be able to:

- Define basic terms: assessment, test, measurement, standardized, validity, reliability, etc.
- Explain the varied purposes of teachers' classroom assessments
- Compare and contrast the three main types of assessment and give examples of each
- Describe common methods of collecting assessment information
- Explain what validity and reliability are and how they influence assessment decisions
- State examples of teachers' ethical responsibilities in collecting and using assessment information

Classrooms are busy places. Every day in every classroom, teachers make decisions about their pupils, the success of their instruction, and the classroom climate. Today was a typical day in Ms. Lopez's classroom. In addition to meeting the school buses in the morning, readying the room for the day's activities, putting the work schedule on the blackboard, reviewing her lesson plans, greeting pupils as they entered the classroom, taking attendance, distributing supplies, reminding pupils of next Saturday's school fair, and monitoring the lunch room, Ms. Lopez also performed the following tasks.

- Assigned grades to her pupils' science tests on the planets
- Referred Aaron to the Special Education Department to be screened for poor gross motor skills
- Completed the monthly school progress report on each pupil in the class
- Moved Tamika from the middle to the high reading group
- Selected Rosa, not Sarah, to deliver a note to Mr. Brown, the school principal
- Decided on topics to cover in next Monday's math lesson
- Met with the special education teacher to review the accommodations Mauricio needed when taking a multiple-choice test
- Stopped the planned language lesson halfway through the period in order to review the previous day's lesson
- Placed pupils who were below the accepted cut-off scores on the statewide basic-skill test in a special remedial group
- Rearranged the class seating plan to separate Jamar and Ramon and to move Claudia to the front of the room so she could see the blackboard better
- Called on Kim twice even though her hand was not raised
- Studied the statewide writing standards to determine what topics to emphasize in instruction
- Switched social studies instruction from discussion to seatwork when the class became bored and unruly
- Previewed and selected a filmstrip on astronomy for next week's science unit

- Encouraged Raul to redraft his English composition to correct spelling and grammar errors
- Decided to construct her own test for the social studies unit rather than using the textbook test
- Sent Antonio to the school nurse when he complained of a headache
- Selected pupils to work together on a cooperative learning exercise in math
- Decided to allow her pupils two more days to complete their poetry portfolios
- Judged that Tabitha's constant interruptions and speaking out in class warranted a note to her parents about the problem
- Assigned homework in science and social studies, but not in math and language
- Checked with the school counselor regarding possible reasons for Joshua's increasingly inattentive class behavior
- Took part in a special education conference to determine whether Maria's Individual Education Plan needed to be altered
- Paired Kim, a class isolate, with Aretha, a class leader, for the project in social studies
- Sent Ralph to the principal because he swore at a teacher and threatened a classmate
- Held a parent-teacher conference with Ivan's parents in which she told them that he was a capable student who could produce better work than he had thus far
- Consulted last year's standardized test scores to determine whether the class needed a review of the basic rules of capitalization

Ms. Lopez's day in the classroom, like those of all teachers, was filled with situations in which she had to make decisions. Some of these decisions concerned individual pupils and some concerned the class as a whole. Some were about instructional matters, some about classroom climate, some about pupil personalities, and some about pupil learning. Some, like the decisions to change Tamika's reading group and to refer Aaron for screening, were infrequently made decisions. Others, like planning topics for instruction, calling on pupils during class, and assigning grades to pupils, were made many times each day.

All of Ms. Lopez's actions resulted from decisions she made, and all her decisions were based upon some type of evidence. Teachers continually observe, monitor, and review pupil performances to obtain evidence for decision making. Teacher decisions are the lifeblood on which classrooms function. Evidence gathering and decision making are necessary and ongoing aspects of teachers' lives in classrooms. Taken together, these decisions serve to establish, organize, and monitor classroom qualities such as pupil learning, interpersonal relations, social adjustment, instructional content, and classroom climate (Clark and Peterson, 1986; Biddle, Good, and Goodson, 1996).

Classroom decisions should be reflective and thoughtful, not impulsive and erratic. The decisions Ms. Lopez made were based upon many different kinds of evidence that she collected. How did Ms. Lopez know that the way to settle down her bored and unruly social studies class was to switch from discussion to seatwork, when there were many other things she might have done to settle the class? What made her decide to move Tamika to the high reading group? Why did she think pairing Kim with Aretha for the social studies project was better than pairing Kim with Claudia, Rosa, or Joshua? Why did she feel that spending two extra days working on the poetry portfolio would be more useful than using the time to introduce some other topic? Why was Rosa, but not Sarah, trusted to deliver a note to Principal Brown? All of these choices were based upon information that helped Ms. Lopez choose a course of action when confronted by the need to make a decision. Think of all the possible sources of evidence Ms. Lopez might have used to help her make these decisions. Notice also that many of the decisions she made were fast paced, practically oriented, and focused on both instructional and social factors. Others involved more thoughtful, lengthy consideration. This book is about the process teachers use to properly gather, evaluate, and use information in classroom decision making.

✖ Purposes of Assessment

Teachers assess for many purposes because they are required to make many different kinds of decisions. The overriding purpose of all assessment is to gather information to facilitate effective decision making. If we review Ms. Lopez's decisions during her classroom day, we can get a sense of the many purposes teachers have for assessment.

Establishing Classroom Equilibrium

An often overlooked purpose of assessment is to establish and maintain the social equilibrium of the classroom. Classrooms are complex social settings in which people interact with one another in a multitude of ways. For classrooms to be positive social and learning environments, order, discipline, and cooperation must be present. Thus, helping pupils to learn well and maintaining order in the classroom are closely related; orderliness is needed if teaching and learning are to be successful. When Ms. Lopez selected Rosa instead of Sarah to deliver a note to Principal Brown, and when she changed the class seating plan to move Jamar and Ramon farther apart, she was making decisions to preserve classroom order and stability. The fact that she allowed Antonio to go alone to the school nurse indicated her trust in him. On the other hand, Tabitha's constant interruptions and speaking out necessitated sending a note to her parents, and Ralph's swearing and fighting led to his being removed from the classroom. Ms. Lopez's efforts to make Kim a part of the classroom society by calling on her even though her hand was not raised was another attempt to create and maintain a viable social and learning environment.

Planning and Conducting Instruction

Many of the decisions Ms. Lopez made focused on planning and conducting classroom instruction. This should not be surprising, since instruction activities are central to the workings of the classroom. The instructional decisions that Ms. Lopez made can be divided into two types: planning decisions and teaching decisions. When Ms. Lopez selected the topics to be included in next Monday's math lesson, previewed and selected the astronomy filmstrip for next week's science unit, decided to spend two extra days on the poetry portfolios, met with the special education teacher to review Mauricio's testing accommodations, selected topics to teach related to the statewide writing standards, and assigned homework in one subject but not another, she was planning future instructional activities. In addition to planning decisions, the actual process of teaching a class also requires constant assessment and decision making. At two points during the day, Ms. Lopez altered her lesson because her pupils were confused and unruly. Once she stopped her language lesson to review the prior day's lesson because pupil responses to her questions indicated that the class did not understand the content of yesterday's language lesson. Another time she switched her method of instruction from discussion to seatwork when the students became silly and lost focus. A great deal of teacher assessment is conducted for the purpose of planning and delivering instruction.

Placing Pupils

Most classroom teachers must make decisions about the placements of their pupils. Whenever a teacher divides pupils into reading or math groups; organizes pupils into cooperative learning groups; pairs or groups pupils for class projects; or recommends that a particular pupil be placed with a particular teacher next year, assessments for placement purposes have taken place. Ms. Lopez made a placement decision when she moved Tamika from the middle reading group to the high reading group. She made another placement decision when she identified pupils who were below the cut-off score on the statewide basic skills test and placed them into a remedial group. Her selection of pupils to work together in a math cooperative learning group was a placement decision. Finally, when she paired Kim, the class isolate, with Aretha for the social studies project she made another placement decision. Note that Ms. Lopez's placement decisions were made for both academic and social reasons.

Providing Feedback and Incentives

Another important reason for classroom assessment is to provide feedback and incentives to pupils. For example, Ms. Lopez used assessment information from Raul's first-draft book report to suggest improvements. She held a parent-teacher conference with Ivan's parents to provide them information about his progress. In both of these cases, information about academic performance was used to provide feedback to pupils or parents about performance. The term used to describe feedback intended to alter and improve students' learning while instruction is taking place is **formative assessment.** In order to provide such feedback, teachers must constantly assess student learning and behavior.

Diagnosing Pupil Problems

Teachers are always on the lookout for pupils who are having learning, emotional, or social problems in the classroom. Having identified such problems, the teacher can sometimes carry out the remedial activities needed, but at other times the pupil must be referred for more specialized diagnosis and remediation outside of the classroom. Thus, Ms. Lopez set up her own in-class group for basic skill remediation, but she recommended that a specialist screen Aaron for his apparent gross motor skill deficiency. She reviewed last year's standardized test performance to determine whether her pupils had a special need for remedial work in capitalization, but she also checked with the school counselor about possible reasons for Joshua's inattentive behavior. Referring Aaron to the Special Education Department for screening was another diagnostic decision. Much of the assessment data teachers gather is used to identify, understand, and remediate pupils' problems and learning difficulties.

Judging and Grading Academic Learning and Progress

A number of Ms. Lopez's decisions involved judging pupils' academic learning and progress. She assigned grades to her pupils' science tests, completed a monthly progress report on each pupil, decided to construct her own test for the social studies unit rather than use the test provided in her textbook, and determined whether Maria's Individual Education Plan was still appropriate for her. Much of a teacher's time is spent collecting information that will be used to grade pupils or make final judgments about their academic progress. The task of grading or making final judgments about students' learning at the end of instruction is termed **summative assessment.**

All of Ms. Lopez's decisions and all of the purposes of assessment just described can be grouped into three general types or areas of assessment. Table 1.1 compares these three assessment types. A first kind of assessment is used by teachers early in the school year to learn about their pupils' social, academic, and behavioral characteristics and needs in order to foster and enhance instruction, communication, and cooperation in the classroom. These assessments, called **sizing-up assessments,** allow teachers to set up and maintain an effective classroom society. Other assessments are used to plan and deliver instruction, and include decisions about what will be taught, how and when it will be taught, what materials will be used, how a lesson is progressing, and what changes in planned activities must be made. These assessments are **instructional assessments.** Many classroom decisions help teachers carry out their official responsibilities as members of the school bureaucracy. Tasks such as grading, grouping, assessing progress, interpreting

TABLE 1.1

Comparison of Three Types of Classroom Assessments

	Sizing-Up	Instructional	Official
Purpose	Provide teacher with a quick perception and practical knowledge of pupils' characteristics	Plan instructional activities and monitor the progress of instruction	Carry out the bureaucratic aspects of teaching, such as grading, grouping, and placing
Timing	During the first week or two of school	Daily throughout the school year	Periodically during the school year
Evidence-gathering method	Largely informal observation	Formal observation and pupil papers for planning; informal observation for monitoring	Formal tests, papers, reports, quizzes, and pupil papers and assignments
Type of evidence gathered	Cognitive, affective, and psychomotor	Largely cognitive and affective	Mainly cognitive
Record keeping	Information kept in teacher's mind; few written records	Written lesson plans; monitoring information not written down	Formal records kept in teacher's mark book or school files

test results, conferencing with parents, identifying pupils for special needs placement, and making promotion recommendations are all part of the official responsibilities a teacher assumes as an employee of a school system. These assessments are **official assessments.** Succeeding chapters will describe these three general types of assessment in greater detail.

Although the focus in this text is on teachers' classroom assessments, there are other groups who take great interest in pupil assessments. National and state policy makers, school administrators, and parents and pupils, in addition to teachers, have many uses for assessments. Table 1.2 shows the broad audience and uses of classroom assessments for varied groups.

Appendix A presents the *Standards for Teacher Competence in Educational Assessment of Students* that were developed jointly by the American Federation of Teachers, the National Council on Measurement in Education, and the National Education Association. These standards provide a

---

TABLE 1.2

Varied Perspectives and Uses of Classroom Assessments

National and state policy makers
- Setting state and national standards
- Developing policies based on assessment
- Tracking the progress of national and state achievements
- Providing resources to improve learning
- Providing rewards or sanctions for pupil, school, and state achievements

School administrators
- Identifying program strengths and weaknesses
- Using assessment to plan and improve instruction
- Identifying instructional needs and programs
- Monitoring pupil achievements over time

Teachers
- Monitoring pupil progress
- Judging and altering classroom curriculum
- Identifying pupils with special needs
- Motivating pupils to do well
- Placing pupils in groups
- Providing feedback to teachers and pupils

Parents
- Judging pupil strengths and weaknesses
- Monitoring pupil progress
- Meeting with teachers to discuss pupils' classroom performance

---

description of the many uses of assessment in the classroom, the variety of methods teachers use to gather information, and the competencies teachers should possess to carry out fair and meaningful classroom assessments. Review these standards and consider what qualities make up good teacher classroom assessments.

✳ Some Definitions: Assessment, Test, Measurement, and Evaluation

The process of collecting, synthesizing, and interpreting information to aid in decision making is called **assessment.** Assessment involves much more than administering, scoring and grading paper-and-pencil tests, as the preceding list of Ms. Lopez's decisions makes clear. Assessment, in its true and richest meaning, includes the full range of information teachers gather in their classrooms: information that helps them understand their pupils, monitor instruction, and establish a viable classroom culture. It also includes the variety of ways teachers gather, synthesize, and interpret that information.

There are differences between assessments, tests, measurements, and evaluations. Assessment is a general term that includes *all* the ways that teachers gather information in their classrooms. Common assessment approaches include tests, observations, interviews, oral questions, portfolios, and projects, among others. A **test** is a formal, systematic, usually paper-and-pencil procedure used to gather information about pupils' behavior. Test results are used to make generalizations about how pupils would have performed on similar but untested behaviors. Tests are only one of many types of assessments.

Measurement is the process of quantifying or assigning a number to pupil performance. The most common example of measurement in the classroom occurs when a teacher scores a quiz or test. Scoring produces a numerical description of performance: Conner got 17 out of 20 items correct on the science test; Tito got a score of 65 percent on his math test; Rhonda's score on the biology test was 49 items correct; Izumi scored 755 on the SAT verbal. In measurement, a numerical score is used to represent the individual's performance.

Once assessment information is collected, it is used to make decisions about pupils, instruction, or classroom climate. **Evaluation** involves judging the quality of a pupil's performance or determining a possible course of action. When assessment information has been synthesized and thought about, the teacher is in a position to make a judgment about the quality of a pupil's performance or the best classroom course of action. Evaluations describe the merit, worth, goodness, or desirability of pupil performance.

Consider a teacher who wishes to assess the mathematics readiness of a transfer pupil in order to decide where to start instruction for that pupil and what instructional methods are likely to be most effective. Notice that the decision to be made guides the assessment information to be collected. To help make the decision, the teacher collected information about the pupil's performance. He gave a paper-and-pencil test of mathematics readiness. The score on the test, 25 percent of the items correct, provided a measurement of the pupil's math readiness. Of course, the teacher used other forms of assessment to determine the pupil's readiness. He talked to the pupil about how he felt about math, watched him perform math exercises, and checked his prior math performance and test scores in his school record file. The teacher then reflected on all the assessment information collected. He evaluated, or made judgments about, the quality of different strategies for providing helpful instruction tailored to the pupil's current math readiness. His final decisions, based on his evaluation, were to recommend a tutor for the pupil to help him catch up to the rest of the class and to begin the tutoring based on the pupil's performance on the readiness test. Box 1.1 summarizes the definitions of *assessment, test, measurement,* and *evaluation*.

It is important to note that assessment carried out by classroom teachers is not the only type of assessment that goes on in classrooms. Just as teachers constantly assess their pupils, instruction, and classroom climate, pupils constantly assess their teacher, instruction, and classroom climate. Just as teachers want to know whether pupils are motivated, hardworking,

---

Box 1.1   Definitions of Common Assessment-Related Terms

Assessment: The collection, synthesis, and interpretation of information to aid the teacher in decision making.

Test: A formal, systematic, usually paper-and-pencil procedure for gathering information.

Measurement: The process of quantifying or assigning a number to performance.

Evaluation: The process of making judgments about the quality or goodness of a performance or a course of action.

---

academically able, and adjusted to the culture of the classroom, pupils want to know if the teacher is fair, gives hard tests, enforces rigid discipline, can be swayed by a "sob story," and likes them as individuals. Pupils have their own ways of gathering information to help them make decisions about their teachers. Many of these methods are similar to the ways teachers gather information about pupils. What do you want to know about your teachers and how do you try to gather assessment information to find out?

Even teacher-pupil and pupil-teacher assessments do not fully exhaust the assessment activities that characterize life in classrooms. Pupils also are constantly assessing each other. The classroom is a public place and it does not take long for most pupils to learn where they stand in the teacher's pecking order in the academic, athletic, social, and other hierarchies established by their peers (Jackson, 1990). Assessment that focuses upon a pupil's personal qualities is as likely to come from classmates as from anyone else, and classroom friendships, cliques, and popularity are based heavily upon these assessments. While these pupil-teacher and pupil-pupil assessments are interesting and extremely important in their own right, they are beyond the scope of this text. It is useful, however, to bear in mind the pervasiveness of classroom assessments and their consequences for both pupils and teachers. The following sections describe the many dimensions of classroom assessments and their associated vocabulary.

❧ Methods of Collecting Assessment Information

Teachers use three primary methods to gather their assessment information: paper-and-pencil methods, observation, and oral questioning. Teachers rely heavily upon each technique to help them obtain the assessment information they need to make classroom decisions.

Paper-and-Pencil Methods

Paper-and-pencil methods refer to assessments in which pupils write their responses to questions or problems. When pupils take a multiple-choice test, complete a written homework assignment, turn in a written report, draw a picture, write an essay, or fill in a worksheet, they are providing paper-and-pencil evidence to the teacher. Paper-and-pencil assessments are of two general types: selection and supply. Multiple-choice, true-false, and matching items are called **selection** or selected response items because, as the name implies, the pupil responds to each question by selecting an answer from the choices provided. **Supply,** or constructed response items, require the pupil to construct or produce a response to a question or task. The length of the response can vary substantially. For example, an essay question usually requires pupils to construct a lengthy, detailed response, while a short-answer or "fill-in-the-blank" question may require only a word, phrase, or sentence. Complex supply productions and constructions such as book reports, math journal, portfolios, science experiments, class projects, and other similar assessments are supply items that are commonly termed *performance assessments.* Notice that a selection-type item provides the maximum degree of control for the question writer, since he or she specifies both the question and the answer choices. A supply-type item provides the question writer with control only over the question itself, since the responsibility for constructing a response resides with the pupil.

Observation Methods

Observation, often called "kid watching," is the second major method teachers use to collect assessment data about pupils, instruction, and learning. As the term suggests, observation involves watching or listening to pupils carry out some activity (observation of process) or judging a product a pupil has produced (observation of product). When pupils mispronounce words in oral reading, consistently give clear and detailed responses, interact well in groups, speak out in class, fight with other pupils, demonstrate excellent concentration, have puzzled looks on their faces, patiently wait their turn, fall asleep in class, or fail to sit still for more than 5 minutes, teachers become aware of these behaviors through observation. Teachers see many pupil behaviors. When pupils submit a science fair project, produce a still-life drawing, set up laboratory equipment, or complete a project in shop class, the teacher also observes and judges the products pupils have produced.

Thus, Ms. Lopez observed that Claudia often squinted when she was writing on the blackboard and decided to move her to the front of the room so she could see the blackboard better. She noticed Antonio with his head on his desk and a grimace on his face and sent him to the school nurse for examination. During the language lesson she saw blank looks on her pupils' faces and got no raised hands when she asked questions, so she stopped to review the lesson from the previous day. Ms. Lopez observed Ralph swearing at another teacher and fighting with a classmate, actions that earned him a trip to the principal's office. These examples show the range of teacher observations and how observations produce information that leads to classroom decisions.

In most classrooms, the teacher's desk faces the pupils' desks, and during instruction, the teacher faces the pupils. The fact that teachers and their pupils are located in a confined space, facing and interacting with one another from 1 to 6 hours per day, means that teachers cannot help but observe a great deal about their pupils.

Some teacher observations are formal and planned in advance, as when teachers assess pupils reading aloud in reading group or presenting an oral report to the class. In such situations, the teacher wants to observe a particular set of pupil behaviors. For example, in reading aloud the teacher might be watching and listening for clear pronunciation of words, changing voice tone to emphasize important points, periodically looking up from the book while reading, and so forth. Because such observations are planned in advance, the teacher has time to prepare the pupils and to identify the particular behaviors that will be observed.

Other teacher observations are unplanned and informal, as when the teacher sees Jamar and Ramon talking when they should be working, notices the pained expression on a pupil's face when a classmate makes fun of his clothes, or observes the pupils' fidgeting and looking out the window during a science lesson. Such spontaneous observations, based on what is often called "kid watching," reflect momentary unplanned happenings that the teacher observes, mentally records, and interprets. Both formal and informal teacher observations are important information gathering techniques in classrooms (McKinley, 1999).

Oral Questioning Methods

Asking oral questions is the third major method teachers use to collect assessment data. Teachers are forever asking questions such as: Why do you think the author ended her story that way? Explain to me in your own words what an improper fraction is. Did you call Ron a nasty name at recess? Raise your hand if you can tell me why this answer is incorrect. Who can summarize yesterday's discussion about the water cycle? Why do you not have your homework today? These questions are used to assess pupils during a lesson. Questioning students is very useful and important during instruction. It can be used to review a previously taught topic, brainstorm a new topic, find out how well the lesson is being understood by pupils, and get the attention of a student who is not paying attention. The teacher can gather the information he or she wants in the course of instruction, without the intrusiveness of administering a paper-and-pencil assessment. Oral questioning is a common feature of all classrooms, and, after lecture, it is the most used instructional activity. Formal oral examinations are used in subject areas such as foreign language, speech, and singing.

Selection, supply, observation, and questioning techniques complement each other in the classroom. Imagine classroom decision making without being able to observe pupils' appearances, reactions, performance, answers to questions, and interactions. Now imagine what it would be like if no paper-and-pencil information could be obtained in classrooms. Finally, imagine what it would be like if teachers could not ask oral questions of their students. Each type of information is needed to carry out the rich and meaningful assessments that occur in classrooms. As a result, teacher mastery of all of these evidence-gathering approaches is important.

In addition to these three primary methods of collecting assessment information, supplementary information can also be obtained from the pupils' prior teachers, school records, the school nurse, and parents. Teachers routinely consult previous teachers to corroborate their own perceptions or reinforce their decisions. Parents frequently volunteer information and respond to teacher queries about their children. While useful, these supplementary sources of information have their limitations and should be treated with caution when making decisions.

⚔ Standardized and Nonstandardized Assessments

The information teachers collect and use in their classrooms comes from assessment procedures that are either standardized or nonstandardized.

Standardized Assessments

Standardized assessment procedures are those that are intended to be administered, scored and interpreted in the same way for all test takers, regardless of where or when they are assessed. Standardized assessments are given to different pupils in different places, but always under identical conditions of administration, scoring, and interpretation. The main reason for standardizing assessment procedures is so that pupils' scores can be compared across schools and states without the conditions of administration, scoring and interpretation distorting the comparisons. The Scholastic Assessment Test (SAT) and the American College Testing Program Test (ACT) are examples of standardized tests, as are nationally administered achievement tests such as the Iowa Tests of Basic Skills, California Achievement Test, Metropolitan Achievement Test, and Comprehensive Tests of Basic Skills. So, too, are the many statewide assessment programs that have sprouted up in recent years. Classroom teachers virtually never construct standardized tests.

Remember that Saturday morning in early December when you took your SAT or ACT? Regardless of whether you were taking the SAT or ACT in a school cafeteria in Sacramento, California, an auditorium in Abilene, Texas, or a classroom in Albany, New York, you were administered the same test, under the same conditions, with the same directions, in the same amount of time as all other students who were taking the test at that time. ("Good morning. Today you will take the Scholastic Assessment Test/ American College Test. Do not open your booklet until I tell you to do so.") Moreover, the results of the test were scored and interpreted the same way for all test takers. These are characteristics of standardized assessments. When Ms. Lopez recommended remedial work for pupils below the cut-off score on the state-mandated basic skills test and consulted the previous year's test scores to determine if the class needed a review of capitalization rules, she was examining information from standardized assessment instruments.

Nonstandardized Assessments

Few teacher-made assessments are standardized. Most are constructed specifically for classroom use and are focused on assessment of the particular instruction provided in that classroom. The information from the nonstandardized assessment is used to provide feedback about the performance of pupils in a single class, not of pupils in other classes. Essentially, teacher-made **nonstandardized** assessment procedures are intended for one-time use with a single group of pupils at a single point in time. Thus, they do not need to be standardized.

When Ms. Lopez assigned grades to her pupils based upon her science test on the planets and decided to construct her own test for the social studies unit, she was relying upon assessment information that was nonstandardized. Many of Ms. Lopez's unplanned observations of her students' behaviors also were nonstandardized assessments. These fleeting, infrequently occurring, unpredictable, seldom repeated classroom observations represent rich and important, though nonstandardized, forms of assessment data. Teachers use these idiosyncratic observations to make decisions about individual pupils and the class as a group.

It is important to note that standardized assessments are not necessarily better than nonstandardized ones. Standardization is only important when one desires to make comparisons among pupils in many different classrooms and locations. If comparison beyond a single classroom is not desired, a standardized assessment procedure is not needed. Standardization has to do with the type of comparison one wishes to make—either within or beyond a single classroom—and the rigidity of administrative conditions that flow from the desired comparison. The quality of most classroom assessments depends more heavily on characteristics such as the clarity of the teacher's questions and their relation to the instruction in that classroom.

❈ Individual and Group Assessment

Assessment procedures can be administered to one person at a time or to a group of pupils simultaneously. The former is called an **individually administered** assessment and the latter is called a **group administered** assessment.

Individually Administered Assessments

Individually administered assessments are collected either under formal conditions or from teacher observation and interaction with a single pupil. Standardized tests like the Stanford-Binet Intelligence Scale (Terman, 1973) or the Wechsler Intelligence Scale for Children (Wechsler, 1974) (WISC), two commonly used school ability tests, are given under controlled conditions to one pupil at a time. As with most individually administered assessments, they are given orally and require that the examiner pay constant attention to the pupil being assessed, since how the pupil interacts with and responds to the examiner provides information that is just as important as the particular score the pupil attains.

One major advantage of individually administered assessments is that a one-on-one assessment provides many opportunities for clinical observation of a pupil. For example, the administrator can observe the pupil's attention span, listening ability, speech, frustration level, and problem-solving strategies, as well as the accuracy of the specific answer the pupil provides. The administrator also has the chance to follow up on a pupil's response in order to clarify or comprehend it more completely. Most standardized, individually administered assessments require that the administrator have a great deal of training and experience, usually beyond what most teachers have. Some individually administered instruments, including the Stanford-Binet and the WISC, can only be given by persons who have been trained and certified to give the test.

It is also clear that teachers focus on, interact with, and assess their pupils individually. When Ms. Lopez moved Tamika to the high reading group, she did so on the basis of assessment evidence she had gathered about Tamika's reading performance. When Ms. Lopez selected Rosa, not Sarah, to deliver a note, she did so because her individual assessment of Rosa's personal qualities indicated that she was a responsible pupil who could be relied upon to carry out a nonsupervised task. Informal observation of her individual pupils helped Ms. Lopez determine which pupils would work well together in cooperative learning activities. When Ms. Lopez sat down with Ivan's parents at a parent-teacher conference, much of the information she conveyed was based upon her assessment of Ivan as an individual. Assigning grades to pupils is also an individualized assessment procedure.

Group Administered Assessments

Group assessments, whether standardized or not, are more efficient to administer than individually administered ones because in the amount of time needed to gather information from a single student, group assessments can gather information from a whole class. However, the cost of this efficiency is the loss of rapport, insight, and clinical knowledge about each examinee that can be obtained from individually administered assessments. Virtually all group administered assessments involve paper-and-pencil tests that permit many pupils to work simultaneously on a task. When the task to be assessed involves procedures such as oral reading, giving a speech, assembling equipment, or reciting a poem, group administered procedures can rarely be used.

Informal group assessment occurs often in the classroom, primarily through teacher observation. Thus, when Ms. Lopez watched the class become silly and unruly during the social studies lesson, she was performing group assessment. Similarly, when her pupils had difficulty answering her questions during the language lesson, she stopped what she was doing to review the previous day's lesson. This is another example of informal group-based assessment.

In summary, assessments vary according to their purpose, method of data collection, degree of standardization, and type of administration. We can use these characteristics to describe the different kinds of assessments. For example, a test such as the SAT or the ACT can be described as a standardized, group administered, paper-and-pencil assessment. An assessment intended to determine how well a student can shoot free throws, use a hand saw, or assemble laboratory apparatus can be described as a standardized, individually administered, performance assessment. Most teacher-constructed classroom tests are nonstandardized, group administered, paper-and-pencil assessments. Finally, teacher's judgments about a pupil's ability to get along with his or her classmates in social situations would likely be based upon nonstandardized, individual, performance assessments.

⚔ Characteristics of Good Assessment: Validity and Reliability

Assessment is the process of gathering, interpreting, and synthesizing information to aid decision making in the classroom. Whether assessment information helps teachers to make *good* decisions depends upon whether the assessment information collected is itself good. We begin our examination into the characteristics of good assessment information with an example.

Mr. Ferris has just finished a 3-week math unit on computing long division problems with remainders. During the unit he taught his pupils the computational steps involved in doing long division problems and the concept of a remainder. He gave and reviewed both homework problems and examples from the text, and administered a few quizzes. Now, at the end of the unit, Mr. Ferris wants to gather assessment information to find out whether his pupils have learned to do computational problems involving long division with remainders. He wants to gather this information to help him make a decision about how well his pupils have learned from his instruction so that he can assign a grade to each pupil for the unit.

To gather the information, Mr. Ferris decided to give a test containing items similar in content, format, and difficulty to those he taught throughout the unit. From the millions of possible long division with remainder items, Mr. Ferris selected ten that were representative of his teaching. Note that if he had picked ten items that covered different content or were much harder, easier, or presented in a different format than what he had taught in class, the results of the test would *not* have provided good decision-making information. To assess how well his students learned from his instruction, his test items must be similar to the content, format, and difficulty of his instruction.

Mr. Ferris recognized this potential pitfall and avoided it by writing ten items with content, difficulty, and format similar to the items taught and practiced in his classroom. He assembled the items into a test, administered the test during one class period, and scored the tests on a scale of 0 to 100. Mr. Ferris then had the assessment information he needed to make a decision about each pupil's grade.

Manuela and Chad each scored 100 on the test and received A's for the unit. Stuart scored 30 and received a D. The grades were based upon Mr. Ferris's evaluation of the quality of their performance on the ten-item test. If one were to ask Mr. Ferris to interpret what Manuela's and Chad's A grades meant, he would likely say, "Manuela and Chad can do long division with remainder items very well." He would also likely say that Stuart's D is "indicative of the fact that he cannot do such items well."

In making these statements, Mr. Ferris illustrates the relationship between assessment data and resulting teacher decisions. Consider carefully how Mr. Ferris described the performance of Manuela, Chad, and Stuart. He said Manuela and Chad "can do long division with remainder items very well." He did *not* say "Manuela and Chad can do the ten items I included on my test very well." He judged and described their performance in general terms rather than in terms of his specific ten-item test. Similarly, Stuart was judged in general rather than test-specific terms.

The logic that Mr. Ferris and all teachers use in making such judgments is that if a pupil can do well on the test items or performances that are actually assessed, the pupil is likely to do well on similar items and performances that were not assessed. If pupils do poorly on the ten test items, it is likely that they also would do poorly on similar, unasked items. Hence, when asked to describe the performance of Manuela and Chad, he indicated that they do very well on long division with remainder problems in general.

Mr. Ferris's ten-item test illustrates a characteristic that is common to virtually all classroom assessments, regardless of whether they are formal or informal, paper-and-pencil, observational or oral, standardized or nonstandardized. The essence of classroom assessment is to look at a *sample* of a pupil's performance or behavior and use that sample to make a generalization or prediction about the pupil's performance on similar, unobserved tasks or behaviors. Mr. Ferris used performance on ten test items to make a generalization about his pupils' likely performance on the millions of similar items that could have been, but were not, included on his test.

Note that this process is not confined solely to assessments of pupils' learning. Teachers often form lasting impressions of their pupils' and classes' personalities, motivation, interests, or self-esteem from a few brief observations made in the first week or two of school. They observe a small sample of the pupils' or classes' behavior and on the basis of this sample make general judgments such as "he is unmotivated," "she is a troublemaker," and "they are hard workers." These are informal generalizations about pupils that teachers routinely make based on only a small sample of the pupils' school behavior.

What if the behavior sample the teacher collects is irrelevant or incomplete? What if the items on Mr. Ferris's test did not reflect his classroom instruction? What if the pupil had an "off day" or the teacher's impatience to finish the test before the bell rang did not permit a pupil to complete the problems and show the pupil's "true" performance? If these things happen, then the decision made about the pupil is likely to be wrong and probably unfair.

Validity

The single most important characteristic of good assessment is its ability to help the teacher make a correct decision. This characteristic is called **validity** and is the key to obtaining high-quality and meaningful assessment decisions. Without validity, assessment data will not lead to correct decisions. When a teacher asks, as all teachers should, "Am I collecting the right kind of information for the decision I want to make?" she is asking about the validity of her assessments (Moss, 1995; Whittington, 1999). For a given classroom decision, some types of evidence are more valid than others. For example, it was more valid for Mr. Ferris to determine his pupils' achievement by giving a test that contained items similar to those he had been teaching than it would have been for him to give items that were much more difficult than those taught or to ask his pupils to write an essay about their feelings toward math instead of taking a test. Similarly, it is more valid to determine pupils' motivation or ability by observing their classroom work over a period of time than it is to base such judgments on the performance of their older siblings or the section of the city they live in. These latter indicators are likely to be less valid for decision making than more direct classroom observation.

Here are some examples of questions that relate to the validity of classroom assessments.

- Does the assessment cover all the important aspects of what I want to assess?
- Does the assessment method allow me to make valid decisions about instruction and assessment?
- Do the assessment questions allow pupils to demonstrate the performance I want to assess?
- Are the directions and wording of the items clear enough that pupils will know what is expected in their answers?
- Is the assessment related to what the pupils have been taught?
- Are scoring procedures clear, consistent, and unbiased?

We shall have more to say about validity throughout this text. At this point it is sufficient to say four things about the validity of assessment information. First, validity is concerned with whether the information being gathered is really relevant and appropriate to make the desired decision. Second, validity is the most important characteristic that assessment information can possess; without it assessment information is of little or no use. Third, concerns about validity pertain to all classroom assessment, not just to those involving formal, paper-and-pencil techniques. Each of the many decisions Ms. Lopez made during her school day was based upon some type of assessment information. It is important, therefore, to ask about the validity—that is, the appropriateness—of the assessment information behind each of Ms. Lopez's many daily decisions. Fourth, the teacher's professional judgment is the main determiner of classroom assessment validity, emphasizing the teacher's responsibility to construct valid assessments. Box 1.2 identifies key concerns in the validity of assessments.

Box 1.2   Key Aspects of Assessment Validity

1. Validity is concerned with this general question: To what extent will this assessment information help me make an appropriate decision?
2. Validity refers to the decisions that are made from assessment information, the assessment approach itself. It is not appropriate to say the assessment information is valid unless the decisions or groups it is valid for are identified. Assessment information valid for one decision or group of pupils is not necessarily valid for other decisions or groups.
3. Validity is a matter of degree; it does not exist on an all-or-nothing basis. Think of assessment validity in terms of categories: highly valid, moderately valid, and invalid.
4. Validity is always determined by a judgment made by the test user.

Reliability

A second important characteristic of good assessment is its consistency, stability, or reliability. Would the assessment results for this person or class be similar if they were gathered tomorrow or a week from now? If not, the results are not reliable. If you weighed yourself on a scale, got off it, then weighed yourself again on the same scale, you would expect the two weights to be almost identical. If they weren't, you wouldn't trust the information provided by the scale. It is unreliable. If assessment information does not produce stable, consistent information, a teacher should exercise caution in using that information to make a decision about a pupil or the class. **Reliability** is the extent to which an assessment consistently assesses whatever it is assessing.

Think of a friend whom you consider to be unreliable. Is he sometimes punctual and sometimes late? When she tells you something or promises to do something, can you rely on what she says? A person who is unreliable is inconsistent. The same holds true with assessment information; unreliable or inconsistent information does not help teachers make sound decisions. An unreliable assessment is generally useless because it provides different information each time it is used, just like the unreliable scale.

Recall that Ms. Lopez observed Tabitha's class interruptions and Joshua's inattentive behaviors over a period of time before deciding to take action. She did this to be sure that she was observing stable, consistent behavior on the part of Tabitha and Joshua. Did they behave the same way at different times and under different circumstances? By observing them over a period of time, Ms. Lopez could have faith in the reliability of her observations. Similarly, Mr. Ferris included ten long division with remainder questions on his test—not just one—so that he would obtain reliable information about his pupils' achievement. He can have more confidence about pupils' learning by testing them on ten items rather than on only one or two.

Because any single assessment provides only a limited sample of a pupil's behavior, no single assessment procedure or instrument can be expected to provide perfect, error-free information (Thorndike, 1990). All assessments contain some unreliability or inconsistency due to factors such as ambiguous test items, interruptions during testing, differences in pupils' attention spans, clarity of test directions, pupils' luck in guessing, changes in pupils' moods, appropriateness of the assessment for the pupils, mistakes in scoring (especially essay and observational assessments), and obtaining too small a sample of behavior to permit the pupil to show consistent, stable performance. These and other factors conspire to introduce some inconsistency into all assessment information. Obviously, we want to minimize the inconsistency of assessments as much as possible. Box 1.3 reviews key aspects of the reliability of assessment information.

One of the main purposes of this text is to suggest methods that can reduce the amount of unreliability in classroom assessments. If a teacher cannot rely upon the stability and consistency of the information gathered during the assessment process, the teacher must be careful not to base important decisions on that information. Thus, along with validity—which asks, "Am I gathering assessment information that is relevant to the decision I wish to make?"—the classroom teacher must also be concerned with reliability—which asks, "How consistent and stable is the information I have obtained?" Once again, validity is concerned with whether or not the targeted characteristic is being assessed appropriately, while reliability is concerned with the consistency of the assessment information.

Consider the following assertion regarding the relationship between validity and reliability: Valid assessment must be reliable, but reliable assessment need not be valid. The first half of the statement is fairly straightforward. One cannot make valid decisions if the assessment data on which the decisions are based is not consistent. So, a valid assessment is always reliable.

As to the second part of the statement, imagine the following scenario. Suppose you ask a pupil in your class how many brothers and sisters he

Box 1.3   Key Aspects of Assessment Reliability

1. Reliability refers to the stability or consistency of assessment information and is concerned with this question: How consistent or typical of the pupils' behavior is the assessment information I have gathered?
2. Reliability is not concerned with the appropriateness of the assessment information collected, only with its consistency, stability, or typicality. Appropriateness of assessment information is a validity concern.
3. Reliability does not exist on all-or-nothing basis, but in degrees: high, moderate, or low. Some types of assessment information are more reliable than others.
4. Reliability is a necessary but insufficient condition for validity. An assessment that provides inconsistent, atypical results cannot be relied upon to provide information useful for decision making.

has. He tells you "six," and you ask him again. He tells you "six." You repeat the question several times and each time the pupil indicates six brothers and sisters. You have assessed the number of his brothers and sisters with consistency; the assessment information you have gathered from him is consistent and reliable. Suppose you then use this reliable information to make a decision about what reading group to place the pupil in—the more brothers and sisters, the higher the reading placement. Because the number of brothers and sisters has little relevance to the pupil's reading performance, a decision based on this information, no matter how reliable, is not valid. If an assessment measures what it is intended to measure, it will do so each time and thus be reliable. However, a reliable test can consistently assess the wrong thing and thus be invalid. In short, a valid assessment is always reliable, but a reliable assessment is not necessarily valid. Succeeding chapters will explore the relationship between validity and reliability in greater detail and offer suggestions for improving the validity and reliability of classroom assessment. These chapters will reinforce the fact that validity and reliability are important criteria for *all* types of classroom assessments, not only for paper-and-pencil assessments.

✄ Ethical Issues and Responsibilities

Thus far we have considered many technical aspects of classroom assessment. However, assessment is more than a technical activity; it is a human activity that influences and affects many people, including pupils, parents, teachers, coaches, college admission counselors, and employers. Think about the different kinds and purposes of assessment described in this chapter, and then think about all the ways people can be affected by them. This will give you a sense of the human side of assessment.

Teaching is a profession that has both a knowledge base and an ethical/moral base. Like other professionals who possess knowledge and expertise their clients do not have and whose actions and judgments affect their clients in many ways, classroom teachers are responsible for conducting themselves in an ethical manner. This responsibility is particularly important in education, because unlike most other professions, pupils have no choice about whether they will or will not attend school. Also, compared to their teachers, pupils tend to be less experienced and more impressionable. Among the ethical standards that cut across all dimensions of teaching are the need to treat each pupil as an individual, to avoid physical or emotional abuse of pupils, to respect diversity, to be intellectually honest with pupils, to avoid favoritism and harassment, to provide a balanced perspective on issues raised in instruction, and to provide the best instruction possible for all pupils (Fenstermacher, 1990; Clark, 1990; Strike and Soltis, 1991; Joint Committee on Testing Practices, 1988; McMillan,1997).

Box 1.4 presents a list of ethical standards for teachers developed by the National Education Association. Note the range of ethical concerns and responsibilities that accompany teaching.

Box 1.4   Ethical Standards for Teachers' Relations with Pupils

Commitment to the Student

The educator strives to help each student realize his or her potential as a worthy and effective member of society. The educator therefore works to stimulate the spirit of inquiry, the acquisition of knowledge and understanding, and the thoughtful formulation of worthy goals.

In fulfillment of the obligation to the student, the educator:

1. Shall not unreasonably restrain the student from independent action in the pursuit of learning.
2. Shall not unreasonably deny the student access to varying points of view.
3. Shall not deliberately suppress or distort subject matter relevant to the student's progress.
4. Shall make reasonable effort to protect the student from conditions harmful to learning or to health and safety.
5. Shall not intentionally expose the student to embarrassment or disparagement.
6. Shall not on the basis of race, color, creed, sex, national origin, marital status, political or religious beliefs, family, social or cultural background, or sexual orientation, unfairly:
   a. Exclude any student from participation in any program
   b. Deny benefits to any student
   c. Grant any advantage to any student
7. Shall not use professional relationships with students for private advantage.
8. Shall not disclose information about students obtained in the course of professional service, unless disclosure serves a compelling professional purpose or is required by law.

Source: From *NEA Handbook,* 1992–1993. Reprinted with permission of the National Education Association.

In simple terms, each of these ethical standards refers to some aspect of a teacher's fairness in dealing with his or her pupils. Clearly, gathering and interpreting valid and reliable data for decision making are fundamental to the fairness of teachers' assessments. Other aspects of fairness include:

1. informing students about teacher expectations and assessments before beginning teaching and assessment;
2. describing for pupils what they are to be assessed on before actual assessment;
3. being cautious about making snap judgments and labeling pupils with emotional labels (e.g., disinterested, at-risk, slow learner) before you have spent time with them;
4. avoiding stereotyping pupils (e.g., "He's just a dumb jock." "Kids from that part of town are troublemakers." "Pupils who dress that way have no interest in school.");

5. avoiding terms and examples that may be offensive to students of different gender, race, religion, culture, or nationality;
6. recognizing that cultural differences do not imply cultural deficits;
7. knowing and protecting pupils' legal rights guaranteed by federal/state law;
8. respecting pupils' diversities or disabilities and insuring that pupil participation and interactions are not limited on the basis of diversity or disability.

There are many other dimensions to classroom fairness. Can you list others? See Appendix A for other important teacher competencies in the assessment of pupils.

This chapter has indicated that classrooms are complex environments calling for teacher decision making in many areas. Within such an environment, teachers are not expected to be correct in every decision they make. That would be an unrealistic standard to hold anyone to, especially in fluid, decision-rich classroom settings where uncertainty abounds. However, teachers should be expected and morally bound to provide defensible assessment evidence to support classroom decisions and actions. This is the least that can be expected in an environment where teacher actions have such vital consequences for pupils.

Chapter Summary

- Every day in every classroom, teachers make decisions about their pupils, their instruction, and their classrooms' climate. Teachers collect and interpret various sources of evidence to help them evaluate and choose suitable courses of action.
- There are many purposes for classroom assessment: establishing classroom equilibrium, planning and conducting instruction, placing pupils, providing feedback and incentives, diagnosing pupil problems, and judging and grading academic learning and progress.
- All the purposes of assessment can be divided into three general categories: sizing-up assessment, which occurs early in the school year and is used by teachers to get to know their pupils; instructional assessment, which includes both planning and delivering instruction to pupils; and official assessments such as grades, which teachers are expected to provide as part of their role in the school bureaucracy.
- Assessment is the general process of collecting, synthesizing, and interpreting information to aid teachers in decision making. A test is a formal, usually paper-and-pencil, way to gather information. Measurement is describing performance numerically. Evaluation is making judgments about what is good or desirable.
- Many forms of assessment evidence are used by teachers, including tests, observations, and oral questioning.
- Standardized assessments are intended to be administered, scored, and interpreted in the same way no matter when or where they are given.

These conditions are necessary because a primary purpose of standardized assessments is to compare the performance of pupils across different classrooms.

- The quality of assessments is determined by their validity and reliability. Validity, the most important characteristic of assessments, is concerned with the collection of information that is most relevant for making the desired decision. Reliability is concerned with the consistency or typicality of the assessment information collected.
- Although assessment is thought of as a technical activity, there are ethical concerns associated with the assessment process. Because teachers' decisions can influence pupils' self- perception and life chances, when assessing, teachers must be aware of their many ethical responsibilities.

Questions for Discussion

1. In what ways do the three general types of classroom assessment described in this chapter interact with each other? For example, how do sizing-up assessments influence instructional assessments? How do instructional assessments influence official assessments?
2. How would you know if your teacher constructed a valid and reliable assessment? What factors would influence validity and reliability?
3. Why is it important for standardized assessment to be administered, scored, and interpreted the same way regardless of where or when the assessment was administered? What are the consequences of not following standardized assessment procedures as stated?
4. Do teachers' ethical responsibilities to their pupils change as pupils get older? How? Are there some ethical responsibilities that remain constant across age levels? What do you think are the three most important ethical responsibilities teachers have toward their pupils?

Reflection Exercise

This chapter described assessment as an aid to teacher decision making. Imagine that you are a teacher and have to size up a new group of pupils at the start of the school year, plan instruction for them, teach them your planned lesson, and assess their learning at the end of instruction. Reflect on how you would carry out each of these activities. List some decisions you would have to make in order to carry out each activity successfully.

Decisions related to sizing up pupils
Decisions related to planning instruction for pupils
Decisions related to teaching the plan to pupils
Decisions related to assessing pupil learning

Activity

Interview a teacher about classroom decision making. Ask the teacher how he or she sizes up students at the start of the school year: what characteristics are considered, on what basis are decisions about pupils made, etc. Ask the teacher to identify the two or three most important decisions made when planning instruction and the three most important decisions made while teaching a lesson. Finally, ask what decisions are important when assessing pupils' learning.

Compare your teacher's responses to your own answers in the preceding Reflection Exercise. How are they the same? How are they different? Why are they different?

Review Questions

1. What are the three main types of classroom assessment? How do they differ in purpose, timing, and the types of information most likely to be used in carrying them out? What are examples of decisions teachers make in the three types of classroom assessment?
2. Explain the difference between: individual and group assessments; standardized and nonstandardized assessments; supply and selection test items; and validity and reliability.
3. How would you explain the concept of validity to a fellow teacher? What examples would you use to make your point?
4. Why are validity and reliability important concerns in classroom assessments? Why is validity more important then reliability?
5. Give an example of teachers' ethical responsibilities for sizing up pupils, providing instruction, and assessing pupil learning.

References

Airasian, P. W. (2000). *Assessment in the classroom: A concise approach.* New York: McGraw-Hill.

American Federation of Teachers, the National Council on Measurement in Education, and the National Education Association (1990). Standards for teacher competence in educational assessment of students, The National Council on Measurement in Education.

Biddle, B., Good, T., & Goodson, I. (1996). *The international handbook teachers and teaching.* New York: Kluher.

Clark, C. M. (1990). The teacher and the taught: Moral transactions in the classroom. In J. Goodlad, R. Soder, and K. Sirotnik, *The moral dimensions of teaching,* (pp. 251–265). San Francisco: Jossey-Bass.

Clark. C. M., & Peterson, P. L. (1986). Teachers' thought processes. In M. C. Wittrock, *Handbook of research on teaching* (pp. 255–296). New York: Macmillan.

Fenstermacher, G. D. (1990). Some moral considerations on teaching as a profession. In J. Goodlad, R. Soder, and K. Sirotnik, *The moral dimensions of teaching* (pp. 130–151). San Francisco: Jossey-Bass.

Jackson, P. W. (1990). *Life in classrooms.* New York: Teachers College Press.

Joint Committee on Testing Practices. (1988). Code of fair testing practices in education. Washington, DC: American Psychological Association.

McKinley, J. (1999). Observational assessments: Validating what teachers see in the classroom. *Education Update, 41,* 5–6.

McMillan, J. H. (1997). *Classroom assessment.* Boston: Allyn and Bacon.

Moss, P. A. (1995). Themes and variations in validity theory. *"Educational Measurement: Issues and Practices, 14,*(5), 5–13.

Strike, K., & Soltis, J. (1991). *The ethics of teaching.* New York: Teachers College Press.

Terman, L. M., & Merrill, M. A. (1973). *Stanford-Binet intelligence scale: Manual for the third revision (Form L-M).* Iowa City, IA: Riverside Publishing Co.

Thorndike, R. L. (1990). Reliability. In H. J. Walberg and G. D. Haertel, *The international encyclopedia of educational evaluation* (pp. 260–273). Oxford: Pergamon Press.

Wechsler, D. (1974). *Manual for the Wechsler intelligence scale for children-revised.* New York: The Psychological Corp.

Whittington, D. (1999). Making room for values and fairness: Teaching reliability and validity in the classroom context. *Educational Measurement: Issues and Practice, 18*(1), 14–22.

Learning about Pupils: Sizing-Up Assessment

Chapter Outline

Chapter Objectives

After reading this chapter, the pupil will be able to:

- Identify features of classrooms that make them social settings and explain the need for teacher sizing-up assessment
- Describe the sources of teacher sizing-up assessments
- Differentiate between cognitive, affective, and psychomotor behaviors
- Distinguish between formal and informal observations
- Identify weaknesses in the validity and reliability of sizing-up assessments and suggest ways to overcome them
- State potential effects of sizing-up assessments on pupils
- Explain strategies that can improve teacher sizing-up assessments

The beginning of the school year is important for both teacher and pupils. These initial days set the tone and lay the foundation for the rest of the year. For both teacher and pupils, these days are the one opportunity to make an initial impression. It is in these early days that a group of diverse individuals begins to come together to form a class. Although most teachers and pupils have been through the beginning of school many times before, uncertainties always accompany the start of a new school year. Each new group of pupils has its own special mix of backgrounds, abilities, interests, disabilities, needs, and personalities that make it unlike any other class the teacher has encountered. In this chapter we explore questions that confront all teachers at the start of the school year: How do I get to know my new pupils, and what do I need to know about them to provide them an orderly, civil learning environment? To discover this information teachers ask and try to answer questions such as the following about their pupils: Will they get along well and be cooperative with each other? Are they academically ready for my curriculum? What intellectual, emotional, and physical strengths and weaknesses do they have? Do some students have disabilities that require classroom accommodations? Are there particularly disruptive pupils in the class? If you were a teacher, what other questions would you add to this list and why?

In the early days of the school year teachers try to learn about each individual pupil and the class as a whole and to organize a classroom society that is characterized by communication, order, and learning (Garcia, 1994). It is very important to understand that a class is more than a group of pupils who happen to be in the same place at the same time. A class is a society, a social system, made up of people who communicate with each other, pursue common and individual goals, and follow rules of order. For example, all classrooms have rules that govern such matters as who can visit the bathroom and when, how tardiness or lost homework will be treated, and how papers are distributed and collected. There also must be rules to govern the flow of communication in the classroom: "Don't talk when the teacher or another class member is talking;" "Raise your hand if you have a question;" "If you know the answer to a question don't blurt it out;" "If you don't know the answer to a question sit quietly and listen." Pupils learn quickly that the fastest way to anger a teacher is not by doing poorly on a homework assignment or a test, but by doing such things as talking out of turn, pushing in line, laughing at the teacher, or engaging in some other breach of classroom etiquette. Establishing a set of classroom rules and routines is one of the most important things a teacher can do to promote positive social and learning environments (Boostrom, 1991). Without rules and routines the classroom would be chaotic, making instruction and learning very difficult (Lieberman and Miller, 1992). Of course, classrooms are more than just social settings, they are also instructional settings in which teachers plan and deliver instruction and assess pupils. And finally, classrooms are places where one member, the teacher, has responsibility for other members, the pupils, thus making it a moral and ethical environment (McCaslin and Good, 1996). At the beginning of the school year the teacher must begin to set up this complex social, academic, and moral society.

Although all classrooms are simultaneously social, academic, and moral environments, the specific features of particular classrooms differ greatly from one another. For example, the academic and socioeconomic backgrounds of pupils, as well as their mix of personalities, learning styles, languages, special needs, and interests, differ from classroom to classroom (Ladson-Billings, 1994; Delpit, 1995). From one year to the next, a teacher cannot count on having similar groups of pupils. Because of such differences, planning and delivering instruction are context-bound activities; that is, the ways that teachers plan and teach are dependent upon the varied characteristics of their pupils. This means, of course, that the teacher must know about the characteristics of his or her pupils. Try to imagine planning and teaching a lesson for a group of pupils you know nothing about. What will interest the pupils? How long can they pay attention? What have they learned previously? What learning needs do they have? What accommodations must be met to help pupils with disabilities learn? Similarly, try to imagine how you would discipline students you did not know. What strategies might work with different pupils? Is a student acting out because she is bored, unable to follow the lesson, or testing the teacher? Teachers size up their pupils at the start of the school year to answer such questions.

In order to know how to group, teach, motivate, manage, accommodate, and reward pupils, the teacher must learn about their individual characteristics. Thus, a first and very important type of classroom assessment that all teachers must conduct takes place at the start of the school year when they must learn about or "size up" the characteristics of each pupil and the class as a whole.

There is a scene in the musical *The King and I* in which Anna, the English governess and teacher, meets the many children of the King of Siam whom she is to instruct. One by one, each child is presented to Anna. The children differ in their confidence, facial expressions, dress, and manner. As each child parades in front of her, Anna sings the song "Getting to Know You": "Getting to know you, getting to know all about you. Getting to like you, hoping that you like me. . . ." This is what the first days are like in most classrooms, as teachers try to learn enough about their pupils to form them into a society that will permit classroom goals to be realized.

All teachers size up their pupils, although the characteristics teachers gather information about differ depending on the goals of schooling at different levels. At the elementary school level, curriculum goals include both academic and socialization outcomes. Elementary teachers were asked about the importance of socialization outcomes in their classrooms. Here are a few of their comments.

> Every spare minute I try to stress good citizenship and cooperation. If these issues arise during instruction, I stop the lesson and remind the students about good classroom behavior and cooperation. Even if a student just took someone's pencil, I would say, "Do you realize. . .?" I think that good citizenship, civility, and cooperation are as important as learning subject matter. Some of them don't get it at home.

> I'm trying to make them good citizens in the classroom community and beyond, not only good learners. I make sure they know what is expected of them by the time they are out of the sixth grade, the difference between right and wrong.

In elementary schools, most pupils spend 5 to 6 hours per day in the same classroom with the same teacher and classmates. Often, much of the instruction is carried out in small groups, so that while one group is occupying the teacher's attention, other pupils must keep themselves busy and productive without constant teacher supervision. Thus, in elementary classrooms, a teacher's initial assessments tend to focus both on pupils' academic capabilities and their general classroom behavior.

In high schools, pupils may already be grouped into tracks and most have already been socialized in appropriate school behavior. The goals of schooling at the high school level are predominantly academic and vocational. Instead of seeing 20 to 25 pupils for 6 hours per day as in the elementary school, high school teachers see 100 to 125 pupils in five different classes lasting about an hour each. While high school teachers are interested in their pupils' affective and personal characteristics, they do not "live" with their pupils in the same way that elementary teachers do. As a consequence, the sizing up done by high school teachers tends to focus on academic characteristics, work habits, behavior, subject matter interest, and attitude. Thus, to suggest that high school teachers are not concerned with emotional and interest outcomes is to overstate the matter. One high school business teacher notes: "I try to prepare my students for life. I want them to know how to key board and balance ledgers, but I am equally concerned that they are respectful, honest, good citizens, and so forth." All teachers are concerned with their pupils' cognitive and affective characteristics, although the relative emphasis on these characteristics differs by grade level.

If sizing-up assessment is not done well, a disorganized, disruptive, unresponsive classroom environment results, one in which communication and learning are inhibited. Each of us can recall a particular classroom in which the social system was characterized by anarchy, where personal impulse replaced social consideration, and where teaching and learning were constantly undermined by futile efforts to establish order.

To summarize, sizing-up assessments are done by every teacher early in the school year to provide information that will help mold the classroom into a viable social and academic environment in which rules, routines, and common understandings are established. By the end of the first few days of the school year, experienced teachers begin to know much about their pupils' home backgrounds, academic knowledge and skills, learning needs, behavior problems, and out-of-school activities. Where and how do teachers amass such information about their pupils so early in the school year?

Gathering Sizing-Up Assessment Information

Many sources of information contribute to sizing-up assessments. Some information comes to teachers before their pupils enter the classroom for the first time. Other information is obtained from a variety of sources during the first weeks of school. Regardless of where the information is obtained, identifying relevant pupil characteristics is becoming more difficult and complex for teachers at all levels. American teachers are increasingly being asked to teach learners who are widely varied in ability, motivation, culture, and language. Issues of poverty, disability, violence, abuse, teen pregnancy, and drugs confront too many of our students and impact their school performance and success (Wiseman, Cooner, & Knight, 1999). However, in spite of this difficult reality, teachers are expected to know and teach all their students. So, during the beginning days of school, each teacher must collect and synthesize a broad range of information about pupils and use this information to form an initial set of perceptions and expectations about them (McCaslin & Good, 1996). These perceptions and expectations will influence the way the teacher plans for, interacts with, and manages pupils and instruction. Teachers also recognize that some important pupil characteristics may not manifest themselves in the first few days of school. Issues such as poverty, violence, abuse, and pregnancy may not be immediately apparent to a teacher, while issues of culture, language, and physical disabilities probably would be easily noted.

The information teachers use to size up pupils comes from a variety of sources, including the school grapevine, comments of other teachers, school records, performance of prior siblings, teachers' formal and informal classroom observations, teacher-pupil conversations, various types of classroom assessments, parent comments, and information from the nurse or special education teacher. In general, teachers gather much of their data about pupils from what pupils say, do, and write. Table 2.1 shows some of the common sources teachers use to size up their pupils.

Preclassroom Sizing-Up Information

The sizing-up process often starts before pupils set foot in the classroom. One might think that pupils would be unknown to a teacher before they meet face-to-face, but this is not always the case. A school is a hotbed of

TABLE 2.1

Some Common Sources of Teachers' Sizing-Up Information

What Pupils Say	What Pupils Do	What Pupils Write
Oral reports	Complete work on time	Homework
Class discussion	Response to prompts	Journals
Responses to questions		Tests
Interaction with others	Involvement in tasks	Portfolios
Oral responses	Performance	Neatness
Fluency	Attention span	Penmanship
Politeness	Get along with peers	Logical thoughts
Choice of words	Talk out in class	Organization

assessment information, and teachers cannot help being exposed to it. The teachers' room in most schools is more than a place where teachers go to eat lunch, correct papers, or plan their next class. It is also a place where opinions are voiced and "stories" about the day's activities are exchanged.

Sit and listen in the teachers' room. Listen to Ms. Espenoza or Mr. Habermas complain about Janos's continual inattentiveness or Jane's defiant behavior in class. Listen to Mr. Gelman praise Lindsay's math effort and conscientiousness. Hear Ms. Karas complain about Jamie's interfering and demanding parents. One does not have to know Janos, Jane, Lindsay, or Jamie personally to begin forming impressions of them as persons and pupils. Many pupils' reputations precede them into the classroom, and teachers who may never have set eyes upon them may already have heard a great deal about their strengths, weaknesses, behaviors, and attitudes. Here are the words of several teachers who were asked what information they had regarding their pupils before the start of the school year and where that information came from.

> School records are kept in the office and are available on all pupils. I could look at these before the school year started to get information about my pupils' abilities, prior school performance, home situation, and disabilities and needed accommodations. I don't do this, because I like the students to start out with a "clean slate" so I can judge them for myself. However, if I know I have a pupil with a physical, emotional, or learning disability, I always review that pupil's office file before the start of classes to help prepare for appropriate instruction and accommodations.

> Sometimes I recognize names of siblings I have taught on my class list. This gives me some idea of the type of student I expect a pupil to be. Usually it is teacher-to-teacher interaction that provides most of my information about my new pupils. After all, the pupil's prior teachers are the people who have seen the child constantly for a year.

> Standardized test scores and previous grades are available in the Principal's Office. I look at these before classes start to get an idea of the

capabilities of my class. I also give pretests and play math games to determine how prepared they are for what I plan to teach.

In my school, classes are assigned by academic level. Before classes start I know whether a class is higher or lower level. This information tells me something about the general ability, interest, and motivation of the pupils and the classes as a whole.

Sometimes when I compare my class list with another teacher's, the other teacher may comment on a pupil, the sibling of the pupil, or the parents of the pupil. Susie's brother was a nice, quiet boy. Sam's sister was defiant and disruptive in class. Andy is the last of the eight Rooney children, thank goodness. Be careful, Mrs. Roberts is overly protective of Peter and very concerned about grades.

The fact that such information is readily available to teachers and can influence their perceptions of pupils before meeting them face-to-face raises an important question. How much should teachers know about their pupils before the start of classes? What are some important pupil characteristics that teachers want to know before the first day of class? For example, most teachers want to know about any important physical or emotional disabilities their pupils might have and accommodations they require. Or, in elementary schools, teachers want to know about problematic or atypical pupil custodial arrangements. One elementary school teacher put it this way: "This is an era of divorce, child snatching, and fierce custody battles. It reassures me to know right from the first day of school who should, and more importantly, who should not, be picking up or dropping off a student." Most teachers agree about the usefulness of having these general types of information available to them at the start of classes.

There is less agreement about the usefulness of other types of sizing-up information gathered before the start of school. Some teachers want all the information they can get and turn to office records, other teachers, and other sources to learn as much as possible about their incoming pupils. A greater number of teachers, however, prefer not to know too much about their pupils until they meet them face-to-face. These teachers often talk about allowing the pupils to enter their classroom with a "clean slate," unencumbered by the perceptions of other teachers or knowledge of the pupils' prior school performance. These teachers say, in essence, I would like to find out about the pupils myself, based upon the way they act with me in my classroom. The advantages and disadvantages of having a great deal of information before classes start will be considered later in this chapter. For the present, it is important to note that information of varied kinds is available to teachers, and that teachers vary in the amount of information they seek prior to first meeting their pupils.

Classroom Sizing-Up Information

A number of teachers were asked to indicate what two or three pieces of information about the pupils in their classes they would like to know by the end of the first days of school. This is another way of asking what types of information are most helpful in setting up a classroom learning society. Not surprisingly, the answers varied according to the grade levels the respondents taught.

In elementary schools, curriculum goals are both academic and social, since elementary school pupils are generally less mature, less socialized, and less independent than their high school counterparts. Consequently, it is generally more difficult for a teacher to organize the classroom society at the elementary school level. Also, the classroom social system is more complex and intricate when pupils and teachers are together 6 hours per day than it is when they are together less than an hour per day as in high school. Given this fact, it is not surprising that most elementary teachers (and some secondary teachers) want to know if their pupils have disabilities such as hearing loss, hyperactivity, speech problems, or other physical infirmities, and how well students with such disabilities will adjust to the classroom's social environment. Few elementary school teachers indicate that information such as test scores, prior reading placement, or interest in mathematics are the things they most want to know about their pupils on the first days of the school year. Rather, they are concerned with information that will help them form 20 or 25 diverse young learners into a unified, orderly classroom society.

At the high school level pupils are more mature, often separated into tracks on the basis of prior performance and vocational plans, and long-term veterans of participation in classroom socialization procedures. Further, the high school classroom society is not as complex as that in the elementary school because pupils and teachers usually are together for only an hour or so at a time. Finally, because instruction in high school classes is focused primarily upon subject matter content, the information initially sought by high school teachers is generally related to the achievement or ability level of their pupils and their interest in the subject matter to be taught.

Thus, both elementary and high school teachers want and need some information about their pupils early in the school year. How do they get the information needed to create a desirable classroom learning environment? How long does it take most teachers to feel that they have correctly sized up the pupils in their classes and how confident are they in these initial assessments? These are important questions to answer because they influence the quality of the assessments teachers make and these assessments, in turn, determine how teachers will perceive and interact with pupils (Kolb and Jussim, 1994; O'Neil and Drillings, 1994).

When teachers were asked what behaviors and traits they observed in the first week or so of school to help them get to know their pupils, they offered these answers.

By the end of the first or second week of school I will know whether each child is going to work hard, care about school, get along with the other pupils, be responsible enough to relay messages for me, and orally express his or her thoughts. I know these things mainly from observing and talking with the children in class. Whether a child volunteers an answer and comments willingly or if he or she needs to be called on to give an answer tells me about the pupil's interest. I watch how they get along with each other and how focused they are on their seat work. The look of interest on their faces tells me about how hard they will work.

I watch the way the pupils enter the classroom. Are they late? Sullen? Quiet? How do they interact with each other and with me? I watch the students' body language and attitude because you can learn a lot about the way a student feels about himself and the class from body language. I'd like to say that students' clothes don't influence me in judging the students, but it is a good indicator of the student's style. Their style usually reflects the way they go about addressing academics.

After the first few days of class I go to the office to review each student's past academic record. I look over test scores, previous grades in my subject area, Individual Education Plan and other teacher's comments if they are there. This information tells me a lot about the differences among students I have in class and what I can expect of them.

I can recognize who is motivated and who is not by the end of the second week of school. I base my judgment on whether or not students complete their homework and raise their hands. I also get a lot of information about the students' interests and personal lives by just talking and listening to them. It's amazing what one can learn by overhearing conversations before and after class and in the hallways.

Note the range of methods used by teachers to help them get to know their pupils, often even before classes start. Some of these sources provide formal written evidence, but much of the information is informal and hearsay. In sizing up pupils, teachers rely heavily on the three main methods of collecting assessment data: paper-and-pencil, observation, and questioning methods. Note also the broad range of information teachers collect about their pupils. Virtually all of this information can be placed into one of three general categories or domains: the cognitive domain, the affective domain, and the psychomotor domain.

The most commonly assessed behavior domain is the **cognitive domain.** Cognitive behaviors include a range of intellectual activities such as memorizing, interpreting, applying, problem solving, reasoning, analyzing, and thinking critically. Virtually all the tests that pupils take in school are intended to measure one or more of these cognitive activities. Most school instruction is focused upon helping pupils attain cognitive mastery of some content or subject area. A weekly spelling test, a unit test in history, a worksheet on proper use of *lie* and *lay*, an essay on the theory of supply and demand, and an oral recitation of a poem all require pupils to demonstrate cognitive thinking behaviors. The Scholastic Aptitude Test, the American College Testing Program Test, state high school graduation tests, the written part of a state driver's test, and standardized achievement tests such as the Iowa Test of Basic Skills and the Stanford, Metropolitan, SRA, and California Achievement Tests all are intended to assess cognitive behaviors.

Ms. Lopez, our elementary teacher in Chapter 1, was relying primarily upon cognitive information about her pupils when she made the following decisions: assigned grades to her pupils, moved Tamika from the middle to the high reading group, planned instruction in math and science, identified pupils for remedial work in basic skills, and consulted last year's standardized test scores to find out whether she needed to review the rules of capitalization for the class. In each case, Ms. Lopez was assessing her pupils' thinking, reasoning, memory, or general intellectual behaviors.

✕ A second domain of behavior is the **affective domain.** Affective behaviors involve feelings, attitudes, interests, preferences, values, and emotions. Emotional stability, motivation, trustworthiness, self-control, and personality are all examples of affective characteristics. Although affective behaviors are rarely assessed formally in schools and classrooms, they constantly are being assessed informally by all teachers. Teachers need to know who can be trusted to work unsupervised and who cannot, who can maintain self-control when the teacher has to leave the classroom and who cannot, who needs to be encouraged to speak in class and who does not, who is interested in science but not in social studies, and who values education and who does not. Teachers also want to know how individual pupils respond to pressure, teasing, failure, and other stressors. Most classroom teachers can describe many affective pupil characteristics based primarily upon their informal observations and interactions with the pupils. From such informal assessment techniques, teachers build up a store of information about each pupil's interests, motivation, values, work ethic, self-control, and personality. Note, however, that determining pupils' affects may take longer than determining their cognitive levels.

Ms. Lopez was relying mainly upon her assessment of pupils' affective behaviors when she selected Rosa, not Sarah, to deliver a note to the school principal and when she changed the class seating plan to separate Jamar and Ramon, who were unable to control themselves when seated together. When she switched the social studies instruction from discussion to seatwork to avoid unruliness, decided to send a note home to Tabitha's parents about her interruptions in class, paired Kim with Aretha in the hopes of overcoming Kim's shyness and reticence, and sent Ralph to the principal for swearing at a teacher, she also was making decisions based upon the affective behaviors of her pupils.

The third behavior domain is the **psychomotor domain,** which includes behaviors of a physical and manipulative nature. Playing a sport, setting up laboratory equipment, building a bookcase, acting in a school play, key boarding, holding a pencil, buttoning a jacket, and playing a musical instrument are examples of activities that require psychomotor behaviors. Although psychomotor behaviors are present and important at all levels of schooling, they are especially stressed in the early elementary grades where tasks like holding a pencil, opening a locker, and buttoning or zippering clothing are important behaviors for pupils to master. Similarly, many physical disabilities such as blindness, inability to walk, lack of hand-eye coordination, or inability to speak affect pupils' psychomotor functioning. Finally, school subjects such as gym, art, shop, and music, among others, are heavily dependent on psychomotor performance.

Ms. Lopez was concerned with her pupils' psychomotor behavior when she moved Claudia to the front of the room so that she could see the blackboard better, sent Antonio to the school nurse because he felt ill, and referred Aaron to the Special Education Department because he continued to exhibit poor gross motor skills. In each case, Ms. Lopez's decision was based upon assessment evidence that pertained to some aspect of a pupil's physical or motor behavior.

Two features of sizing-up assessments deserve special attention. First, much of the information used in these assessments comes from informal teacher observations. Most teachers do not rely heavily on tests or formal measurements to determine pupil characteristics. If they seek such information—and many do not—they often go to the school record folders where past performance, including both triumphs and failures, is usually recorded. For the most part, however, teachers observe, listen, and talk to their pupils to frame their sizing-up assessments. Second, because sizing-up information is obtained early in the school year and largely by means of informal observations, teachers may be exposed to only a small sample of each pupil's behavior. Because teachers can observe any given pupil only part of the time, it is inevitable that these mainly informal observations will be incomplete and limited to what the pupils happened to be doing when the teacher glanced their way.

Thus, during the early days of the school year, teachers have their antennae up, searching the environment for indicators of pupil characteristics. Sometimes their search leads them to expected places: school record folders, prior teachers' perceptions, formal and informal observations, and the ways pupils interact with them and their peers. The search also leads to some unexpected places that would, on the surface, seem to have little to do with the main task of the school: the ways pupils dress, their posture and body language, overheard snatches of pupils' hallway discussions, and who they "hang around" with. Once collected, the sizing-up information teachers gather is translated into descriptions of pupils.

✂ Forming Pupil Descriptions

The many sources of sizing-up information are synthesized into teacher descriptions of pupils such as:

> Mara (a first grader) comes from a family in which her older siblings have had many, many problems in their school careers. But Mara seems to be a little better than her brothers and sisters, because she is able to identify differences in pictures and in word sounds. She seems to like school and gets along well with her classmates. She will be one of the best of her family but she will be a slow learner. I have taught all her other siblings in this school. Mara listens well and follows directions to some extent, and seems content. I believe she will be below average.

> Alfrado (a first grader) is a handsome young man with big brown eyes and a smile all the time, even his eyes smile. He tries to please, is well behaved, and does well in his work. He joins in with any group activity that is going on and his written and oral work have been competent. Alfredo is well liked by his classmates. I'm expecting him to be one of the class leaders this year.

Saleene (a fifth grader) walks into class each day with a worried and tired look. Praising her work, or even the smallest positive action, produces a broad smile though its impact is brief. She is inattentive, even during class exercises we do step by step. Saleene has a hearing disability that makes it hard for her to follow directions and classroom discussions. She is shy, but sometimes will ask for help. But before she gives herself a chance, she will put her head down on her desk and close her eyes. Her self-esteem is low. I am concerned that she will be this way all year.

David (an eighth grader) is a smooth talker, an extrovert. He dresses well and is a nice kid with a good head on his shoulders. Unfortunately, David is very unmotivated, most likely because of his family background. He's street smart, loves attention, and has a good sense of humor. He is able to "dish it out" but can also take it. David is loud in class but not to the point of disruption; he knows where to draw the limit. If only he had some interest and more determination, the kid could go a long way.

Jim (an eleventh grader) is athletic and good-natured. He is flirtatious with the girls and sometimes with his teachers. He doesn't go beyond the bounds of good taste and is respectful in class. His ability is average. He is a handsome boy who will be a class leader.

These are rich and detailed pupil descriptions. Each includes many characteristics of pupil behavior and background (Goodson, 1992). Cognitive, affective, and psychomotor characteristics are included among the teachers' descriptions. A number of the descriptions make a prediction about how the pupil will perform during the school year. Consider what these teachers have said about their pupils after a week or two of school: "I believe she will be below average." "I'm expecting him to be one of the class leaders this year." "I am concerned that she will be this way all year." "If only he had more interest and determination, the kid could go a long way." "He is a handsome boy who will be a class leader." As a whole, these teacher descriptions provide strong testimony to the fact that teachers size up their pupils.

What is perhaps the most remarkable aspect of these assessments is that each was provided by a classroom teacher after 10 or so days at the start of the school year. The fact that teachers size up pupils is not in itself remarkable—people in any social situation size each other up. What is important to consider, however, is the speed at which teacher impressions are formed. Only the most timid and quiet pupils escape initial sizing up, and then only for a few extra days or weeks.

Sizing-up assessments produce a set of perceptions, expectations, and labels that influence the manner in which the teacher plans for, instructs, and interacts with the pupils throughout the school year (O'Neil and Drillings, 1994; Merryfield, 1994; Good and Brophy, 1997). This is, after all, the purpose of sizing-up assessment: to help the teacher get to know the pupils so he or she can organize them into a classroom society and know how to interact with, motivate, and teach them. Clearly the teachers represented above have achieved their purposes. Not only do they describe diverse and multiple characteristics of their pupils, they also make predictions about their performance through the upcoming school year. First impressions have an important impact in the classroom.

To get a sense of the importance of sizing-up assessment for teachers and pupils, imagine that it is the middle of January and you have been called in to substitute for the regular sixth grade teacher at the Martin Luther King Middle School, who is away at a computer workshop. The classroom teacher has provided you with detailed lesson plans describing the activities and the subject matter scheduled to be covered. You have a good sense of what you are to teach. Just after the bell rings, a boy in the back of the room raises his hand and asks to go to his locker to get a book he has forgotten. Should you let him go? Can he be trusted to return with the book in a minute or two, or will he wander the corridors for an hour? What is the classroom teacher's policy on forgotten books? A few minutes later two girls get up and start to leave the room. "We always go to the library to see Ms. Flanders for extra help at this time on Wednesday. We'll be back in about an hour." Is this true? Will they return when they say they will? Can the class be relied upon to answer these questions if asked? Shortly thereafter, a boy and girl start arguing over the last copy of a reference book. The argument grows louder and begins to disturb the class. How should you react? What strategy will pacify this particular boy and girl? Later, you assign the pupils some written math homework and they respond, "Ms. Gozinta (the classroom teacher) never gives us math homework on Wednesday. Wednesday is a science homework day." Is it? You don't know the answers to any of these questions. As a substitute, you are an outsider, a stranger to the classroom society, with little knowledge about classroom routines and pupil personalities. Ms. Gozinta knows the answers to all these issues because she is a founding member of the classroom society, the person who has used sizing-up assessment to help form that society.

Sizing-up assessment provides the teacher with the kinds of practical, "nitty-gritty" knowledge that helps the classroom function (Bullough, Knowles, and Crow, 1992; Solas, 1992). Caught up in the many demands of the classroom, the teacher cannot solve problems or reach decisions based upon abstract principles or generalities. The teacher must deal with classroom situations that require specific knowledge about the actors in those situations. What the teacher does to stop Mark's misbehavior will differ from what he does to stop Shannon's. Sue needs special attention and reinforcement to perform well, but Kinu needs to be left to himself to do his best. Norman has a difficult home situation and requires special warmth and reinforcement, but Meredith must be nagged into doing her work.

Teachers as a group have often been looked down upon because, it is said, their profession lacks a unique body of professional knowledge and expertise that can be applied in all situations. Although it is true that much of teachers' knowledge is less scientific, theoretical, and generalizable, it is also true that much of what teachers do in their classrooms requires situation-specific, not generic information (Airasian, 1990). Situation-specific knowledge is what teachers need to solve the practical problems and dilemmas they face. Given the diversity among students in most classrooms, teachers must attend to each pupil's unique cognitive, affective, and psychomotor needs. Sizing-up assessment helps teachers know what is unique about their pupils so that appropriate instructional activities can be planned, classroom

Box 2.1   Characteristics of Sizing-Up Assessment

1. **Sizing up is done at the start of the school year.** Most teachers can describe the personal, social, and academic characteristics of each pupil and the class as a whole after the first 2 weeks of school.
2. **Sizing up is pupil-centered.** Pupils and their characteristics are the focus of assessment.
3. **Informal observation is used.** Much of the information about pupil behavior and performance is collected through spontaneous, informal observations.
4. **Observations are synthesized into perceptions.** Teachers put together their observations in idiosyncratic ways to form generalized perceptions of pupils.
5. **Impressions are rarely written down.** Unlike test scores or grades, which are written down in rank books or report cards, the perceptions formed from sizing-up assessments are unwritten and selectively communicated.
6. **Observations are broad and diverse.** Teachers attend to a broad range of cognitive, affective, and psychomotor characteristics when they size up their pupils.
7. **Early impressions tend to become permanent.** Teachers are very confident about the accuracy of the sizing-up assessments they perform in the first days of school. Initial perceptions are very stable from the first week of school to the end of the school year.

problems managed, and classroom events understood. It provides perceptions and expectations that the teacher will use continually throughout the school year. Box 2.1 reviews the main characteristics of sizing-up assessment.

✸ Characteristics of Sizing-Up Assessments

The practice of sizing up pupils is not unexpected or unusual. Bear in mind that classroom sizing-up assessments are simply a special case of our natural tendency to observe and make judgments about people on the basis of what we have seen or heard about them. Observing and judging people are ways of bringing order into social situations. They facilitate "knowing" or "labeling" others so that it is no longer necessary to interact with them as if they were complete strangers. In schools, sizing-up assessment provides a frame of reference within which social interaction and meaningful instruction can take place. When a teacher remarks that she feels "at home" with a class and speaks about "my class" or "my group," the teacher has likely completed or nearly completed the sizing-up process. Remember also that sizing-up activities are a two-way street; as you are sizing up your pupils, they will be sizing up you.

Imagine what it would be like if you could not size up your pupils, friends, or roommates; if you never could know their likes and dislikes, biases, attitudes, values, personalities, interests, and phobias. Without such information, every interaction with them would always be the same—two complete strangers with no information, perceptions, or understandings of each other attempting to communicate. Sizing-up assessments are a necessary aspect of communication, because they provide the context within which social relationships develop.

Teachers differ, however, in the accuracy, completeness, and appropriateness of their sizing-up assessments and predictions. The rapidity and the heavy reliance on informal observations during sizing-up assessment increases the likelihood of unreliable and invalid decisions. An assessment process based on quickly obtained, often incomplete evidence, should be monitored closely. Consequently, teachers have an ethical responsibility to make sizing-up assessments as valid and reliable as possible and to understand the potential consequences of poor or inaccurate sizing-up assessments.

Stability of Sizing-Up Assessments

Teachers' initial impressions of their pupils can "stick" and remain quite stable over time. Once a teacher forms an impression, it is likely to stay relatively unchanged during the school year. One factor prompting this stability is that once a teacher has an impression of a pupil, even an incorrect one, the teacher feels a degree of closure and security because the pupil is now felt to be "known." This sense of closure and security may explain why teachers are generally confident of their initial pupil perceptions and why they rarely indicate concern or uncertainty about their accuracy.

The security of "knowing" a pupil may also explain why teachers act to maintain a consistent and stable perception of the pupil after their initial impression is formed (Kuhn, 1991). If a teacher believes a pupil has high ability and the pupil succeeds on a difficult test, the teacher is likely to attribute the success to the pupil's high ability. The teacher's belief is reinforced. If, on the other hand, an unexpected outcome occurs—such as the perceived high-achieving pupil performing poorly on a test—the teacher is likely to attribute the pupil's performance to some external factor such as the pupil having an "off" day. The teacher acts to maintain the initial impression of the pupil. For whatever the reason, teachers' initial sizing-up assessments and expectations tend to remain stable over the school year, unless substantial evidence is available to alter the teacher's view.

Observation in Sizing-Up Assessment

Observation is an important classroom assessment strategy. It is relied upon heavily by teachers in many decision-making situations, and in particular for situations related to sizing-up assessment. Classroom observations are of two types: formal and informal. Table 2.2 contrasts the features of these two types.

TABLE 2.2

Comparison of Informal and Formal Classroom Observation

Informal Observation	Formal Observation
Naturalistic: Permits only naturally occurring behaviors to be observed	**Predetermined:** Constructed so pupils will have to demonstrate a desired behavior
Idiosyncratic: Viewed from each individual's unique perspective	**Generalizable:** Capable of being applied across many pupils and situations
Subjective: Interpretations based on individual's own judgments	**Objective:** Interpretations based on external or empirical verification
Descriptive: Assessment information results in narrative descriptions	**Numerical:** Assessment information results in numerical descriptions
Covert: Information rarely written down	**Overt:** Information recorded and reported

Informal observations have five characteristics that distinguish them from formal observations and these traits are important to recognize when using informal observations for sizing up pupils (Arends, 1994; Borich, 1990). Informal observations are: (1) naturalistic, (2) idiosyncratic, (3) subjective, (4) descriptive, and (5) covert. Consider each of these characteristics in turn.

1. *Informal observation is naturalistic.* Informal observation takes place in a natural setting, not in an artificial, structured one. In formal observation, a situation is constructed that requires pupils to demonstrate a particular behavior. For example, if a teacher wants to determine how well pupils can give a 5-minute prepared speech, the teacher could require each student to prepare and give such a speech. If the teacher wants to see how well a group of children interact with one another, the teacher could ask those children to do a group project. In both of these examples, the teacher constructs a formal situation that permits observation of the desired pupil behaviors.

In informal observation, events are observed as they spontaneously occur. What the observer sees is neither planned nor controlled; it simply happens as part of the natural flow of classroom events. Informal observations can provide a more realistic picture of pupil behaviors than formal observations, where the artificial structuring may evoke atypical or unnatural behaviors. Furthermore, some pupil characteristics such as motivation or interest are difficult to assess in formal, structured ways. However, it is important to note that informal observations can be collected only about those behaviors that occur naturally. This means that some pupil behaviors may not be observed because, for whatever the reason, they did not occur spontaneously in the classroom. It also means that teachers can observe only those behaviors that the pupils are willing to show them.

2. *Informal observation is idiosyncratic to the person doing the observation and the person being observed.* Each person views the world from some perspective, with some set of ideals, preferences, attitudes, and beliefs. This perspective influences the way the person perceives and interprets observations and events. This is true for all observers, especially teachers in the classroom.

Moreover, because informal observations are unplanned, different pupils are observed at different times and under different circumstances. Consequently, informal observations result in different characteristics being observed for different pupils, different opportunities for pupils to show behavior, and different types of evidence being gathered across pupils. The information gathered about a pupil is also idiosyncratic, because it is unique to that pupil in many ways.

3. *Informal observation is subjective.* The teacher is the primary information gatherer in the classroom. But in order to be of use, the teacher's informal observations must be interpreted. There is an important difference between an observation and the interpretation a teacher attaches to that observation. Most interpretations are subjective because they depend largely upon the perspective of the teacher-interpreter. Bear in mind that the explanation or reason for an observed behavior is not always clear, and sometimes explanations that seem clear are wrong. Few single observations, especially informal ones made in the first few days of school, can be explained without the collection of additional information.

For example, suppose you observe a pupil sitting with her head on the desk during a lesson. What does this observation mean? Is she tired? Is she bored? If she's bored, is it because she has already learned what you're teaching, or because her background knowledge is too poor to understand it? Is she showing her disdain for you or the class? Does she want attention? There are many possible explanations for the observed behavior, and the way a teacher responds to the behavior will depend very much upon the interpretation given it. One interpretation may result in scolding and harsh words, another in extra help, and still another in a note to the parents. Notice that once sizing-up perceptions are formed in the teacher's mind, they become the perspective from which further interpretations are made, making them doubly influential. Once pupils have been sized up, interpretations of classroom events and the teacher's responses to these events will depend as much upon who the student is as upon what the student does.

There can be many different interpretations of an observed behavior. When different people observe the same behavior and agree upon its meaning, we say that the observation is **objective.** When different people observe the same behavior and each interprets it differently, we say the observation is **subjective.** Interpretations of informally observed behaviors, especially those related to attitudes, values, or personality traits, tend to be subjective. Similarly, the quicker classroom behaviors unfold, the less time there is for objective reflection; consequently, the likelihood that interpretations will be subjective increases.

4. *Informal observation is descriptive.* In informal observation, the information collected tends to be descriptive, not numerical. Teachers summarize their particular observations of pupils by using general labels like "motivated," "creative," "high achieving," "self-confident," and "lazy." Often, these general labels ignore and hide the specific observations on which they were based. Teachers observe so many things about pupils that they must simplify the information to make it useful to them. In order to simplify, they construct a model of the pupil by synthesizing information into a few general categories or labels. The pace and complexity of classroom life encourages the need for simple descriptive terms to characterize pupils.

5. *Informal observation is covert, or unrecorded.* The interpretations and descriptions resulting from informal observations are rarely written down. Teachers carry their perceptions of pupils in their minds, preferring not to commit them to paper because they often include affective judgments about pupils that the teacher may regard as private. Also, because the perceptions are based largely upon informal observation, there is little hard evidence to support a teacher's perception if he or she is challenged on it. However, when prompted, teachers can provide rich and detailed descriptions of their pupils.

In summary, informal observation is naturalistic, which limits it to events that occur as part of the natural flow of classroom activities. It is idiosyncratic, limited by each teacher's particular perspective and each pupil's particular observed behavior. It is subjective, based upon personal, often unverified, interpretations made by the classroom teacher. It is descriptive, summarizing perceptions into a general, oversimplified but usable portrait of a pupil that is qualitative rather than quantitative. It is covert, residing in the teacher's head, not in a formal, written record. These five characteristics have important implications for the quality of sizing-up assessments that are based wholly or largely on teachers' informal observations.

✖ The Validity and Reliability of Sizing-Up Assessments

It is appropriate to examine the quality of the sizing-up assessments that teachers construct in their classrooms. How well do these assessments capture the reality of pupil characteristics? How aware are teachers of their influences on pupils? In this section we examine the main problems that can diminish the validity and reliability of sizing-up assessments and the decisions that are based upon them. Validity and reliability work hand in hand to ensure that the perceptions formed from sizing-up assessment are appropriate and trustworthy, leading to good decisions about pupils.

Problems That Affect Validity

Validity is concerned with the collection of *appropriate* evidence—that is, evidence that is related to the pupil characteristic under consideration. Central to the validity of assessment information is the question "Does the evidence I have gathered tell me about the characteristic I wish to judge?" There are two main dangers that occur during sizing-up assessment that diminish the validity of the information gathered: stereotyping and logical error. **Stereotyping** occurs when a member of a group is assumed to have characteristics associated with that group. **Logical error** occurs when the wrong indicators are used to determine a pupil's status and characteristics.

Stereotyping

Stereotyping refers to situations in which a teacher's personal prejudices or beliefs interfere with the ability to make a fair and objective assessment of a pupil (Steele, 1997). When this happens, the validity of the sizing-up assessment is reduced. All of us have personal prejudices or beliefs; we prefer some things to other things and some kinds of people to other kinds. We have beliefs, interests, ideas, and expectations that differentiate us from other people. However, when these likes, dislikes, beliefs, and prejudices interfere with our ability to make fair pupil assessments, there is a real problem.

Teachers' personal prejudices or stereotypes about particular groups often lead to unfair, invalid pupil perceptions. When teachers think or make statements like "This pupil comes from Old Town, and kids from Old Town are poor learners and discipline problems," "Girls are no good in math," "Everyone knows that members of that group have no interest in school," "Parents who don't show up at school have no interest in education and expect little in the way of school performance from their children," or "He's just another dumb jock," they are expressing their personal prejudices or stereotypes of what certain people are and how they think those people behave. The person is labeled because he or she belongs to a particular club, race, disability group, gender, social class, language group, nationality, or religion. Being labeled and stereotyped without a fair chance to show one's true characteristics can injure pupils and inhibit their learning. Thus, during sizing-up assessment, teachers should be particularly sensitive to possible gender, race, culture, disability, and social class stereotypes when making judgments. Recognize that stereotyping is a validity concern because it deals with the issue of whether the group stereotype used to size up a pupil is valid and appropriate for that particular individual.

Stereotyping is of particular concern with regard to teachers' racial, cultural, disability, and language prejudgments and stereotypes. While the variety of pupil languages, cultures, races, and disabilities in American classrooms is quickly increasing, the variety of teachers who teach these pupils is not increasing as quickly. When sizing up pupils, teachers who are not familiar with pupils' cultures and languages often interpret what are really cultural *differences* as if they were cultural *deficits* (Ladson-Billings, 1994; Delpit, 1995) Similarly, teachers' stereotypes or personal beliefs can produce invalid sizing-up assessments for students who are different from the teacher. For example, many Americans, including many teachers, believe that the majority of children of color are poor, come from single-family homes, and live on public assistance. In fact, none of these beliefs are true regarding children of color. How might a teacher who erroneously believes these misconceptions perceive a pupil of color on the first day of school? Do you think he or she might have some prejudgments or stereotypes that could influence initial perceptions of the pupil? The dangers of prejudgment are real and consequential. Teachers must strive to recognize their personal beliefs and stereotypes and judge each individual pupil on the basis of how he or she actually performs in class. Each pupil is an individual entitled to be judged on his or her own merits, not on the basis of stereotypes and personal beliefs. Guaranteeing this right is a teacher's ethical responsibility.

Are stereotypes always wrong? Of course not. There typically is some truth that perpetuates stereotypes: many kids from Old Town have behavior problems and are weak academically; many families do have a consistently poor record in school; many females do achieve lower than males in math and science; many athletes do poorly in their studies; and the failure of parents to participate in school activities is sometimes a sign of low interest and lack of concern about their children's school performance. It is because there is *some* truth to these stereotypes that they persist and are so dangerous when sizing up pupils. It is vital that teachers recognize that stereotypes and personal prejudices are not universally true and thus cannot be relied upon when making sizing-up assessments. There is no way a teacher can know whether a particular female does well in math and science, whether an athlete is a good student, whether a pupil with a speech disability has a compensating accommodation, or whether a pupil has a behavior problem until the teacher observes that particular female, athlete, or pupil. Succumbing to stereotypes severely limits the validity of sizing-up assessments.

Logical Errors

When teachers select the wrong indicators to assess a pupil's characteristics, they lower the validity of their sizing-up assessments. A logical error occurs when teachers mistakenly assume that the behavior they observe provides information about the pupil characteristic they wish to describe. For example, when someone says, "Mr. Graves is warm and friendly in his interactions with pupils. They must learn a lot from him," we very likely are hearing a logical error. Warmth and friendliness with pupils *may* contribute to pupil learning, but warmth and friendliness by themselves are certainly no guarantee that pupils will learn. The person who made this statement is assuming that two observed characteristics, warmth and friendliness, also provide information about a third unobserved characteristic, pupil learning. If the assumption is incorrect, the observer has made a logical error by linking warmth and friendliness to pupil learning. Logical errors lead to invalid assessment and incorrect decisions.

Earlier in this chapter a number of teacher comments indicated the behaviors or characteristics teachers looked for in the first few days of school in order to size up their pupils. Some of these teachers reported that they judged pupils' academic and personality characteristics by observing their body language, disabilities, posture, attendance, volunteering answers, and so on. From these observations teachers formed perceptions of their pupils' abilities, personalities, self-concept, motivation, and home background. It is appropriate to question the validity of such perceptions. That is, do observations of disability, body language, posture, and so forth provide the best information to judge pupils' ability, personality, or self-concept? Is body language a good indicator of personality, or are there other, better and more valid indicators that should be examined? Is a pupil's learning style or disability a good indicator of motivation, or are there more relevant characteristics that provide a more valid indication of motivation? These are important validity questions.

It is tempting to read a great deal into a single observation, especially at the start of the year when teachers want to quickly characterize each pupil in order to size up and organize their classes. It would be convenient, for example, to read a whole series of inferences about a pupil's motivation, attention span, interest in the subject, self-concept, and leadership based on the pupil's eager hand raising. Maybe all the interpretations would prove to be correct, but it is wrong and dangerous not to recognize the difference between information that is directly observed and interpretations of that information. This distinction and the problems it can lead to were noted in the prior section on observation in sizing-up assessment. When observation of one characteristic is used to infer about other unobserved characteristics, the potential for logical errors—and therefore invalid assessment—is great.

A fifth grade teacher described Mihaly's first day in school this way: "I knew right away that Mihaly was cooperative and a hard worker. He was the first pupil to complete his 'Summer Vacation' essay, and instead of wasting his free time, he offered to get the dictionary and help the other children with their spelling." Is being cooperative and a hard worker the only valid interpretation of Mihaly's behavior? What are some others, and how might you go about determining which is correct?

Recognize that the labels teachers use to describe pupils are based on interpretations of their pupils' behaviors. For example, teachers do not directly observe characteristics such as "motivation," "intelligence," "leadership," "self-confidence," "aggressiveness," "anxiety," "shyness," "intolerance," and the like. Rather, they observe a pupil behaving in some way, interpret what they think the behavior signifies, and give the behavior a name like "motivated," "leadership," "interest," or "anxious." It is the *name* given to the behavior that attaches to the pupil in sizing-up assessment, not the specific behavior that prompted the teacher to use the name. Teachers remember that a pupil is a bully, self-confident, aggressive, aloof, motivated, or shy, but they rarely remember the specific observations that led them to label the pupil in that way.

Most teachers recognize the dangers stereotyping and logical error introduce to validity, as the following statements indicate.

> I don't like to hear anything about a student's behavior from past instructors. Every teacher is different, just like every student is different. A student may have a negative experience with one teacher, but a positive experience with another teacher. I prefer to make my own decision about every child.

It is so easy to be influenced by what other teachers tell you. Many times I have known a child without ever having met him—and he has had to pay the consequences of my ignorance.

There are both positive and negative consequences of relying on prior knowledge about pupils or going to school records to size-up pupils before school starts.

I remember the time I stereotyped three of my female students based on their wardrobe—not too bright and mainly superficial—in the first days of class. Yet when it came time for formal assessment, these three individuals ranked the highest in the class.

From the class list, one does notice "familiar" names. These could be the troublemakers, intellectuals, highly motivated, or the siblings of previous students. Information about the names comes from various sources. It could be personal relations with a family, teachers' room conversations, town gossip, or just plain exposure to students in other classes. It's easy to be aware of these things, but I make it a rule to never let this become my first impression.

Reliability of Sizing-Up Assessments

Reliability is concerned with collecting *enough* evidence to be reasonably certain that the pupil's typical performance is being observed. Teachers ask, "Is the evidence gathered indicative of the pupil's typical or normal performance?" Whether formal or informal, teachers' assessments are based upon samples of their pupils' behavior. These samples are used to make generalizations about the pupils' typical behavior. This process is analogous to political polling, in which a sample of people is asked whom they will vote for in the next election and the sample responses are used to infer the likely voting pattern of the entire electorate. Similarly, teachers observe samples of a pupil's behavior and use those samples to form perceptions to characterize the pupil. The concern in both political polling and teacher assessment is how well the observed sample represents the electorate's or the pupil's general behavior. Reliable information captures consistent and stable pupil characteristics.

The nature of sizing-up assessments creates special reliability problems. For example, the spontaneity of informal observation limits what teachers are able to see and what pupils are willing to show. Also, the time available to observe pupils is often brief, since attention must be distributed among many pupils and classroom activities. The lack of time for prolonged observation reduces the opportunity to assess stable and typical pupil behavior patterns. The fewer the opportunities to observe a pupil, the more difficult it is to judge whether the assessment information is typical of the pupil's behavior. The sample of behavior that is observed under these circumstances may not be a reliable indicator of a pupil's typical behavior. Many teachers recognize this problem, particularly as it applies to sizing-up assessments at the start of the school year. Consider the following comments from teachers.

First impressions are so important. They can either make or break a child. It all depends on how much opportunity a particular teacher gives to a student to prove himself before passing a judgment. Unfortunately, so many children get stuck with the short end of the stick early in the year—and pay for it throughout the rest of the school year.

The first days are very difficult. The students will not even present their "normal" classroom behaviors to you in the first three days. They are somewhat intimidated and uncomfortable; they don't know you. Even kids who are badly behaved in the first three days, they're just feeling you out, they're testing, trying to see how far they can get.

It's easy to misinterpret some deviant behavior as being a big problem when in fact it might be the uncomfortableness of a new situation. A child's behavior in the beginning few days of class is not always the typical behavior of that child.

Carol breaks up with her boyfriend a week before the beginning of school, leaving her depressed and unmotivated. Does Carol's English teacher know the reason for this behavior? Is her assessment of Carol after 1 day of school correct? Josh had been a below average student his first 2 years of high school. He had never fulfilled his potential before, but now wants to go to college. He is finally motivated to work hard. Can he overcome the teacher's lounge grapevine and prove himself to his new teachers? The teacher's view of the pupil plays a large role in the pupil's view of him or herself and, consequently, in the pupil's academic achievement. If Carol's teacher views her as a disinterested student based on the first week of school, then, even though Carol normally is a very energetic and motivated student, there is a strong possibility that Carol will respond to being treated as disinterested by being disinterested. Josh, by the same token, has been labeled as a poor student and will most likely have to overcome his reputation by extraordinarily hard work.

Because John hit Stephan in the nose this morning out in the schoolyard doesn't necessarily mean that he will be the class bully. It may be that he has had a very bad day and Stephan said something to push him over the edge. You must give each child half a chance to show you what he or she is typically made of.

The implication of these comments is that teachers must be sure they collect enough information about pupils before solidifying their perceptions and using them to label pupils. There are times, such as the start of the school year, when pupils' behavior may not be indicative of their normal behavior. They may be nervous, uncomfortable with a new teacher, not yet settled into school after summer vacation, or intimidated by the teacher or new classmates. Any of these or other factors may distort pupils' behavior until they feel more settled and comfortable in class. In short, what is typical behavior cannot be determined by observing a pupil just once or for just one day, especially at a time when the pupil may feel uncomfortable in new surroundings.

It is important to note that because teachers are reluctant to change their initial impressions of pupils there is no guarantee that those perceptions are reliable. In fact, one of the most harmful consequences of sizing-up assessment occurs when teachers refuse to admit that their initial assessments were inaccurate.

In order to determine the reliability of sizing-up assessment it is necessary to observe pupil behavior multiple times. A single behavior is insufficient. Conversely, a teacher trying to remember every behavior a particular student showed in one day is likely to forget much of what has been seen, thus lowering reliability. For example, Stiggins (1997) notes that our personal observations and exchanges with pupils provide a great deal of information about them. He uses the term *personal communication* to describe six common forms of teacher-pupil exchanges: questioning, conferencing, classroom discussions, oral examinations, and pupil journals. Teacher conversations with others who know the pupil or pupils also can provide information. These teacher-pupil interactions are often used, consciously or unconsciously, to inform teachers' sizing-up assessments. What kinds of information could a teacher gather about students from each of the six forms of personal communication?

As noted earlier, informal personal communication tends to be subjective. That is, the usefulness and reliability of the information gathered is dependent on the memory and interpretations of the teacher. Two problems can limit the reliability of all forms of personal communications with pupils. First, because of the limits of the human mind and memory, teachers may "lose" or forget important pieces of information about a student. Most of the six personal communication approaches involve dealing with many students over short time periods, thus taxing the depth and accuracy of teacher memory. If memory is faulty or incomplete, the reliability of the information is lowered. Second, because teachers can observe any given pupil only part of the time, it is inevitable that their observations will be partial and limited, thus producing unreliable information (McCaslin and Good, 1996). Personal communications are varied, often brief, and focused on a large number of pupils, thereby increasing the possibility that insufficient information will be obtained to provide reliable interpretations about pupil characteristics. Thus, while varied personal communication approaches help teachers gather valuable information about pupils, teachers should also recognize the potential reliability problems of selective memory and insufficient information.

The reliability of teachers' perceptions differs with different pupil characteristics. Studies reveal that, in general, classroom teachers are fairly accurate in their early predictions of pupils' cognitive performance as measured by test scores (Alexander, Entwisle, and Dauber, 1993). Of course some teachers are more accurate than others, but overall, teachers are reasonably accurate judges of pupils' ability and achievement. This result, however, does not mean that even the most accurate teacher is correct about every pupil. It simply means that when teachers are asked to rank their pupils from best to worst in academic performance early in the school year, they can reliably put pupils in a high, medium, or low classification. It does not mean that teachers can rank their pupils individually from highest to lowest. Teachers are also accurate in identifying many pupils' psychomo-

TABLE 2.3

Threats to the Validity and Reliability of Sizing-Up Assessments

Validity Threats

1. Stereotyping: labeling pupils based on prior information, first impressions, or personal theories (e.g., girls do poorly in math and science, athletes do worse in school than nonathletes, etc.)
2. Logical errors: judging pupils based on the wrong characteristics (e.g., judging pupils' motivation based on how they are dressed, judging pupils' ability by their culture or disability, etc.)

Reliability Threats

1. Inadequate sampling: making decisions about a pupil based on a single observation or piece of information
2. Generalizing: observing performance or behavior in one setting (playground) and assuming the pupil's performance or behavior will be the same in a different setting (classroom)

tor behaviors. Teachers can generally see many pupils' physical disabilities and other psychomotor skills are also readily observable.

The reliability of teachers' assessments of pupils' affective behaviors such as motivation, interest, activity, self-concept, emotional development, and social adjustment is less well examined and, consequently, less well established. Teachers do perceive differences between pupils on affective behaviors, but the accuracy of teachers' affective perceptions is lower than their perceptions of pupils' cognitive and psychomotor characteristics. Thus, regardless of the particular evidence gathered to support sizing-up decisions, it is important to recognize the potential of unreliable decisions based on too little information.

Table 2.3 summarizes the threats to validity and reliability that we have just discussed. For the most part, these threats are a result of the informal assessment process itself and the subjective, idiosyncratic, naturalistic context in which these assessments are made. Considering the helter-skelter nature of most classrooms and the relatively short time available to form initial perceptions of pupils, one can see the potential for assessments to be based upon information that is not valid or reliable.

Sizing-Up Effects on Pupils

If sizing-up assessments were private, if they were kept in the teacher's head and had no influence on pupils, there would be few problems with them. But that is not the case. The initial impressions and perceptions formed about pupils can influence the way teachers perceive, treat, interact with, and make decisions about them throughout the school year. Teachers' sizing-up assessments influence their academic, social, and personal expectations for both individual pupils and the entire class. These predictions and expectations, in turn, influence the way teachers interact with pupils and the class. Teachers' beliefs about pupils' capabilities can have great impact on pupils' self-perception and achievement.

One potential effect of sizing-up assessment on pupils is the creation of a **self-fulfilling prophecy** (Oakes and Lipton, 1999; Good and Brophy, 1997; Arends, 1994). The process of a self-fulfilling prophecy contains a number of steps. First, a teacher's sizing-up assessment leads the teacher to expect certain behaviors or levels of performance from a pupil. Second, the teacher interacts with the pupil based on the teacher's expectations. Third, the teacher communicates the expectations to the pupil. Fourth, the teacher's behavior toward the pupil affects the pupil. Fifth, the student begins to conform to the teacher's expectations. Sixth, the pupil's behavior reinforces the teacher's expectations for the pupil. This cycle continues until the pupil conforms to the teacher's initial perception. Thus, if a teacher expects that a pupil is incapable of learning (whether or not that belief is correct), and the teacher communicates this expectation to the pupil, the chances are good that the teacher's initial expectation will become a reality. Needless to say, it is the teacher's ethical responsibility to avoid this situation by making sizing-up assessments as fair and accurate as possible for all pupils.

A second influence of teachers' sizing-up assessments relates to the consequences of stereotyping. "Any time a student takes a test, especially one that compares her with other students, and any time her performance is public, such as when she answers aloud in class, this student is vulnerable to the judgments of others. However, there can be an added burden of vulnerability when the student is acutely aware that her lack of knowledge or difficulty with language is associated with all the negative judgments about her race, speakers of her first language, or others of her social class" (Oakes and Lipton, 1999, pp. 200–201). Similar vulnerability can occur with pupil gender, disability, or culture. Stereotyping raises problems such as being negatively stereotyped, being judged or treated stereotypically, conforming to the stereotype, and other threats (Steele, 1997).

The negative consequences of stereotyping are many. Common examples include internalizing the stereotype with a resulting sense of inadequacy; extreme or undue pressure to perform well; and emotional distress (Steele and Aronson, 1995; Steele, 1992). A more subtle consequence occurs when belief in a stereotype leads to lack of encouragement or teacher efforts to improve pupils' performance. Thus, a teacher who believes that a blind student cannot function successfully in a regular classroom setting is unlikely to try to help or encourage the pupil.

A third influence of sizing-up assessments on pupils concerns the teacher's communication of their sizing-up perceptions to pupils. The classroom is a public place in which most activities occur in the presence of others. Consequently, it is hard *not* to communicate perceptions. If you were to wander into a first grade classroom soon after the start of the school year and you asked any pupil in the class to name the best and worst readers, chances are very good that the pupil could tell you. Even though the groups may be called the Sparrows, Cardinals, and Barn Owls, or be identified by the title of their text (no thinking teacher would overtly identify these groups as top, middle, and low readers), the pupils quickly and accurately decipher the pecking order from highest to lowest. Ask the pupils who the teacher likes best, who tries the hardest, who is the smartest, or who the teacher dislikes, and you will get similar replies. Remember, we are talking about first graders who are relatively new to schooling and who have only been with the teacher a short time. To emphasize, the classroom is a public place where teacher actions and interactions convey almost as much as overt labels. Pupils learn more in classrooms than subject matter. They also learn about themselves and how others perceive them.

Teachers communicate their sizing-up assessments in many ways (O'Neil and Drillings, 1994; Good and Brophy, 1997). Offhand comments tell individuals and the class a great deal about the teacher's perceptions: "Oh Robert, can't you even remember what we just talked about?" "All right Sarah, will you tell the rest of the class the answer it can't seem to understand.'" "Didn't Ruby read that paragraph with a lot of expression?" "No Sid, don't bother, this work is too hard for you." Sometimes perceptions are conveyed indirectly, as when a teacher waits patiently for one pupil to think through a problem but allows another only a few seconds; expresses encouragement and assurance to one student but says "at least try" to another; encourages one pupil to "think" but another to "take a guess." Tone of voice, physical proximity, gestures, seating arrangements, and other signals all tell pupils how they are perceived in the classroom.

To summarize, we have seen that sizing-up assessments are largely based upon information that is gathered in the first few days of school, that teachers form these assessments quickly, and that they remain fairly stable throughout the school year. Available evidence also suggests that teachers are reasonably accurate in predicting the academic performance of their pupils, but less so in predicting their social or personal qualities. Finally, sizing-up assessments spawn perceptions and expectations, which in turn influence teachers' interactions with pupils. Because sizing-up assessments can be so influential in setting expectations, influencing pupil-teacher interactions, and affecting pupils' performance and self-perception, it is important to examine more closely the process through which such assessments are made. It also is necessary to identify the dangers inherent in that process and the strategies teachers can use to improve their initial pupil assessments.

⚔ Improving Sizing-Up Assessments

Having examined some of the problems endemic to sizing-up assessments, we now turn to some of the strategies that teachers can use to overcome these problems. The strategies suggested here are all simple, manageable actions that teachers can take to enhance the validity and reliability of their sizing-up assessments. However, they will not produce perfect information collection or decision making. As long as pupil perceptions are heavily influenced by teachers' interpretations of pupil behavior, total elimination of error will remain an elusive goal. The teacher's ethical responsibility, therefore, is to do everything possible to minimize errors and to revise judgments when initial impressions prove to be wrong.

1. *Be aware of sizing-up assessment and of its effects on pupils.* Sizing-up assessment is such a natural teacher behavior that teachers are often unaware that they are doing it. But doing it they are, because it is a necessary prerequisite to bringing order into the classroom social setting. If a teacher does not realize that sizing-up assessment is occurring and does not recognize the dangers of forming incorrect impressions of pupils, little can be done to improve the assessment process. Teachers must be aware that they attach labels to pupils very early in the school year and they must be sensitive to the consequences of making incorrect judgments based on incomplete or prejudiced observations. Consequently, awareness of sizing-up assessment—of its legitimate role in the classroom, its influence on pupil-teacher interactions, and its dangers—is the necessary first step in improving the process.

2. *Treat initial impressions as hypotheses to be confirmed or corrected by subsequent observations and information.* Initial impressions based upon informal observations should be considered tentative hypotheses that need to be confirmed or disproved by subsequent observation and information. Not all initial impressions made by teachers are correct. The less information a teacher has gathered about a pupil, the greater the amount of interpretation and subjective analysis the teacher must perform to define the pupil's characteristics and the greater the likelihood of error in judgment. In areas such as achievement and ability, teachers are reasonably accurate in sizing up their pupils' performance levels. In their initial assessments of pupils' affective traits such as interest, motivation, aggression, boredom, or self-confidence, teachers are less accurate because it takes longer to size up affective characteristics. Regardless of whether the focus is cognitive or affective pupil characteristics, no teacher's initial perceptions are correct all the time.

One method to improve sizing-up assessment and the perceptions that result from it is to try to refrain from judging and labeling pupils on the basis of hearsay or a single, brief observation. When a doctor sees a patient, the doctor goes through a series of information-gathering stages to diagnose or "size up" the patient's problem. The physician asks the patient about the problem and its symptoms. On the basis of this information the doctor forms a first, general impression of what diagnoses fit the symptoms. But doctors do not stop with this initial information gathering. They ask further questions to narrow the range of possible diagnoses. "Does it hurt when you breathe?" "How long has it been like this?" "Does it seem to be worse?" "Is it worse before or after eating?" "Is the pain consistent or intermittent?" "Have you had a fever?" Synthesizing the information gathered from these two stages of questioning might lead the doctor to an accurate diagnosis. If not, more information will be collected until the proper diagnosis is made. This medical example provides a good model for classroom teachers when they carry out sizing-up assessments. Confirm the first impression with subsequent observations and information and do not be afraid to change an incorrect first impression.

3. *Use direct indicators to gather information about pupil characteristics.* Teachers must interpret their observations in order to use them in sizing-up pupils. Some observations require less interpretation than others do because they are more valid, that is, more closely related to the pupil characteristic under consideration. Other observations that are less related to the characteristic of interest require a more complex and error-prone chain of reasoning to characterize the pupil. **Direct indicators** are those that are closely related to the characteristic of interest, while **indirect indicators** are those that are not closely related and consequently require a number of interpretive leaps by the teacher. The more relevant the observed behavior is to the pupil trait a teacher wishes to describe, the more valid the resulting information, and the more confident a teacher can be about a perception based on it.

Assume that a teacher wants to determine a pupil's motivation to learn. He could do this in a variety of ways. He could ask the previous year's teacher about the pupil's motivation to learn or he could (as did a number of teachers quoted earlier) determine motivation by observing the pupil's neatness, dress, and choice of peers. He could also watch the pupil for behaviors such as staying after school to complete work and asking questions about topics discussed. There are many indicators the teacher could use to assess motivation.

There are, however, differences in the validity of the information provided by different indicators. The pupil's dress and choice of friends are indirect indicators of the pupil's motivation to learn. In order to infer a connection between pupil dress and motivation, the teacher has to make a number of assumptions: (1) that the way a person dresses tells something about his or her personality; (2) that for this particular pupil, clothes reflect personality rather than income level, fashion, or parental guidance; (3) that there are particular kinds of dress that are more indicative of motivation to learn than others; (4) that the teacher knows what those styles are and what they indicate about motivation; and (5) that today's clothes represent the pupil's typical style of dress. Each of these assumptions may be wrong, which would invalidate the process of judging a student's motivation by his dress. In short, the more assumptions needed to support an interpretation, the more likely it is that errors will occur. Lack of validity is a main problem with indirect indicators.

Suppose the teacher asks last year's teacher about the pupil's motivation to learn. In this case the teacher is using a more direct indicator than the pupil's style of dress. However, by relying on the judgment of last year's teacher, the teacher assumes: (1) that both teachers define motivation to learn in the same way; and (2) that the pupil has not changed a great deal since last year. In the end, the best way for the teacher to determine motivation to learn is by direct observation of the pupil's classroom activities, such as asking questions, staying after school to complete work, spending spare time on lesson-related topics, and so on. These are more direct indicators, because the behaviors of interest are closely related to motivation and are observed directly. Note that the teacher still has to make assumptions about how typical the observed behavior is and whether the pupil is faking the apparent motivation. Nevertheless, direct observation is much more likely to produce valid sizing-up information than the use of indirect indicators.

In sizing-up assessments, teacher-pupil encounters are brief and the tendency is for the teacher to focus on superficial, indirect characteristics such as dress, facial expression, helpfulness, general appearance, and so on. The teacher then reads into these superficial observations, inferring that they indicate evidence of more complex traits and personality factors like motivation, self-concept, trustworthiness, self-control, and interest. Such generalizations are likely to be invalid because, as noted, they are based upon a chain of assumptions which are unlikely to be completely true. The moral is to avoid overgeneralization from indirect indicators; good assessment involves gathering information that is directly related to the pupil characteristic being assessed.

4. *Supplement informal observations with more formal, structured activities.* There is no rule requiring the exclusive use of informal observations to size up pupils. In fact, the informal nature of most observations means that the teacher does not have control over many of the behaviors that occur, especially in the first few days of school. Many teachers recognize this limitation and introduce more structured activities to supplement their ongoing sizing-up observations.

In order to get maximum benefit from formal assessment activities at the start of the school year, it is important that teachers plan the activities in advance and structure classroom events so that time is available to observe and interact with pupils. Setting up seatwork assignments or simple group activities can provide the teacher with an opportunity to circulate about the room and observe pupils' work habits and interpersonal skills. It also can provide time for teachers to meet one-on-one with pupils to have them read aloud or talk about their interests. It is also useful to structure classroom activities to permit the observation of one or two specific pupil characteristics per day (e.g., cooperation in groups, mastery of content prerequisites, study habits, reference knowledge and skills).

Some school systems collect samples of pupils' work into portfolios. These portfolios often accompany the pupils as they progress from grade to grade. They provide a new teacher with concrete examples of a pupil's work as well as a cumulative record of performance across grades. Note that having actual samples of a pupil's work from previous years is quite different from the hearsay evidence teachers accumulate through the school grapevine. Portfolios will be described more fully in Chapter 9. The following list provides a representative sample of the kinds of formal activities that teachers can engage pupils in during the first week of school to broaden sizing-up assessments.

- Administer textbook review or diagnostic pretests in subject areas to assess pupils' entering levels.
- Require pupils to keep a journal during the first week of school or write an essay on "What I Did Last Summer" to assess pupils' experiences, writing skills, and thought processes.
- Carry out group discussions or group projects to assess how pupils interact and work in groups.
- Let pupils read aloud to determine reading facility.
- Play classroom games based on spelling words, math facts, geographical knowledge, or current events to assess general knowledge, interest, and competitiveness.
- Use games related to listening skills to assess pupils' abilities to follow directions and process auditory information.
- Have pupils do paired introductions describing each pupil's activities, pets, etc.

To summarize, structured exercises, activities, and work samples accomplish two goals in sizing-up assessment. First, they provide information about pupil interests, styles, and academic performance that is not always obtainable from informal observations. Second, they require all pupils to perform the same behavior and thereby permit comparisons among pupils on desired characteristics. Structured activities are important and useful supplements to informal observations in the process of sizing up pupils. They also generally provide more direct and thus more valid pupil assessments.

5. *Observe long enough to be fairly certain that you have perceived the pupil's typical behavior.* It is evident that a very important feature of good information is that it represents the *typical* behavior of a pupil. It is for this reason that rushing to make judgments in the first few days of school or basing perceptions solely upon first impressions can produce both invalid and unreliable assessments. To obtain data that are reliable, the teacher must look for consistent patterns of behavior, not for one-time, never-to-be-repeated behaviors. This caution is especially appropriate since, once formed, teacher perceptions tend not to change much. The greater the consequences that an assessment is likely to have for pupils, the higher the standard of certainty a teacher should strive for in information gathering.

There is no standard amount of time or number of observations that can insure that assessment data represent stable, typical pupil behavior. This will vary according to the observational skills of the teacher, the number of characteristics being observed, the opportunity to observe characteristics of interest, and the nature of the pupil being observed. However, a good rule of thumb to follow is to make sure the behavior on which one wishes to base a perception is observed at least twice. This "see it twice" principle will guard against isolated, atypical behaviors being accorded too much influence in forming a perception of the pupil. Don't let a single test performance, classroom incident, lunchroom behavior, or peer interaction—good or bad—define a pupil's character, ability, or personality. Give pupils the benefit of the doubt before passing judgment; give them a fair chance to show their typical behaviors and characteristics.

Box 2.2   Strategies to Improve Sizing-Up Assessment

1. Recognize that sizing-up assessment is taking place; without this awareness, it is difficult to improve the process.
2. Let first impressions represent initial hypotheses to be confirmed or rejected by additional information.
3. Observe important pupil behaviors directly rather than inferring them from ancillary behaviors and characteristics.
4. Supplement informal observation with more formal, structured assessments such as pretests and games. Pick one pupil characteristic per day and structure classroom activities that encourage pupils to demonstrate that characteristic.
5. See behaviors at least twice before judging pupils.
6. Determine whether different types and source of information (e.g., informal observation, formal observation, tests, or other teachers' comments) provide similar information about pupil characteristics.

6. *Determine whether different kinds of information confirm each other.* Astronomers use the method of "triangulation" to locate stars. Essentially, this method involves measuring a star's position relative to two other positions. The three positions (the star's and two others) form a triangle that allows the astronomer to plot the star's position in space with confidence. A form of triangulation is also relevant for classroom assessment, particularly the kind that goes on in the first few days of school.

Teachers can have more confidence in their assessments if they are based upon two or more kinds of supporting evidence. For example, are test scores supported by classroom performance? Are classroom observations of a pupil's needs consistent with those identified by last year's teacher and the pupil's parents? Do classroom behavior patterns persist in the lunchroom and on the playground? Does the classroom teacher's judgment of a pupil's oral reading and comprehension skills match those of last year's teacher and of the pupil's test performance?

Each of these questions represents a form of triangulation in which multiple sources of information are used to corroborate the teacher's perception of a pupil. Such corroboration permits the teacher to be more confident about his or her impressions of the pupil's true characteristics and behaviors. Bear in mind that it is better if the present teacher forms her own impressions of the pupil before obtaining corroborative information from other sources. By doing this, the teacher's perceptions will not be influenced or prejudiced by the perceptions of others. Box 2.2 summarizes the six strategies for improving the validity and reliability of sizing-up assessments.

Chapter Summary

- In the first few days of school, teachers must learn about their pupils and organize them into a classroom society characterized by communication, order, and learning.
- Sizing-up assessments help teachers form perceptions and expectations for their pupils that determine the flow of classroom activities and communication.
- Information for sizing up pupils comes from a variety of sources, including the school grapevine, comments of other teachers, school records, performance of siblings, classroom observations, and pupil comments, body language, performance, and dress. From these sources of information, teachers construct rich descriptions of pupils, usually within the first two weeks of school.
- Sizing-up assessments are a natural part of social interaction. In classrooms they lead teachers to form and often communicate expectations of pupils. Moreover, teachers' first impressions of pupils tend to remain stable, although they are not always accurate. As a consequence, teachers must consider carefully when sizing up and labeling pupils at the start of the school year.
- The process of sizing up involves four steps: collecting information, interpreting the information, synthesizing the information, and naming the characteristic the information describes.
- Much of sizing-up assessment is based on informal observations of pupils. Because of this, informal observations can be limited in their usefulness because they are naturalistic, idiosyncratic, subjective, descriptive, and covert.
- Two main problems affect the validity of sizing-up assessments: stereotyping and logical error. Steroptyping occurs when a teacher's prior knowledge, first impression, or personal beliefs interfere with the ability to make a fair and objective assessment of a pupil. This is a special concern when teachers know little about the racial, cultural, disability, and language characteristics of their pupils. They are likely to interpret cultural differences as cultural deficits. Logical error occurs when teachers use the wrong kind of information to judge pupil characteristics—for example, when they judge interest by a pupil's dress or appearance.
- Reliability is a special problem in sizing-up assessment because the process takes place so quickly and is based upon many fleeting observations, making it difficult to assess pupils' typical or consistent performance. Teachers should not label pupils based on only one or two observations.
- Six suggestions for improving sizing-up assessments are: (1) be aware of sizing-up assessment and of its potential effects on pupils; (2) treat initial impressions as hypotheses to be confirmed or corrected by subsequent observation and information; (3) use direct, low-interpretation indicators to gather information about pupil characteristics; (4) supplement

informal observations with more formal, structured activities; (5) observe long enough to be fairly certain that you have perceived the pupil's typical behavior; and (6) determine whether different kinds of information confirm each other.

Questions for Discussion

1. How does the fact that a classroom is a social setting influence teachers' planning, teaching, grading, managing, and interacting with pupils?
2. What are the advantages and disadvantages of examining a pupil's school (cumulative) record before the start of school? Under what circumstances would you examine a pupil's record before meeting the pupil in class?
3. How much must teachers really know about a pupil's home and family background? What home and background information is absolutely essential for teachers to know? Why? Do a teacher's information needs differ for elementary and high school pupils? What information does a teacher have no right to know about a pupil's home or background?
4. Why do teachers rely so heavily on informal observation when sizing up pupils?
5. What ethical responsibilities do teachers have when collecting and using their sizing-up information?

Reflection Exercises

1. Did you ever have a teacher who liked or disliked you? Who trusted or did not trust you? Who thought you were smart or dumb? Who had perceptions about your ability, character, motivation, or effort? How could you tell the teacher felt that way about you? What did the teacher do or say to communicate that perception to you? How do you know you were reading the teacher's message correctly? What can you do to control the messages you send to pupils?
2. What are the three most common ways teachers transmit their feelings and attitudes about students to them? How can a teacher become aware of the perspectives he or she is transmitting to pupils?
3. Do pupils size each other up? Why and for what reasons?

Activities

1. Interview a classroom teacher. What information does the teacher have about pupils before the first day of class? What are the sources of that information? How much does the teacher rely upon the comments of other teachers when getting to know a new class? If the teacher could know only two specific characteristics of each pupil at the end of the first day of class, what would these be? Why? What information is most useful for managing pupils in the classroom? Add three questions of your own to this list. Why did you select those three questions?

2. List three structured group activities that you could use to begin sizing up your pupils at the start of school. What kinds of information would your activities provide?

Review Questions

1. What factors make a classroom a social setting or society? How do these factors influence teachers' assessment responsibilities?
2. What is sizing-up assessment? How is it done? How does it differ from other types of classroom assessments? What are three dangers that can reduce the validity and reliability of sizing-up assessment?
3. Why are sizing-up assessments important? What do they help teachers accomplish?
4. What are some differences between formal and informal observation?
5. What are the main problems of validity and reliability in sizing-up assessment and assessments for planning and delivering instruction?
6. What are some strategies teachers can use to improve sizing-up assessments?

References

Alexander, K. L., Entwisle, D. R., & Dauber, S. L. (1993). First-grade classroom behavior: Its short- and long-term consequences for school performance. *Child Development, 64*(3), 801–814.

Arends, R. I. (1994). *Learning to teach.* New York: McGraw-Hill.

Boostrom, R. (1991). The value and function of classroom rules. *Curriculum Inquiry, 21*(2), 194–216.

Borich, G. (1900). *Observation skills for effective teaching.* Columbus, OH: Merrill.

Bullough, R. V., Knowles, J. G., & Crow, N. A. (1992). *Emerging as a teacher.* New York: Routledge.

Delpit, L. (1995). *Other people's children: Cultural conflict in the classroom.* New York: The New Press.

Garcia, E. (1994). *Understanding and meeting the challenge of student cultural diversity.* Boston: Houghton Mifflin.

Good, T. L., & Brophy, J. E. (1997). *Looking in classrooms.* New York: Longman.

Goodson, I. (1992). *Studying teacher's lives: Problems and possibilities.* New York: Teachers College Press.

Kolb, K. J. & Jussim, L. (1994). Teacher expectations and underachieving gifted children. *Roeper Review, 17,* 26–30.

Kuhn, D. (1991). *The logic of argument.* New York: Cambridge University Press.

Ladson-Billings, G. (1994). *The dreamkeepers.* San Francisco: Jossey-Bass.

Lieberman, A., & Miller, L. (1992). *Teachers—Their world and their work: Implication for school improvement.* New York: Teachers College Press.

McCaslin, M., & Good, T. (1996). Listening to students. New York: Harper-Collins.

Merryfield, M. M. (1994). Shaping the curriculum in global education: The influence of student characteristics on teacher decision making. *Journal of Curriculum and Supervision, 9*(3), 233–249.

Oakes, J., & Lipton, M. (1999). *Teaching to change the world.* New York: McGraw-Hill.

O'Neil, H. F., & Drillings, M. (1994). Motivation: Theory and research. Hillsdale, NJ: Lawrence Erlbaum Associates.

Solas, J. (1992). Investigating teacher and student thinking about the process of teaching and learning using autobiography and repertory grid. *Review of Educational Research, 62*(2), 205–225.

Steele, C. M. (1992). Race and the schooling of black Americans. *The Atlantic Monthly* (April), 68–78.

Steele, C. M. (1997). A threat in the air: How stereotypes shape intellectual identity and performance. *American Psychologist, 52*(6), 613–629.

Steele, C. M., & Aronson, J. (1995). Stereotype threat and the intellectual test performance of African Americans. *Journal of Personality and Social Psychology, 69,* 797–811.

Stiggins, R. J. (1997). *Student-centered classroom assessment.* Columbus, OH: Prentice Hall.

Wiseman, D. L., Cooner, D. D., & Knight, S. L. (1999). *Becoming a teacher in a field-based setting.* Belmont, CA: Wadsorth.

3

Lesson Planning: Objectives, Standards, and Accommodations

Chapter Outline

❖ Education, Curriculum, and Instruction

❖ The Instructional Process

❖ Characteristics of Objectives

❖ Stating Cognitive Objectives: Bloom's Taxonomy

❖ A Second Dimension of Objectives: Three Types of Knowledge

❖ Other Sources of Objectives

❖ Improving Planning Assessment

❖ Addressing Pupil Accommodations

Chapter Objectives

After reading this chapter, the pupil will be able to:

- Define basic terms: achievement, curriculum, objective, etc.
- Differentiate between education, curriculum, instruction, and objectives
- Describe the instructional process
- Describe the process of teacher planning, including pupil characteristics, teacher characteristics, and instructional resources
- Explain the use of Bloom's Taxonomy and factual, conceptual, and procedural knowledge in developing objectives
- Write and identify well-stated educational and instructional objectives
- State the role and limits of textbook objectives
- Explain the use and formats of statewide and district-wide standards
- Describe teachers' responsibilities in dealing with pupils with disabilities
- Match accommodations to common disabilities

Sizing-up assessments provide the initial information about pupils that helps teachers to form a classroom society and to plan formal instruction. While all teachers learn more about their pupils as the school year passes, the initial sizing-up assessment activities that tend to dominate the first weeks of school quickly give way to a second set of assessment activities, planning and carrying out instruction. This chapter describes assessment issues associated with the important task of planning instruction. It also provides information about pupil disabilities and their accommodations. Assessment activities associated with actually carrying out or delivering instruction are described in Chapter 4.

✖ Education, Curriculum, and Instruction

A major purpose of schools is to educate pupils. But what does it mean to educate? Under what circumstances can a teacher claim credit for helping to educate a pupil? To **educate** means to help change pupils in beneficial ways, to help them to know, do, and understand new things. When teachers help pupils learn to read, identify parts of speech in a sentence, use the scientific method, write a cohesive paragraph, translate a French sentence to English, or apply the Pythagorean Theorem, they are helping to educate pupils. Of course, pupils are also educated in nonschool settings, primarily their home and in peer groups. However, the skills, behaviors, attitudes, and interests that are primarily learned through classroom instruction represent the school's and teacher's contribution to a pupil's total education.

A **curriculum** describes the skills, performances, attitudes, and values pupils are expected to learn in school. The methods and processes used to teach pupils' these things are called **instruction.** Lectures, discussions, worksheets, projects, cooperative learning, experiments, learning logs, homework, and portfolios are just a few of the instructional approaches that teachers employ to teach their curricula and educate their pupils.

Pupils learn many things during their school years and it is clear that many sources contribute to their learning: TV, maturation, peer groups, family, and formal school instruction, among others. The term **achievement** is used to describe school-based learning, and terms like **ability** and **aptitude** are used to describe learning that is not solely a result of school instruction, but rather the product of broader, nonschool influences. Because the focus of schooling is to help pupils attain knowledge, skills, and understandings, almost all of the formal tests that pupils take in school assess their achievement. The Friday spelling test, the unit test on chemical equations, the math test on regrouping, the oral recitation of a memorized poem, the autobiographical book report, as well as midterm and final examinations all seek to assess pupil achievement—that is, what was learned from the instruction provided. The focus in teachers' classrooms is on the achievement of pupils.

✄ The Instructional Process

The instructional process is comprised of three steps. The first step is *planning instruction,* which includes identifying important and desirable things for pupils to learn, selecting materials to foster pupil learning, and organizing learning experiences into a coherent, reinforcing sequence to facilitate learning. The second step follows logically from the first. It involves *instructing* or teaching pupils based on the planned lesson. The third step is *assessing,* determining whether pupils have learned from the instruction provided.

Figure 3.1 shows these three steps and the relationships among them. Notice that the diagram is presented as a triangle, rather than as a straight line. This indicates that the three steps are interrelated in a more complicated way than a simple one-two-three sequence. For example, in planning instruction (step 1), one has to consider the characteristics of pupils and the resources and materials available to help them learn (step 2). Similarly, the information gained at the time of assessment (step 3), can be useful in judging the appropriateness of the learning experiences provided for pupils (step 2) and the suitability of their intended learning (step 1). These pieces are interdependent in the instructional process. Note that the instructional process illustrated in the diagram is equally applicable to instruction focused on large or small chunks of material. The process of planning, instructing, and assessing pupil learning can be done for a textbook unit or chapter as well as for a single day's lesson.

All three steps in the instructional process require teacher decision making, and thus require teachers to collect assessment information to help them make informed decisions. Step 3, assessing pupil learning, obviously involves the collection and synthesis of information about how well pupils are learning or have learned. Steps 1 and 2 also are dependent upon teacher assessment. For example, when a teacher decides what subject matter skills,

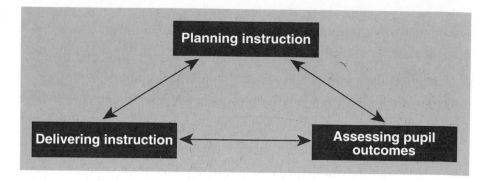

FIGURE 3.1   *Steps in the Instructional Process*

topics, and understandings pupils should be taught, the teacher bases the decisions on information about pupil readiness, disabilities, available instructional materials, and time available to teach. During instruction the teacher is constantly "reading" the class to obtain information to help make decisions about lesson pace, pupil attention, comprehension, interest and the like. Thus, the entire instructional process, not just the formal assessment step, depends on teacher decisions.

Teachers' Views of the Instructional Process

The processes of planning and providing instruction are important activities for classroom teachers. Not only do they occupy a substantial amount of their time, but teachers define their teaching rewards in terms of their instructional success.

In one study, Lortie (1975) asked teachers about the things that gave them the most pride and satisfaction in their craft. Teachers talked mainly about the tangible outcomes that resulted from their instruction and stewardship of pupils. Sometimes they spoke about pupils they helped to succeed against difficult odds.

> I think when you have one or two children in a class who might not have the advantages at home that some children have, you might lean a little bit towards that child. . . or make some inward excuses for him. Then when you see that child has really grasped something, it's worth its weight in gold.

> I have had many, many happy moments and I have seen many of them go a long way. They probably might have never gone anywhere if it hadn't been for the little I had to contribute in their life along the line.

Sometimes they spoke about graduates who come back to school to thank them.

> Ordinarily, I get the greatest satisfaction from the people who come back after they're in college and they may say that they didn't realize how much teaching could help them. A student may say he's better prepared than the average. That's the proof of the pudding; that's the most pleasing thing.

Sometimes they spoke more directly about class achievements.

> I feel proud at the end of the year when every one of my youngsters can read. That's about the only time.

> If I work all year and there is a good median at the end of the year in my reading, I feel rather proud. . . . The children give you a nice feeling of accomplishment.

For these teachers, the rewards of teaching were identified in terms of the impact that the teachers' instruction and mentoring had upon pupils. Pride in teaching did not come from collecting lunch money, planning field trips, meeting the morning bus, and the thousand other semiadministrative tasks teachers perform. It came from the teachers' knowledge that they had taught pupils to do, think, or perform some things they otherwise would have been unable to do, think, or perform.

Because the classroom is where pride in teaching is forged, it is not surprising to find that teachers guard their classroom instructional time jealously. When teachers were asked what made for a good day in school, they emphasized uninterrupted time spent with their classes.

> I most enjoy having the children to myself without interruption. I can accomplish a lot.

> It's a day when I do nothing but teach. When I don't have to collect money, go to assemblies, or count out how many want pizza or baked macaroni for lunch. No interruptions, the kids focused on instruction, and a sense of making progress, that's a great day!

In light of these teacher comments, it should not be a surprise that planning and carrying out instruction are important aspects of teachers' classroom lives.

Teacher Planning

Teachers plan in order to modify the curriculum to fit the unique characteristics of their pupils and resources. To plan, teachers reflect on and integrate information about their pupils, the subject matter to be taught, the curriculum they are following, their own teaching experience, the resources available for instruction, the classroom environment, and other factors. Their reflection and integration of these factors leads to an instructional lesson plan. The plan helps teachers allocate instructional time, select appropriate activities, link individual lessons to the overall unit or curriculum, sequence activities to be presented to pupils, set the pace of instruction, select the homework to be assigned, and identify techniques to assess pupil learning.

Planning help teachers feel comfortable about instruction by providing them with a sense of understanding and personal ownership over the planned teaching. Planning helps teachers in four ways. First, it helps reduce teachers' uncertainty and anxiety about instruction by providing them with a sense of purpose and subject matter focus. Second, planning affords teachers an opportunity to review and become familiar with the subject matter they will teach, before actually beginning to teach. Third, plans include ways to get instruction started, activities to be pursued, and a framework to use during the actual delivery of instruction. Fourth, plans link daily lesson plans to more general and integrative units or curriculum topics.

Classrooms are complex environments that are informal rather than formal, ad hoc rather than linear, ambiguous rather than certain, process-oriented rather than product-oriented, and people-dominated rather than concept-dominated. The realities and strains of the classroom call for order and direction, especially when teachers are carrying out formal instruction. In such a world, some form of planning and organization is needed.

Planning instruction is a context-dependent activity that includes consideration of pupils, teacher, and instructional materials. A lesson that fails to take into account the needs and prior knowledge of the pupils or that poorly matches lesson aims to lesson instruction is doomed to failure. Similarly, a lesson that does not take into account the context in which it will be taught can also lead to difficulty.

Teachers have a great deal of control over many classroom features associated with lesson planning. For example, most teachers have control over the physical arrangement of the classroom, the rules and routines pupils must follow, the interactions with pupils, the kind of instruction planned and the nature of its delivery, and the methods used to assess and grade pupils. However, there are important features that teachers do not control. For example, most teachers have little control over the number and characteristics of the pupils in their classes, the size of their classroom, the quality of their instructional resources, and the state and district curriculum guidelines. In planning, teachers must arrange the factors they do control to compensate for the factors they do not.

Table 3.1 describes two teachers' classrooms. Teachers normally would have little classroom control over the characteristics in each of these

TABLE 3.1

Comparison of Two Classroom Contexts

Classroom A	Classroom B
22 pupils	34 pupils
Range of pupil abilities	Mainly low-ability pupils
Strong pupil self-control	Poor pupil self-control
Good prerequisite skills	Range of prerequisite skills
Intense parental interest	Moderate parental interest
10-year-old textbooks	New textbooks
Mandated district curriculum	Teacher-selected instructional topics
Poor school library	Excellent school library
Small classroom size	Large classroom size
Individual pupil desks	Pupils sit at four-person tables
Little colleague support	Strong colleague support

classrooms. Imagine that these classrooms are at the same grade level in the same school and that the teachers are each planning a lesson on the same topic. How might these different classroom characteristics influence the ways these two teachers plan instruction? What features are especially influential in determining teaching plans? Which characteristics would be advantageous to a teacher and which ones might be disadvantageous? Do you think the teachers would construct identical instructional plans? In what ways might they differ? The following discussion examines in more detail how pupil and teacher characteristics as well as instructional resources can affect instructional planning.

Pupil Characteristics

Initial and extremely important considerations when planning instruction are the present status and needs of the pupils. What are they developmentally ready to learn? What topics have they mastered thus far in the subject area? How complex are the instructional materials they can handle? How well do they work in groups? What disabilities do they have and how are they accommodated? What is the range of classroom pupils' culture and language? What are their learning styles? The answers to these questions provide needed and valuable information about what and how to teach. Note that teachers obtain much of the information to answer these questions from their sizing-up assessments.

Planning in elementary school classrooms generally is more complex than planning in high school classrooms. This is because the range of pupil characteristics that must be considered is broader in lower grades. For example, in addition to content, the elementary teacher must take into account pupil readiness, behavior, and learning styles, as well as how a lesson will fit with other lessons to be given that day. The ebb and flow of elementary school activities from small-group instruction to seatwork to large-group instruction and back again make consideration of pupil characteristics such as independence, work habits, and attention span very important. When the teacher is working with one reading or math group, seatwork for pupils not in that group must accommodate their learning abilities and allow them to work independently and quietly.

In addition, the elementary teacher often works with many different pupil groupings that use different instructional materials geared to the group level. Plans for each group differ according to the ability, prior achievement, needs, and socialization levels in the group. Further, most elementary school teachers are responsible for planning instruction in all subjects, not just one or two as is typical at the high school level. Planning is a complex and time-consuming task for these teachers.

When planning instruction, an initial, and extremely important, consideration is the present status and needs of the pupils. At the start of the school year, most teachers begin instruction by reviewing subject matter concepts and skills normally mastered in the prior grade or course. The information gained in such a review provides the most direct evidence about pupils' readiness and needs. It is especially important to assess readiness and needs in those subjects that are sequentially organized, such as mathematics, foreign languages, and reading. The structure of these subjects is such that concepts and ideas build upon one another. For example, in order to do long division problems correctly, a fourth or fifth grader must be able to use the processes of addition, subtraction, regrouping, and multiplication. Thus, it would make little sense for a fifth grade teacher whose pupils did not understand regrouping and multiplication to teach only long division, even though it might be the normal focus of fifth grade mathematics instruction.

In other subjects, such as social studies and English, the content is not as sequential and interdependent as in math, reading, and foreign languages. The "expanding horizons" focus of elementary school social studies texts, for example, moves from homes and neighborhoods to communities to regions of America to U. S. history to world history. For the most part, each year's text and content is distinct from the prior or succeeding year's. In this case, the teacher has more discretion in planning what to stress.

It is obvious that pupil characteristics such as disability, readiness, independence, and self-control should be taken into account in planning instructional activities. To ignore these factors would be irrational. However, it is very important to recognize that much of the needed information comes to teachers from their initial sizing-up assessments. Consequently, it is crucial that teachers strive to make their initial sizing-up assessments as valid and reliable as possible.

Teacher Characteristics

Many teachers do not consciously consider their own characteristics when planning instruction, although these characteristics do influence their instruction. In particular, teachers' content knowledge, instructional preferences, personalities, and physical limitations are important factors in planning and delivering instruction.

It is impossible for teachers to have equal knowledge of all the topics they teach, nor can they be expected to keep abreast of all advances in subject matter knowledge or pedagogy. Consequently, the topics teachers choose to teach, the accuracy and currency of their topical coverage, and their teaching methods are influenced by their knowledge limitations.

Just as pupils' personalities influence the way instruction is planned and provided, teachers' personalities and preferences affect planning and teaching. Some teachers feel uncomfortable using certain instructional techniques and consequently avoid them. Some teachers feel uncomfortable leading classroom discussions, others dislike independent projects or field trips, and still others avoid working with small groups. While individual preferences are to be expected among teachers, it is important to understand that when carried to the extreme, such preferences can result in an overly narrow repertoire of teaching methods, inhibiting the teacher's ability to choose the method best suited to a particular type of learning.

Finally, because teaching can be a rigorous, fatiguing activity, teachers should consider their own physical limitations when planning instruction. This caution is especially appropriate for beginning teachers, whose enthusiasm and lack of experience often leads them to overestimate what they can physically accomplish in the classroom. One of the most common comments heard from college students experiencing their first full-time classroom practicum is how mentally and physically draining a day in the classroom can be.

Instructional Resources

The instructional resources available to a teacher can influence not only the nature of instruction but also the learning outcomes that can be sought. The term *resources* is used here in its broadest sense to include teaching supplies, administrative and collegial support, equipment, classroom space, technology, aids or volunteers, textbook quality, time, and more. Each of these resources influences the nature of instruction and the quality of pupil achievements.

A biology teacher may want his class to learn about the internal organs of a frog by having each pupil perform a dissection. However, if the school has no biology laboratory and no dissecting equipment, the teacher must forgo this activity. A third grade teacher may wish to set up a learning center in his classroom to pursue pupil outcomes related to independent study and research skills. However, if the classroom is too small or if the resource materials needed to supply the center are not available, a center is unrealistic. If the classroom is too small to have pupils work in small groups, many useful instructional activities cannot be used. Conversely, the availability of classroom aides or volunteers who read to pupils, work with small groups, or serve as "microscope moms" during a unit on the microscope can free the classroom teacher to plan and pursue enrichment activities that might not have been possible otherwise.

Time

Another important, though often overlooked, resource that greatly influences teacher planning is time. Because there is never enough time to teach pupils all the important skills and concepts in a subject area, teachers must carefully match their instructional time to their intended instructional outcomes. Each teacher's decisions about what content to stress or omit is based in part on the instructional time available. When a teacher skips a concept, unit, or chapter in a textbook, the teacher is saying, "All other things being equal, I prefer to spend my limited instructional time focusing on other topics and skills that are more important." While teachers make decisions about the allocation of instructional time daily, it is often in the last few weeks of the school year that these decisions become most apparent. The end of the school year always seems to arrive before all the planned topics can be taught. At this point, explicit decisions about how to allocate scarce time are made: "We must cover subtraction of fractions before the end of the year, but we can omit rate, time, and distance word problems." "If I don't finish parts of speech this year, next year's teacher will be upset. I'll take the time from the poetry unit to work on parts of speech." Time is a limited resource that has important consequences for planning instruction.

Instructional Materials

A final resource that influences what is taught and learned in classrooms is the textbook. In most classes, the textbook is very influential in determining instructional plans. A number of studies have shown that a large part of students' learning time (up to 85 percent) and a large part of the teacher's instructional time are focused on textbook use (Woodward and Elliott, 1990). Textbooks provide a level of content knowledge that few teachers possess. Further, textbooks structure the content around units or topics, thereby helping to sequence the content taught. Finally, the teacher's edition of the textbook provides teachers with lesson questions, test items, instructional activities, and other teaching resources.

Teacher's editions of most textbooks are supplemented with resources that help teachers plan, deliver, and assess instruction, and it is not surprising that so many teachers rely heavily upon them. In a real sense, textbook publishers have made it possible for teachers to abdicate their planning, teaching, and assessment decision making. Relinquishing these responsibilities, however, reduces the classroom teacher from a professional decision maker to a mindless technician carrying out the instructional program of others. Obviously, overreliance on the suggestions of textbook authors should be discouraged.

It is a responsibility of all teachers to assess the status and needs of their pupils, the curriculum requirements of their state or community, and the resources available when planning instruction for their pupils. In the end, the decision about what to emphasize rests with the individual classroom teacher, who knows her pupils better than anyone else and who is in the best position to plan and carry out instruction that is suited to their needs. Table 3.2 summarizes the main types of information that are important to consider in planning instruction.

Once information about pupil, teacher, and instructional resources is collected, the task of the teacher is to weigh and synthesize this information into a set of instructional or lesson plans. Starting with a general idea of what will be done during an instructional unit, teachers move through a series of successive specifications to focus on daily instruction. In a very real sense, teachers mentally rehearse the learning activities they contemplate using in the classroom, visualizing the teaching activities as they will unfold in their classroom. There are many steps in lesson planning and many options teachers have in their planning. However, the core features of lesson plans have four parts, as shown in Box 3.1.

A good teacher does more than just present any old curriculum to pupils. A good teacher plans instruction, chooses appropriate instructional

TABLE 3.2

Areas to Consider When Planning Instruction

Pupil Characteristics	Teacher Characteristics	Instructional Resources
Prior knowledge	Content knowledge	State curriculum standards
Prerequisite skills and knowledge	Instructional method preferences	Time
Work habits, socialization	Assessment preferences	Textbook materials
Special learning needs	Physical limitations	Technology
Learning styles		Collegial and administrative support
Cultural/language differences		Other resources (space, aids, equipment)
Disabilities		

Box 3.1 Components of a Lesson Plan

Objectives: Description of the things pupils are to learn from instruction: what pupils should be able to do after instruction (e.g., the pupils can write a summary of a story, the pupils can differentiate adverbs from adjectives in a given passage).

Materials: Description of the resources, materials, and apparatus needed to carry out the lesson (e.g., overhead projector, clay, map of the United States, Bunsen burners, video on the civil rights movement, etc.).

Teaching activities and strategies: Description of the things that will take place during instruction; often includes factors such as determining pupil readiness, identifying how the lesson will start, reviewing prior lessons, providing advanced organizers, specific instructional techniques to be used (e.g., discussion, lecture, silent reading, demonstrations, seatwork, game, cooperative activities, etc.), sequence of techniques, providing pupils practice, and ending the lesson.

Assessment: Description of how pupil learning from the lesson will be assessed (e.g., homework assignment, oral questions, writing an essay, etc.).

materials, provides a conducive learning environment, attends to pupils' disabilities, arranges the teaching sequence, teaches, evaluates pupil learning, and plans future instruction accordingly. Clearly, a great deal of decision making must be considered when planning and delivering instruction. The following sections describe objectives, a key aspect of instructional planning.

✂ Characteristics of Objectives

In our everyday activities, objectives help us focus on what's important; they remind us of what we want to accomplish. Objectives in teaching describe the kinds of content and processes teachers hope their pupils will learn from instruction. Objectives are particularly crucial in teaching because teaching is an intentional and normative act. Teaching is intentional because teachers teach for a purpose; they want pupils to learn something as a result of teaching. Teaching is also normative because what teachers teach is viewed by them as being worthwhile for their pupils to learn. In fact, it would be unethical for teachers to teach things that they did not believe were beneficial to pupils.

Because teaching is both intentional and normative, it always is based on objectives. Normative teaching is concerned with selecting objectives that are worthwhile for pupils to learn. Intentional teaching is concerned with issues of how teachers will teach their objectives—what learning environments they will create and what methods they will use to help pupils learn the intended objectives. Although teachers' objectives may be explicit or implicit or clear or fuzzy, it is best that objectives be explicit, clear, and measurable. Regardless of how they are stated and what they are called, objectives are present in all teaching. Other names for objectives are "learning targets," "educational objectives," "instructional objectives," "behavioral objectives," "pupil outcomes," and "curriculum objectives," among others. Whatever they are called, objectives are an important aspect when developing lesson plans. Teachers cannot help pupils meet their objectives if they do not know what their objectives are. Similarly, if teachers don't identify their objectives, instruction and assessment will be purposeless.

Types of Objectives: Global, Educational, and Instructional

Objectives can range from very general to very specific. Compare the following two objectives: "The pupil can add three one-digit numbers," and "The pupil will become mathematically literate." Each is an objective, but clearly the former objective is more specific than the latter. Notice how different instructional time, learning activities, and range of assessments would be needed for the two objectives. Because objectives vary widely in specificity, a more limited framework for discussing objectives is commonly used. Three levels of abstraction represent degrees of objective specificity: global, educational, and instructional (Krathwohl and Payne, 1971). Note that regardless of the type or specificity of an objective, its focus should always be on *pupil* learning and performance.

Global objectives, often called "goals," are broad, complex pupil learning outcomes that require substantial time and instruction to accomplish. They are very general, encompassing a large number of more specific objectives. Examples of global objectives include: "The pupil will become a life-long learner," "The pupil will become mathematically literate," and "Pupils will learn to use their minds well, so that they may be prepared for responsible citizenship, further learning, and productive employment in our nation's economy." Because they are broadly inclusive, global objectives are rarely used in classroom assessment unless they are broken down into more narrow objectives. A global objective is something currently out of reach, something not ready to be realized, something to focus and excite the imagination. Global objectives mainly provide a rallying cry that reflects what is important in education policy. The breadth encompassed in global objectives makes them difficult for teachers to use in planning classroom instruction. Narrower objectives are needed to meet classroom needs.

Educational objectives represent a middle level of abstraction. Examples of educational objectives include: "The pupil can interpret different types of social data," "The pupil distinguishes between facts and hypotheses," and "The pupil can read Spanish poetry aloud." Educational objectives are more specific than global objectives. They are sufficiently narrow to help teachers plan and focus teaching, and sufficiently broad to indicate the richness of the objective and to suggest a range of possible student outcomes associated with the objective.

Instructional objectives are the least abstract and most specific type of objective. Examples of instructional objectives include: "The pupil can correctly punctuate sentences," "Given five problems requiring the pupil to find the lowest common denominator of a fraction, the pupil can solve at least 4 of 5," and "The pupil can list the names of the first five U.S. presidents." Instructional objectives focus teaching on relatively narrow topics of learning in a content area. These concrete objectives are used in planning daily lessons. Table 3.3 illustrates the difference in degree of breadth among the three types of objectives.

Table 3.4 compares the purpose, scope, and time frame for achievement of the three types of objectives. The most useful objectives in classroom teaching are educational and instructional objectives. Educational objectives are used when planning units of instruction, while instructional objectives are applied when planning daily instruction. Most of the discussion of objectives in this text focuses on educational objectives. Planning lessons at the level of educational objectives provides teachers with sufficient breadth of content to develop units of instruction that can then be broken down into instructional or daily objectives.

The distinctions among these three levels of objectives are far more than semantic. The level at which an objective is stated influences its use in planning, instructing, and assessing. For example, the perspectives of teachers planning instruction and assessment for a global objective such as "The pupil will become mathematically literate" are quite different from those of teachers planning instruction and assessment for an instructional objective such as "The pupil will write common fractions in their lowest terms." Global objectives do not deal with specifics, while instructional objectives deal mainly with specifics. Thus, the level at which an objective is stated—global, educational, or instructional—has an impact on the manner in which processes such as planning, instructing, and assessing will be structured and carried out.

TABLE 3.3

Comparison of the Breadth of Objectives

Global Objective	Educational Objective	Instructional Objective
The pupil will acquire competency of worldwide geography.	The pupil will gain knowledge of devices and symbols in maps and charts.	Given a map or chart, the pupil will correctly define 6 of the 8 representational devises and symbols on it.
The pupil will be aware of the roles of civics and government in the U.S.	The pupil will interpret various types of social data.	The pupil can interpret bar graphs describing population density.
The pupil will know how to repair a variety of home problems.	The pupil will use appropriate procedures to find solutions to electrical problems in the home.	Given a home repair problem dealing with a malfunctioning lamp, the pupil will repair it.

TABLE 3.4

Relationship of Global, Educational, and Instructional Objectives

Levels of Objectives	Scope	Time to Accomplish	Function
Global	Broad	One or more years	Provide vision
Educational	Intermediate	Weeks or months	Develop curriculum, plan instruction, and define suitable assessments
Instructional	Narrow	Hours or days	Plan teaching activities, learning experiences, and assessment exercises

❈ Stating Cognitive Objectives: Bloom's Taxonomy

Having examined three levels of objectives, we now turn to some classifications of cognitive processes that are commonly used by teachers when they develop their objectives. Cognitive objectives focus on intellectual activities such as memorizing, interpreting, applying, problem solving, reasoning,

TABLE 3.5

Types of Cognitive Process Identified in Bloom's Taxonomy

Taxonomy Level	Related Verbs	General Description
1. Knowledge	Remember, recall, identify, recognize	Memorizing facts
2. Comprehension	Translate, rephrase, restate, interpret, describe, explain	Explaining in one's own words
3. Application	Apply, execute, solve, implement	Solving new problems
4. Analysis	Break down, categorize, distinguish, compare	Breaking into parts and identifying relationships
5. Synthesis	Integrate, organize, relate, combine, construct, design	Combining elements into a whole
6. Evaluation	Judge, assess, value, appraise	Judging quality or worth

analyzing, and thinking critically. Virtually all the tests that pupils take in school are intended to measure one or more of these cognitive processes, and instruction is usually focused on helping pupils attain cognitive mastery of some content or subject area. A weekly spelling test, a unit test in history, a worksheet on proper use of *lie* and *lay*, an essay on supply and demand, a rate and distance problem, and translating French to English are all cognitive activities.

The many cognitive processes have been organized into six general categories. This organization is presented in the *Taxonomy of Educational Objectives: Book 1, Cognitive Domain* (Bloom et al., 1956). Commonly referred to as Bloom's Taxonomy, or the Cognitive Taxonomy, it is widely used by teachers to describe and state cognitive objectives.

A taxonomy is a system of classification. Bloom's cognitive taxonomy is organized into six levels, with each successive level representing a more complex type of cognitive process. Starting with the simplest and moving to the most complex, the six cognitive taxonomic processes are: knowledge, comprehension, application, analysis, synthesis, and evaluation. It is important to note that in Bloom's Taxonomy "knowledge" refers only to memorizing and remembering information. It does *not* include other kinds of cognitive processes. Table 3.5 provides some action verbs indicative of each cognitive process of Bloom's Taxonomy, and the general description of each process. Below are sample objectives derived from Bloom's Taxonomy with the taxonomic category shown in parentheses.

The pupils can identify the correct punctuation marks in a writing assignment. (knowledge)

The pupils can integrate the information from the science experiment into a
   lab report. (synthesis)
The pupils can punctuate correctly in a writing task. (application)
The pupils can translate French sentences to English. (comprehension)
The pupils can distinguish facts from opinions in eight newspaper
   editorials. (analysis)
The pupils can categorize paintings by their historical periods. (analysis)
The pupils can judge the quality of varied persuasive essays. (evaluation)
The pupils can add previously unseen proper fractions. (application)

Consider the following three objectives: (1) "The pupil will learn to use their minds well, so that they may be prepared for responsible citizenship, further learning, and productive employment in our nation's economy"; (2) "The pupil can read Spanish-language poetry"; and (3) "The pupil can correctly punctuate sentences." Although they represent a global, educational, and instructional objective respectively, these objectives have common characteristics. First, all are stated in terms of what the pupil is to learn from instruction. Objectives describe *pupil learning,* not teacher learning or the activities teacher or pupils engage in during instruction. Instructional activities are not objectives, although activities are an important aspect of lesson planning and must be described. Second, each objective contains two parts: some content for pupils to learn and a process to show their learning. The content in the three objectives above are, respectively, "citizenship skills," "Spanish-language poetry," and "sentences." The cognitive processes are "develop," "read," and "punctuate." Another way to think about an objective's content and process is in terms of nouns and verbs. The content is the noun and the process is the verb. Thus, at a minimum, an objective is stated in terms of the content (noun) and process (verb) the pupil is expected to learn. Third, notice that the nouns and verbs differ from one objective to another because different subject matters, grade levels, and teaching styles require different objectives.

Objectives such as those shown above are widely used to guide teachers' planning, instruction, and assessment. For example, the objective "The pupils can categorize paintings by their historical periods" is focused on analysis (categorize) by identifying relationships. Or, the objective "The pupil can explain in his/her own words the meaning of a second-year-level French paragraph" is focused on comprehension (explain). Note that the verbs in the objectives we have examined (e.g., summarize, add, remember, categorize, explain, etc.) are *not* labeled using Bloom's generic taxonomy names (e.g., knowledge, comprehension, analysis, etc.). Instead, they are described using narrower, more specific verbs. These more specific and observable cognitive verbs are preferred over the generic taxonomy names because they more clearly indicate the particular process (verb) the pupils will be expected to carry out. Table 3.6 provides a number of these more precise verbs for each taxonomic category that can be used in stating clear objectives.

TABLE 3.6

Examples of Terms Used to Write Educational Objectives for Each Category of Bloom's Taxonomy

Knowledge	Comprehension	Application	Analysis	Synthesis	Evaluation
count	classify	compute	break down	arrange	appraise
define	compare	construct	diagram	combine	conclude
identify	convert	demonstrate	differentiate	compile	critique
label	contrast	illustrate	discriminate	create	criticize
list	discuss	solve	outline	design	grade
match	distinguish		separate	formulate	judge
name	estimate		subdivide	generalize	recommend
quote	explain			generate	support
recite	generalize			group	
repeat	give examples			integrate	
reproduce	infer			organize	
select	interpret			relate	
state	paraphrase			summarize	
	rewrite				
	summarize				
	translate				

❊ A Second Dimension of Objectives: Three Types of Knowledge

We have seen that there are six cognitive processes that help describe objectives. However, although widely used and very useful, Bloom's Taxonomy has a limitation. It was published in 1956, about 45 years ago, at a time when the primary learning theory was behaviorism, an approach that viewed students as passive recipients of learning provided by their teachers and parents. The view was that learning entailed pupils' accumulation and remembering of varied pieces of information.

In recent years, the behavioristic approach has been challenged. Students no longer are viewed as passive recipients taking in others' knowledge. Current learning theories move away from passive, rote learning to a more constructivist approach in which students are viewed as being active learners and constructors of their own knowledge (Airasian and Walsh, 1997; Bereiter and Scardamalia, 1998; Oakes and Lipton, 1999). Pintrich (in press) notes that ". . . learners come into any instructional setting with a broad array of different types of knowledge they use to 'make sense' out of the information they encounter as well as their own experiences in the situation. Learners are not passive recipients of teachers' information. The process of 'making sense' involves the activation of their prior knowledge as well as the various process categories that operate on that knowledge." The view of students as active learners and interpreters who construct their own knowledge has lead to a greater emphasis on different kinds of student knowledge. That is, students should be able to deal with different forms of knowledge just as they deal with different forms of cognitive processes. Thus, meaningful objectives and learning should focus on both process (verbs) and content (nouns).

Consider an objective commonly used by most English teachers: "The pupils can state the main idea of a short story." The process (verb) is "state" and the content (noun) is "main idea." But there are multiple ways that pupils can learn to know a main idea. Which does the teacher want? One way pupils can learn a main idea is to memorize the teacher's statement of it during instruction. To know the main idea in this case, the pupils have only to remember what the teacher stated in class. Another way to learn a main idea is to have pupils infer it based on their interpretation of the key aspects of the short story. This kind of learning calls for more than memory and requires pupils to know about main ideas in a quite different way than simple memorization. Pupils must define the main idea for themselves. Finally, pupils can learn a main idea by following a set of steps the teacher has taught them to help find main ideas. For example, the teacher may have taught pupils the following simple four-step procedure to help identify main ideas: (1) carefully examine the topic sentence for important terms or characters; (2) examine sentences that are related to the topic sentence; (3) read the final sentence (the "clincher") for ideas that reinforce the main idea in the topic sentence; and (4) state the main idea.

Because these are three different ways to show main ideas, there should be a different objective for each way. Thus, for remembering the teacher's statement of the main idea, the objective would be: "The pupils can remember the main idea of a short story." For knowing the main idea by inferring it, the objective would be: "The pupils can understand the concept of a main idea in a short story." Finally, for knowing the main idea by applying a procedure for finding main ideas, the objective would be: "The pupil can apply a procedure to find the main idea of a short story."

Which one of these three objectives will be emphasized? It is important to recognize that which one of the three objectives is emphasized will influence greatly the nature of the "main ideas" pupils will be exposed to. Note also that the type of content knowledge teachers emphasize has an important impact on the way pupils will be taught (to remember, to understand, or to apply). The same is true of the way pupils will be assessed. The objective "The pupils can state the main idea of a short story" does not indicate the type of knowledge the teacher wishes the pupils to learn. Too often, objectives like this one end up being taught and assessed in a different way than the teacher wanted because the type of content knowledge is not explicit. This usually ends up with the objective emphasizing memorization.

Two additional examples help indicate the need to pay attention to the content part of an objective. Given the objective "The pupils can explain the water cycle," we can identify the verb (explain) and the noun (water cycle). But how does the teacher want the pupils to explain: explain from memory, explain the concepts underlying the process that governs the water cycle, or explain the order of steps that take place when the water cycle is in process? Finally, given the objective "The student can list three causes of the Civil War," the verb is "list" and the noun is "causes." We can ask about the type of knowledge the pupils are to explain. Is it remembering three causes the teacher stated in class, or is it inferring from original readings of the time what three main causes were? Two teachers pursuing this objective could state the same objective, but teach and assess it in very different ways.

Teachers should think about and include information about the knowledge dimension of objectives for three reasons: (1) pupils are expected to master different types of knowledge and these types should be made explicit when teachers formulate objectives; (2) different types of knowledge often call for different types of instruction; and (3) different types of knowledge often call for different types of assessment. Further, clarity of the objectives, both in content and process, is essential for aligning lesson plans and instruction. Without clear alignment, plans may not be implemented in instruction as the teacher planned.

The preceding examples suggest that there are three main types of content knowledge that teachers should focus on when stating objectives. Just as the cognitive processes (verbs) of Bloom's Taxonomy encompass a range of six different processes, types of content (nouns) encompass a range of three different types. These three types predominate in teachers' objectives, instruction, and assessments. They are factual knowledge, conceptual knowledge, and procedural knowledge (Pintrich, in press; Wiggins and McTighe, 1998; Marzano, Pickering, and McTighe, 1993).

Factual knowledge encompasses knowledge of specific facts. It is usually linked with the taxonomy process of remembering (knowledge in Bloom's Taxonomy). Common forms of factual knowledge include dates, definitions, terminology, names, vocabulary words, and facts. Factual knowledge, as the name suggests, involves pupils showing their recall of information. There is nothing to figure out in factual knowledge; either you know it or you don't. Questions such as "What is the capital of Kentucky?", "What was the date on which World War I ended?", and "Who was the nineteenth President of the United States?" require factual knowledge. Factual knowledge is important in its own right and also because it is the basic information that pupils build on to move to other kinds of learning. Factual knowledge is generally linked to the process of remembering. That is, we typically remember factual knowledge.

Conceptual knowledge encompasses categories and related groupings. Factual knowledge is characterized by singular, unrelated bits of information. Conceptual knowledge deals with larger, more systematically organized forms of knowledge. Conceptual knowledge builds on factual knowledge by integrating pieces of information into more organized, related concepts. For example, conceptual knowledge could include the concept trees, which might include particular types of trees such as maple, birch, oak, dogwood, and palm. Other examples of concepts are literature, principles of learning, educational assessments, communicable diseases, and state or city government agencies. For each of these concepts, you probably could identify one or more examples that fit within it.

Consider the difference between factual and conceptual knowledge. Remembering the definition of *irony* is factual knowledge. Explaining what irony is in one's own words, describing the attributes of irony, and knowing when to use irony show conceptual knowledge. Conceptual knowledge reflects pupils' understanding of irony, not only their recall of its definition. Conceptual knowledge is generally linked to the process of understanding. That is, we typically understand conceptual knowledge.

Finally, **procedural knowledge** is concerned with how to do things. The process of solving simultaneous equations, finding the lowest common denominator of a fraction, conducting historical research, finding capital cities on a world map, shooting a free throw, constructing scoring rubrics, and developing a grading system are all examples of procedural knowledge. The essence of procedural knowledge is knowing how to apply methods or strategies to carry out a multistage process. It is important to recognize that a pupil who understands conceptual knowledge of some type is not automatically able to apply that knowledge to a situation or problem. There is an important difference between understanding a concept (conceptual knowledge) and actually applying a procedure (procedural knowledge). The pupil may understand irony but may not be able to use a procedure to identify irony in short stories. Procedural knowledge is generally linked to the process of applying. That is, we typically apply procedural knowledge. Table 3.7 summarizes the characteristics of the three types of content knowledge described.

TABLE 3.7

Types of Knowledge

Type of Knowledge	Related Nouns	General Description
Factual	Terminology, names, facts, definitions, dates	Knowledge of specific facts
Conceptual	Classifications, categories, generalizations, theories, principles	Knowledge of concepts and categories
Procedural	Methods, criteria, recipes, algorithms, strategies, steps in a process	Knowledge of how to apply methods and procedures

Combining Cognitive Processes and Types of Knowledge

We have seen that objectives can be categorized into three levels of abstraction. We have seen that educational and instructional objectives are most commonly used by classroom teachers. We have examined Bloom's six cognitive processes and three types of content knowledge. Here we join cognitive processes with types of content knowledge. Neither a description of cognitive process alone nor a description of types of knowledge alone make an objective. Objectives contain both a description of the process the pupils are expected to carry out and the type of knowledge they should use to execute it. The clarity provided by the dual dimensions helps teachers refine their intents, guide their instruction, and develop their assessments. To illustrate how the process and knowledge dimensions work in stating objectives, Figure 3.2 is helpful.

The figure has two dimensions, process and knowledge. The top dimension lists the six categories of Bloom's Taxonomy. Each process contains its taxonomy name, a brief description of the process, and common terms associated with the process. The three processes most commonly used in teachers' objectives are the first three of Bloom's Taxonomy—knowledge, comprehension, and application.

The side dimension lists the three types of content knowledge. Each type is named, followed by a brief description of each type, and common terms associated with each type of knowledge.

Objectives derive from the intersection of a process and a type of knowledge. There are many areas of intersection, but three key areas form the basis for the great majority of teachers' classroom objectives. They are remembering factual knowledge, understanding conceptual knowledge, and applying procedural knowledge. These three intersections are noted on Figure 3.2. The combination of process and type of knowledge helps teachers align objectives with instruction and assessment. Here are some examples of objectives from the process-knowledge intersections.

Remembering Factual Knowledge

The pupils can remember addition facts totaling 10.
The pupils can recall definitions of social studies terms.
The pupils can recall important dates in the Civil War.

Understanding Conceptual Knowledge

The pupils can translate a German paragraph into English.
The pupils can explain in their own words the meaning of a short story.
The pupils can describe in their own words the theory of relativity.

Applying Procedural Knowledge

The pupils can carry out the steps in solving simultaneous equations for
   two unknowns.

PROCESS

	KNOWLEDGE Memorizing facts (remember, recall, identify, define)	COMPREHENSION Explain in one's own words (translate, rephrase interpret, explain, describe)	APPLICATION Use procedures to solve problems or do tasks (execute, carry out a process, implement a plan, develop)	ANALYSIS Break into parts, identify relationships (contrast, discriminate, differentiate, distinguish)	SYNTHESIS Combine elements into a whole (integrate, organize relate, combine)	EVALUATION Judge quality or worth (assess, compare, appraise, value)
TYPES OF KNOWLEDGE						
FACTUAL Knowledge of specific facts (terminology, names, facts, definitions, dates)	Remembering factual knowledge					
CONCEPTUAL Knowledge of concepts and categories (classifications, categories, theories, generalizations, principles)		Understanding conceptual knowledge				
PROCEDURAL Knowledge of how to apply methods and procedures (methods, techniques, criteria, steps in a process)			Applying procedural knowledge			

FIGURE 3.2 *Combining Cognitive Processes and Types of Knowledge*

Adapted from Anderson, L. W. and Krathwohl, D. R. (in press). A taxonomy for learning, teaching, and assessing: A revision of Bloom's Taxonomy of educational objectives. New York: Addison-Wesley-Longman.

The pupils can execute a plan for constructing a science fair project.
The pupils can develop a set of criteria to judge a persuasive essay.

While it is not necessary to use the nouns and verbs shown in Figure 3.2, they will be useful in writing objectives, planning instruction, and identifying appropriate assessments to determine pupil learning.

For objectives involving Bloom's analysis, synthesis, and evaluation processes, it is very likely that more than one type of process and knowledge will be involved. That is, factual, conceptual, and procedural knowledge will occur in various combinations in objectives focused on analysis, synthesis, or evaluation. For example, consider this objective: "The pupils will combine separate elements of a story into a unified whole." The process portion of the objective is "combine," a form of synthesis, and the knowledge part of the objective is "elements of a story." To carry out this objective, both conceptual and procedural knowledge likely will be needed. Pupils will need conceptual knowledge to help them determine the function of a topic sentence, what goes into a summary, how summaries are organized, what writing style is appropriate for a summary, and so on. Thus, conceptual understanding will be important. But pupils then will need to apply their procedural knowledge to actually carry out the task of combining the elements of the story into a unified whole. Recognizing that two forms of knowledge and process are needed to attain the objective helps teachers plan and carry out instruction that takes into account both types of knowledge and process. This is one of the benefits of linking process and content knowledge.

It is not unusual for more complex processes such as analysis, synthesis, and evaluation to rely on multiple types of knowledge for their mastery. These complex processes and knowledge types are important and should be taught. However, in most classrooms, these multiknowledge and multiprocess types of objectives will represent a relatively small portion of objectives. Most classroom objectives are focused on remembering factual knowledge, understanding conceptual knowledge, and applying procedural knowledge as prerequisites for accomplishing the more complex processes. The three basic process-knowledge links serve as relevant prerequisites for more complex objectives. Teachers should use factual, conceptual, and procedural types of knowledge to identify what process and knowledge are needed as prerequisite to the more complex processes. Doing this can help instruction by clarifying the meaning of an objective and providing appropriate instructional strategies.

We have worked our way from identifying three different levels of abstraction for objectives to focusing attention on the middle-level abstraction of educational objectives. We have dissected objectives into cognitive processes and kinds of content knowledge. When the processes and content types were united into a two-dimensional we were able to link types of content knowledge to particular cognitive processes. As we have seen, a focus on process and knowledge makes objectives clearer for teachers and pupils. In addition, suitable instructional activities and assessments result from the two dimensions.

Stating Objectives

While different paths can be followed to state objectives, three common steps are used by teachers to state objectives. First, identify the process (verb) that best represents the activity the pupils are to perform. Second, identify the type of knowledge (noun) that describes the information the pupils will work with. Tables 3.5 and 3.7 provide examples of processes and types of knowledge that can guide the selection of these components when stating objectives. Third, check for the compatibility of the process and knowledge. If you want pupils to remember information, be sure you focus on factual knowledge. If you want pupils to understand information, focus on conceptual knowledge. If you want pupils to apply information, focus on procedural knowledge. Using these steps will yield objectives that give a clear focus to what pupils are to learn, as well as how they will be taught and how they will be assessed. They will ensure clear alignment among objectives, instruction, and assessment.

Questions About Objectives

Objectives are usually the starting point in the instructional process because they identify the desired outcomes of instruction. Some have called stating objectives a "backward approach" to planning because it starts by defining the intended end result (Wiggins and McTighe, 1998). Because objectives are important, a few common issues and questions about objectives require attention.

1. *Is it necessary to write down one's objectives?* Beginning teachers and students in a teaching practicum usually are required to write objectives for their lessons. Even if you are an experienced teacher, listing your objectives is useful because it reminds you to focus on what pupils are expected to get out of instruction, not just what your teaching activities will be. Annual review of existing objectives is an important part of any teacher's classroom assessment responsibilities. Each year, important new content and processes are identified and added to the curriculum. Further, different pupil groups require different objectives. It is a good idea to inform pupils of the objectives, perhaps by having students list them in their notebooks or by writing them on the board.

2. *What are higher-level objectives?* Cognitive processes can be divided into lower-level objectives, such as memorizing and remembering, and higher-level objectives requiring more complex thinking behaviors. Higher-level processes, or higher-order thinking skills (HOTS), include activities such as analyzing information, applying facts and rules to solve new problems, comparing and contrasting objects or ideas, and synthesizing disparate pieces of information into a single, organized idea. Higher-level objectives include all but the lowest level of Bloom's Taxonomy.

Whether an objective is higher or lower level depends on how it is taught. Regardless of the wording of an objective, if pupils are taught only to remember information from the teacher, it is a lower-level objective. In the following examples, the lower-level objective calls only for memorization, while the higher-level objective calls for a more complex behavior. Recognize that any of the following higher-level objectives could also be lower-level objectives depending on how they are taught. For example, in the first set of objectives, if pupils were previously taught specific new sentences using the vocabulary words, the objective would be lower level. Only if the pupils constructed their own, non-taught sentences could the objective be classified as higher level.

Lower level: The pupil can state a definition of each vocabulary word. *memory*.
Higher level: The pupil can construct new sentences using each vocabulary *applying* word correctly.

Lower level: The pupil can match quotes from a short story to the characters who said them.
Higher level: The pupil can infer the motives of the protagonist and the antagonist in a short story.

Lower level: The pupil can write the formula for the Pythagorean Theorem.
Higher level: The pupil can use the Pythagorean Theorem to solve new word problems involving the length of ladders needed by the fire department.

All teachers should be aware of the difference between lower- and higher-level thinking skills and should strive to incorporate some higher-level objectives in their plans and instruction.

3. *How many objectives should I state in a subject area?* The answer to this question depends in part upon the time available and the specificity of the objectives: the longer the period of instruction and the more specific the objectives, the more objectives one can state and teach. Also, as noted, higher-level objectives usually take longer to teach and learn, so fewer of them can be taught in a given instructional period. It takes longer for pupils to interpret graphs than to memorize a formula. Teachers who have hundreds of objectives for the year's instruction either are expecting too much of themselves and their pupils or are stating their objectives too narrowly. On the other hand, teachers who have only five or ten objectives for the school year are either underestimating their pupils or stating their objectives much too broadly.

4. *Are there any cautions I should keep in mind regarding objectives?* Objectives are generally stated before instruction actually begins. However, although they are framed before instruction, objectives should not be followed slavishly when circumstances during instruction suggest the need for adjustments. Because objectives are written *before* instruction starts and because it is difficult to anticipate the flow of classroom activities during instruction, teachers must exercise discretion regarding how closely they will follow the objectives they initially stated prior to the start of instruction.

✂ Other Sources of Objectives

Textbook Objectives

Modern textbooks and their accompanying teacher aids provide a great deal of information to help teachers plan, deliver, and assess their instruction. The richest and most used source of information is the teacher's edition of the textbook. Figure 3.3 illustrates the range of resources found in most teacher's editions of textbooks. While not every textbook or instructional package provides every one of the resources listed in Figure 3.3, most provide a majority of them, and many provide more. At the very least, one can

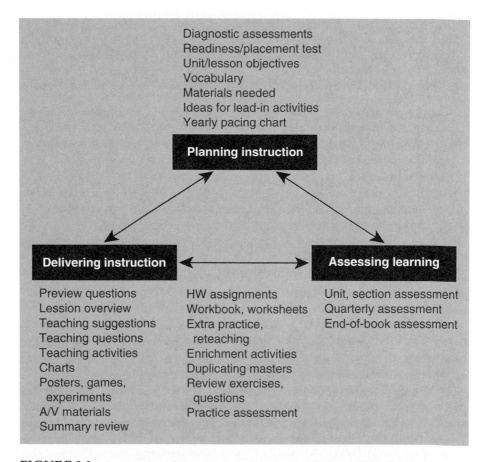

FIGURE 3.3 *Instructional Resources in Teacher's Editions of Textbooks*

count on finding objectives, teaching suggestions, instructional activities, and assessment instruments. While the most instructional aids and materials are generally found in elementary school texts, the disparity between elementary, middle, and high school texts is diminishing. More objectives and instructional aids are appearing in high school texts and even college texts. If you have never seen a teacher's edition of a textbook or the resources that accompany it, visit your curriculum library or a local school to examine some. Review a number of teacher's editions and compare the objectives and resources provided for planning, teaching, and assessment they provide the teacher. Pay special attention to the introductory sections of the teacher's edition, which describe the resources and materials provided.

The objectives and other resources that accompany textbooks can be very useful to the classroom teacher—so useful that a teacher might be tempted to rely exclusively upon them. To do so, however, is to abdicate one's assessment and decision-making responsibilities, which require a teacher to carefully assess the adequacy of the textbook objectives and other materials in terms of pupil needs and resources.

Textbook authors cannot tailor objectives, plans, and assessments to each varied user. They cannot take the status, needs, readiness, and resources of all teachers and classes into account when stating objectives, so they offer objectives and materials that they think most teachers would agree with and accept. It is the responsibility of all classroom teachers to assess the suitability of the textbook objectives and materials for their own particular situation. Blindly following the suggestions in the teacher's textbook can undermine the classroom teacher's responsibility to determine objectives and instructional activities that are well matched to the needs of pupils.

Teachers should assess textbook objectives and lesson plans using three screens (Brophy and Alleman, 1991). If the text material appears useful after these screens have been applied, a teacher may use it to help focus instruction and assess pupil learning. The three screens include: (1) Are the objectives and text materials clearly stated? (2) Are they suitable for pupils in this particular classroom? (3) Do they exhaust the kinds of objectives and activities these pupils should be exposed to? Box 3.2 provides specific questions that should be asked when reviewing the appropriateness of textbook objectives and lesson plans. Note that most of these questions involve objectives, indicating the importance of stating clear and achievable objectives when planning lessons.

The first screen examines the way the objectives and lesson plans are stated. Do they contain a clear description of the process and content knowledge the pupils will learn and the instructional activities that enhance learning? Most, though not all, textbook objectives do provide a clear description of the desired process and content. In the event that the author's objectives are vague and ambiguous, the teacher must define these terms, recognizing that his or her definition may differ from the author's and thus may not be reflected in the instructional suggestions and materials that accompany the text.

Box 3.2 Basic Factors to Consider When Examining Textbook Objectives and Lesson Plans

Textbook Objectives

1. **Clarity:** Are objectives clearly stated, especially the process and knowledge?
2. **Comprehensiveness:** Do the objectives include most learner outcomes for this topic?
3. **Level:** Do the objectives include both higher- and lower-level thinking behaviors?
4. **Prerequisites:** Do pupils have the prerequisite skills needed to master the objectives?
5. **Time:** Can pupils reasonably be expected to master the objectives in the time available for instruction?

Lesson Plans

1. **Pertinence:** Do plans help foster the stated objectives?
2. **Level:** Do plans include activities for fostering both higher- and lower-level objectives?
3. **Realism:** Are plans realistic given pupil ability, learning style, reading level, attention span, and so on?
4. **Resources:** Are the resources and materials needed to implement plans and activities available?
5. **Follow-up:** Are follow-up materials (e.g., worksheets, enrichment exercises, and reviews) related to the objectives and do they reinforce lesson plans and activities?

The second screen examines appropriateness for the particular pupils in a teacher's class. When teachers develop their own objectives and plans, they take into account the status, needs, and readiness of the pupils. Not to do so is to risk irrelevant instruction. Textbook authors, however, can only state a single set of objectives and plans for all the classes and pupils who will use the book. Often, these objectives and plans are more suitable for some classes than for others. Consequently, teachers must ask: Do my pupils have the prerequisites needed to master the textbook objectives? Can they be taught these objectives in a reasonable amount of time? Will the lesson activities interest them? Do the lesson activities pertain to all the important objectives in the unit?

The final screen examines completeness. Do the textbook objectives exhaust the important outcomes pupils should learn? Lesson plans in textbooks tend to emphasize structured, didactic methods (remember factual knowledge) in which the teacher either tells pupils things or elicits brief re-

TABLE 3.8

Advantages and Disadvantages of Textbook Objectives and Lesson Plans

Advantages	Disadvantages
Convenient, readily available objectives and plans	Designed for teachers and pupils in general, not necessarily for a given teacher or class
Can save valuable time in planning	
Provide an integrated set of objectives, plans, activities, and assessments	Heavy emphasis on lower-level objectives and activities
Contain many ancillary materials for planning, instructing, and assessing	Lesson activities tend to be didactic and teacher-led
	If accepted uncritically, can lead to inappropriate instruction for pupils

sponses to questions. Lessons using such objectives are easier to devise and present than less structured, more complex ones. Relatively few textbook objectives call for synthesis or analysis of ideas, themes, or topics. Although teachers commonly omit topics from a text when teaching, they rarely introduce new topics that are not in the text. If teachers wish to include or emphasize higher-level objectives in their instruction, they may be forced to break this pattern and introduce additional objectives that round out pupil learning. Table 3.8 summarizes the advantages and disadvantages of textbook objectives and lesson plans.

State and School District Learning Standards

In recent years, the term *objective* no longer is the sole term used to describe statements of intended pupil learning. The growth of standards-based education in which statewide and district-wide learning outcomes are called **standards,** has become common in the United States. Presently, almost every state has developed mandated standards to focus and guide instruction in the classrooms of their states (Olson, 1999). These mandated statewide and district-wide learning standards are a response to perceptions that today's school pupils are performing considerably lower in school than pupils of prior years. To rectify this problem, legislatures and boards of education in most states and many school districts have mandated defined learning standards for teachers to teach and pupils to learn. Standards-based education seeks to reduce inequity, uneven teacher performance, haphazard assessments, lack of school accountability, and heterogeneous curricula. Table 3.9 indicates some of the pros and cons of standards-based education.

TABLE 3.9

Some Pros and Cons of Common State Standards

Pros	Cons
Provide all students access to a broad and balanced curriculum	Unlikely to serve all students equally
Set clear outcomes for instruction and assessment	Can take attention away from subject areas not included in the standards
Promote cultural cohesion	Often emphasize a "transmission" model of instruction
Provide state authority over school outcomes	Can reduce professionalism of teachers by removing many of their decisions about planning and delivering instruction

In most states and in many districts assessments are administered to pupils to determine how well they are performing on the mandated standards. These assessments can have important consequences for teachers, pupils, and administrators. The consequences of the assessments encourage teachers, pupils, and administrators to emphasize the standards in instruction. Chapter 11 describes the construction and interpretation of the state and district assessments. Here, we focus on examples of standards adopted in varied states or school districts. The following examples were chosen more for their variety than for their excellence.

Depending on the state and district, standards can encompass a variety of subject areas, grade levels, and formats. For example, Figure 3.4 shows one of the six standards comprising the Colorado Model Content Standards for Reading and Writing, "Students write and speak using conventional grammar, usage, sentence structure, punctuation, capitalization, and spelling." Information that describes what is necessary to meet the standard is provided, and what pupils in three grade groups (K–4, 5–8, and 9–12) should be taught and should learn in Colorado is described.

Compare the Colorado fourth grade reading and writing standards to the fourth grade English standards of the State of Virginia in Figure 3.5. The Virginia standards are developed on a grade-by-grade approach, unlike the grade groupings in the Colorado standards. That is, in Virginia each individual grade has its own set of learning standards. The Virginia standards are lengthy and more specific than the Colorado standards, thus providing a sharper focus for teachers to plan and carry out their instruction on the standards. Notice that although different states present their standards with varied specificity, in almost all cases the teacher must interpret and translate the standards into day-to-day instruction.

Students write and speak using conventional grammar, usage, sentence structure, punctuation, capitalization, and spelling.

In order to meet this standard, students will

- know and use correct grammar in speaking and writing;
- apply correct usage in speaking and writing;
- use correct sentence structure in writing; and
- demonstrate correct punctuation, capitalization, and spelling.

In grades K–4, what students know and are able to do includes
- knowing and using subject/verb agreement;
- knowing and using correct modifiers;
- knowing and using correct capitalization, punctuation, and abbreviations; and
- spelling frequently used words correctly using phonics rules and exceptions.

In grades 5–8, what students know and are able to do includes
- identifying the parts of speech such as nouns, pronouns, verbs, adverbs, adjectives, conjunctions, prepositions, and interjections;
- using correct pronoun case, regular and irregular noun and verb forms, and subject-verb agreement involving comparisons in writing and speaking;
- using modifiers, homonyms, and homophones in writing and speaking;
- using simple, compound, complex, and compound/complex sentences in writing and speaking;
- punctuating and capitalizing titles and direct quotations, using progressives, and correct paragraphing in writing;
- using prefixes, root words, and suffixes correctly in writing and speaking;
- expanding spelling skills to include more complex words;
- demonstrating use of conventional spelling in their published works; and
- using resources such as spell checkers, dictionaries, and charts to monitor the spelling accuracy.

In grades 9–12, what students know and are able to do includes
- using pronoun reference correctly in writing and speaking;
- using phrases and clauses for purposes of modification and parallel structure in writing and speaking;
- using internal capitalization and punctuation of secondary quotations in writing;
- using manuscript forms specified in various style manuals for writing (for example, indenting for extended quotation, precise placement and form of page numbers, appropriate line spacing); and
- refining spelling and grammatical skills and becoming a self-evaluator of their writing and speaking.

FIGURE 3.4 *State of Colorado Reading, Writing, and Speaking Standards*

Standards of Learning for Virginia Public Schools (SOLs). Reprinted by permission of Virginia Department of Education, P.O. Box 2120, Richmond, Virginia 23218-2120.

GRADE FOUR

The fourth-grade student will communicate orally in large- and small-group settings. Students will read classics and contemporary literature by a variety of authors. A significant percentage of reading material will relate to the study of math, science, and history and social science. The student will use text organizers, summarize information, and draw conclusions to demonstrate reading comprehension. Reading, writing, and reporting skills support an increased emphasis on content-area learning and on utilizing the resources of the media center, especially to locate and read primary sources of information (speeches and other historical documents) related to the study of Virginia. Students will plan, write, revise, and edit narratives and explanation. The student will routinely use information resources and word references while writing.

Oral Language
4.1 The student will use effective oral communication skills in a variety of settings.
 • Present accurate directions to individuals and small groups.
 • Contribute to group discussions.
 • Seek the ideas and opinions of others.
 • Begin to use evidence to support opinions.
4.2 The student will make and listen to oral presentations and reports.
 • Use subject-related information and vocabulary.
 • Listen to and record information.
 • Organize information for clarity.

Reading/Literature
4.3 The student will read and learn the meanings of unfamiliar words.
 • Use knowledge of word origins; synonyms, antonyms, and homonyms; and multiple meanings of words.
 • Use word-reference materials including the glossary, dictionary, and thesaurus.
4.4 The student will read fiction and nonfiction, including biographies and historical fiction.
 • Explain the author's purpose
 • Describe how the choice of language, setting, and information contributes to the author's purpose.
 • Compare the use of fact and fantasy in historical fiction with other forms of literature.

FIGURE 3.5 *Standards of Learning for Virginia Public Schools, Fourth Grade English*

SOURCE: Virginia Department of Education, P.O. Box 2120, Richmond, Virginia 23218-2120.

Figure 3.6 shows a sample mathematics standard used in the state of New Mexico. The standard is stated in the top left corner. The New Mexico standards are grouped into grade levels as in Colorado, and benchmarks describe what pupils are expected to be able to do at the end of grades 4, 8, and 12. A **benchmark** indicates what pupils should be able to achieve at a

- Explain how knowledge of the lives and experiences of individuals in history can relate to individuals who have similar goals or face similar challenges.

4.5 The student will demonstrate comprehension of a variety of literary forms.
  - Use text organizers such as type, heading, and graphics to predict and categorize information.
  - Formulate questions that might be answered in the selection.
  - Make inferences using information from texts.
  - Paraphrase content of selection, identifying important ideas and providing details for each important idea.
  - Describe relationship between content and previously learned concepts or skills.
  - Write about what is read.

4.6 The student will read a variety of poetry.
  - Describe the rhyme scheme (approximate, end, and internal).
  - Identify the sensory words used and their effect on the reader.
  - Write rhymed, unrhymed, and patterned poetry.

Writing

4.7 The student will write effective narratives and explanations.
  - Focus on one aspect of a topic.
  - Develop a plan for writing.
  - Organize writing to convey a central idea.
  - Write several related paragraphs on the same topic.
  - Utilize elements of style, including word choice, tone, voice, and sentence variation.
  - Edit final copies for grammar, capitalization, punctuation, and spelling.
  - Use available technology.

4.8 The student will edit final copies of writings.
  - Use subject-verb agreement.
  - Avoid double negatives.
  - Use pronoun "I" correctly in compound subjects.
  - Use commas in series, dates, and addresses

Research

4.9 The student will use information resources to research a topic.
  - Construct questions about a topic.
  - Collect information, using the resources of the media center.
  - Evaluate and synthesize information for use in writing.
  - Use available technology.

FIGURE 3.5 *Continued*

given grade level. The benchmarks for Colorado and New Mexico are assessed at the end of the fourth, eighth, and twelfth grades, the benchmark grades. In Virginia, the benchmarks are assessed each year because Virginia standards are developed for each grade level. In general, benchmarks are more specific than standards.

MATHEMATICS
Number and Operation Concepts

STANDARD	BENCHMARKS		
	K–4	5–8	9–12
Students will understand and use numbers and number relationships. **5** For sample lesson relating to this standard see page: M-20	Students will construct number meanings through everyday experiences and the use of physical materials; describe the numeration system by relating counting, grouping, and place value concepts; develop numbers sense for whole numbers, fractions, and decimals; explore the relationships among mixed numbers, fractions, and decimals; and interpret the multiple uses of numbers in everyday life.	Students will represent and use numbers in a variety of equivalent forms including integers, fractions, decimals, percents, exponents, and scientific notation; expand number sense skills to include integers and rational numbers; apply the relationships among fractions, decimals, and percents to ratios and proportions; and represent numerical relationships in one- and two-dimensional graphs.	Students will extend number-sense skills to include irrational numbers; apply number-sense skills within the real number system; apply ratios, proportional, and percents in more complex mathematical situations; and analyze and interpret numerical relationships in one- and two-dimensional graphs, both manually and using tools such as graphing calculators and computers.

FIGURE 3.6 *State of New Mexico Mathematics Standards for Number and Operation Concepts*

Samples of the New Mexico Content Standards. Reprinted with permission.

In addition to standards and benchmarks, teachers in New Mexico are also provided with suggestions for how to prepare pupils to learn the standards as well as strategies for instruction. Figure 3.7 shows the New Mexico K–4 math benchmarks, an overview of an instructional math activity, and a set of instructional procedures to teach portions of the K–4 math benchmarks. Similar benchmarks, overviews, and instructional procedures are available for other math levels and for other New Mexico standards such as language arts.

The Glenview Public School District in Glenview, Illinois, has developed standards for pupils in a number of subject areas and grade levels. Figure 3.8 shows a portion of the study and research skills standards for the eighth grade. In addition to each standard, the Glenview District provides an indication of how long instruction on a standard should take, whether the objective reinforces prior learning or is a new topic for study, how the objective will be assessed, and the intended level of Bloom's Taxonomy.

Standards-based education has become a common feature of schooling. As the previous examples illustrate, standards determined by states and school districts can differ greatly in terms of specificity and whether the standards are focused on individual grade levels or on groups of grade levels. Standards for a given subject area such as math or reading can vary greatly from state to state and district to district. The most common subject areas for which standards are written are math, English/language arts, science, and history/social studies. Fewer subject standards are written for foreign languages, health, and arts and humanities.

In summary, there are three main sources of objectives: teachers, textbooks, and state or district standards. In many situations the teacher develops his or her own set of objectives focused on his or her pupils and classroom context. In other situations, objectives are chosen from the teacher's edition of the textbook being used. Finally, statewide and district-wide standards and benchmarks are provided to help teachers focus on important pupil outcomes emphasized in instruction. While the form, nature, or source of objectives can vary, it is important that all teachers include objectives or standards in their instructional planning.

✖ Improving Planning Assessment

In planning instruction, there are a few common guidelines that teachers can follow to strengthen the effectiveness of their planning.

1. *Perform complete sizing-up assessments of pupils' needs and characteristics.* Because the purpose of instruction is to help pupils do things they were unable to do before instruction, planning responsive lessons requires that the needs and characteristics of pupils be taken into consideration. Knowledge of pupils' readiness, abilities, and attention spans help the classroom teacher determine how long lessons should be, whether they should involve whole-class or small-group activities, and whether they should be teacher-led or

MATH CONTENT STANDARD 5:

Students will understand and use numbers and number relationships.

This sample lesson may also apply to the following content standards:

i
- Language Arts 1, 3, 10
- Modern, Classical and Native Languages 1, 6
- Social Studies 10, 12, 14

Incorporates Technology

Career Readiness Standard 3

NOTES:

_____

_____

_____

_____

_____

_____

_____

_____

_____

_____

_____

_____

_____

K-4 BENCHMARKS:
- Construct number meanings through everyday experiences and the use of physical materials.
- Describe the numeration system by relating counting, grouping, and place value concepts.
- Interpret the multiple uses of numbers in everyday life.

for a complete listing of benchmarks see Content Standards and Benchmarks *section*

OVERVIEW:

The students count the number of school days beginning with the first day of school. A long strip of paper (counting strip) is placed on a wall. Near the classroom calendar are three boxes taped together. The box to the far right is labeled "ones", the middle box is labeled "tens", and the box to the left is labeled "hundreds". Each day the students add a straw to the ones' box. When there are ten straws in the ones' box, the straws are bundled together with a rubber band and placed in the tens' box. When there are ten bundles in the tens' box, those are put together with a large rubber band and placed in the hundreds' box. Students count the number of straws in the boxes each day and then add the number to the counting strip.

When the students are getting close to 100 straws in the boxes and 100 on the counting strip, a "100th Day of School Celebration" is planned and celebrated on that day. Plans for the celebration may include one hundred cookies, a cake cut up into 100 pieces, asking students to bring 100 of something (shells, beans, marbles, etc.), a parade, a school-wide celebration, hanging 100 links across the room, making stacks of 100 cubes, etc.

METHODOLOGY

FOCUS OF LESSON: Students will use physical materials on a daily basis to consturct number meanings and to participate in numeration system activities involving counting, grouping, and place values.

PROCEDURE:

1. On the first day of school set up the place-value boxes and counting strip described in the overview. Explain to the students what the boxes and counting strip are for. Materials to use with the place-value boxes might include straws, popsicle sticks, unifix cubes, Cuisenaire rods, etc. Place a supply of whatever you use near the boxes for easy access each day. A calendar can be incorporated by placing the boxes near the classroom calendar.

2. Establish a daily routine so that each day one student adds a straw to the boxes and adds a number to the counting strip while the class participates by helping count the straws in the boxes and suggesting how to write the number on the counting strip. Count by ones, tens, hundreds.

3. The numbers on the counting strip can be color-coded by groups of ten until reaching 100, and then the color pattern can be repeated. The counting strip can be used to teach even and odd numbers. It can also be used as a classroom reference for students while solving math problems. Students can use sentence strips to write about events on certain days and then display them under the number for that day.

4. Reinforce concepts of place value, grouping, and counting in other activities using manipulatives and problem solving. Race to 100 is a game that students can play in small groups. In this game each student has a place mat with three sections, ones, tens, and hundreds. They also have dice, Cuisenaire rods, or unifix cubes. Students take turns rolling the dice. The number they roll indicates the number of Cuisenaire rods or cubes they should take and put on the place mat. When they have ten ones, they trade them in for a ten, ten-tens trade for one hundred. The race can go to 100 or higher. One student can play the role of the banker.

5. The "100th Day of School Celebration" can be celebrated in the classroom or school-wide. Some excellent books to use to expand on the activities include *The 100th Day of School* by Angela Shelf, *Every Day Counts* by Patsy F. Kanter, and *Calendar Math Guide* published by DC Heath.

More than one language may be used.

Provides opportunities for integration of math and language arts.

Provides opportunities for teacher to observe students' understanding of place value concepts.

FIGURE 3.7 *State of New Mexico K–4 Math Benchmarks, Including Overview and Suggested Instructional Approaches*

STUDY AND RESEARCH SKILLS

This component includes developing organization and research skills needed to find appropriate resources, judging resources as relevant or not relevant to a given topic, categorizing and synthesizing information, taking notes in class, and studying for exams.

1. The learner will be able to identify the kinds of information a dictionary contains and locate information in a dictionary.
   Instructional hours: 3.0
   Scope: Reinforce
   Source: Comprehensive Tests of Basic Skills *(CTBS)*, Level 19/20 week tested: 28.
   Bloom's taxonomy: Comprehension

2. The learner will be able to follow directions.
   Instructional hours: 0.5
   Scope: Grade Level Expectation
   Source: Foundation Core Curriculum, Language Arts Intermediate Series
   Bloom's taxonomy: Application

3. The learner will be able to identify the purpose for a graphic organizer, use organizational skills to complete a graphic organizer, and choose the most appropriate title for a graphic organizer.
   Instructional hours: 5.0
   Scope: Reinforce
   Source: Comprehensive Tests of Basic Skills *(CTBS)*, Level 19/20 week tested: 28.
   Bloom's taxonomy: Analysis

4. The learner will be able to select appropriate reference sources.
   Instructional hours: 1.0
   Scope: Reinforce
   Source: Foundation Core Curriculum, Language Arts Intermediate Series
   Bloom's taxonomy: Comprehension

5. The learner will be able to identify, develop and understand the correct bibliography format for a book.
   Instructional hours: 1.0
   Scope: Reinforce
   Source: Comprehensive Tests of Basic Skills *(CTBS)*, Level 19/20 week tested: 28.
   Bloom's taxonomy: Knowledge

6. The learner will be able to follow oral and written test directions.
   Instructional hours: 5.0
   Scope: Reinforce
   Source: Illinois Goal Assessment Program *(IGAP)*, Reading Grade 8 week tested: 26.
   Bloom's taxonomy: Comprehension

FIGURE 3.8   *Sample Study and Research Eighth Grade Standards for the Glenview, Illinois Schools*

Reprinted by permission of EdVISION, Inc.

7. The learner will be able to be familiar with various testing formats, such as multiple choice, essay, fill in the blank, and matching.
   Instructional hours: 0.5
   Scope: Reinforce
   Source: Illinois Goal Assessment Program *(IGAP)*, Reading Grade 8 week tested: 26.
   Bloom's taxonomy: Comprehension

8. The learner will be able to identify pertinent information for notes and note cards.
   Instructional hours: 2.0
   Scope: Reinforce
   Source: Comprehensive Tests of Basic Skills *(CTBS)*, Level 19/20 week tested: 28.
   Bloom's taxonomy: Analysis

9. The learner will be able to use library software to locate resource materials and download resource information.
   Instructional hours: 2.0
   Scope: Reinforce
   Source: Foundation Core Curriculum, Language Arts Intermediate Series
   Bloom's taxonomy: Synthesis

FIGURE 3.8   *Continued*

pupil-directed. The more valid and reliable pupil and class sizing-up assessments are, the more appropriate the lesson plans are likely to be.

2. *Use sizing-up assessment information when planning.* A teacher may have done an exceptional job of sizing up pupils, but if the teacher does not use that information when planning lessons, it is useless. Planning involves fitting instruction to pupil needs and characteristics, and it is the teacher's responsibility to plan accordingly.

3. *Do not rely entirely and uncritically on textbooks and their accompanying aids when planning.* As we have seen, teacher's edition textbooks can provide much of the information needed to plan, carry out, and assess instruction, but usually not all. It is important to match the suitability of textbook plans and assessments with pupil characteristics and needs. Teacher's guides should be assessed, adapted, and supplemented to provide the best possible instruction to each teacher's class.

4. *Include a combination of lower-level and higher-level objectives.* The instructional activities offered in most teacher's editions are heavily weighted toward whole-class practices such as recitation, teacher presentation, and seatwork. Such practices normally emphasize lower-level objectives. It is important, therefore, that lesson plans and activities (whether textbook or teacher-made) include *both* lower- and higher-level objectives.

5. *Include a wide range of instructional activities and strategies to fit your pupils' instructional needs.* Teachers who use the same strategy (e.g., lecture, seatwork, or board work) every day with little change or variety create two problems. First, they risk boring pupils and reducing their motivation to attend to the repetitive activity. Second, by limiting their teaching repertoire to a single or very few strategies, they may not be reaching pupils whose learning styles, handicaps, or language backgrounds are best suited to some other method (e.g., small-group instruction, learning games, hands-on materials). It is important to include varied teaching strategies and activities in lesson plans.

6. *Align objectives, teaching strategies, and planned assessments.* Objectives describe the desired results of instruction. Teaching strategies and activities represent the means to achieve those results. Assessment is a measure of the success of the objectives and instruction. In order to reach the desired ends, the means must be relevant and appropriate. Without pupil ends clearly in mind, it is difficult to judge the adequacy of an instructional plan or the quality of an assessment. Box 3.3 shows the relationship between statements of ends (objectives) and statements of means (teaching activities).

7. *Recognize one's own knowledge and pedagogical limitations.* Teachers assess many things when planning instruction, but one often neglected area is assessment of themselves. Content knowledge limitations may lead a teacher to omit an important topic, teach it in a perfunctory or superficial manner, or provide pupils with incorrect information. Likewise, preferences for one or two teaching methods may deprive pupils of exposure to other methods or activities that would enhance their learning. When a teacher's knowledge limitations and pedagogical preferences outweigh pupil considerations in determining what is or is not done in classrooms, serious questions must be raised about the adequacy of the teacher's instructional plans.

Box 3.3   Examples of Instructional Means and Ends

Means: Read a short story silently.
End: The pupils can summarize a short story in their own words.

Means: Show a film about computers.
End: The pupils can differentiate between computer hardware and software.

Means: Do seatwork on p. 47–8 in math book.
End: The pupils can calculate the areas of square and triangles.

Means: Discuss the organization of the periodic table.
End: The pupils can plan an element in its periodic group when given a description of the element's properties.

Box 3.4   Guidelines in Planning Instruction

- Perform complete sizing-up assessments of pupils' needs and characteristics.
- Use sizing-up assessments when planning.
- Do not rely entirely and uncritically on textbooks and their accompanying aids when planning.
- Include a combination of lower- and higher-level objectives.
- Include a range of instructional activities and strategies.
- Match educational objectives with teaching strategies and activities.
- Recognize one's own knowledge and pedagogical limitations and preferences.
- Include assessment strategies in instructional plans.

---

8. *Include assessment strategies in instructional plans.* The object of planning and conducting instruction is to help pupils learn new content and behaviors. Consequently, lesson plans should include some formal measure or measures to determine whether pupils have learned the desired objectives and to identify areas of misunderstanding or confusion. While informal assessments about pupil enthusiasm and participation can be useful, they are not substitutes for more formal assessments such as follow-up seatwork, homework, quizzes, or oral questioning. Box 3.4 summarizes the guidelines to follow in planning lessons.

✴ Addressing Pupil Accommodations

Initially it may seem odd to introduce pupil disabilities and accommodations in a chapter focused on objectives and planning instruction. However, on reflection, it is not really odd at all. Pupil disabilities and particularly pupil accommodations are very important aspects that must be addressed in a teacher's instructional planning.

In recent years there has been increasing emphasis on integrating pupils with disabilities into regular classrooms. Prior "pull out" programs that educated pupils with disabilities in classrooms separate from the majority of pupils are diminishing with the growing emphasis on inclusion of special pupils with their nondisabled peers (Sawyer, McLaughlin, and Winglee, 1994; Ferguson, 1995). Increased inclusion has placed greater responsibility and challenge on the classroom teacher, who is often charged with educating pupils with varied disabilities (Hoy and Gregg, 1994; Roach, 1995). In this section we will examine laws that define how pupils with disabilities must be diagnosed, instructed, and assessed, as well as accommodations that can make assessment more valid and appropriate for such pupils.

Legal Issues

The enactment of Public Law 94-142, the Education for All Handicapped Children Act of 1975, mandated that free public education be provided for *all* school-age children, including those with disabilities, many of whom had been excluded from a free public education. Public Law 94-142 also prescribed assessment procedures and practices for pupils identified as having special needs. Public Law 101-476, the Individuals with Disabilities Education Act of 1990 (IDEA), extended the rights of pupils with disabilities by requiring a free and appropriate education for preschool pupils with disabilities. Public Law 101-476 called for the placement of pupils with disabilities in the least restrictive environment. The least restrictive environment provision requires that, to the maximum degree possible, pupils with disabilities should be educated in classrooms with pupils who do not have disabilities. Section 504 of the Rehabilitation Act of 1973 reinforced and expanded protection of pupils with disabilities by broadening the definition of what constitutes a disability. These acts have substantially increased classroom teachers' responsibilities for identifying, instructing, and assessing pupils with disabilities (Phi Delta Kappan, Special Issue on Inclusion, 1995). Box 3.5 describes the major provisions of IDEA. More wide-ranging discussion of legal issues in educating such pupils can be found in Ordover and Boundy (1991), Rothstein (1990) and Overton (1996).

The law requires school systems and teachers to identify and assess all children who have disabilities or are at risk of having their learning impaired because of some cognitive, affective, or psychomotor disability. The range of conditions that qualify as disabilities is large, spanning from physical disabilities and hearing or visual impairments to emotional disorders, learning disorders, and speech impairments. Although the manner of identifying such pupils varies greatly, the classroom teacher is a primary source, especially in the preschool, elementary, and middle school grades. These teachers spend a great deal of time each day with a small group of pupils and thus are in an advantageous position to observe and identify pupils' strengths, weaknesses, needs, and potential disabilities. One of the teacher's official assessment responsibilities is to identify pupils suspected of having a special learning need or disability.

The law requires formal assessment of a pupil who has been identified as likely to have a disability that impacts his or her learning. The assessment helps determine whether the pupil does have special needs, what the needs are, and how they may best be addressed in instruction. Referrals for such pupil assessments can come from teachers, parents, counselors, physicians, and others. The composition of the assessment team that reviews a referred pupil varies, but it is usually made up of some or all of the following individuals: one or more special education teachers, the pupil's classroom teacher(s), specialists in areas of the pupil's perceived needs, parents, child advocates, counselors, and a social worker. The assessment conference must be carried out according to the following procedures and guidelines:

- A parent must have written notice, in nontechnical language and in the parent's native language, that a school system proposes to conduct an assessment. Prior notice is needed for a "preplacement" assessment to determine whether a child needs special education, as well as subsequent assessments.

Box 3.5   Major Provisions of IDEA

Free and Appropriate Public Education

All children are entitled to a free and appropriate public education, regardless of the nature or severity of their disability.

Nondiscriminatory Assessment

Requires the establishment of procedures to ensure that testing and evaluation materials and procedures utilized for evaluation and placement of children with disabilities will be selected and administered so as not to be culturally or racially discriminatory.

Development of an Individual Education Plan (IEP)

Requires the development of a written IEP for each child with a disability that will include a statement of current levels of educational achievement, annual and short-term goals, specific educational services to be provided, dates of initiation and duration of services, and criteria for evaluating the degree to which the objectives are achieved.

Due Process

Requires an opportunity to present complaints with respect to any matter relating to the identification, evaluation, or educational placement of a child. Specific due process procedures include: (a) written notification to parents before evaluation, (b) written notification when initiating or refusing to initiate a change in educational placement, (c) an opportunity to obtain an independent evaluation of the child, and (d) an opportunity for an impartial due process hearing.

Privacy and Records

Requires that educational and psychological records pertaining to a child remain confidential except to those individuals who are directly involved in a child's education and who have a specific reason for reviewing the records. Further, the law provides an opportunity for the parents or guardian of a child with a disability to examine all relevant records with respect to the identification, evaluation, and educational placement of the child.

Least Restrictive Environment

Requires to the maximum extent appropriate that children with disabilities be educated with children who are not disabled in as normal an environment as possible.

Related Services

Requires that support services (e.g., psychological, audiology, occupational theory, music therapy) be available to assist the child with a disability to benefit from special education.

Source: Adapted from individuals with Disabilities Education Act, P.L. 101–476.

- Parental consent must be obtained before pupils are assessed.
- Assessments must not be racially or culturally discriminatory.
- Assessments must be in the pupil's native language.
- No single test or procedure can be the basis for deciding that the pupil has a disability and requires help through instructional accommodations.
- Assessments must be conducted by a multidisciplinary team, including at least one teacher knowledgeable about the pupil's area of disability; the assessment must include all areas related to the pupil's disability including health, vision, hearing, emotional status, etc.
- The assessments used must have proven validity applicable to the decision to be made.
- Formal tests and assessments of the pupil must be administered by trained individuals.
- A written report must be presented after the assessment process is complete.

Although these procedures say little about the role of the classroom teacher, it is often the teacher who identifies a pupil's disability. Common areas of disability such as oral expression, listening comprehension, written expression, reading fluency, comprehension, and attention deficit are best identified by the classroom teacher. If an assessment is conducted, the teacher will provide important information about a pupil's classroom performance and behavior at the assessment conference.

If a pupil is identified as having a disability, the results of the assessment conference will be used to develop appropriate educational objectives, instructional approaches, and assessment methods for the pupil. Here again, the classroom teacher's recommendations are important in deciding how and what the pupil will be taught and assessed. Because the emphasis in assessment and instruction is on the individual pupil, not the identified disability, each assessed pupil is treated as an individual and the most suitable educational arrangement for that pupil is the primary focus (Hoy and Gregg, 1994). Two pupils with the same disability may have different objectives, instruction, and assessment strategies.

The specific educational plan developed for a pupil is called an **Individual Educational Plan** (IEP), and must include information about the pupil's present level of educational performance, annual goals and short-term objectives, prescribed educational services, degree of inclusion in regular education programs, and assessment criteria for determining achievement of the goals and objectives. In essence, the IEP defines a pupil's special needs and the ways that the teacher must modify objectives, instructional strategies, and assessment methods to best suit the pupil's needs and learning style. Box 3.6 lists the required parts of an IEP. Examination of these parts shows how a pupil's IEP relates to the planning, instruction, and assessment of the pupil. Once the IEP is developed and agreed upon, it may not be unilaterally changed by school personnel or the classroom teacher.

Box 3.6   Required Contents of an IEP

1. A statement of the child's present levels of educational performance, including academic achievement, social adaptations, prevocational and vocational skills, psychomotor skills, and self-help skills.
2. A statement of annual goals which describes the educational performance to be achieved by the end of the school year under the child's individualized education program.
3. A statement of short-term instructional objectives, which must be measurable intermediate steps between the present level of educational performance and the annual goals.
4. A statement of specific educational services needed by the child (determined without regard to the availability of services), including a description of
   a. all special education and related services which are needed to meet the unique needs of the child, including the type of physical education program in which the child will participate, and
   b. any special instructional media and materials which are needed.
5. The date when those services will begin and length of time the services will be given.
6. A description of the extent to which the child will participate in regular education programs.
7. A justification of the type of educational placement that the child will have.
8. A list of the individuals who are responsible for implementation of the Individual Education Plan.
9. Objective criteria, evaluation procedures, and schedules of determining, on at least an annual basis, whether the short-term instructional objectives are being achieved.

Source: Federal Register, 41(252), p. 5692.

Decisions about pupils' disabilities and accommodations focus on placing pupils in the least restrictive environment, which enables them to be educated in the most normal environment their disabilities allow. The overriding purpose of referral, IEP development, and placement in the least restrictive environment is to ensure that pupils receive an education appropriate for their needs.

Disabilities and Accommodations

In 1997, the National Academy of Science reported that 5 million pupils are eligible for assistance under IDEA. That is about 10 percent of the school pupils in the U.S. Four areas account for the major portion of pupil disabilities: disabilities related to speech and language; mental retardation; severe emotional problems; and specific learning problems such as learning disabilities, physical limitations, attention deficits, and behavioral problems. The range of pupil disabilities and their appropriate accommodations is wide. Because the focus here is on the classroom, the discussion of specific disabilities and their accommodations centers on classroom issues and accommodations. Even limiting discussion to the classroom leaves a wide variety of disabilities and accommodations to consider, and each particular disability can range from severe to mild.

Some classroom disabilities are treated with medication. The widespread use of Ritalin to combat attention deficit disorder (ADD) is the classic example. Other disabilities are so severe that they require intense one-on-one interactions between a special needs teacher and the pupil. Many of these pupils are taught in special classrooms to meet their needs. In other cases, pupils with disabilities may split their time between a special education classroom and a regular classroom. Finally, many pupils with disabilities spend their whole day in a regular classroom, some with an aide and some without an aide (Phi Delta Kappan, Special Issue on Inclusion, 1995).

As noted, an important aspect of planning and delivering instruction is accommodating pupil needs and disabilities. (We will consider assessment accommodations in Chapter 7.) Clearly, pupil needs and disabilities span a broad range, from pupils with severe cognitive, affective, and/or psychomotor disabilities to pupils with mild attention problems (Cegelka and Berdine, 1995; Cartwright, Cartwright, and Ward, 1995). While it is not possible here to address all available accommodation strategies for instruction, we will review a sample of useful strategies to illustrate the breadth of options. For an excellent in-depth survey of strategies to accommodate varied pupil needs and disabilities see Price and Nelson (1999, Chapter 6).

Common Disabilities and Accommodations

For a hearing impaired pupil the teacher can

- use written rather than oral directions,
- speak slowly and distinctly,
- use sign language.

For a vision impaired pupil the teacher can

- use large print,
- listen to recorded materials,
- let other pupils read out loud,
- seat pupil near the blackboard.

For a pupil with poor comprehension the teacher can

- state directions orally and in writing,
- increase available time,
- sequence directions,
- shorten directions.

For a pupil with a lack of attention the teacher can

- repeat major points,
- change the tone of voice,
- call pupil's name before questioning,
- ask frequent questions,
- have the pupil write down directions.

Common Disabilities and Accommodations for Planning and Instructing

Accommodations when planning content:

- If students have fallen behind in the curriculum, teach what is most generalizable.
- Teach learning strategies along with teaching content area.
- Select content based on student interests; for example, allow pupils to read the sports page to practice reading skills.

Accommodations when planning objectives:

- Pretest before teaching to make sure the objective is appropriate for the students.
- Determine whether the objective can be altered for some students; for example, can pupils who have poor writing skills demonstrate their knowledge orally?

Accommodations when deciding on instructional methods:

- Recognize that pupils with some learning and behavior disabilities often need very explicit directions.
- Evaluate the level of structure pupils need to be successful; do not assume that all students learn best with unstructured approaches.
- If pupils have fallen behind in the curriculum use time-efficient methods.
- Be sure pupils have the necessary skills to be successful in the instructional method being used.

Accommodations when planning the lesson:

- Provide directions, procedures, and rules; describe them orally and in writing.
- Follow up by asking questions or by having pupils repeat or paraphrase what they are to do.
- Repeat key words often, using the same wording.
- Ask for frequent active responses.
- Break up information: teach a couple of steps, practice, teach a couple more steps, practice. Keep reminding pupils of the whole task. Stop often to summarize.
- Point to steps on a written list as they are demonstrated.

Common Nondisability Teacher-Pupil Issues

Dealing with an argumentative pupil

- Do not confront the pupil in a group situation.
- Evaluate the situation that led to the confrontation.
- Allow the pupil to have his or her say.
- Do not make threats that cannot be backed up.

Dealing with cleaning up classroom work sites

- Establish and reinforce clean-up rules.
- Practice cleaning up.
- Praise pupils who are neat and begin to clean up first.
- Make a check list of clean-up tasks.

Dealing with pupil disrespect

- Inform the pupil that such behavior is not acceptable.
- Make the consequences of future disrespect clear.
- Try to determine the basis for the pupil's disrespect.
- Have an individual conference or a conference with a mediator such as the pupil's advisor.
- Model respect to students.

In addition to the above, there are many other strategies for pupils with specific disabilities. For example, for pupils who have difficulty maintaining attention, provide a seat near an adult or quiet peers; seat them away from high traffic areas of the classroom; seat them at a single desk, not a table; provide more breaks or task changes; and use more active participation activities. For pupils having difficulty beginning a task, provide a cue card of steps on the desk that the pupil can check off as steps are completed; go to the pupil quickly at the start of the task and help him or her get started (indicate that you will return to check progress); and provide a peer helper. For pupils having difficulty organizing, list assignments and materials needed on the board or a transparency; have students use notebooks with pocket dividers; color code materials needed for various subjects; and provide time to gather books and materials at the start and end of school (Nissman, 2000; Price and Nelson, 1999).

These accommodations represent only a few of the ways lessons can be planned to help pupils get the most out of instruction. Based on the knowledge gained from sizing-up assessment and the teaching of initial lessons, teachers should begin to identify needs and appropriate accommodations for pupils. With this knowledge, teachers can plan and implement accommodations for students who need them to learn most effectively, thus improving the validity of their instruction and assessments.

Chapter Summary

- Education is the process of helping pupils acquire new skills and behaviors. A curriculum is the statement of the things pupils are expected to learn in school or in a course. Instruction includes the methods used to help pupils acquire the desired skills and behaviors. Changes in pupils brought about through formal instruction are called achievements.
- The instructional process is comprised of three steps: identifying desirable ways for pupils to learn, selecting materials and providing

experiences to help pupils learn, and assessing whether pupils have learned. All three of these steps require teacher decision making and therefore involve assessment.

- Planning instruction involves teachers understanding and modifying the curriculum and instruction to fit the needs and characteristics of their pupils. Planning helps teachers reduce anxiety and uncertainty about their instruction, review and become familiar with the subject matter before teaching, select ways to get the lessons started, and integrate lessons into units.

- Planning is dependent upon the context in which instruction takes place and must take into account both the classroom characteristics teachers control (e.g., arrangement of the classroom, methods of instruction, or strategies for assessment) and those they do not (e.g., pupil characteristics, classroom size, or instructional resources).

- Four basic elements that teachers should include in their lesson plans are educational objectives, materials needed, teaching strategies and activities, and assessment procedures. Lesson plans should be written down in advance of instruction.

- Objectives are statements that describe what pupils are expected to learn from instruction. Objectives have three general levels of abstraction— global, educational, and instructional—that range from broad to moderate to narrow. Classroom teaching relies primarily upon educational and instructional objectives.

- Bloom's Taxonomy describes important cognitive processes: knowledge, comprehension, application, analysis, synthesis, and evaluation.

- A second dimension of objectives includes three types of content knowledge: factual knowledge, conceptual knowledge, and procedural knowledge.

- Linking cognitive processes and content knowledge produces three important forms of objectives: remembering factual knowledge, understanding conceptual knowledge, and applying procedural knowledge. Combining cognitive processes and content knowledge in objectives strengthens the alignment of objectives, instruction, and assessment.

- Higher-level educational objectives require pupils to do more than just memorize facts and rules. Higher-level objectives involve behaviors that require application, analysis, synthesis, or evaluation of content and ideas.

- Although educational objectives are useful in planning instruction, the fact that they are stated before instruction begins means that they may need to be amended once instruction is under way. It is appropriate to make such adjustments based on pupil readiness.

- Planning instruction is greatly influenced by textbooks and their accompanying aids and resources. Although it is appealing to uncritically accept a textbook's objectives, plans, activities, and assessments, teachers must remember that every class is different. They must assess the textbook and its resources in light of their own classes' unique needs, readiness, and learning styles.

- Statewide standards describe outcomes that pupils in a state are expected to learn. One important aim of statewide standards is to homogenize desired outcomes statewide. Almost every state has developed statewide standards.
- Standards are usually accompanied by statewide assessments that provide information about how pupils, teachers, or schools are doing in meeting the state standards.
- Lesson planning can be improved by avoiding the following mistakes: not knowing pupils' learning needs and characteristics; ignoring pupil needs and characteristics in planning; relying uncritically on the textbook and its accompanying aids; emphasizing only lower-level educational objectives in plans; using a narrow range of instructional strategies and activities; ignoring the relationship between objectives and teaching activities; failing to recognize one's own content and teaching strategy weaknesses; and omitting assessment from plans.
- An important part of planning instruction is to take into account pupil disabilities and their accommodations.
- Pupils who are identified as having a disability may be given an Individual Education Plan (IEP) that defines the services and accommodations that pupils should receive.
- There is a wide range of accommodations for pupils with special needs.

Questions for Discussion

1. What pupil characteristics are most important to take into account when planning instruction? How realistic is it to expect a teacher to plan instruction that takes into account the important needs of all the pupils?
2. Which subject areas are most difficult to plan for? Why?
3. What would be the characteristics of a class that would be easy to plan for? What would be the characteristics of a difficult-to-plan for group?
4. Why do you think that many teachers describe stating objectives as "backward planning"? Is "backward planning" useful? Why?
5. What are the advantages and disadvantages of using textbook objectives and materials?
6. What activities will help teachers plan for statewide standards and assessments?
7. What are the most common disabilities that pupils have? How might they influence planning, instruction, and assessment?

Reflection Exercise

List as many factors as you can (at least 20) that influence pupils' learning and behavior in school.

Put an X beside the three factors you think are most important for pupil learning.

Put a *Y* beside factors that you think a teacher would discover through
    sizing-up assessment.
Put a *Z* beside all the factors you think a teacher has little control over.
Pick the three factors that a teacher is likely both to know about and be able
    to influence in the classroom.

Activities

1. Write two objectives each for remembering factual knowledge,
   understanding conceptual knowledge, and applying procedural
   knowledge.
2. Pick a cognitive, affective, and psychomotor disability and provide two
   accommodations for each disability.
3. Develop a lesson plan in a topic of your choice. Include the four
   components of lesson plans discussed in the chapter.

Review Questions

1. Explain the differences among education, achievement, instruction, and
   curriculum.
2. How does sizing-up assessment contribute to planning and delivering
   good instruction to pupils? In what ways does sizing-up assessment
   influence classroom decisions?
3. What are the differences between Bloom's six cognitive processes and
   the three types of content knowledge?
4. How are objectives that combine cognitive process and content
   knowledge better than objectives that include only one of these
   elements?
5. What are the advantages and disadvantages of teacher's editions of
   classroom texts? What cautions should teachers exercise when using
   teacher's editions?
6. What are common errors made in planning instruction and how can they
   be overcome?
7. How do objectives influence decisions about instruction and assessment?
8. What are important guidelines for planning instruction?

References

Airasian, P. W., & Walsh, M. E. (1997). Constructivist cautions. *Phi Delta Kappan, 78,*
    444–449.
Bereiter, C., & Scardmalia, M. (1998). Beyond Bloom's Taxonomy: Rethinking
    knowledge for the knowledge age. *International Handbook of Education Change,*
    675–692.
Bloom, B. S., et al. (1956). *Taxonomy of educational objectives: Handbook 1: Cognitive
    Domain.* New York: McKay Publishing.

Brophy, J., & Alleman, J. (1991). Activities as instructional tools: A framework for analysis and evaluation. *Educational Researcher, 20*,(4), 9–23.

Cartwright, P. G., Cartwright C. A., & Ward, M. (1995). *Educating special learners.* Boston: Wadsworth Publishing.

Cegelka, P. T., & Berdine, W. H. (1995). *Effective instruction for students with learning difficulties.* Needham Heights, MA: Allyn and Bacon.

Ferguson, D. L. (1995). The real challenge of inclusion. *Phi Delta Kappan, 77,* 281–287.

Hoy, C., & Gregg, N. (1994). *Assessment: The special educator's role.* Pacific Grove, CA: Brooks/Cole.

Krathwohl, D. R., & Payne, D. A. (1971). Defining and assessing educational objectives. *Educational Measurement.* R. L. Thorndike. Washington, D.C., American Council on Education: 17–41.

Lortie, D. C. (1975). *School teacher.* Chicago: University of Chicago Press.

Marzano, R. D., Pickering, D., & McTighe, J. (1993). *Assessing student outcomes: Performance assessment using the dimensions of learning model.* Alexandria, VA: Association for Supervision and Curriculum Development.

Nissman, B. (2000). *Teacher-tested classroom management strategies.* Upper Saddle River, NJ: Merrill.

Oakes, J., & Lipton, M. (1999). *Teaching to change the world.* New York: McGraw-Hill.

Olson, L. (1999). "In search of better assessments." *Quality Counts 99, Education Week* (January 11), 17–20.

Ordover, E. L., & Boundy, K. B. (1991). *Educational rights of children with disabilities.* Cambridge, MA: Center for Law and Education.

Overton, T. (1996). *Assessment in special education: An applied approach.* Englewood Cliffs, NJ: Merrill.

Phi Delta Kappan (1995). Race, Testing and I.Q., 77,(4), 265–328.

Pintrich, P. (in press). The knowledge dimension. In L. W. Anderson and D. R. Krathwohl (eds.). *A taxonomy for learning, teaching, and assessing: A revision of Bloom's taxonomy of educational objectives.* New York: Addison-Wessley-Longman.

Price, K. M., & Nelson, K. L. (1999). *Daily planning for today's classroom.* Belmont, CA: Wadsworth Publishing.

Roach, V. (1995). Supporting inclusion. *Phi Delta Kappan, 77,* 295–299.

Rothstein, L. F. (1990). *Special education law.* New York: Longman.

Sawyer, R. J., McLaughlin, M. J., & Winglee, M. (1994). Is integration of students with disabilities happening? An analysis of national data trends over time. *Remedial and Special Education, 15(4),* 204–215.

Wiggins, G., & McTighe, J. (1998). *Understanding by design.* Alexandria, VA: Association for Supervision and Curriculum Development.

Woodward, A., and Elliot, D. L. (1990). Textbooks: Consensus and controversy. In D. L. Elliott and A. Woodward, *Textbooks and schooling in the United States. The eighty-ninth yearbook of the National Society for the Study of Education, Part I* (pp. 141–161). Chicago: University of Chicago Press.

C H A P T E R 4

Assessing During Instruction

Chapter Outline

❖ Teachers' Tasks During Instruction: Two Metaphors

❖ Aligning Objectives and Instruction

❖ Teacher Thinking During Instruction

❖ Instructional Assessment

❖ The Quality of Instructional Assessments: Validity and Reliability

❖ Improving Assessment During Instruction

❖ Questioning: Purposes and Strategies

Chapter Objectives

After reading this chapter, the pupil will be able to:

- Distinguish between planning and delivering instruction
- Align objectives and instruction for three types of knowledge
- Find and critique state standards that provide instructional suggestions
- Explain the use of level of tolerance and practical knowledge
- Identify problems that influence validity and reliability in instructional assessment
- Write or ask higher-level and lower-level questions and convergent and divergent questions
- Cite strategies for effective questioning

The assessment activities that teachers carry out when planning instruction are very different from those carried out when delivering instruction. The most obvious difference is the time at which assessment occurs. Planning assessments take place before or after instruction, while instructional assessments take place during instruction. Planning assessments are developed during quiet time, when the teacher can reflect and try to identify appropriate objectives, content topics, and assessment activities for pupils. Instructional assessments take place on the firing, during teaching, and are focused upon making instantaneous and very specific decisions about what to do, say, or ask next in order to keep instruction flowing smoothly. Planning instruction allows the teacher to consider, weigh, and synthesize many kinds of information in making decisions. Conversely, assessments during instruction require the teacher to rely heavily on informal pupil cues such as attention, facial expressions, posture, and questions. Table 4.1 compares the principal characteristics of planning and instructional assessments.

Although discussed separately, it is important to understand that planning and delivering instruction are integrally related. The instructional process constantly cycles from planning instruction to delivering instruction to revised planning to delivering, and so on. There is a logical, ongo-

TABLE 4.1

Characteristics of Planning and Instructional Assessments

Planning Assessment	Instructional Assessment
1. Occurs before or after instruction	1. Occurs during instructions
2. Carried out away from class	2. Carried out in front of class
3. Allows for reflective decisions	3. Requires instantaneous decisions
4. Focuses on identifying objectives, content, and activities	4. Focuses on pupil reactions to content and activities presented
5. Based on many kinds of formal and informal evidence	5. Based mainly on informal pupil cues and responses

ing, and natural link between the two processes and both are necessary for successful teaching.

Although good planning reduces uncertainty during instruction, it rarely eliminates it. The teaching process must, to some extent, be free-flowing and adaptable, allowing for interruptions, digressions, and unexpected happenings. What the teacher does influences what the pupils do, which in turn influences what the teacher does, and so on throughout the instructional process. To understand the process of assessment during instruction, it is necessary to look beyond the teacher's written lesson plans to examine the classroom as a learning society.

❧ Teachers' Tasks During Instruction: Two Metaphors

Once instruction begins, teachers have a twofold task to accomplish. First, they must deliver the instruction that they have planned. Second, they must constantly assess the progress and success of their instruction so that they can modify it if necessary. For many reasons, things do not always go as planned during instruction. Interruptions, misjudgments about pupil readiness, shifts in pupil attention or interest, and various spontaneous events such as fire drills or the first snow flakes of the winter all operate to alter planned instruction. Thus, the teacher must read the classroom society minute by minute, sensing its mood and making decisions about what to do next.

In some respects it is appropriate to consider a teacher as being part actor, one whose task is to "read" the audience's reaction to the instructional "performance." While the classroom teacher has a much more complex task than the actor, the notion of "reading the audience" is a useful one when thinking about the teacher's instructional assessments. Indeed, one teacher interviewed about his teaching performance said, "A theatrical sense is something that you can't learn, but a good actor can sense his audience. He knows when a performance is going well or not going well, simply by the feeling in the air. And it's that way in the classroom. You can feel when the kids are resistant" (Jackson, 1990, p. 122).

Thus, once instruction begins, the teacher engages in an ongoing process of observing and assessing its progress and the pupils' reactions to it. This is a complicated task, since instruction, assessment, and decision making are all taking place simultaneously. For example, during a class discussion,

> . . . a teacher must listen to student answers, watch other students for signs of comprehension or confusion, formulate the next question, and scan the class for possible misbehavior. At the same time, the teacher must attend to the pace of the discussion, the sequence of selecting students to answer, the relevance and quality of the answers, and the logical development of the content. When the class is divided into small groups, the number of simultaneous events increases, and the teacher must monitor and regulate several different activities at once (Doyle, 1986, p. 384).

This quote suggests that teaching is not only similar to acting, but also is similar to being a circus ringmaster who must keep a variety of activities

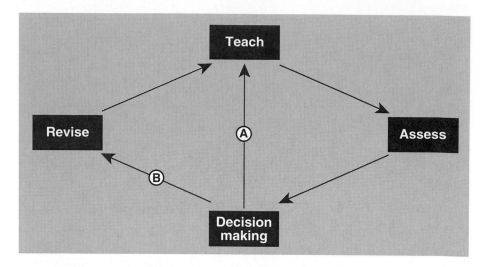

FIGURE 4.1   *Steps in Interactive Instructional Assessment*

going on simultaneously. Teachers must make many decisions as part of the instructional process.

Figure 4.1 illustrates the instructional process. Once teaching begins, the teacher constantly assesses its progress by observing pupil reactions and questioning. On the basis of these reactions and responses, the teacher makes a decision about how instruction is going. If the teacher decides that the lesson is progressing satisfactorily, the teacher continues teaching as planned (path A). If the teacher senses a problem such as lack of pupil understanding or interest, the teacher revises the planned instructional activity to alleviate the problem and initiates another teaching activity or strategy (path B). This cycle can be repeated many times in the course of a single lesson.

⚔ Aligning Objectives and Instruction

Teachers use many different instructional approaches when planning instruction. Madeline Hunter's (1982) Lesson Design Cycle Model, Robert Slavin's (1995) Cooperative Learning Models, and Howard Gardner's (1995) work on multiple intelligences are a few of the many available approaches to instruction. Each approach involves a set of steps or a variety of strategies. For example, Gardner's approach divides intellectual or thinking abilities into seven distinct kinds of intelligence: linguistic (using words), logical/mathematical (using reasoning), spatial (using images and pictures), musical (using rhythms), interpersonal (using interpersonal interactions), intrapersonal (using meditation or planning), and body/kinesthetic (using physical activities). Accepting Gardner's approach to multiple intelligences—or any other approach to learning—has implications for classroom instruction. For example, Gardner would argue that his approach demands that teachers teach a broader range of outcomes using a broader range of styles that engage pupils in different intellectual activities. While simultaneously implementing the seven multiple-intelligence categories in classrooms may be very difficult for teachers, Gardner's theory reminds teachers that there is more than one way for all pupils to learn and be assessed. Different types of intended learning often require different instructional strategies and different assessments (Wiggins and McTighe, 1998). How might instruction and assessment based on a cooperative learning approach differ from instruction and assessment in a multiple-intelligence approach?

Consider three different approaches to planning lessons that are commonly used by beginning teachers: direct instruction, informal presentation, and structured discovery (Price and Nelson, 1999). Direct instruction, also called supervised practice, is teacher-directed. It can be characterized as "I (the teacher) do it, we (teacher and pupils) do it, and you (pupils) do it." That is, the teacher demonstrates a process, the pupils and teacher perform it together, and then the pupils are expected to do it alone. This approach is useful to teach intended factual or procedural outcomes.

Informal presentation involves the teacher lecturing to students. It is a classical lecture format in which the teacher describes to the pupils the things they are to listen to and learn. While direct instruction focuses on pupils doing something, informal presentation focuses on pupils listening. Structured discovery involves the pupils "discovering" teacher-planned information or concepts. The teacher knows in advance what the pupils are to "discover" and structures activities, explorations, and examples so that the pupils will "discover" the intended information or concept. This format can be conducted with pupils cooperatively or individually. There are, of course, many additional approaches to lesson planning and teaching (Arends, 1997; Borich, 1996).

In Chapter 3 we noted that different kinds of knowledge require different kinds of instructional approaches. Remembering factual knowledge calls for different cognitive processes than understanding conceptual knowledge. While it is beyond the scope of this text to list all the varied instructional approaches associated with factual, conceptual, and procedural knowledge, a number of illustrative instructional strategies for teaching each type of knowledge can be presented. These instructional strategies do not exhaust all of the possibilities available. Further, no single strategy is useful in all instructional situations and with all subject areas and types of pupils.

Before teaching in any instructional situation, it is important to know what facts, concepts, and procedures are needed for pupils to learn something new. It is critical to determine what pupils know or don't know about what they are to learn so that the teacher can start instruction at a level appropriate to the pupils' readiness. If pupils do not remember needed factual knowledge, it may be fruitless to begin instruction at the level of conceptual knowledge. Similarly, trying to teach pupils to apply procedural knowledge will be difficult if the conceptual knowledge that underlies a procedure is not available to the pupil. Knowing where pupils are starting instruction from provides a guide for the teacher to determine needed instructional strategies to help the pupils attain desired objectives. Following are instructional strategies that are useful in helping pupils develop factual, conceptual, and procedural knowledge.

Remembering Factual Knowledge

Factual knowledge involves remembering specific facts, dates, vocabulary, and terms. When pupils are expected to achieve objectives dealing with remembering factual knowledge, instructional practices such as the following are useful for teaching.

Instructional Practices: Remembering Factual Knowledge

- Direct instruction
- Drill and practice
- Memorization strategies:
  - Connect factual knowledge with mental pictures, emotions, or physical sensations.
  - Create mnemonic devices.
- Repetition strategies: Use flash cards, games, quizzing, or matching exercises (e.g., matching definitions with meanings or dates with events).
- Questioning
- Inside-outside circle: Each student writes a question on the front of an index card and the answer on the back. Students are divided into two groups, and the groups form circles, one inside of the other. Students should turn and face each other. Students facing each other become partners. Each pair asks their questions and reviews the answers. The members of the pairs switch index cards. The inside circle rotates to the left or right and the process is repeated.

Understanding Conceptual Knowledge

Conceptual knowledge involves understanding concepts and categories. When pupils are expected to achieve objectives dealing with understanding conceptual knowledge, instructional practices such as the following are useful for teaching.

Instructional Practices: Understanding Conceptual Knowledge

- Brainstorming
- Visual organization: Use images such as graphic organizers, diagrams, mapping, webbing, Venn diagrams. Have students create their own maps or diagrams of the concept.
- Concept attainment: Differentiate between examples and non-examples of a concept. Teachers provide students with examples of the concept followed by non-examples of the concept, and then solicit student-generated examples and non-examples.

- Analogizing: Provide students with an analogy that will give them an initial idea of the concept. The analogy should compare the new concept to one the student is already familiar with (e.g., Federal laws are similar to rules in a classroom).
- Questioning
- Subcategorizing: Organize the concept by breaking it into subcategories (e.g., food groups—meat, dairy, vegetables, grains—or federal government—executive, legislative, and judicial branches).
- Linking concepts: Develop and present students with a taxonomy of relevant concepts.
- Rule-example-rule technique: Define the key rule or principle—for example, "supply and demand." Then cite examples of the principle such as, "When Florida experiences an extremely cold winter, orange crops are destroyed. Consequently, the price of oranges increases, because the supply of oranges has decreased." Then reinforce the rule/principle by reviewing the definition or by presenting another example and having students predict the outcome.
- Summarizing techniques: Have students summarize, explain or paraphrase the concept in their own words.
  - Relay summary: Students are grouped into teams of four to five people. Each team is given a blank piece of paper. Each member of the team writes a summary sentence and then passes the piece of paper on to the next member of the team. Each member adds a sentence related to the concept without repeating ideas already recorded. Teams continue until the time limit expires or the entire team has written the required number of summary sentences.
  - Last word: The concept studied becomes the acronym for the activity. Students generate characteristics of the concept and use the letters of the concept to form the first word in each line. For example, the concept "learning" might elicit the following responses:
    Learning has several different levels.
    Educate students by using a variety of instructional strategies.
    Assessments should indicate if students have learned.
    Reinforce concepts by using summary activities.
    New ideas and concepts can be linked to prior knowledge.
    Indicate objectives for student learning.
    Number each step in a process to help students learn procedures.
    Games are an effective method to review for tests.

Applying Procedural Knowledge

Procedural knowledge involves applying processes or procedures. When pupils are expected to achieve objectives dealing with applying procedural knowledge, instructional practices such as the following are useful for teaching.

Instructional Practices: Applying Procedural Knowledge

- Analogizing: Present a comparison of the new problem or process in familiar terms.
- Think-aloud modeling: The teacher verbally explains the process pupils would use to solve the problem.
- Flow charts, sequencing charts
- Guided practice, feedback and correctives, independent practice
- Extended practice until procedure becomes routine
- Means-ends analysis: Define the problem then decide how to solve the problem. Have students plan a solution method for the problem.
- Scaffolding: Task assistance, simplification strategies, increase student independence—move away from need for assistance.
- Elaboration: Mnemonics, summarizing, paraphrasing
- Demonstrations: Lab experiments

As noted previously, these instructional strategies are not the only ones available to teach remembering factual knowledge, understanding conceptual knowledge, and applying procedural knowledge. Also, some strategies such as questioning, writing, and recalling, are applicable to more than one kind of knowledge. What is important, however, is that the instructional strategies shown above illustrate that, in many cases, different approaches are needed to teach different kinds of knowledge. Thus, it is important to identify the type of knowledge needed to align with the objective.

Instructional Approaches from State Standards

In most cases, teachers develop their own instructional methods to help pupils learn the objectives the teacher has stated. However, some standards-based approaches provide suggested or example instructional methods that are linked to particular standards and benchmarks. One of the main aims of standards-based approaches is to focus teachers and pupils on a limited number of desired common learning outcomes. The aim is to have consistency of purpose and instruction across a state. While not all states furnish instructional suggestions for teaching standards, many do. Thus, teachers are provided suggestions for how to teach particular statewide standards. For many teachers, these suggested instructional methods help clarify the intent of a standard and focus the teacher on ways to instruct pupils. Often, the suggested instructional methods are linked to statewide assessments, thus illustrating for teachers and pupils how the instructional activities relate to the assessments of the standards.

Figures 4.2, 4.3, and 4.4 illustrate examples of instruction linked to statewide standards. For each figure, the standard or benchmark is stated, the grade level(s) encompassed by the standard is listed, and suggestions or examples of instructional methods that correspond to the standard are

LEARNING STANDARD 9:

*Students will identify the basic facts and essential ideas
in what they have read, heard, or viewed.*

**Grades
PreK–4**

Standard

Identify the basic facts and
ideas in what they have read,
heard, or viewed, drawing on
such strategies as recalling
prior knowledge, previewing
illustrations and headings to
make predictions, listening to
others' ideas, and comparing
information from several
sources.

**Examples
Focusing and Planning:**

PreK–2: Students and their
teacher read together *Dan the
Flying Man,* a predictable book
which uses repeating phrase.
When they reach the part on
each page that tells where Dan
flies next, the teacher reminds
students to use the pictures, the
rhyming pattern, and their
knowledge of beginning sounds
to figure out new words.
Students demonstrate use of
these strategies in their
independent reading to figure
out other books' essential ideas.
Monitoring and Assessing:
After reading Patricia Lauber's
*Volcano: The Eruption and
Healing of Mt. St. Helens,* the
students are unclear if the
eruption is related to the
eruption of volcanoes in Japan.
Students generate their own
ideas and then the teacher
provides a video on the
volcanoes around the Pacific
Rim. The students brainstorm
what they learned from the video
and are now able to place Mt.
St. Helens in a broader context.

FIGURE 4.2 *State of Massachusetts English Language Arts Standard and
Related Instructional Planning and Assessment*

Reprinted by permission of The Massachusetts Department of Education

given. While teachers do not have to use the standards-based instructional
activities, they are provided to indicate what the standards are about and
how they likely will be assessed. Thus, just as teachers, textbooks, and state
standards can provide learning outcomes, they also can provide instructional strategies to teach the learning outcomes.

9–12 BENCHMARKS:

- **Interpret and draw three-dimensional objects.**
- **Represent problem situations with geometric models and apply properties of figures.**

METHODOLOGY

FOCUS OF LESSON: The objective of this lesson is to provide students with an understanding of:

- the technological development of bridges through history;
- the scientific and mathematical principles that apply to the physical science of bridge building; and
- the construction techniques and creative skills that are necessary for designing and building a good bridge.

PROCEDURE: Students will work in teams to:

- observe different styles of bridge construction by researching in the library media center, studying photographs, and by visiting several bridges within the vicinity;
- write a summary of their activities in which they:
1. Discuss various factors that influence bridge design and construction.
2. Discuss strengths of triangles versus squares.
3. Identify and design a model bridge and develop a materials list.
4. Build model bridge.
5. Discuss strategies used and/or difficulties encountered in drawing a blueprint and constructing a model bridge.
6. Discuss results of the bridge's capacity to bear weight and its efficiency.

FIGURE 4.3   *State of New Mexico Math Benchmark with Objective and Instructional Guides*

❧ Teacher Thinking During Instruction

Researchers have addressed the question of what teachers think about when they are teaching by asking teachers to recall what they were thinking about at certain points in their teaching (Bullough, Knowles, and Crow, 1992). When asked, only a small number of teachers indicated that their thoughts were related to their objectives. Teachers rarely referred to an objective as a basis for their thoughts or actions during instruction. Also, a large proportion of teachers' instructional thoughts were focused on the adequacy of their instruction and how it should be changed for a particular pupil or for the entire class. Teachers described much of their thinking in terms such as these:

INTERMEDIATE

3. Study of the major social, political, cultural, and religious developments in world history involves learning about the important roles and contributions of individuals and groups.

Students:
- investigate the roles and contributions of individuals and groups in relation to key social, political, cultural, and religious practices throughout world history
- interpret and analyze documents and artifacts related to significant developments and events in world history
- classify historic information according to the type of activity or practice: social/cultural, political, economic, geographic, scientific, technological, and historic.

This is evident, for example, when students:
- read historic narratives, biographies, literature, diaries, and letters to learn about the important accomplishments and roles played in individuals and groups throughout world history.
- explain some of the following practices as found in particular civilizations and cultures throughout world history: social customs, child-rearing practices, government, ways of making a living and distributing goods and services, language and literature, education and socialization practices, values and traditions, gender roles, foods, and religious/spiritual beliefs and practices
- develop a map of Europe, the Mediterranean world, India, South and Southeast Asia, and China to show the extent of the spread of Buddhism, Christianity, Hinduism, and Confucianism; explain how the spread of these religions changed the lives of people living in these areas of the world (Adapted from *National Standards for World History*)
- write diary accounts, journal entries, letters, or new accounts from the point of view of a young person living during a particular time period in world history, focusing on an important historic, political, economic, or religious event or accomplishment
- study the historical writings of important figures in world history to learn about their goals, motivations, intentions, influences, and strengths and weaknesses.

FIGURE 4.4   *State of New York Fifth to Eighth Grade Standards, Benchmarks, and Instructional Strategies*

I was trying to get him to see the relationship between the Treaty of
     Versailles and Hitler's rise to power, without actually telling him.
I was thinking about a worksheet that would reinforce the idea.
I decided that it was necessary to review yesterday's lesson.
I was thinking about how I could give her a clearer explanation of the concept.

The largest proportion of teachers' thoughts concerned the effectiveness of their instruction—how pupils were attending to and profiting from the instruction. This last category of teacher thinking is closest to the concept of "reading one's audience," and was expressed through thoughts such as:

I realized that they didn't understand the concept at all.

I thought, "At least everyone is concentrating on the topic."

I figured I'd better call on Larry, just to make sure he was with us on the idea of the lesson.

I asked Mike to explain it because I thought he would know it and could explain it in a way many pupils could understand.

Thus far we have seen that instructing is different from planning but there are links between the two. Instructing takes place in a more complicated setting than planning and it relies very heavily on the teacher's assessments of moment-to-moment classroom events. During instruction, the teacher is concerned mainly with the flow of instruction and pupils' responses to it. Conversely, when planning, a teacher's concern is mainly with the level of pupil readiness, the content to be presented, and appropriate teaching approaches. The following section describes the kinds of evidence teachers rely upon to help them make decisions about the success, problems, and outcomes of their interactive instruction.

✎ Instructional Assessment

Once relevant information about pupils, teacher, and instructional resources are identified, the teacher's task is to synthesize this information into a set of instructional plans. When planning, teachers try to visualize themselves teaching, mentally viewing and rehearsing the learning activities they contemplate using in the classroom. This mental dress rehearsal provides instructional direction for both pupils and teacher.

In a very real sense, any instructional act is a result of a decision by the teacher. However, sometimes it is difficult to see all the decisions teachers make during instruction because many of them occur so quickly and so naturally that they become fleeting, forgotten occurrences in the ebb and flow of classroom events. During instruction, teachers collect assessment data to help monitor factors such as

- Interest level of individual pupils and the class as a whole
- Apparent or potential behavior problems
- Appropriateness of the instructional technique or activity being used
- Most appropriate pupil to call on next
- Appropriateness of the answer a pupil provides
- Pace of instruction
- Amount of time being spent on the lesson and its activities
- Usefulness and consequences of pupils' questions
- Smoothness of transitions from one concept to another and from one activity to another

- Usefulness of examples used to explain concepts
- Degree of comprehension demonstrated by individual pupils and the class as a whole
- Desirability of starting or ending a particular activity

Information gathered about these factors leads to decisions about other activities. For example, depending upon the appropriateness of the answer one pupil gives, the teacher may try to (1) draw out a better answer from the pupil, (2) seek another pupil to provide a more complete answer, or (3) ask the next logical question in the content sequence. Decisions about the progress of a particular instructional technique may lead to a variety of decisions about halting, changing, or continuing the technique. A teacher who notices active or potential behavior problems in the class must make additional decisions about whether and how to handle the problems. In short, the need to respond to a variety of immediate classroom situations allows teachers little time to reflect on what they are doing or the motives for their actions. However, in spite of these instructional realities, most teachers are quite confident that they have a good sense of their teaching effectiveness, suggesting that they are paying attention to the cues in their environment.

Assessing Abnormal and Normal Behavior

Over time, through observations and experience, teachers establish **levels of tolerance** that indicate what is normal pupil or class behavior. These tolerance levels vary from class to class and teacher to teacher. For example, in some classrooms, "normal" tolerance of noise during seatwork is very low; pupils are not permitted to interact, converse, or speak out. In other classrooms, "normal" tolerance permits more noise, pupil movement around the room, and conversation. Tolerance levels are also established for individual pupils. When we hear a teacher say things like, "Tarig acted out much more than usual today. He must be upset about something"; "Anush is mad at her parents again because she had that sulky expression and didn't say a word in class"; or "Eugenio turned in a sloppy, unfinished homework assignment today. Something's wrong," we are witnessing teacher decision making based upon pupil behaviors that are "out of tolerance" based upon normal pupil behavior.

Part of the process of "reading" the class during instruction involves knowing when the class or some pupils are exhibiting "out-of-tolerance" behaviors that call for a response from the teacher. Thus, a large proportion of teachers' decisions during instruction result from monitoring signals and signs that tell the teacher whether the pupils' behavior is in or out of tolerance.

But teachers' decisions during instruction are not based solely on perceptions of unusual pupil behavior. Many relate to normal classroom routines. For example, many teacher decisions are the result of a pupil's question ("If Pedro doesn't understand I'd better review this topic for the whole class") or the teacher's need to choose a pupil to respond during instruction ("Lilli hasn't raised her hand to answer for three days; I'll call on her").

Likewise, when there is a transition point in the lesson from one activity to another, when the teacher anticipates a problem teaching a concept, when there is insufficient time to complete planned activities, or when there is a shortage of materials, the teacher must make a decision about the course and nature of subsequent instruction.

Teachers are bombarded by stimuli that tell them about the progress and success of their teaching. During instruction they monitor, assess, dismiss, or act upon these stimuli. Given the pace and complexity of classroom instructional activities and the need to keep instruction flowing smoothly, it is no surprise that teachers rely heavily on informal assessments like student attention, responsiveness, questions, or facial expressions to monitor instruction. Of course, this does not mean that formal evidence has no place in assessment during instruction, but formal assessment procedures usually break the flow of the lesson and thus are not extensively used while teachers and pupils are interacting during instruction.

What types of indicators do teachers use to monitor and determine the success of their instruction? Teachers indicated how they knew when their instruction was successful. Their responses were enlightening with regard to the cues teachers respond to during instruction.

It is easy to tell when things are not running as planned. Children get impatient, facial expressions become contorted, their body language, voice level, and eyes tell the story of their reaction to instruction. By asking the children questions and listening to the responses you can tell whether or not they are actually comprehending the lesson.

If my class is day dreaming, looking blankly out the window and unresponsive that tells me something. At times like these I have to decide what to do, since I don't want the pupils to think that by acting disinterested they always can make me change my plans.

I look for blank or wandering stares. I jump around the room during instruction, moving up and down rows. If their eyes follow me, there's a good chance they're taking an interest in what I'm saying. I also listen for additional noise in the classroom like sighs or shuffling papers and feet.

Some examples of a good lesson are when the pupils are eager to be called on, raise their hands, give enthusiastic answers, look straight at me, scream out answers, show excitement in their eyes. During a bad lesson, the kids have their heads on the desk, look around the room, play with little objects at their desks, talk to their neighbor, or go to the bathroom in droves.

The Need for Practical Knowledge

Caught up in the special demands of instruction, teachers rarely can deal with broad issues, questions, or decisions. Instead, they deal with specific pupils and situations. A teacher must focus on disciplining Xavier when he misbehaves, not on trying to apply general theories of classroom behavior and management. A teacher must have at her fingertips insights and strategies that will suggest how to explain a difficult concept to Joyce, not a list of general techniques for teaching complex principles. Furthermore, disciplining Xavier or explaining something to Joyce probably call for different techniques than disciplining Anastasia or explaining something to Tabatha. Teachers must know who can be pushed for a correct answer, who responds to reinforcement, who needs encouragement, and who can be relied on to help Martha with her accommodation.

While general theories of behavior or instruction provide some direction for a teacher, they cannot alone identify the reason why Clarise can't understand or Derrick won't listen. Clarise's and Derrick's teachers must pull together their own personal knowledge about these pupils to decide what is the best course of action to take. They must have a store of practical knowledge that fits pupils and the class as a whole in order to enable them to carry out instruction and manage the classroom.

Most of the observations, interpretations, and decisions that occur during instruction are made on the basis of the teacher's practical knowledge of the pupils. **Practical knowledge** comprises those beliefs, insights, perceptions, and habits that enable teachers to do their work in school and in the classroom. Practical knowledge, in contrast to theoretical knowledge, is time-bound and situation-specific. It is relevant to a particular class and to particular individuals in the class. It changes from year to year as the characteristics of pupils and the class change. Each class has its own personality, strengths, weaknesses, and challenges, and every year the teacher must rely upon sizing-up assessments to help build up a new store of practical knowledge about the new class. Consider how the following teacher comments underscore the importance of practical knowledge.

> . . . the teacher's job is to recognize each student's particular needs, even very minor needs. The amount of attention the teacher gives a student or the tone of voice she uses to speak to or reprimand a student must be considered in terms of the student's individual needs and make up. Moreover, the teacher must recognize when a student is troubled, simply by the look on his or her face. The teacher must recognize potential behavior problems before they occur and know how to prevent them.

> The room was alive with enthusiasm and curiosity; twenty of the twenty-one students were watching me demonstrate exchanging air from one underwater cup to another to displace the water. Letty's attention was everywhere but on the experiment, so I asked Letty to come up to the front and try to displace the water with air. Knowing Letty, I knew that this would gain her interest, but not make her uncomfortable. Letty got up and smiled as she hurried to the front of the room to demonstrate to the class. If I had tried that with Peter or James, they would have fallen apart.

> Of course every child is different. Some children will do anything to impress a class. Those kids I ask to speak to later, alone. Another child I may scold in front of his or her peers. There is one child who all I have to do is give a look and that's enough. Teaching and discipline are heavily personality based. What works for one pupil or class may not be the solution for another.

To summarize, the direction, flow, and pace of instruction will be dictated by the "chemistry" of the classroom at any given time. The assessment task of the teacher during instruction is to monitor the progress and success of the lesson. In most classrooms, this monitoring boils down to assessing the appropriateness of the instructional procedures and the pupils' reaction to them. Decisions that teachers make during the instructional process are prompted by (1) unusual pupil behavior that requires a response or action on the teacher's part and (2) typical issues that arise during instruction, such as responding to a pupil's question, deciding who to call on next, and deciding whether to move on to the next topic. The assessment information that teachers gather when they monitor their instruction comes mostly from the pupils. Judging by the comments of teachers, heavy reliance is placed on pupil characteristics such as body language, facial expressions, involvement in the lesson, responses to questions, and questions asked. Cues such as these plus the teacher's practical knowledge support the quick decision making needed during classroom instruction.

⚔ The Quality of Instructional Assessments: Validity and Reliability

Because there is little time for a teacher to reflect on what is observed or to collect additional information during instruction, teachers must make decisions and act on the basis of incomplete and uncertain evidence. Good teachers are quite successful in overcoming these difficulties and carrying out informative instructional assessments. In spite of the success of some teachers, however, it would be naive and inappropriate to overlook validity and reliability problems associated with assessment during instruction.

Problems That Affect Validity

Validity is based on collecting evidence that will help the teacher correctly interpret pupil performance and make appropriate decisions about the pupils and the suitability of the instructional activities. As mentioned previously, during instruction teachers assess these areas by observing pupil attentiveness and monitoring the verbal reactions and responses pupils provide. An important validity question to ask is, Do physical and verbal reactions of pupils provide the information teachers need to make appropriate decisions about the success of instruction? Two potential problems threaten the validity of this assessment evidence: (1) the lack of objectivity by teachers when they observe and judge the instructional process and (2) the incompleteness of the indicators teachers use to make decisions about instruction and learning.

Objectivity of the Teacher/Observer

Being a participant in the instructional process can make it difficult for the teacher to be a dispassionate, detached observer of his or her own instruction. Teachers have a stake in the success of instruction and derive their primary rewards from it; they have a strong personal and professional investment in the instructional process. Every time the teacher makes a favorable judgment about instruction or pupil learning, the teacher is also rewarding him or herself. Because teachers rely heavily on their observations to assess instruction, one can ask whether teachers see only what they want to see—that is, only those things that will give them reinforcement. If so, the evidence they use to assess their instruction is potentially invalid. Teachers who become selective observers may pay too little attention to poorer learners or only call on pupils who will give a correct answer in order to maintain a false sense of instructional effectiveness.

Evidence of invalid assessments of instruction is not hard to find. For example, the types of questions teachers ask can influence their sense of personal effectiveness. Simple, factual questions are likely to produce more correct pupil responses than open-ended, complex ones. Concentration on lower-level, rote skills and information, rather than on higher-level skills and processes, can ensure more pupil participation and mastery. Teacher comments such as "This topic is too hard for my pupils, so I'll skip over it" may be a realistic appraisal of pupil readiness, or may simply be a way for teachers to avoid difficult instructional disappointments. In short, the desire to achieve teaching satisfaction may influence the teacher's observations and produce invalid conclusions about the success of instruction, with harmful consequences for pupils.

Incompleteness of Instructional Indicators

The primary indicators that teachers use to monitor their instruction include pupil reactions such as facial expressions, posture, participation, questions, and attending behavior. Using such indicators, the teacher—like an actor—"reads" the class to judge the success of his or her performance.

The main task of the actor is to engage the audience and to maintain a style and pace that will involve and please the audience. Teachers also strive for involvement and pleasure from their "audience," because these help maintain pupil interest and attention. But the teacher's task requires much more than maintaining the involvement and pleasure of pupils; it also requires that pupils learn from the process. The real criterion for determining teachers' instructional success is *pupil achievement.*

For the most part, however, teachers gauge their instructional success using indicators that focus on the *process* of instruction rather than its learning *products.* Attention is centered upon the immediate activities that are transpiring in the classroom: the flow, pace, and pupils' reactions. Teachers are right to focus attention on these factors during their instruction, but involvement and attention are only intermediate goals that lead to another key goal, pupil learning. Yet, if we reconsider the earlier comments teachers made about the indicators they use to monitor instruction, we see that few mention direct evidence of pupil learning. Rarely did a teacher define successful instruction in terms of pupil accomplishments as a result of instruction. The assumption seems to be that if pupils are engaged in the instructional process—if they have a light in their eyes, are sitting up straight, or yelling out answers—then learning is taking place. This may or may not be the case. Being involved in instruction does not necessarily result in desired learning.

In Chapter 2, logical errors and their effect on assessment validity were introduced. In brief, a logical error occurs when one reads more into a pupil behavior than the behavior warrants, when a conclusion goes beyond the available evidence. When a logical error is made, the validity of the decision made is called into question. Evidence concerning pupil involvement, attention, and participation in instruction may not mean that learning—the targeted characteristic—is taking place. Valid assessment of instruction should include appropriate information about *both* pupil involvement and learning. If it does not, only the intermediate goals of instruction will be assessed, and judgments about the ultimate goal—how well pupils are learning—may be invalid.

Problems That Affect Reliability

Reliability is concerned with stability or consistency of the assessment information that is collected. If the message of some observation or indicator changes each time it is observed, the teacher cannot rely upon the evidence to help in decision making. One of the difficulties in collecting reliable evidence about the instructional process stems from the fast pace of classroom instruction. Observations are made, interpretations produced, and action taken all in a matter of seconds, thus providing the teacher little opportunity to corroborate observations and interpretations. The less the opportunity to observe at length, the less confidence teachers can have in the reliability of the observations they have made. In this regard, an important problem in the reliability of instructional assessment is the difficulty of obtaining an adequate sampling of pupil reactions.

Inadequate Sampling of Pupils

Teachers obtain most of their information regarding the success of instruction by observing their pupils. The broader the group of pupils observed, the more reliable the information will be regarding the class' reaction to instruction.

However, because of seating arrangements and an unconscious preference for certain pupils, teachers often use a narrow sample of pupils when assessing instruction. When pupils are grouped at tables, as they are in many elementary classrooms, teachers often focus more attention and interaction on pupils at certain tables than at others. Or, in order to maximize their feelings of success during instruction, teachers may ignore their poorer learners. By unconsciously grouping low-achieving pupils at certain tables or areas in the classroom, teachers may reinforce this pattern.

In all these situations, a significant portion of the class is ignored or undersampled by teachers who seek to determine the success of instruction. It must be understood, however, that problems of narrow sampling during instruction result as much from the rapidity of classroom events as from the teacher's inattention to particular class members. It is extremely difficult for teachers to see everything that is going on in the classroom because so

TABLE 4.2

Validity and Reliability Problems of Instructional Assessment

Validity Problems

1. Lack of objectivity by the classroom teacher
2. Concentrating instruction on objectives and assessments that will provide the teacher maximum reinforcement but which narrow instruction for pupils
3. Focusing on instructional process indicators (e.g., facial expressions, posture, or participation) without also considering instructional outcome indicators (e.g., pupil learning)

Reliability Problems

1. Fast pace of classroom activities and decision making inhibit the collection of corroborative evidence
2. Focusing on a limited number of pupils to obtain information about the process of instruction and pupil learning

many things happen at once. This makes it difficult for the teacher to interpret what is going on at any particular time.

"The unexpressed, fleeting nature of reflection in action (during instruction) makes it difficult to study and model; the amount of time available to reflect on any particular action event is very small, leading to brief and often shallow reflections and decisions . . ." (Airasian and Gullickson, 1997). Because it is difficult to reflect in depth on classroom events and problems during instruction, it is even more important for teachers to reflect on the meanings of classroom events and problems after instruction. Why did the lesson go astray? Why were the pupils so disinterested? Why is Donaldo being so disruptive? How could I improve this lesson the next time I present it? Questions such as these are difficult to answer during instruction, but they can and should be addressed after instruction. Table 4.2 summarizes validity and reliability problems in instructional assessment.

❈ Improving Assessment During Instruction

In basketball we talk often about a player who has a shooting "touch." Beyond the mechanics of knowing how to shoot a basketball, the player has an intangible ability to put the ball into the basket with unusual success. Likewise, an actor's ability to "read" the audience and react to it goes beyond the technical aspects of acting; it involves a special sensitivity to the audience. Just as the basketball player needs "touch" and the actor must be able to "read" an audience, successful instructional assessment depends upon a teacher's "feel" for the instructional process. This "feel" is dependent in large measure upon the teacher's sizing-up assessments and practical knowledge of the pupils' typical behavior. It permits the teacher to anticipate instructional problems, select the correct instructional procedure from the many options available, and utilize a few valid indicators to determine how instruction is going.

Assessments during instruction depend in some measure on an intangible, unarticulated process. To try to describe the instructional assessment process by spelling out a detailed list of rules and procedures would be to corrupt the natural flow of classroom events and likely destroy the process altogether. Teachers will always have to rely in part upon their "feel" for the classroom situation when gathering assessment information and making decisions during instruction. This fact, however, does not mean that the process cannot be made more valid and reliable, so that decision making is improved and pupil learning enhanced.

To improve assessment during instruction does not mean to make the teacher an automaton blindly following a set of prescribed rules. It is, after all, the "feel" of teachers for their pupils and classroom situations that makes it impossible for machines to replace teachers. However, keeping the following recommendations in mind during instruction should improve the validity and reliability of the assessment process.

1. *Include a broad sample of pupils when assessing instruction.* As discussed earlier, teachers evaluate themselves largely in terms of pupil involvement and attention during instruction. Consequently, they may observe or call on only those higher-achieving pupils whose behaviors or answers are likely to reinforce their perception of instructional success. Likewise they may be tempted to focus on lower-level instructional activities that are more easily attained by their pupils. To avoid these pitfalls, an effort must be made to sample a wide range of pupils in the class.

Do not wait for hands to be raised to determine if pupils are following what is going on. Scan the room when a question is posed, surveying the eyes of the pupils. If they know the answer, they will look you in the eye and raise their hands. If they look away, begin cleaning the tops of their desks, or suddenly develop an interest in reading the text, they probably don't understand the question or don't know the answer. Directing attention only at the few pupils who always know the answer may mean that the teacher loses touch with the class as a whole. Unless the teacher attends to a wide range of pupils, evidence about the progress and success of instruction may be unreliable.

2. *Supplement informal assessment information with more formal information about pupil learning.* In order to get a more complete and reliable picture of instructional success, teachers should supplement their informal observations with more formal types of evidence taken from sources such as homework papers, chapter and lesson review exercises, and worksheets. Each of these are valuable sources of information that can tell the teacher something about how well pupils have mastered the lesson objectives. They should be examined closely to help identify misunderstandings and problem areas. If most pupils' homework fails to demonstrate mastery of the concept of regrouping when subtracting, the next instructional segment could begin by reviewing this concept and talking through the solutions to the homework problems. If the workbook exercise shows that pupils cannot differentiate between a fact and an opinion, succeeding instruction that will clarify the difference should be planned.

3. *Use appropriate questioning techniques and strategies to assess pupil learning.* During instruction, teachers have a limited number of ways to determine if pupils are learning the desired objectives. It is impractical to stop instruction to give a quiz or test every time instructional effectiveness is in doubt. Similarly, most paper-and-pencil procedures like worksheets and homework take time to complete and, consequently, cannot provide the immediate feedback that teachers need. Therefore, to gather information about pupil learning during instruction, teachers rely heavily on oral questions. Oral questions are the major instructional assessment technique for most classroom teachers, with some teachers asking as many as 300 to 400 questions per day (Morgan and Saxton, 1991; Christensen, 1991). Questions facilitate learning by stimulating thinking and inquiry and provide assessment information to teachers.

Except for lecturing, questioning is the most dominant teaching strategy at all levels of education and, together with discussion, comprise the most common form of pupil-teacher interaction. Further, the types of questions teachers ask influence pupils' views of the subject matter and their learning of it. For example, rote, recall types of questions emphasize memorization of facts, while application, analysis, and synthesis questions emphasize higher-level uses of the content.

✎ Questioning: Purposes and Strategies

Purposes of Questioning

During instruction, teachers ask questions for many reasons (Morgan and Saxton, 1991; McMillan 1997; Stein, Grover, and Henningsen, 1996), some of which are identified below.

1. *To promote attention.* Questioning is a way to keep pupils' attention during a lesson, a way to engage them actively in the process of learning.
2. *To promote deeper processing.* Questioning lets pupils verbalize their thoughts and ideas, thereby promoting the thinking and reasoning that lead to deeper processing of information.
3. *To promote learning from peers.* Questioning allows pupils to hear their peers' interpretations and explanations of ideas, processes, and issues. Often, other pupils explain things in ways that are more in tune with the minds of their peers.
4. *To provide reinforcement.* Questioning is used by teachers to reinforce important points and ideas. The questions teachers ask cue pupils regarding what and how they should be learning.

5. *To provide pace and control.* Questions that require brief, correct responses keep pupils engaged in learning and require them to pay continuous attention. Questions that are more general and open-ended slow the pace of instruction so pupils can reflect upon and frame their answers and explanations.

6. *To provide diagnostic information.* Questions provide the teacher with information about pupils and class learning. Teachers' questions can supplement their informal observations of pupil learning in the least disruptive way. Also, for group or cooperative learning activities, questioning of group members after completion of their task is a useful way to assess the success of the group.

Types of Questions

Not all teacher questions are alike. There are higher- and lower-level questions and convergent and divergent questions. **Convergent questions** have a single correct answer: What is the capital of Brazil? Who is credited with the discovery of radium? How many corners does a cube have? **Divergent questions** may have many appropriate answers: What are the benefits of a good education? Describe some differences between the American and French systems of government. What kinds of jobs do people in your neighborhood have? Divergent questions tend to demand more thought than convergent questions, although it should be recognized that both types are important to use during instruction (Wiggins and McTighe, 1998).

Christensen (1991) has developed a typology of questions that shows the breadth of information that can be obtained from varying types of questions.

• Open-ended questions	What is your reaction to this poem?
• Diagnostic questions	What is the nature of the problem in this short story?
• Information questions	What was the last state to be admitted to the United States?
• Challenge questions	What evidence is there to support your conclusion?
• Action questions	How can we go about solving the problem of high school dropouts?
• Sequence questions	Given limited resources, what are the two most important steps to take?
• Prediction questions	What do you think would happen if the government shut down for 3 months?
• Extension questions	What are the implications of your conclusion that grades should be abolished in schools?
• Generalization questions	Based on your study of classroom assessment, how would you sum up the general concept of validity?

Questions also can be categorized by whether they require higher or lower levels of pupil thinking. Lower-level thinking, requiring recall or memorization, resides in the lowest category of Bloom's Taxonomy. All succeeding levels of the taxonomy are considered higher level, because they require pupils to perform processes more complicated than pure memorization, such as understanding conceptual knowledge and applying procedural knowledge.

Lower-level questions generally begin with words such as "who," "when," "what," and "how many." Examples of such questions are: In what years did the American Civil War take place? What is the definition of *taxonomy*? Where is the city of Beijing located? How much is 9 times 8? Such questions focus on factual information that the pupil is expected to remember and produce when questioned. Higher-level thinking often depends upon factual knowledge.

Most teachers want their pupils to apply, analyze, and synthesize the factual knowledge they have attained in order to help them solve new problems. Higher-level questions typically start with words such as "explain," "predict," "relate," "distinguish," "solve," "contrast," "judge," and "produce." Examples of such questions are: Explain in your own words what the main idea of the story was. Predict what will happen to the price of oil if the supply increases but the demand remains the same. Distinguish between statements that are facts and statements that are opinions in the passage we have just read. Give three examples of how the self-fulfilling prophecy might work in a school. Questions such as these pose tasks that require pupils to think and to go beyond factual recall. Note that if the answers to these questions had been specifically taught to pupils during instruction, they would not be higher-level questions, because pupils could answer them from memory, rather than having to construct an answer for themselves.

The questions teachers ask should match the learning objectives they set for their pupils. Although most teachers want their pupils to attain both lower- and higher-level outcomes from instruction, they tend to focus instruction and classroom questions on lower-level questions. Only about 10 to 20 percent of teachers' classroom questions are higher-level ones. Pupils are not frequently asked to explain ideas in their own words, apply knowledge in unfamiliar situations, analyze components of an idea or story, synthesize different pieces of information into a general statement or conclusion, or judge the pros and cons of particular courses of action. This emphasis on lower-level questions also can be found in some teacher's edition textbooks and assessments of statewide standards.

Four factors explain this emphasis on lower-level questions. First, memory-focused questions are utilized heavily in the lesson plans found in the teacher's editions of most textbooks. Reliance on the textbook often results in instruction that overemphasizes lower-level cognitive questions. Second, lower-level questions are the easiest for pupils to answer, because they usually have already been taught. Focusing questions at lower levels gives pupils the best chance to reply correctly, and thus promotes a feeling of instructional success among teachers. Third, teachers themselves are most likely to know the answers to lower-level questions, so they feel more confident in asking such questions. Finally, lower-level questions are much easier to create than higher-level questions. While Bloom's Taxonomy provides a useful model, it is less important to ask questions at specific taxonomic levels than it is to focus generally on asking a range of questions that stimulate both memory and reflection. Box 4.1 provides examples of each level of questioning in Bloom's Taxonomy for a unit on the solar system.

Box 4.1   Sample Questions for Each Level of Bloom's Taxonomy

UNIT: Solar System

Knowledge: What are the names of the nine planets in the solar system?

Comprehension: Explain in your own words the important characteristics of the moon.

Application: How would you determine the distance between the earth and Mars?

Analysis: What are three differences between the sun and the moon?

Synthesis: What is one characteristic that all the planets in the solar system have?

Evaluation: Which planet is most like the earth? Explain why.

Higher-level questions require teachers to have a greater mastery of a subject area than lower-level questions. Teachers must be confident about the "hows" and "whys" of the subject area in order to ask for and judge responses that are less predictable and more complex than responses to recall questions. These obstacles are real and may dissuade many teachers from introducing more high-level questions into their instruction. However, the cost of ignoring such questions is great: a less-rich academic climate and a message to pupils that only rote learning is desired and valued.

Questioning Strategies

The following strategies can be used to increase the effectiveness of oral questioning.

1. *Ask questions that are related to the objectives of instruction.* Teachers' questions communicate what topics are important and in what ways these topics should be learned, so there should be consistency among objectives, instruction, and questioning. This consistency is especially important when higher-level objectives are stressed. It is useful to prepare a few higher-level questions before instruction begins and then incorporate them into the lesson plan.

2. *Avoid global, overly general questions.* Do not ask, "Does everyone understand this?" because many pupils will be too embarrassed to admit they do not and others will think they understand what has been taught when in reality they do not. Ask questions that probe pupils' comprehension of what is being taught. Similarly, avoid questions that can be answered with a simple yes or no unless the pupils are also expected to explain their answers.

3. *Involve the entire class in the questioning process.* Do not call on the same pupils time after time. Occasionally call on nonvolunteers in order to keep everyone attentive. Arranging pupils into a circle or a U and

asking questions in a variety of ways in order to adapt them to pupils' varying ability levels increases pupil participation. Finally, support the response efforts of weak pupils and encourage everyone who tries.

4. *Be aware of patterns in the way questions are distributed among pupils.* Some teachers call on high-achieving pupils more frequently than low achievers, on girls more than boys, or on those in the front rows more than those in the back. Other teachers do the opposite. Be sensitive to such questioning patterns and strive to give all pupils an equal opportunity to respond.

5. *Allow sufficient "wait time" after asking a question.* This permits pupils to think about and frame a response. Pupils need time to process their thoughts, especially when the question is a higher-level one. Remember, silence after a question is good because it means the pupils are thinking. Three to five seconds is a suitable "wait time" that permits most pupils, even the slower ones, to think about an answer to the question. Giving pupils time to think also leads to improved answers.

6. *State questions clearly and directly in order to avoid confusion.* Avoid vague questions or prompts like "What about the story?" or "Talk to me about this experiment." If pupils are to think in desired ways, the teacher must be able to state questions in ways that focus and produce that type of thinking. Clarity focuses thinking and improves the quality of answers. Again, preparing key questions before teaching a lesson is a useful practice.

7. *Probe pupil responses with follow-up questions.* Probes such as "Why?" "Explain how you arrived at that conclusion," and "Can you give me another example?" indicate to pupils that the "whys" or logic behind a response are as important as the response itself and will encourage them to articulate their reasoning.

8. *Remember that instructional questioning is a social process that occurs in a public setting.* Consequently, all pupils should be treated with encouragement and respect. Incorrect, incomplete, or even unreasonable answers should not evoke demeaning, sarcastic, or angry teacher responses. Be honest with pupils; do not lie to or try to bluff them when they pose a question that you cannot answer. Find the answer and report it to pupils the next day.

9. *Allow private questioning time for pupils who are shy or difficult to engage in the questioning process.* If possible, allow private questioning time for these pupils, perhaps during seatwork or study time. Then, as they become more confident in their private responses, gradually work them into public discussions, first with small groups and then with the whole class.

10. *Recognize that good questioning also involves good listening and responding.* In addition to framing good questions, it is important to be both a good listener and responder to pupils' answers to questions. Good listening means hearing the meaning and implications of pupils' responses. Good responding means following up a pupil's answers with comments that will benefit the pupil.

Chapter Summary

- During instruction, teachers must accomplish two tasks simultaneously: They must deliver instruction to pupils and they must constantly assess the progress and success of that instruction.
- Instructional assessments are more spontaneous and informal than planning assessments and focus on indicators such as body language, facial expressions, inattentiveness, and pupil questions.
- Studies of teachers' thoughts during instruction indicate that most attention is given to how learners are attending to and profiting from instruction, followed by teachers' own thoughts about their instructional actions.
- Among the factors teachers monitor and assess during instruction are: pupil interest and behavior, instructional pace, usefulness of examples, most appropriate pupil to call on, and need to begin or end an activity.
- When delivering instruction, there should be an alignment between the objectives and the instruction. Different types of instruction are needed for objectives such as remembering factual knowledge, understanding conceptual knowledge, and applying procedural knowledge.
- Because of its informal, spontaneous nature, assessment during instruction must overcome some validity problems, including lack of objectivity of the classroom teacher regarding the success of instruction and the tendency to judge instructional success by facial expressions and participation, not by actual pupil achievement.
- Reliability problems during instructional assessment center on the difficulty of observing pupils given the fast pace of instruction and the fact that teachers often observe or call on only some pupils in the class, thus limiting their perception of the whole class' interest and understanding.
- Instructional assessments can be improved by observing a broader sample of pupils, supplementing informal assessment information with more formal information, and using appropriate questioning techniques during instruction.
- Questioning is the most useful strategy a teacher can employ to assess the progress of instruction. It gives the teacher information about pupil learning, lets pupils articulate their own thoughts, reinforces important concepts and behaviors, and influences the pace of instruction.
- Good questioning technique includes: asking both higher- and lower-level questions, keeping questions related to the objectives of instruction, involving the whole class in the process, allowing sufficient "wait time" for pupils to think about their responses, probing responses with follow-up questions, and never demeaning or embarrassing a pupil for a wrong or unreasonable answer.

Questions for Discussion

1. How might the fact that a teacher is the planner and deliverer of instruction and the assessor of its success negatively influence the ways the teacher plans and delivers instruction?
2. In what situations should a teacher change instruction in response to pupil interest and attentiveness, and in what situation should a teacher not change instruction?
3. Under what circumstances would you call on a shy pupil who never raises a hand for oral questions?

Reflection Exercises

1. In what ways might the lesson plans of an experienced teacher differ from those of an inexperienced teacher?
2. Can the alignment between objectives and instruction be too strict? What are the consequences of this?
3. What is "practical knowledge" and how do teachers acquire it?

Activities

1. Select a unit or chapter in a textbook. Use the content of your unit or chapter to write an objective for each of Bloom's six cognitive processes based on your topic. See Box 4.1 for an example.
2. Interview a teacher about how he or she knows when a lesson is going well or poorly. Ask the teacher to recall a recent lesson and ask what his or her main thoughts were during the lesson.

Review Questions

1. What strategies of oral questioning can a teacher use to make assessment during instruction more valid and reliable?
2. How is assessment different for planning instruction and delivering instruction?
3. How do decisions about objectives influence decisions about instruction and assessment?
4. What are the main kinds of evidence teachers collect to assess instruction and what are the problems with this kind of evidence?
5. What are the purposes of oral questioning?
6. What does it mean for objectives to be aligned with instruction?
7. What are the validity and reliability issues in delivering instruction?
8. What are some instructional approaches that align to objectives based on remembering factual knowledge, understanding conceptual knowledge, and applying procedural knowledge?

References

Airasian, P. W., & Gullickson, A. R. (1997). *Teacher self-evaluation tool kit.* Thousand Oaks, CA: Corwin Press, Inc.

Arends, R. I. (1997). *Classroom instruction and management.* New York: McGraw-Hill.

Borich, G. (1996). *Effective teaching methods.* Englewood Cliffs, NJ: Merrill.

Bullough, R. V., Knowles, J. G., & Crow, N. A. (1992). *Emerging as a teacher.* New York: Routledge.

Christensen, C. R. (1991) The discussion teacher in action: Questioning, listening, and response. In C. R. Christensen, D. A. Garvin and A. Sweet, *Education for Judgment.* Boston: Harvard Business School Press.

Doyle, W. (1986). Classroom organization and management. In M. C. Wittrock, *Handbook of research on teaching* (pp. 392–431). New York: Macmillan.

Gardner, H. (1995). *Frames of mind: The theory of multiple intelligence.* New York: Basic Books.

Hunter, M. (1982). *Mastery teaching,* El Segundo, CA: TIP Publications.

Jackson, P. W. (1990). *Life in classrooms.* New York: Teachers College Press.

McMillan, J. H. (1997). *Classroom assessment.* Boston: Allyn and Bacon.

Morgan, N., & Saxton, J. (1991). *Teaching, questioning, and learning.* New York: Routledge.

Price, K. M. & Nelson, K. L. (1999). Daily planning for today's classroom. Belmont, CA: Wadsworth Publishing.

Slavin, R. E. (1995).*Cooperative learning: Theory, research, and practice.* Needham Heights, MA: Allyn and Bacon.

Stein, M. K., Grover, B. W., & Henningsen, M. (1996). Building student capacity for mathematical thinking and reasoning: An analysis of mathematical tasks used in reform classrooms. *American Educational Research Journals, 33,*(2), 455–488.

Wiggins, G., & McTighe, J. (1998). *Understanding by design.* Alexandria, VA: Association for Supervision and Curriculum Development.

Official Assessment: Developing Tests and Assessments

Chapter Outline

❖ Formative and Summative Assessment
❖ Developing Formal Assessments
❖ Preparing Official Assessments: Four Concerns
❖ Preparing Pupils for Official Assessments

Chapter Objectives

After reading this chapter, the pupil will be able to:

- Contrast official assessment with sizing-up and instructional assessment
- Differentiate formative and summative assessment
- Explain the difference between good teaching and effective teaching
- Describe the decisions needed to develop and plan official assessment
- Identify the pros and cons of using textbook tests
- State activities that help prepare pupils for official assessments

Thus far we have seen that assessment plays an important role in class-rooms and that teachers use assessment to help them

- Get to know pupils early in the school year
- Establish the classroom as a learning community with rules and order
- Select appropriate educational objectives for pupils
- Develop lesson plans
- Select and critique instructional materials and activities
- Monitor the instructional process and pupil learning during instruction

✂ Formative and Summative Assessment

Much of the evidence that supports teachers' decisions comes from informal observations and perceptions. Rarely written down or saved in formal records, they are used to guide teachers' interactions with pupils during both instructional and noninstructional classroom encounters. These observations and perceptions help teachers make moment-to-moment decisions about specific pupil problems, control of the class, what to do next in a lesson, and how pupils are reacting to instruction. Such assessments are used primarily to "form" or alter ongoing classroom processes or activities, and are called **formative assessments.** They provide information when it is still possible to influence or "form" the everyday processes that are at the heart of teaching.

Although critical to teachers' decision making, informal assessments should be supplemented by more formal kinds of evidence. Such formal assessments usually come at the end of a classroom process or activity, when it is difficult to alter or rectify what has already occurred. Called **summative assessments,** they are used mainly to assess the outcomes of instruction and are exemplified by end-of-chapter tests, projects, term papers, and final examinations. Table 5.1 contrasts formative and summative assessments.

Summative assessments represent a third type of classroom assessment called **official assessment.** Official assessment is more formal and systematic than either sizing-up or instructional assessment. It helps teachers to make decisions that the school bureaucracy requires of them: testing, grading, and grouping pupils; recommending whether pupils should be pro-

TABLE 5.1		

Comparison of Formative and Summative Assessments

	Formative	Summative
Purpose	To monitor and guide a process while it is still in progress	To judge the success of a process at its completion
Time of assessment	During the process	At the end of the process
Type of assessment technique	Informal observation, quizzes, homework, pupil questions, and worksheets	Formal tests, projects, and term papers
Use of assessment information	Improve and change a process while it is still going on	Judge the overall success of a process; grade, place, promote

moted or placed in an honors section; and referring pupils to special education services if they have special needs. The most common form of official assessments are unit and chapter achievement tests and report card grades.

Unlike sizing-up and instructional assessments that are based largely on informal assessments, official assessments are usually formal, appearing in report cards, school record folders, and standardized test reports, as well as in reading group or ability level designations. Further, most official assessment decisions are about individual pupils rather than groups or classes. Usually we grade, promote, honor, and place individuals, not groups. Because they have important public consequences for pupils and must often be defended by teachers, official assessments are generally based upon formal, systematically gathered evidence like that generated by tests or other formal assessment procedures. In the classroom, official assessments almost always focus on pupils' cognitive performance, usually how well pupils have learned what has been taught.

Official assessments and their resulting decisions are summative in nature because they usually are administered at the end of a unit of instruction or the end of a grading period. As a consequence, summative assessments occur much less frequently than formative assessments.

Teachers have mixed emotions about official assessments, and especially about tests, as the following comments show.

> I hate giving them. I find the testing situation to be one where tests become public expressions of what I already knew about the kid and what the kid already knew about the subject matter. In other words, I knew who would get A's and who would get F's because I taught the class. I knew who knew it and who didn't, so when kids take a test it is a public transmission to say "yes, you know it or "no, you don't know it."

I need to use tests in algebra for grading my students and having objective information I can show parents when they complain about their child's grade. With so much emphasis on grades, I'm sure my students work mostly for a test grade and not for their enjoyment or understanding of the subject matter.

The pressure to perform is too great for anyone, let alone a seven year old who's still trying to figure out what in the world he needs education for. Because the school system requires it, I test my students once a week in math and vocabulary and about once every two weeks in science, social studies, and religion. The only advantage I see in testing is that it gives the teacher a number on which to base the student's academic progress.

Each test gives me some feedback on what I'm doing right and what I'm not, as well as what the class is learning best. I like to give a large number of tests to get this feedback and because I feel that the larger the number of test grades, the better indication I have of a pupil's learning.

My tests are helpful in that they offer concrete evidence to show parents if the student is deficient in an area. I'll tell a parent that Johnny can't add and they'll sometimes respond "I know he can add when he wants to." Then I show them a classroom test which shows Johnny's deficiency. One drawback to the tests, especially in the early grades, is that a child sometimes will become upset during testing, either because the child is having difficulty with the test or because the child wants to be doing something more enjoyable.

The statewide standards are supposed to focus and guide my instruction and assessment. In some respects they are useful because they specify specifically what pupils are to learn, but it is also true that many of my students are not well prepared enough to begin instruction where the standards decree they should. This causes problems with planning my instruction.

Although teachers differ in their views of official assessments, it is clear that no matter how teachers feel about them, they must use them at least some of the time in their classrooms.

Despite their sometimes lukewarm endorsement by teachers, it is a grave mistake to underestimate the importance of official assessments. Official assessments have important consequences for pupils and should be taken quite seriously by teachers. They provide the teacher with additional information about pupil learning. Moreover, pupils, their parents, and the public at large consider them to be very important and take them very seriously. The grading, placement, promotion, and other decisions that result from official assessments can influence pupils' lives both in and out of school. They are the public record of a pupil's school accomplishments and are often the sole evidence a parent has of how his or her child is doing in school. The following teacher comments illustrate the degree of importance parents and students attach to official assessments.

Every year at open house I can count on at least one parent asking how much test scores count in the final grade and another asking me if I allow children to make up a poor test grade in some way. Test scores are like the currency of the classroom for many of them.

When my students move on to the middle school, parents always ask if low scores and grades mean a lower group placement in middle school.

The kids are forever asking "Do we have to know this," "Is this going to be on the test," and "Will this be a big part of the test?" They define what's valuable and important in terms of what's going to be tested at the end of the chapter.

Grades and test scores are the heart of the permanent record folder that follows pupils from school to school and from teacher to teacher during their academic careers. Furthermore, pupils' performance on national and statewide testing programs often provides the evidence the public uses to judge the general level of performance in schools. While there are problems in using such summative information to judge the success of schools, the fact remains that public, official assessment information does much to shape people's opinions and attitudes about the status of pupils, schools, and education in general. Therefore, although official assessment occurs infrequently in comparison to sizing-up and instructional assessment, its perceived importance necessarily makes it a central part of any classroom's activities. This chapter and succeeding chapters view the four main types of official assessment that classroom teachers use to gather information about pupils' achievement: teacher-made tests, textbook tests, standardized tests, and performance assessments, including portfolios.

However, before addressing formal assessments it is important to examine the difference between good teaching and effective teaching. Good teaching refers to the *process of instruction* (were pupils taught?) while effective teaching refers to the *outcomes of instruction* (did pupils learn?). Good teaching depends on how teachers organize and present their instructional activities in order to engage pupils in the learning process. A good teacher is one who, among other things, provides a review at the start of a new lesson, maintains an appropriate level of lesson difficulty, emphasizes important points during instruction, gives pupils practice doing what they are expected to learn, and maintains an orderly classroom.

Effective teaching goes one step beyond good teaching to focus upon what pupils have actually learned from instruction. An effective teacher is one whose pupils learn what they have been taught. Clearly there is a relationship between good and effective teaching: The better the teaching, the more likely that it will be effective. Teachers who misjudge the level of their pupils' ability, fail to review or point out important concepts to pupils, and permit disciplinary problems to distract from instruction have a poorer chance of producing learning than good teachers.

✵ Developing Formal Assessments

Sizing-up and instructional assessment focus primarily on the instructional process, while formal assessment focuses primarily upon pupil learning at the completion of that process. In short, official assessments seek to obtain evidence about teaching effectiveness. This is another way of saying that official assessment must be matched to the objectives, activities, and instruction provided. It is impossible to assess pupils' school-based achievement if the things that are assessed do not match the things pupils were taught. If teachers implement fair and representative assessment approaches that show what pupils have learned from instruction, they will have gone a long way toward having valid and reliable information on which to base official decisions. Matching objectives with assessments is a teacher's important ethical responsibility.

The overall aim of assessing pupil achievement is *to provide pupils a fair opportunity to demonstrate what they have learned from the instruction provided.* It is not to trick pupils into doing poorly, to entertain them, or to insure that most of them get A grades. It is not to determine how much total knowledge pupils have accumulated as a result of all their learning experiences, both in and out of school. It is simply a means of letting pupils show what they have and have not learned from the things they have been taught in the classroom.

Good official assessments of classroom achievement possess three main characteristics:

- The pupils are assessed on things they were taught.
- The exercises or questions in the assessment provide a representative sample of the objectives and instructional emphases.
- The assessment exercises, questions, directions, and scoring procedures are clear, unambiguous, and appropriate for the pupils.

If these three characteristics are reflected in official assessment procedures, the information gathered will provide a valid and reliable foundation from which the teacher can make decisions about pupil learning.

Preparing Official Assessments: Four Concerns

When teachers have completed instruction on a unit or chapter, they usually administer a formal assessment to determine pupil learning. To develop an assessment, the teacher must ask and answer a number of questions. The teacher must decide:

1. What should be tested?
2. What types of assessments should be used?
3. How long should the assessment take?
4. Should a teacher-made test or a textbook test be used?

Mr. Wysocki's Class

Mr. Wysocki is a seventh grade English teacher who is teaching one of his classes how to write descriptive paragraphs. Based on his sizing-up assessments, the pupils' previous curriculum, the textbook, and other instructional resources available to him, Mr. Wysocki decided that the unit would focus upon the following educational objectives:

- The pupil can explain in his or her own words the three stages of the writing process (e.g., prewriting, writing, and editing). (understanding conceptual knowledge)
- The pupil can select the topic sentence in a given descriptive paragraph. (understanding conceptual knowledge)
- The pupil can write a topic sentence for a given descriptive topic. (applying procedural knowledge)
- The pupil can construct a descriptive paragraph with a topic sentence, descriptive detail, and a concluding statement. (applying procedural knowledge)

The first objective was not included among the objectives covered by Mr. Wysocki's textbook, so he added it to his instructional plans. The last three objectives were included in his textbook chapter on writing descriptive paragraphs. However, also included among the textbook chapter objectives were: "The pupil will correct grammatical errors in a descriptive paragraph" and "The pupil will write down details that are presented in a descriptive paragraph read aloud." Mr. Wysocki had recently completed a unit on identifying written grammatical errors, so he decided to omit this text objective. Also, since he knew that listening skills were a major part of the eighth grade curriculum, he decided to omit the text objective concerned with listening skills. Thus, Mr. Wysocki based his objectives for the unit on his assessment of his pupils' needs, the statewide English standards, the pupils' prior instruction, the textbook objectives, the time available for instruction, and the curriculum emphases pupils were likely to encounter in the next grade. He adapted his plans to fit his particular class, textbook resources, and classroom context.

Once the objectives were identified, Mr. Wysocki developed lesson plans for them. In selecting instructional activities, he considered his pupils' ability levels, prior experiences, and attention spans; suggestions from the textbook; and the additional resources that were available to supplement and reinforce the textbook. With the objectives and the planned activities identified, Mr. Wysocki commenced instruction.

First, he introduced pupils to the three steps in the writing process: (1) prewriting, which involves thinking about one's intended audience, identifying one's purpose, and jotting down ideas; (2) writing; and (3) editing what one has written. Next, he gave pupils topics and had them describe how they would go through the three steps. He had them give reasons why each step was necessary for good writing. He then introduced them to the concept of a paragraph. He had them read descriptive paragraphs and try to find a common structure. He noted that a paragraph is made up of a topic sentence, detail sentences, and a concluding sentence. Then he had the pupils identify the topic sentences in several paragraphs. Later, he gave them topics and had them write their own topic sentences.

Instruction went fairly well, although pupils had a hard time finding the common structure in paragraphs. This meant that Mr. Wysocki had to give additional explanation to the class. Also, even after instruction, his end-of-lesson assessments indicated that many pupils had the mistaken idea that the topic sentence always came first in a paragraph, so he devised a worksheet in which many of the topic sentences were not at the start of the paragraph.

Finally, Mr. Wysocki had pupils write descriptive paragraphs. First he had them all write on the same topics so pupils could compare topic sentences and the amount of detail in each other's paragraphs. He thought this strategy might be useful because pupils could learn from one another's efforts. Homework assignments were returned to pupils with suggestions for improvement and pupils were required to edit and rewrite their paragraphs. Later, pupils were allowed to construct descriptive paragraphs on topics of their choice.

Not all teachers would have taught their pupils in this fashion; different teachers have different pupils, resources, and styles. But Mr. Wysocki did what he judged was best for his particular class. He used instructional procedures that gave pupils practice on the things they were expected to learn, provided feedback on pupil performance during instruction, and revised his plans based upon his observations during instruction. Mr. Wysocki's performance demonstrates the characteristics of a good teacher.

After all these activities, Mr. Wysocki felt that he had a fair sense about how well the class had mastered the four objectives. Although he knew something about the achievement of each pupil, he wasn't sure about anyone's achievement of all four objectives. He felt a formal assessment of his pupils' achievement would provide information about each pupil's mastery of all he had taught. Also, because the various steps in writing a descriptive paragraph had been taught separately, the assessment would provide Mr. Wysocki with an opportunity to see how well his pupils were able to pull things together. Then he would not have to rely upon incomplete, informal perceptions when grading his pupils. However, to develop the assessment, he had to make some decisions about the nature of the test he would administer.

What Should Be Tested?

The first important decision when preparing to assess pupil achievement is to identify the information and skills that will be tested. A good achievement test is one that provides pupils a fair chance to show what they have learned from instruction. Therefore, in deciding what to test, it is necessary to focus attention upon both the intended objectives and the actual instruction that was provided. Objectives represent what the teacher planned to teach, but this may not be the same as what was actually taught. Usually the two are very similar, but sometimes the realities of the classroom make it necessary to add or omit an objective once teaching begins. In the final analysis, the things that were actually taught are most important in deciding what to test.

Thus, Mr. Wysocki knew that he had to gather information about how well pupils could explain in their own words the three stages of the writing process, select the topic sentence in a paragraph, write a suitable topic sentence themselves, and compose a descriptive paragraph with a topic sentence, detail sentences, and a summarizing statement. But what about other important skills such as taking notes or knowing the difference between a descriptive paragraph and an expository paragraph? These are useful skills. Shouldn't they also be on Mr. Wysocki's test?

The answer to these questions is no. There will always be more objectives to teach than there is time to teach them. There will always be important topics and skills that have to be omitted from tests because they could not be taught. This is why thoughtfully planning instruction in terms of pupil needs and resources is so important. Including untaught objectives on an achievement test diminishes the test's validity, making it less than a true assessment of what pupils have learned from classroom instruction. Assessing untaught objectives usually means that pupils have to call on their individual out-of-school backgrounds and experiences, an unfair basis on which to determine pupils' learning.

By confining his test questions to what he actually taught, Mr. Wysocki knows that all of his pupils, whatever their abilities, backgrounds, or interest levels, will have had an opportunity to learn the things being tested. He can say to himself, "I decided what the important objectives were for pupils, I provided instruction on those objectives, I gave pupils practice performing the objectives, I gave extra attention to those who seemed to be having difficulty, and I gave a test that asked pupils to do things similar to those I taught. The results of the test should fairly reflect how much the pupils have achieved in this unit."

What Types of Assessments Should Be Used?

Mr. Wysocki also wondered about how he should gather information about his pupils' achievement. Should he give a paper-and-pencil test and, if so, what kinds of test items should he use? Should he observe his pupils performing the targeted skills and rate the quality of their performance? Should he develop a group project?

The key to gathering appropriate information about learning is found in the objectives and the instruction provided. The targeted process and type of knowledge contained in an objective determine the type of assessment approach to use. Each of Mr. Wysocki's objectives contains the process and knowledge that pupils will be taught and assessed on. The processes in Mr. Wysocki's objectives are, respectively: explain, select, write, construct. The areas of knowledge in his objectives are, respectively: three stages of the writing process, topic sentences, and descriptive paragraph. The processes in three of the objectives—"explain," "write," and "construct,"—are most validly assessed using **supply questions** that require pupils to produce (supply) their answer. Open-ended essay or short-answer questions should be used to assess such processes. The remaining process, "select," requires **selection questions** that ask pupils to choose (select) the topic sentence. A multiple-choice question could be used to assess learning of this objective. To summarize, the targeted process and type of knowledge contained in an objective determine the type of assessment approach to use.

Many teachers feel that only essay tests are good. Others use multiple-choice items as much as possible, and still others believe that tests should contain a variety of question types. Talking with teachers about the kinds of questions they use in their tests may yield responses similar to the following:

> I always give the kids essay tests because that's the only way I can see how well they think.

> Multiple choice items are easy and fast to score, so I use them most of the time to test pupils' achievement. Besides, most standardized tests like the SAT are made up of multiple choice questions, so my tests give the pupils practice with this kind of item.

> I make sure that every test I make up has some multiple choice questions, some fill in questions, and at least one essay question. I believe that variety in the kinds of questions keeps students interested and gives all students a chance to show what they know in the way that's best for them.

> I just use the tests that come with the textbook; they seem to have a good mix of question types and they are supposed to be related to the curriculum.

Each of these teachers cites a reason for following a particular classroom assessment approach. The reasons cited are neither wrong nor inappropriate, but they are secondary to the main purpose of achievement testing, which is to permit pupils to show how well they have learned the instruction they were taught. Thus, no single assessment type is applicable all the time, just as no testing formula is always appropriate. What makes a particular assessment type useful or not useful depends on whether it matches the objectives and instruction provided to the pupils. Hence, Mr. Wysocki knew that he needed supply-type questions to assess objectives that involved pupils explaining in their own words, writing a topic sentence, and constructing a descriptive paragraph. He also knew that he needed multiple-choice questions to assess pupils' ability to select topic sentences in paragraphs.

How Long Should the Assessment Take?

The length of a test depends on a number of factors, including the age and attention span of the pupils, the type of test questions used, and the importance of each educational objective.

Age and Attention Span

Because time for testing is limited, choices must be made in deciding the length of a test. Usually, practical matters such as the age of the pupils or the length of a class period are most influential. The stamina and attention span of young pupils is less than that of older ones, so a useful strategy to follow with elementary school pupils is to test them often using short tests that assess only a few skills or behaviors. This strategy is obvious in most kindergarten and first grade classrooms where worksheets and workbooks are used so extensively that assessment and instruction are continual and virtually indistinguishable. Formal tests are practically nonexistent in the lower elementary grades, except, perhaps, for the 10-word spelling test that some teachers may give each Friday. Otherwise, the word *test* has little meaning to pupils in the lower elementary grades because testing is not a unique event, but rather an integral part of their instruction. Because of typical attention spans, tests lasting 15 to 30 minutes, depending upon the grade and group, are recommended for elementary pupils.

Some school subjects such as history, social studies, and English are composed of relatively discrete, self-contained units. In other subjects such as mathematics, foreign language, and science, knowledge must be built up in a hierarchical sequence. Whereas topics in history may stand on their own, topics in mathematics usually cannot be understood unless prior math topics are mastered. Consequently, when teaching in a hierarchical subject area it is useful to test frequently, to keep pupils on task in their studying and to make sure they grasp the early ideas that provide the foundation for subsequent, more complex ideas.

Testing in middle, junior, and high schools is usually restricted by the length of the class period. Most teachers at these levels plan their tests to last almost one complete class period. Mr. Wysocki is a seventh grade teacher in a school where the class periods are 50 minutes long. He wanted a test that would take about 40 minutes for most pupils to complete. A 40-minute test would allow time for distribution and collection of the tests, as well as a few minutes for those pupils who always want "one more minute" before handing in their test.

In the end, each teacher must learn by experience what is the best length and arrangement for assessing a given class. One general rule of thumb is to allow enough testing time for almost every pupil to complete the test.

Type of Test Questions

Another factor influencing the length of a test is the type of questions that are used. It takes longer for pupils to construct their own responses to questions than it does for them to select an answer from multiple-choice options. Essay questions require planning and thinking time before the actual writing, so a test with all essay questions will normally include fewer questions than one with all multiple-choice items. Mr. Wysocki knew that most of the questions on his test would require the pupils to construct their own responses. He also knew that at least one question would require pupils to plan and write a descriptive paragraph.

In deciding how many questions to ask, Mr. Wysocki tried to balance two factors: (1) the instructional time spent on each objective and (2) the importance of each objective. Usually the most important objectives tend to be the more general ones, which call for the integration of several narrower objectives. Thus, even though a great deal of instructional time was spent on writing topic sentences, Mr. Wysocki values this skill less for its own sake than for its contribution to the more general objective of constructing a descriptive paragraph. Therefore, the number of questions dealing with this narrow skill will not be proportional to the instructional time he spent on it. This is especially the case since he knows that writing a descriptive paragraph will be the most time-consuming task on the test.

Given these considerations, one might reasonably ask, "Why not omit questions about writing a topic sentence altogether, since pupils will include topic sentences in their descriptive paragraphs? Why not test only the general objective and omit the more specific ones that are part of it?" There are two main reasons why more specific objectives should not be excluded from classroom achievement tests. First, the broader, inclusive nature of the general objectives usually restricts their coverage on tests. In the 40 or so minutes Mr. Wysocki has to test his pupils, he can reasonably ask them to construct only one or two descriptive paragraphs, and he can do this only if he does not test some of the other objectives he has been teaching. If his test did consist of two essays, his 40 minutes of testing would produce only two examples of topic sentences. This would raise the question about whether these two occurrences provide an adequate sample of each pupil's ability to write topic sentences. In short, Mr. Wysocki would have to be cautious in generalizing about pupil performance on the basis of two examples.

Second, Mr. Wysocki thought that writing topic sentences was an important enough skill to state it as a separate objective. Because he spent considerable time teaching the objective, he should test it separately. When teachers focus their tests solely upon their general, integrative objectives, pupils may answer questions incorrectly because they cannot successfully integrate the separate skills they have learned. Pupils often get no credit on such questions, even though they may have learned all the more specific skills that they were taught.

Thus, it is not necessary to include an equal number of questions for each objective, but all or most objectives should be assessed by some items. On the basis of these factors and the instruction he had provided, Mr. Wysocki felt a test with the following format would be fair to pupils and provide him with a valid and reliable assessment of their learning.

- Have pupils *explain* in their own words the three stages of the writing process (e.g., prewriting, writing, and editing). Use a short-essay question.
- Have pupils *select* the topic sentence in a given descriptive paragraph. Use three multiple-choice items, each consisting of a paragraph and a list of possible topic sentences from which the pupil has to select the correct one.
- Have pupils *write* a topic sentence for a given descriptive topic. Use three short-answer questions that give the pupils a topic area and require them to write a topic sentence for each area.

- Have pupils *construct* a descriptive paragraph using a topic sentence, descriptive detail, and a concluding statement. Use an essay question in which each pupil writes a descriptive paragraph on a topic of his or her choice. The paragraph cannot be on a topic the pupil used previously during instruction and practice.

Should a Teacher-Made Assessment or a Textbook Assessment Be Used?

Textbooks and instructional packages include a variety of resources, and teachers are inevitably confronted by the question of whether to use the textbook test or to construct their own. The very availability of textbook tests is seductive and causes many teachers to think, "After all, the test comes with the textbook, seems to measure what is in the chapter I'm teaching, looks attractive, and is readily available, so why shouldn't I use it?" Mr. Wysocki asked himself the same question.

Note that a decision about using a textbook test or constructing one's own cannot be answered in the abstract. That decision must come *after* the teacher has identified the topics and behaviors that need to be tested. Until then, one cannot judge the usefulness of any test, be it a textbook or teacher-made test. The decisions Mr. Wysocki had already made provided the basis for determining whether a textbook test would be suitable for his purposes.

It would be very convenient and time-saving if Mr. Wysocki could use his textbook test to assess his pupils' achievement. Many teachers do rely heavily upon them. However, because the quality and appropriateness of such tests vary according to the skill of the test constructor, it is important to understand the criteria that should be used to judge whether they provide valid and reliable assessment of pupil achievement. Box 5.1 identifies important points to consider when judging textbook tests. Regardless of whether teachers are constructing their own tests or judging the adequacy of textbook tests, they must consider the same basic validity issue: Do the items on the test match the instruction provided to pupils?

When Mr. Wysocki was planning instruction on his descriptive paragraph unit he omitted two textbook objectives dealing with correcting grammatical errors and writing details from orally read descriptive paragraphs. He also added an objective about the three stages of writing that was not in the textbook. As soon as Mr. Wysocki made the decision to modify the text objectives, it became very important for him to pay particular attention to whether or not the textbook test was a fair and representative measure of *his* classroom instruction.

The more a teacher alters and reshapes the textbook curriculum, the less valid its accompanying tests become. As one teacher put it, "The textbook tests look good and can be time savers, but they often don't test exactly what I've been doing in the classroom. Every time I change what I do from what the text suggests I do, and every time I leave out a lesson or section of

---

Box 5.1   Key Points to Consider in Judging Textbook Tests

1. The decision to use a textbook test must come *after* a teacher identifies the objectives that he or she has taught and now wants to assess.
2. Textbook tests are designed for the typical classroom, but since few classrooms are typical, most teachers deviate somewhat from the text in order to accommodate their pupils' needs.
3. The more classroom instruction deviates from the textbook objectives and lesson plans, the less valid the textbook tests are likely to be.
4. The main consideration in judging the adequacy of a textbook test is the match between its test questions and what pupils were taught in their classes:
   a. Are questions similar to the teacher's objectives and instructional emphases?
   b. Do questions require pupils to perform the behaviors they were taught?
   c. Do questions cover all or most of the important objectives taught?
   d. Is the language level and terminology appropriate for pupils?
   e. Does the number of items for each objective provide a sufficient sample of pupil performance?

---

the text from my instruction, I have to look at the text test carefully to make sure it's fair for my pupils." In the end, Mr. Wysocki decided to construct his own end-of-unit test.

Note that it is possible to combine textbook items and teacher-constructed items into an assessment. Often the textbook test has some appropriate assessment items that can be used in conjunction with the items the teacher has constructed. This approach is commonly used by many teachers. The key issue, however, is the relevance of the assessment items to the instruction provided the pupils.

To summarize, both textbook and teacher-made tests should (1) clearly relate to the objectives of instruction, (2) include enough questions to assess all or most of the objectives, and (3) use assessment methods suited to the backgrounds and prior experiences of the pupils (Joint Advisory Committee, 1993). Tests that meet these criteria will provide a valid indication of pupil learning. Box 5.2 provides a summary of common problems teachers encounter in judging achievement tests.

❖ Preparing Pupils for Official Assessments

Mr. Wysocki's actions point out that fair and valid assessment includes a number of steps: selecting appropriate educational objectives, providing good instruction on them, and determining how pupil learning of the objec-

> **Box 5.2   Common Problems in Developing or Selecting Tests to Assess Pupil Achievement**
>
> 1. Failing to consider objectives and instructional emphases when planning a test
> 2. Failing to assess all of the important objectives and instructional topics
> 3. Failing to select item types that permit pupils to demonstrate the desired behavior
> 4. Adopting a test without reviewing it for its relevance to the instruction provided
> 5. Including topics or objectives not taught to pupils
> 6. Including too few items to assess the consistency of pupil performance
> 7. Using tests to punish pupils for inattentiveness or acting out

tives is best assessed. With these decisions made, Mr. Wysocki could then determine whether a textbook test or a teacher-made test was most appropriate. After these initial decisions, other tasks arise, including preparing pupils for testing, constructing clear and valid test questions, scoring pupils' tests, and assigning grades to pupils based on their test performance.

The remaining sections of this chapter discuss how to prepare pupils for testing. Many of these practices may appear to be common sensical things that all teachers would normally do. However, such is not the case. It is remarkable how often these commonsense practices are ignored or overlooked. Failure to carry out these activities can jeopardize the validity of tests.

Issues of Test Preparation

We use tests and other assessments to help make decisions about pupils' learning in some content area. A pupil's performance on a test or assessment is meant to represent the pupil's mastery of a broader body of knowledge and skills than just the specific examples included on the test or assessment. Remember from Chapter 1 that when Mr. Ferris described Manuela's and Chad's scores of 100 on his long division with remainder test, he said, "Manuela and Chad can do long division with remainder items very well." He did not say, "Manuela and Chad can do the 10 specific long division with remainder items that were on my test." Thus, tests and other assessments gather a sample of a pupil's behavior and use that sample to generalize about how the pupil is likely to perform if confronted with similar tasks or items. For example, the performance of a pupil who scores 90 percent on a test of poetry analysis, chemical equation balancing, or capitalization rules is interpreted as indicating that the pupil has mastered about 90 percent of the general content domain he was taught and tested on. The specific tasks or test items are selected to represent the larger group of similar tasks and items.

Throughout this chapter, two points have been stressed. First, assessment of pupil achievement should provide a fair and representative indication of how well pupils have learned what they were taught. Second, in order to do this, tests must ask pupils to respond to tasks or test items similar to those taught during instruction. Thus, when deciding whether to construct or select a test and when reviewing with pupils prior to the test, it was stressed that, as much as possible, the review and the test should be similar to the things pupils were taught. The important word is *similar*.

Objectives, instruction, and the test *should* all be related to each other. After all, the purpose of an achievement test is to determine how well pupils have learned what they were taught. By definition, an achievement test must be related to instruction, and instruction is, in a real sense, preparation for the test. The important question, however, is: When does the relationship between objectives, instruction, and the test becomes so close that it is inappropriate or unethical?

There is an important ethical difference between teaching to the test and teaching the test itself. Teaching to the test involves teaching pupils the general skills, knowledge, and processes that they need to answer the questions on the test. This is an appropriate and valid practice. It is what good teaching and testing are all about. But teaching the test itself—that is, teaching pupils the answers to specific questions that will appear on the test—is neither appropriate nor ethical. It produces a distorted, invalid picture of pupil achievement. Such a test will give information about how well pupils can remember the specific items they were taught, but it will not tell how well they can do on questions that are similar, but not identical, to the ones they have been taught. Teachers have an educational and ethical responsibility not to corrupt the validity of pupils' achievement test performance by literally teaching them the exact items that will be on the test.

The National Council on Measurement in Education Task Force (Canner et al., 1991) has provided guidelines for what is appropriate and inappropriate test preparation practice. Its basic guideline states that no test preparation practice should raise pupils' test scores without also raising their mastery of the general content being tested (Popham, 1991). The task force guidelines categorize the following test preparation practices as *inappropriate* or *unethical*.

- Focusing instruction only on the task or item formats used on the test
- Using examples during instruction that are identical to test items or tasks
- Giving pupils practice taking actual test items

The task force does indicate that it is appropriate and helpful to teach pupils general test-taking skills that will improve their understanding of testing practices.

The most difficult test preparation practice to classify is teachers' limiting instruction to the text objectives. When working with a predetermined curriculum, it is appropriate for teachers to confine their instruction to the objectives that will be tested, so long as they do not prepare the pupils for the specific test items that will be used to measure these objectives. However, it is improper for teachers to consciously exclude important objectives from their instruction solely because those objectives are not on the test. Instead of linking assessment to the curriculum objectives, such teachers have let the test objectives define their curriculum.

The following sections describe actions that teachers should carry out to prepare their pupils for achievement tests. As you read these sections, bear in mind the preceding list of inappropriate practices. Also bear in mind that concern about test preparation is not confined to paper-and-pencil tests, but also includes other assessment strategies and tasks.

Provide Good Instruction

The single most important thing a teacher can do to prepare pupils for formal classroom achievement tests is to provide them with good instruction. Earlier it was noted that good teaching includes activities such as providing a review at the start of a new lesson, setting an appropriate difficulty level for instruction, emphasizing important points during instruction, giving pupils practice on the objectives they are expected to learn, and maintaining an orderly classroom learning environment. These practices will prepare pupils for testing better than anything else a teacher might do. A primary ethical responsibility of teaching, therefore, is to provide the best instruction possible, without corrupting the achievement test in the ways described above. In the absence of good instruction, all aspects of assessment are greatly diminished.

Review Before Testing

While teaching a unit or chapter, many objectives are introduced, some early and others at the end of instruction. Because the topics pupils most remember are the ones most recently taught, it is good practice to provide pupils a review prior to formal testing. The review can take many forms: a question and answer session, a written or oral summary of main ideas, or administration of a review test. The review serves many purposes: to refresh pupils on objectives taught early in the unit, to provide one last chance to practice important behaviors and skills, and to afford an opportunity to ask questions about things that are unclear. Often, the review exercise itself provokes questions that help pupils grasp partially understood ideas.

The review should cover the main ideas and skills that were taught. Many teachers fail to conduct a review because they feel the review might "tip pupils off" to the kinds of things that will be on the test. This is faulty reasoning. A review is the final instructional act in the chapter or unit. It provides pupils an opportunity to practice skills and clarify misunderstandings about the content. If the review focuses mainly on peripheral topics and behaviors in an attempt to "protect" the areas to be tested, pupils will not be afforded a final practice on the important outcomes. They will not have their questions answered, and, after experiencing a few irrelevant review sessions, will cease taking them seriously.

The purpose of a review, especially a review for a test or assessment, is to prepare pupils for the test. In essence, the review is the teacher's way of saying, "These are examples of the ideas, topics, and skills that I expect you to have learned. Go over this review and see how well you have learned them. Practice one last time before I ask you to demonstrate your learning on the test that counts toward your grade. If you have questions or difficulties, we'll go over them before the test. After that, you're on your own." A classroom achievement test should not trick pupils, make them answer topics they haven't been taught, or create a high-anxiety test situation. It should give pupils a fair chance to show what they have learned. A pertinent review prior to the test will help them do this.

Notice that the review exercises or questions should be similar, but not identical, to the exercises or questions that will make up the final test. If they are the actual test questions, then a valid assessment of pupil learning cannot be obtained, because the test will have been reduced to a short-term memory exercise rather than a measure of long-term mastery of general learning objectives. Most textbooks contain chapters or unit reviews to use prior to testing. Go to your curriculum center or library or to a local school and examine the chapter tests and reviews in a variety of textbooks.

Ensure Familiarity with Question Formats

If a classroom test contains questions that use an unfamiliar format, pupils should be given practice with that format prior to testing. The need for such practice is especially important in the elementary grades where pupils first encounter matching, multiple-choice, true-false, short-answer, and essay questions. Pupils must learn what is expected of them for each type of question, and how to record their answer. One opportune time to familiarize pupils with question formats is during the review exercises prior to the chapter or unit test. Pretest practice with new types of question and response formats can reduce anxiety and permit a more valid assessment of pupil learning. In addition to familiarizing pupils with new types of questions and response formats, there is a general set of test-taking guidelines that can help pupils do their best on tests. These guidelines will not enable pupils to overcome the handicaps of poor teaching and lack of study, but they can help focus pupils during testing. For example, it is helpful for pupils to know that when taking a test they should:

- Read test directions carefully.
- Find out how questions will be scored. Will all questions count equally? Will points be taken off for spelling, grammar, neatness?
- Pace themselves to ensure that they can complete the test.
- Plan and organize essay questions before responding.
- Attempt to answer all questions. On most classroom tests, guessing is not penalized, so pupils should guess when they don't know the answer.

- When using a separate answer sheet, check often to make certain that pupils are marking their responses in the correct place.
- Be in good physical and mental condition at the time of testing by avoiding late-night cram sessions.

Another set of skills, called **testwise skills,** help pupils identify errors on the part of the question writer that provide clues to the correct answer. For example, when responding to multiple-choice questions, the testwise pupil applies the following probabilities:

- If the words "some," "often," or similar vague words are used in one of the options, it is likely to be the correct option.
- The option that is longest or most precisely stated is likely to be the correct one.
- Any choice that has grammatical or spelling errors is not likely to be the correct one.
- Choices that do not attach smoothly to the stem of the question are not likely to be correct.

Teachers should be aware of common test errors so they can guard against them when they construct or select test items. Ensure that pupils who answer test questions correctly do so because they have mastered the content or skill taught so the validity of the test will be strong.

There are many other testwise strategies that pupils use to overcome a lack of content knowledge. More detailed descriptions of these can be found in Chapter 6. With regard to one's own classroom tests, it is best to make pupils aware of such general test-taking skills and then concentrate on writing fair, appropriate test questions that do not contain errors that can be "psyched out." Chapter 6 describes how to write or select test questions that have few of the faults that testwise pupils thrive on.

Scheduling the Test

It has already been recommended that teachers not administer an achievement test immediately after completing instruction on a chapter or unit in order to provide pupils the opportunity to review, study, and reflect on the instruction before being tested. However, there are other considerations about the times when pupils are most likely to show their best performance. For example, if a teacher were to test pupils the day of the school's championship football game, the period after an assembly or lunch, or on the first day after a long school vacation, it is likely that pupils would give a subpar test performance. Likewise, a teacher should not schedule a test on a day that he will be away just so the substitute teacher will have something to keep the pupils busy. The substitute may not be able to answer pupils' questions about either the test or the meaning of particular questions. Furthermore, if it is an elementary classroom, the presence of a stranger in the classroom may make the pupils uncomfortable and unable to do their best.

In the elementary school there is more flexibility in scheduling tests than in the middle or high school, where 50-minute periods and departmentalized instruction mean that pupils must be in certain places at certain times. The algebra teacher who has a class immediately after lunch has no choice but to test his pupils then. While no teacher has complete control over scheduling tests, it is useful to bear in mind that there are some times when pupils are able to perform better on tests than others.

Giving Pupils Information About the Test

Usually the beginning of a chapter or unit review alerts pupils to the fact that a formal assessment for grading purposes should be anticipated. It is a good idea, however, to let them know when the test will be given, what areas will be covered, what types of questions it will contain, how much it counts, and how long it will take. These factors undoubtedly influence your own test preparation. By providing this information, the teacher can help reduce some of the anxiety that inevitably accompanies the announcement of a test. When information is provided, the test becomes an incentive to make pupils study.

The hardest achievement test for pupils to prepare for is the first one they take in a class. Even if a teacher provides detailed information about topics to be covered, types of items, number of questions, and the like, pupils always have some uncertainty about the test. It is not until they take a teacher's first test that they get a sense of how that teacher tests and whether the review given by the teacher can be trusted as a basis for test preparation. Once pupils know the teacher's style, they have a sense of what to expect on subsequent tests and whether the teacher's pretest information is useful.

Of course, unless a teacher has thought about the nature of the test to be given, it is impossible to provide the pretest information pupils need to prepare for the test. The specifics of test content, types of questions, and test length need to be considered well before the test is given. Hastily planned tests too often focus mainly on memorization skills and fail to cover a representative sample of the instruction provided to pupils. Thus, in order to inform pupils about test characteristics, a teacher cannot put off planning the test until the last minute.

Chapter Summary

- Official assessments help teachers make decisions that the school bureaucracy requires of them, such as assigning grades, recommending pupils for promotion, placing pupils in groups, and referring pupils to special education services.
- Unlike formative sizing-up and instructional assessments, official assessments are summative—that is, based on formal, systematically gathering end-of-instruction evidence.

- The main types of official assessment instruments are teacher-made tests, textbook tests, standardized tests, and standards-based assessments.
- Official assessments are taken very seriously by pupils, parents, school administrators, and the public at large because they result in tangible consequences for pupils.
- Good official assessments have three features: (1) pupils are expected to perform what the teacher has stated in the objectives and instruction; (2) the questions provide a representative sample of the things pupils were taught; and (3) the questions, directions, and scoring procedures are clear and appropriate. Incorporating these three features in official assessments will provide valid and reliable information for decision making.
- Because the aim of official assessments is to provide pupils a fair opportunity to show what they have learned from instruction, it is very important that assessments reflect what pupils were taught. This is the most basic requirement for official assessments.
- The methods used to gather information about pupil learning are dependent on the objectives and instruction provided. Methods that permit the pupils to show the behaviors taught are essential for valid assessment. Use multiple-choice, matching, or true-false questions when pupils are taught to "choose" or "select" answers; short-answer or essay questions when pupils are taught to "explain," "construct," or "defend" answers; and actual performances when pupils are taught to "demonstrate" or "show."
- Test length is determined by the age and attention span of the pupils and the type of test questions used.
- The decision whether to construct one's own test or use a textbook test depends upon how closely instruction followed the lead of the textbook. The more a teacher supplements or omits from the textbook, the less likely the textbook test will be a valid indication of pupils' learning.
- Preparing pupils for official assessments requires careful teacher thought and planning. First and foremost, teachers should provide the best instruction possible prior to assessment. Good instruction should be followed up by a review that gives pupils a chance to ask questions and practice important behaviors and skills that will be tested. Use of textbook review tests is one way to prepare pupils. Pupils, especially those in early elementary grades should be given practice with item formats that they are not familiar with before testing. Pupils should be informed in advance of the time, nature, coverage, and format of the test.
- The test should be scheduled, when possible, at a time that will permit pupils to show their best work.
- In preparing pupils for testing, the teacher should *not* focus instruction only on item formats used on the test, use classroom examples taken directly from the test, or give pupils practice taking the actual test. These practices corrupt the validity of the test results. Instruction should be focused on the general skills and knowledge teachers want pupils to learn in a subject area, not on the specific questions that will be asked about those areas on the test.

Questions for Discussion

1. What are some things that a teacher can do to help prepare students for classroom testing? What are some dangers of test preparation that should be avoided?
2. If higher-level thinking requires pupils to work with material and concepts they have not been taught specifically, what are some ways to prepare pupils to take tests that include higher-level items?
3. What are some of the differences between a good teacher and an effective teacher? How could you tell whether you were seeing good, effective, or both good and effective teaching?
4. How do official assessments differ from sizing-up and instructional assessments?
5. What are the criteria for judging the goodness of a classroom achievement test? Aside from what is on the test, what other information would you need to judge a test's validity and reliability?

Reflection Exercise

In planning, delivering and assessing, Mr. Wysocki tried to attend to the needs of all of his pupils. All models of lesson planning recommend that teachers take into account the needs of their pupils when planning and delivering instruction. As a pupil, how could you tell whether a teacher had planned and delivered a lesson that took your needs into account? What factors limit a teacher's ability to take into account the needs of all pupils? When faced with these limitations, what should a teacher do?

Activity

Select a chapter from a teacher's edition of a textbook. Read the chapter and examine the aids and resources provided for planning, delivering, and assessing instruction. Compare the objectives of the chapter to the suggestions for instruction provided by the textbook author. Will the suggested instructional experiences help pupils attain the objectives? Is there a match between objectives and instructional experiences? Examine the end-of-chapter test. Is it a good test in terms of the chapter's objectives and the instructional suggestions? Do the types of test items used match the objectives? What is the proportion of higher- and lower-level items in the test? Are there opportunities for pupils to remember factual, understand conceptual, and apply procedural knowledge?

Review Questions

1. What is the fundamental purpose of assessing pupils' achievement? What decisions must a teacher make when preparing to assess pupil achievement?

2. How should the validity of an achievement test be determined?
3. List some ethical and unethical ways to prepare pupils for achievement testing? Why are the unethical ways you identified unethical?
4. What factors should be considered in determining whether to use a textbook test or construct your own?
5. In what way are the methods used to gather information about pupil learning dependent on the teacher's objectives and the instruction provided?
6. What are the characteristics of a good official assessment?

References

Canner, J., et al. (1991). *Regaining trust: Enhancing the credibility of school testing programs. A report from The National Council on Measurement in Education Task Force.* National Council on Measurement in Education. Mimeo.

Joint Advisory Committee (1993). Principles for fair student assessment practices for education in Canada. Edmonton, Alberta: University of Alberta.

Popham, J. W. (1991). Appropriateness of teachers' test preparation practices. *Educational Measurement: Issues and Practice, 10,*(4), 12–15.

Paper-and-Pencil Test Questions

Chapter Outline

❖ Types of Test Items: Selection and Supply

❖ Higher-Level Test Questions

❖ General Guidelines for Writing and Critiquing Test Items

❖ Aligning Instruction with Paper-and-Pencil Assessments

Chapter Objectives

After reading this chapter, the pupil will be able to:

- Define basic item-writing terms: selection items, supply items, item stem, specific determiner, etc.
- Distinguish between higher-level and lower-level test items
- Write correctly stated supply and selection items
- Identify and correct flaws in supply and selection items
- Link varied types of instruction (e.g., remembering, understanding, and applying) to appropriate types of assessment

At most grade levels, paper-and-pencil tests are the most commonly used procedure for gathering formal evidence about pupil learning. These tests may be constructed by teachers, textbook publishers, statewide test constructors, or standardized test publishers. We have seen that a good assessment plan takes many things into consideration: identifying important instructional objectives, selecting question formats that match these objectives, deciding whether to construct one's own test or use one from the textbook, providing good instruction, and providing a review and information about the test. The success of these important preparatory steps can be undone, however, if the actual test questions are poorly constructed, unclear, or subjectively scored. Such problems do not give pupils a fair chance to show what they have learned and, consequently, do not provide a valid basis for decision making. No matter whether one is concerned with teacher-made, textbook, statewide, or standardized tests, it is important that teachers be able to differentiate between well-constructed and poorly constructed test questions.

Tests are composed of short communications called questions or **items.** Each question must be brief and must set a clear problem for the pupil to think about. Each question must also be complete in itself and independent of other questions. Further, because pupils will mentally debate the nuances of each word to be sure they are not misinterpreting the intent of the item, it is crucial that questions be stated in clear, precise language. This chapter examines and contrasts different types of paper-and-pencil test questions and provides general guidelines for writing or judging the adequacy of each kind of item. It also illustrates the link between educational objectives and student assessments.

❈ Types of Test Items: Selection and Supply

There are two basic types of paper-and-pencil test items: selection items and supply items. As their names suggest, **selection items** are those in which a pupil selects the correct answer from among a number of options presented, while **supply items** are those in which the pupil supplies or constructs his or her own answer. Within the general category of selection items are multiple-choice, true-false, and matching questions. Supply items consist of short-answer or completion (also called fill-in-the-blank) items and essay items. Each type of paper-and-pencil item is discussed in the following pages.

Selection Items
Multiple Choice

Multiple-choice items consist of a **stem,** which presents the problem or question to the pupil, and a set of **options,** or choices, from which the pupil selects an answer. The multiple-choice format is widely used in achievement tests of all types, primarily to assess learning outcomes at the recall and comprehension levels. However, with suitable introductory material, it can also be used to assess higher-level cognitive processes involving application, analysis, and synthesis. Item 3 below is an example of a multiple-choice item that assesses a higher-level behavior. The main limitations of the multiple-choice format are that it does not allow pupils to construct, organize, and present their own answers, and it is susceptible to guessing.

Notice that the multiple-choice examples in this chapter always identify the options with capital letters. While the choice of capital or lower case letters may not be important in middle and high schools, capital letters are strongly recommended for use in elementary schools. The reason is that many elementary pupils have difficulty differentiating lowercase *b* from lowercase *d*. Using capital letters removes this confusion. The following are examples of multiple-choice items.

1. You use me to cover rips and tears. I am made of cloth. What am I?
   A. perch
   B. scratch
   C. patch
   D. knot
2. The basic purpose of the Marshall Plan was to
   A. provide military defense for Western Europe
   B. develop industry in African nations
   C. help American farmers during the Great Depression
   D. rebuild business and industry in Western Europe
3. Read the following passage.
   (1) For what men say is that, if I am really just and am not also
       thought just, profit there is none, but the pain and the loss on the
   (3) other hand is unmistakable. But if, though unjust, I acquire the
       reputation of justice, a heavenly life is promised to me. Since then
   (5) appearance tyrannizes over truth and is lord of happiness, to
       appearance I must devote myself. I will describe around me a
   (7) picture and shadow of virtue to be the vestibule and exterior of my
       house; behind I will trail the subtle and crafty fox.
   Which one of the following states the major premise of the passage?
   A. For what men say (line 1)
   B. if I am really just (line 1)
   C. profit there is none, but the pain and the loss (line 2)
   D. appearance tyrannizes over truth and is lord of happiness (line 5)
   E. a picture and shadow of virtue to be the vestibule and exterior of
      my house (lines 6–8)

Note that if pupils have not previously encountered this passage, it is a higher-level one. However, if the passage was discussed in class, the item is likely a lower-level one.

True-False

The true-false format requires pupils to classify a statement into one of two response categories: true-false, yes-no, correct-incorrect, or fact-opinion. True-false items are used mainly for assessing recall and comprehension behaviors, although they also can be used to assess higher-level skills (Frisbie, 1992). The main limitations of true-false questions are that they are susceptible to guessing and it is often difficult to find statements that are unqualifiedly true or false. The following are typical true-false items.

1. The first ten amendments to the U. S. Constitution are called the Bill of Rights.   **T.   F.**

2. Read the statement. Circle T if it is true and F if it is false. If the statement is false, rewrite it to make it true by changing only the underlined part of the statement.

    The level of the cognitive taxonomy that describes recall and memory behaviors is called the synthesis level.   **T.   F.**

3. In the equation $E = mc^2$, when the value of m increases the value of E also increases.   **T.   F.**

Matching

Matching items consist of a column of **premises,** a column of **responses,** and directions for matching the two. The matching exercise is similar to, but more efficient than, a set of multiple choice items. Unlike multiple-choice items that have a different set of choices for each item, matching items use the same set of choices for all the premises. A matching exercise is a compact, easy-to-construct, fast way to assess factual material. The main disadvantage of this format is that it is limited to assessing mainly lower-level behaviors. Following is an example of a matching exercise.

On the line to the left of each invention in Column A, write the letter of the person in Column B who invented it. Each name in Column B may be used only once or not at all.

Column A
(1) telephone
(2) cotton gin
(3) assembly line
(4) vaccine for polio

Column B
A. Eli Whitney
B. Henry Ford
C. Jonas Salk
D. Henry McCormick
E. Alexander Graham Bell

Supply Items
Short-Answer and Completion Items
Short-answer and completion items are very similar. Each presents the pupil with a question to answer. The short-answer format presents the problem with a direct question (e.g., What is the name of the first president of the United States?), while the completion format presents the problem as an incomplete sentence (e.g., The name of the first president of the United States is _____.). In each case, the pupil must supply his or her own answer. Typically the pupil is asked to reply with a word, phrase, name, or sentence, rather than with a more extended response. Short-answer and completion items are fairly easy to construct and diminish the likelihood of pupils guessing answers. However, they tend to assess mainly factual knowledge or comprehension. Following are some examples of short-answer and completion items.

1. In what U. S. city is the Empire State Building located? _____
2. Scientists who specialize in the study of plants are called _____.
3. Next to each state write the name of its capital city.
   Alaska _____
   Kentucky _____
   Massachusetts _____
4. In a single sentence, state one way that inflation lowers consumers' purchasing power.

Essay Items
Essay questions give pupils the greatest opportunity to construct their own responses. Pupils have freedom to decide how to approach the question, what ideas to include, how their points will be organized, and what conclusions they will draw. Essay questions are most useful for assessing higher-level cognitive processes. The essay question is the main way teachers assess pupils' ability to organize, express, and defend their ideas. The principal limitations of essay items are that they are time-consuming to answer and score, permit the testing of only a limited amount of pupils' learning, and place a premium on writing ability. Some examples of essay questions follow.

1. Explain in your own words three ways water helps people to live and work.
2. Some people who have studied the painting *Mona Lisa* say the printing is successful because it evokes a calming, serene attitude in its viewer. Others say it is successful because its subject portrays the essence of womanhood. Describe aspects of the painting that you think produce these two reactions. Which do you feel is the more powerful and why? (20 minutes)
3. "In order for revolutionary governments to build and maintain their power, they must control the educational system of their country."

Discuss this statement using your knowledge of the American, French, and Russian Revolutions. Do you agree with the statement as it applies to the revolutionary governments in these three countries? Include specific examples to support your conclusion. Your answer will be judged on the basis of the similarities and differences you identify in the three revolutions and the extent to which your conclusion about the statement is supported by specific examples. You will have 40 minutes to complete your essay.

Table 6.1 provides a comparison of selection and supply questions across a number of characteristics. It shows that both selection and supply

TABLE 6.1

Comparison of Selection and Supply Test Items

	Selection Items	Supply Items
Types of Items	Multiple-choice, true-false, matching, interpretive exercise	Short-answer, essay, completion
Behaviors Assessed	Factual knowledge and comprehension; thinking and reasoning behaviors like application and analysis when using interpretive exercises	Factual knowledge and comprehension; thinking and reasoning behaviors like organizing ideas, defending positions, and integrating points
Major Advantages	1. Items can be answered quickly so a broad sample of instructional topics can be surveyed on a test. 2. Items are easy and objective to score. 3. Test constructor has complete control over the stem and options so the effect of writing ability is controlled.	1. Preparation of items is relatively easy; only a few questions are needed. 2. Affords pupils a chance to construct their own answers; only way to test behaviors such as organizing and expressing information. 3. Lessens change the pupils can guess the correct answer to items.
Major Disadvantages	1. Time-Consuming to construct. 2. Many items must be constructed. 3. Guessing is a problem.	1. Time-consuming to score. 2. Covers small sample of instructional topics. 3. Bluffing is a problem.

questions can be used to assess pupils' higher- and lower-level thinking processes. Supply questions are much more useful than selection questions in assessing pupils' ability to organize thoughts, present logical arguments, defend positions, and integrate ideas. Selection questions, on the other hand, are more useful when assessing application and problem-solving skills. Given these differences, it is not surprising that knowing which kind of items will be on a test can influence the way pupils prepare for the test. In general, supply items encourage global, integrative study, while selection items encourage a more detailed, specific focus.

Table 6.1 also shows that while supply and selection items consume approximately the same amount of total time to construct and score, each format allocates its time differently. Selection items are time-consuming to construct, but can be scored quite quickly. Supply items are less time-consuming to construct, but are much more time-consuming to score.

⚔ Higher-Level Test Questions

There is a growing emphasis on teaching and assessing pupils' higher-level thinking. As the following quotes show, teachers recognize the importance of pupils learning how to understand and apply their knowledge. They know that knowledge takes on added meaning when it can be used in real-life situations.

> Facts are important for pupils to learn in all subjects, but if pupils do not learn how to understand and use the facts to help them solve new problems, they haven't really learned the most important part of instruction.
>
> The kids need to go beyond facts and rote learning. You can't survive in society unless you can understand think, reason, and apply what you know.
>
> It would be so boring to only teach facts. Some recall or memorization is needed of course, but day after day of memorization instruction would be demeaning to my pupils and me. I have to make room in my curriculum for more complex thinking and reasoning skills such as understanding and applying new knowledge.
>
> What is more exciting for a pupil and her teacher than that moment when a pupil's eyes light up with recognition that her or she can solve a new problem? Something that was confusing all of a sudden became clear and a whole new skill is born. That kind of excitement doesn't come very often when instruction is focused on rote, memorization-oriented behaviors.

Essay questions provide an important tool to assess higher-level thinking. Good essay questions require pupils to organize, understand, apply, integrate, and defend ideas. Questions that can be answered using only factual knowledge are better tested by more structured item types such as multiple-choice, true-false, or completion items. The following examples show how essay questions can elicit higher-level thinking from pupils. In all cases it is assumed that the pupils have been taught material similar, though not identical, to that in the items.

1. Explain whether the reasoning in the following statements is correct or incorrect.
   All dogs have tails.
   This animal has a tail.
   Therefore this animal is a dog. (seventh grade English)
2. In what ways were the events leading up to the start of World War I the same as the events leading up to the start of World War II? In what ways were they different? Focus your answer on military, social, and economic factors. (high school history)
3. Describe in your own words how an eclipse of the sun happens. (fifth grade science)
4. Why are some parts of the world covered by forests, some parts by water, some parts by grasses, and some parts by sand? Tell about some of the things that make a place a forest, an ocean, a grassland, or a desert. (fourth grade social studies)

Many people believe that the only way to test higher-level thinking skills is with essay items. That is not the case! Any test question that demands more from a pupil than memory is a higher-level item. Thus, any item that requires the pupil to solve a problem, interpret a chart, explain something in his or her own words, or identify the relationship between two phenomena qualifies as a higher-level thinking item. Similarly, any assessment that requires pupils to demonstrate their ability to carry out an activity (e.g., give an oral talk, construct a mobile, or read an unfamiliar foreign language passage aloud) also qualifies as being higher level.

Interpretive Exercises

The **interpretive exercise** is a common form of multiple-choice item found in many teacher-made, standardized, and statewide assessments that can be used to assess higher-level thinking. An interpretive exercise presents the pupil with a map, a passage from a story, a poem, a chart, a data table, or a cartoon. The pupil is expected to answer questions by interpreting or understanding the presented material. Interpretive exercises can be used to test higher-level behaviors such as recognizing the relevance of information, identifying warranted and unwarranted generalizations, applying principles, recognizing assumptions, interpreting experimental findings, and explaining pictorial materials. Figures 6.1 and 6.2 show examples of interpretive exercises.

In each interpretive exercise pupils are given some introductory material to read or examine. To answer the questions posed, pupils have to interpret, understand, apply, or analyze the information presented. Interpretive exercises contain all the information needed to answer the questions posed. If a pupil answers incorrectly, it is because he or she cannot do the thinking or reasoning required by the question, not because the pupil failed to memorize background information.

1. The cartoon illustrates which of the following characteristics of the party system in the United States?
   Ⓐ Strong party discipline is often lacking.
   B The parties are responsive to the will of the voters.
   C The parties are often more concerned with politics than with the national welfare.
   D Bipartisanship often exists in name only.
2. The situation shown in the cartoon is *least* likely to occur at which of the following times?
   A During the first session of a new Congress
   B During a political party convention
   C During a primary election campaign
   Ⓓ During a presidential election campaign

FIGURE 6.1 *Interpretive Exercise 1*

From *Making the Classroom Test: A Guide for Teachers*, p. 6. Copyright © 1973 by Educational Testing Service (Princeton, N.J.). Used by permission of the publisher. Reprinted by permission of Army Times Publishing Company.

Percentage of population between the ages of 25 and 34 who have completed secondary and higher education, by gender, for large industrialized countries: 1989

Country	Males		Females	
	Secondary Education	Higher Education	Secondary Education	Higher Education
United States	85.7	24.9	87.4	23.5
Japan	89.3	34.2	91.8	11.5
Germany	94.5	13.3	88.2	10.3
United Kingdom	79.7	12.8	73.7	9.5
France	65.6	8.	60.4	7.1
Italy	40.9	6.9	41.2	6.5
Canada	82.1	16.9	84.8	15.2

Source: Data from "The Condition of Education: 1992," Washington, DC: National Center for Education Statistics, U.S. Department of Education, 1992.

Directions: The following statements refer to the data in the table above. Read each statement and mark your answer according to the following key.

Circle: S if the statement is supported by the data in the table.
             R if the statement is refuted by the data in the table.
             N if the statement is neither supported nor refuted by the data.

Ⓢ   R   N   1. Across all seven countries, the percentage of men between the ages of 25 and 34 who have completed higher education is greater than the corresponding percentage of women.

S   R   Ⓝ   2. College admissions policies give preferential treatment to male applicants over female applicants.

S   R   Ⓝ   3. It is more difficult to get into college in Germany than in Japan.

S   Ⓡ   N   4. When males and females are combined, the U.S. has the second-highest secondary school completion percentage for young adults between the ages of 25 and 34.

FIGURE 6.2   *Interpretive Exercise 2 comparing seven countries on levels of education.*

The principle of testing pupils' higher-level skills by providing them with necessary information and then asking questions that require them to use that information in various ways can be applied beyond the realm of interpretive exercises. In a physics test, for example, pupils could be given a list of formulas that might be helpful in solving the problems on the test.

The pupils' task would be to figure out which formulas were needed for each problem. Providing the formulas makes the test a better assessment of higher-level thinking than if the formulas were not provided, since pupils would get questions wrong because of their inability to match formulas to problems, rather than their failure to memorize the formulas. Of course, if one of the teacher's objectives was to have the pupils memorize formulas, providing the formulas along with the test would not be a useful strategy. Compare what might be tested in these two versions of the same question:

Version 1

In one or two sentences, describe what Henry Wadsworth Longfellow is telling the reader in the first two verses of his poem "A Psalm of Life," which we read in class but did not discuss.

Version 2

In one or two sentences describe what Henry Wadsworth Longfellow is telling the reader in these verses of his poem "A Psalm of Life."

Tell me not, in mournful numbers,
    Life is but an empty dream!
For the soul is dead that slumbers,
    And things are not what they seem.

Life is real! Life is earnest!
    And the grave is not its goal;
Dust thou art, to dust returnest,
    Was not spoken of the soul.

Because the first version relies entirely upon the pupil's memory of Longfellow's poem, if a pupil does poorly, the teacher does not know whether the pupil failed to remember the poem, or remembered the poem but could not interpret what Longfellow was trying to say. In the second version, where memory is made irrelevant by providing the needed verses, a pupil's inability to interpret the poem's message is the most plausible explanation for doing poorly. Removing the need to memorize pertinent information in order to answer a higher-level question permits a purer assessment of the higher-level behavior of interest. However, this approach is useful only when memorization is not a focus of the test. If a teacher wants pupils to memorize poems, formulas, rules, and the like, it makes no sense to provide them on the test.

The main disadvantages of interpretive exercises are (1) the difficulty of constructing them and (2) the heavy reliance they often place on reading ability. Pupils who read quickly and with good comprehension have an obvious advantage over pupils who do not. This advantage is particularly evident when the test involves reading and interpreting many passages in a limited amount of time.

Most teachers do not construct their own interpretive exercises, preferring to use exercises supplied by textbook publishers or other sources. Regardless of whether one is constructing or selecting an interpretive exercise, the exercise should meet five general guidelines before it is used to assess pupil achievement.

1.   *Relevance* The exercise should be related to the instruction provided pupils. If it is not, it should not be used.
2.   *Similarity* The material presented in the exercise should be new to the pupils, but similar to material presented during instruction.
3.   *Brevity* There should be sufficient information for pupils to answer the questions, but the exercises should not become tests of reading speed and accuracy.
4.   *Answers not provided* The correct answers should not be found directly in the material presented. Interpretation, application, analysis, and comprehension should be needed to determine correct answers.
5.   *Multiple questions* Each interpretive exercise should include more than one question to make most efficient use of time.

Like the essay question, the interpretive exercise is a useful way to assess higher-level thinking. However, unlike the essay question, interpretive exercises cannot show how pupils organize their ideas when solving a problem or how well they can produce their own answers to questions. Table 6.2 summarizes the pros and cons of the different types of paper-and-pencil test items.

✖ General Guidelines for Writing and Critiquing Test Items

Whether writing your own test items or selecting those prepared by others, there are three guidelines that are important in ensuring good tests: (1) cover important objectives; (2) write clearly and simply; and (3) review items before testing. Following these guidelines will help avoid the most common weaknesses in achievement test items and thereby permit a fair assessment of pupil learning. This section discusses and illustrates these guidelines.

Cover Important Content and Behaviors

Tests should reflect both the lower- and higher-level objectives emphasized in instruction. One caution to keep in mind when preparing tests is not to focus exclusively on lower-level knowledge and skills. Studies examining the nature of the test items that classroom teachers use have found that the vast majority assess remembering factual knowledge, a lower-level behavior. (Marso and Pigge, 1989, 1991). From elementary school to the university, items that stress remembering are used much more extensively than items that assess higher-level thinking and applying. With the possible exception of math and science tests, 95 to 100 percent of the items on teacher-made or textbook tests assess remembering factual knowledge (Marso and Pigge, 1991).

The reason for this is that it is much easier to write a short-answer or multiple-choice question that tests factual knowledge than it is to write a question that probes pupils' understanding, application, or other higher-level objectives. Try this yourself. Write both a short-answer and a multiple-choice question that asks pupils to identify the name of the house in which

TABLE 6.2

Advantages and Disadvantages of Types of Test Items

Item Type	Advantages	Disadvantages
Multiple-Choice	1. A large number of items can be given in a short period 2. Higher- and lower-level objectives can be assessed 3. Scoring is usually quick and objective 4. Less influenced by guessing	1. Takes substantial time to construct items 2. Not useful when "showing your work" is required 3. Often hard to find suitable options 4. Reading ability can influence pupil performance
True-False	1. A large number of items can be given in a short time 2. Scoring is usually quick and objective	1. Guessing correct answer is a problem 2. Difficult to find statements that are clearly true or false 3. Items tend to stress recall
Matching	1. An efficient way to obtain a great deal of information 2. Easy to construct 3. Scoring is usually quick and objective	1. Focus is mainly on lower-level outcomes 2. Homogeneous topics are required
Short-Answer	1. Guessing is reduced; pupil must construct an answer 2. Easy to write items 3. A broad range of knowledge can be assessed	1. Scoring can be time-consuming 2. Not useful for complex or extended outcomes
Essay	1. Directly assesses complex higher-level outcomes 2. Takes less time to construct than other item types 3. Assesses integrative, holistic outcomes	1. Difficult and time-consuming to score 2. Provides a deep but small sample of pupils' performance 3. Bluffing and the quality of writing can influence scores
Interpretive Exercise	1. Assesses integrative and interpretive outcomes 2. Assesses higher-level outcomes 3. Scoring is usually quick and objective	1. Heavily dependent on pupils' reading ability 2. Difficult to construct items

the president of the United States lives. You should find this a fairly simple task. Now write a short-answer and a multiple-choice item that assesses pupils' understanding of the main responsibilities of the president. This is a more difficult, thought-provoking task.

Similarly, while it is more important that fourth grade pupils know about the forces that influence climate, many teachers find writing a question that asks students to name a country that has a desert climate easier than writing a question that asks them about the factors that produce a desert climate. Remembering specific factual knowledge is appropriate in some instances (e.g., when testing memorization of multiplication tables, foreign language vocabulary, rules of grammar, etc.). However, in far too many instances the richness of instruction is undermined by the use of test items that trivialize the breadth and depth of the concepts and applications taught.

Each of the following examples shows the objective taught, the test item used to assess it, and an alternative item that would have provided a more suitable (valid) assessment of the objective.

1. *Objective:* Given a description of a literary form, the pupils can classify the form as fable, mystery, folktale, or fantasy.
   Poor item: What kind of stories did Aesop tell? _____
   A. fables
   B. mysteries
   C. folktales
   D. fantasies

   Better item: A story tells about the year 2020 AD and the adventures of a young Martian named Zik, who traveled to other worlds to capture strange creatures for the zoo at Martian City. This story is best classified as a
   A. fable
   B. mystery
   C. folktale
   D. fantasy

2. *Objective:* The pupils can describe similarities and differences in chemical compounds and elements.
   Poor item: Chlorine and bromine are both members of a chemical group called the _____.

   Better item: Chlorine and bromine are both halogens. What similarities do they possess that makes them halogens? What are two differences in their chemical properties?

3. *Objective:* The pupils can explain how life was changed for the Sioux Indians when they moved from the forests to the grasslands.
   Poor item: What animal did the Sioux hunt on the grasslands?

   Better item: What are three changes in the life of the Sioux that happened when they moved from the forests to the grasslands?

Both the pressure of time and a failure to understand the difference between instructionally important assessments and trivial, isolated ones cause many teachers to focus their test questions on memorized details rather than upon more higher-level content. The temptation to settle for trivial items increases as teachers put off the task of preparing a test. It takes less time to reduce a complex concept to a few memory items than it takes to write or find a higher-level item that reflects the complexity of the concept as it was taught. Furthermore, using mostly memory items influences pupils' study habits and the perceptions of what is important in the subject area.

Note that these cautions pertain to teacher-made tests and to textbook tests. The fact that a ready-made test is available with a textbook is no reason for a teacher to assume that the test adequately assesses his or her instruction on the chapter or unit. Each classroom teacher has a responsibility to decide about the suitability of a textbook test for assessing his or her instructional emphases.

Occasionally, teachers and textbooks overcomplicate test items. Consider the following item, which was given to sixth graders to test their mastery of applying the procedure to calculate simple interest.

John borrowed $117.55 from Bob at an interest rate of 9.73% a year.
How much simple interest must John pay Bob at the end of 15 months?

The numbers in this example are difficult and almost ensure that many sixth grade pupils will make computational errors. Unless the teacher was specifically testing computational accuracy, the following example would better assess the pupils' ability to apply the procedure.

John borrowed $150.00 from Bob at an interest rate of 9.00% a year.
How much simple interest must John pay Bob at the end of 1 year?

The latter item assesses pupils' mastery of simple interest without complicating the computation so much that errors are likely to occur.

There are two main reasons for ensuring that the questions in an achievement test reflect the cognitive process and type of knowledge that were emphasized during instruction. First, if there is not a good match between instruction and the test questions, pupils' performance on the test will be a poor indication of their actual learning, thus leading to invalid decisions. Pupils may have learned what was taught, but be unable to show their mastery because of an invalid test. Furthermore, the low grades that usually accompany such invalid tests can diminish pupils' academic aspirations and expectations.

Second, tests that do not align with objectives and instruction have little positive influence in motivating and focusing pupil study. If pupils find little relationship between what they are taught and what they are tested on, they will undervalue instruction. Each of us can remember instances when we prepared well for a test based upon the teacher's instruction and review, only to find that the test contained many questions that focused either on picky, isolated details or on types of problems that were not discussed in class. Recall how you felt and reacted when you tried to prepare for the next test given by that teacher.

The problem of mismatch between tests and instruction can be overcome to a large degree by thinking about testing well in advance of the day the test is to be given. In daily lesson planning and while preparing a unit or chapter review for pupils, one can consider test issues by identifying main points, examining textbook unit or chapter tests, and selecting or writing appropriate test questions. With some preplanning, tests that assess the important aspects of instruction can be prepared.

Writing Paper-and-Pencil Items: Six Rules

If test items do not clearly identify the question to be answered, use ambiguous words or sentence structure, contain inappropriate vocabulary, or contain clues to correct answers, the test will not be a valid indicator of pupil achievement and will not be useful for grading or any other decisions. The most important skill in writing or selecting good test items is the ability to express oneself clearly and succinctly. Test items should be: (1) briefly stated so pupils do not spend a disproportionate amount of time reading, (2) clearly expressed so pupils will know what their task is, and (3) capable of standing alone, since each item should represent a separate assessment.

The following sections contain confusing or inappropriate test items. As you read them, notice not only their particular faults, but also how often those faults are the result of poor or confusing language. The teachers who wrote these items knew what they wanted to assess and were convinced that they had clearly stated that intent. Unfortunately, this was not always the case.

Rule 1: Avoid Wording and Sentence Structure That Is Ambiguous and Confusing

Pupils must understand the test questions. If the wording or sentence structure is confusing and prevents pupils from figuring out what they are being asked, pupils will not have an opportunity to demonstrate their learning. Consider the following test items.

Example 1. All but one of the following is not an element. Which one is not?
   A. carbon
   B. salt
   C. sugar
   D. plastic

Example 2. Maine is not the only state that does not have a border with a neighboring state.   **T.   F.**

In examples 1 and 2, the wording and sentence construction is awkward and confusing. A pupil has to sort through multiple negatives to try to figure out what is being asked. While the content being tested is relatively simple, the way the items are worded creates interpretive difficulties for pupils. It is better, therefore, to phrase questions briefly, directly, and in the positive voice, as shown in these revised versions.

Which one of these is an element?
   A. carbon
   B. salt
   C. sugar
   D. plastic

Maine has a common border with three other states.   **T.   F.**

Other items, such as examples 3 and 4, are more than just confusing, they are virtually incomprehensible.

Example 3. What is the relative length of the shortest distance between Chicago and Detroit and Sacramento? _____

Example 4. The _____ produced by the _____ is used by the green _____ to change _____ and _____ into _____. This process is known as _____.

What would be a reasonable answer for each of these questions? Taken individually, the words in example 3 are not overly difficult, but their sequencing makes their intent unclear. Example 4 is so mutilated by blank spaces that a pupil has to be a mind reader just to figure out what is being asked. Pupils will get items like examples 3 and 4 wrong regardless of how well they have mastered the information and skills they have been taught. It is unfair for teachers who mark pupils wrong on such unclear or ambiguous items to say to complaining pupils, "You should have known what I meant." It is the teacher's responsibility to construct clear test items. The following changes overcome the problems in examples 3 and 4.

Which is closer to Sacramento, Chicago or Detroit?

The process in which green plants use the sun's energy to turn water and
carbon dioxide into food is called _____.

If a pupil answers the revised items incorrectly, it is because the pupil did not know the desired answers, not because the pupil didn't understand the items. Of course, some pupils may still answer incorrectly, and that is acceptable. Remember, the purpose of a test item is not to guarantee correct answers, but to give pupils a fair chance to show how much they know about the things they were taught. To do this, test items must be readily comprehended.

Another factor that prevents pupils from being able to focus quickly and clearly on the question being posed is the use of ambiguous words or phrases. Read examples 5, 6, and 7 and try to identify the problem in each of them that could cause pupils difficulty in deciding how to answer.

Example 5. George Washington was our best president.   **T.   F.**

Example 6. The most important city in the Southeast United States is
   A. Atlanta
   B. Miami
   C. New Orleans
   D. Tuscaloosa

Example 7. Write an essay in which you consider the future of atomic energy.

Each example contains an ambiguous term that might be puzzling to pupils and make their choice of an answer difficult. The true-false example contains the word "best," which is undefined. Did the teacher mean that Washington was the first president? That he established many of the procedures followed by succeeding presidents? That he was both a statesman and a soldier? Until pupils know what the teacher means by the word "best" they will have difficulty responding. Example 6 has the same fault. What does the phrase "most important" mean? Most important in what sense? Each of these cities is important is many ways and each could be justified as being "most important" in some way.

Words like "greatest," "most important," "best," and similar ambiguous terms should be replaced by more specific language. Note the rewritten versions of examples 5 and 6.

George Washington was both commander of the Continental Army and a President.   **T.   F.**

The main transportation center for train and airplane traffic in the Southeast United States is

    A. Atlanta
    B. Miami
    C. New Orleans
    D. Tuscaloosa

In example 7, the teacher wants the pupils to "consider" the future of atomic energy. Does the teacher mean compare and contrast atomic energy to fossil fuel; discuss the relative merits of fission versus fusion as a means to generate energy; or explain the positive and negative consequences of increased use of atomic energy? It is not clear. The item needs to be made more specific for pupils to respond in the way the teacher desires. Thus, the item could be rewritten as:

> Describe two advantages and two disadvantages of increased use of atomic energy in the automobile manufacturing process.

The teachers who wrote examples 1–7 knew precisely what they wanted to ask pupils, but were unable to write items that clearly conveyed their intents. Part of the problem is that the teachers knew too well what they wanted and assumed that the pupils would know their intentions equally well. Rarely is this the case. Teachers must say precisely what they mean, not assume or hope that their pupils will interpret their test items in the ways intended.

Rule 2: Use Appropriate Vocabulary

The difficulty of test questions can be influenced dramatically by the level of their vocabulary. If pupils cannot understand the vocabulary used in test questions, their test scores will reflect their vocabulary deficiencies rather than how much they have learned from instruction. Every teacher should take into account the vocabulary level of his or her pupils when writing or selecting items for achievement tests.

Note the differences in the following three ways of writing a true-false question to assess pupils' understanding of capillary action, a principle which explains how liquids rise in narrow passages.

The postulation of capillary effectuation promotes elucidation of how pliant substances ascend in incommodious veins.   **T.   F.**

The thesis of capillary execution serves to illuminate how fluids are elevated in small tubes.   **T.   F.**

The principle of capillary action helps explain how liquids rise in small passages.   **T.   F.**

Clearly, vocabulary level can affect pupils' ability to understand what is being asked in a test question. Inappropriate vocabulary will decrease test validity. Sentence structure can also influence pupil understanding of test questions. Simple declarative sentences are most appropriate for younger pupils, while longer and more complex sentences can be used for older pupils.

Rule 3: Keep Questions Short but to the Point

Items should quickly focus pupils on the question being asked. Examine these questions.

Example 8. Switzerland
   A. is located in Asia
   B. produces large quantities of gold
   C. has no direct access to the ocean
   D. is a flat arid plain

Example 9. Billy's mother wanted to bake an apple pie for his aunt and uncle who were coming for a visit. Billy had not seen them for many months. When Billy's mother saw that she had no apples in the house, she sent Billy to the store to buy some. Her recipe called for 8 apples to make a pie. If apples at the store cost 30 cents for two, how much money will Billy need to buy eight apples?
   A. $.30
   B. $.90
   C. $1.20
   D. $2.40

In example 8, the item stem is too short and does not clearly set the problem for the pupil. That is, after reading the item stem "Switzerland," pupils still have no idea of the question being asked. Only after reading the stem *and* all the options does the point of the item begin to become clear. In multiple-choice items the stem should set the problem clearly so that the pupil knows what is being asked before going on to the options. The item could be written more directly as:

Which of the following statements about the geography of Switzerland is true?
   A. It is located in Asia.
   B. It is a flat arid plain.
   C. It has no direct access to an ocean.
   D. It has a tropical climate.

The teacher's intent in example 9 is to find out whether pupils can correctly determine the cost of some apples. The item contains a great deal of information that is unrelated to the math question being asked. The information about the aunt and uncle's visit, how long it had been since Billy last saw them, or the lack of apples in the house is distracting, difficult for poor readers, and takes time away from other items. A more direct way to state the item is:

To make an apple pie Billy's mother needed 8 apples. If apples cost 30 cents for two, how much will 8 apples cost?
 A. $.30
 B. $.90
 C. $1.20
 D. $2.40

The failure of test items to focus pupils on their task can be a problem in short-answer and completion items as well as multiple-choice items. Blanks should come at the end of short-answer or completion items so pupils know what kind of a response is required when they reach the blank. Compare these two items and notice how placing the blank at the end of the question helps pupils get a quicker grasp of what the item is about.

_____ and _____ are the names of two rivers that meet in Pittsburgh.

The names of two rivers that meet in Pittsburgh are _____ and _____.

Matching items can also be written to help focus pupils more quickly on the questions being asked. Look over example 10 and suggest a change that would help focus pupils more clearly on the questions they have to answer.

Example 10. Draw a line to match the president in Column A with his accomplishment in Column B. One accomplishment will not be used.

Column A	Column B
G. Washington	Signed the Emancipation Proclamation
T. Jefferson	President during the New Deal
U. Grant	First president of the United States
F. Roosevelt	Head of Northern troops in Civil War
R. Nixon	First president to resign from office
	Main author of the Declaration of Independence

Matching items are similar to multiple-choice items, so the stem of the item should set the question clearly. Most matching items can be improved by placing the column that contains the lengthier descriptions on the left and the column that contains the shorter descriptions on the right. The longer descriptions focus pupils on the question better than the short descriptions. Notice how a minor change like reversing Columns A and B helps the test taker in identifying his or her task.

Draw a line to match the president in Column B with his accomplishment in Column A. One accomplishment will not be used.

Column A	Column B
Signed the Emancipation Proclamation	G. Washington
President during the New Deal	T. Jefferson
First president of the United States	U. Grant
Head of Northern troops in Civil War	F. Roosevelt
First president to resign from office	R. Nixon
Main author of the Declaration of Independence	

Rule 4: Write Items That Have One Correct Answer

With the exception of essay questions, most paper-and-pencil test items are designed to have pupils select or supply one best answer. Selection items ask pupils to choose a single answer from the options provided. Completion and short-answer items are mainly used to assess fairly specific aspects of instruction, so ideally they should be written to elicit a single correct response from pupils. With this goal in mind, read examples 11, 12, 13, and 14. See how many correct answers you can provide for each item.

Example 11. Who was George Washington?

Example 12. Ernest Hemingway wrote _____.

Example 13. _____ was born in France.

Example 14. Where is Dublin located?
- A. in the Northern Hemisphere
- B. near England
- C. in Ireland
- D. south of Scotland

Each of these items has more than one correct answer. George Washington was the first president of the United States, but he also was a member of the Continental Congress, commander of the Continental Army, a Virginian, a surveyor, husband of Martha, a slaveowner, a man with false teeth, and many other things. Faced with such an item, pupils ask themselves, "Which of the many things I know about George Washington should I answer?" Similarly, Ernest Hemingway wrote books, letters, in Spain, sitting down, and with a pencil, as well as specific novels such as *The Old Man and the Sea*. Millions of people were born in France, making millions of potential correct answers. In example 14, all four answers are possible.

The pupil's dilemma, of course, is deciding which of the many possible correct answers the teacher is looking for. The pupil should not have to be a mind reader in order to determine precisely what the teacher wants to know. It is the responsibility of the teacher or the textbook test writer to phrase questions specifically enough so that the pupil does not need a crystal ball to figure out which of many possible answers is being sought.

Examples 11, 12, 13, and 14 can be restated so that pupils know precisely what is being asked of them. Notice how each question asks specifically for a name or a country, thus indicating to pupils the nature of the expected correct answer.

What was the name of the first president of the United States?

In what country was Jean-Jacques Rousseau born?

The name of the author of *The Old Man and the Sea* is _____.

In what country is Dublin located?
- A. England
- B. France
- C. Germany
- D. Ireland
- E. Spain

Items with more than one possible correct answer occur much more often in short-answer and completion formats than in selection formats. Unless short-answer or completion items are stated specifically and narrowly, the teacher can expect many different responses. The dilemma for the teacher then becomes whether to give credit for answers that are technically correct but not the desired ones. Stating the short-answer or completion item narrowly at the start will prevent such dilemmas.

Rule 5: Give Information About the Nature of the Desired Answer

While the failure to properly focus pupils is common to all types of test items, it is most often a concern in essay items. Despite pupils' freedom to structure their own responses, essay questions should still require pupils to demonstrate mastery of key ideas, understandings, or concepts they were taught. An essay question, like any other type of test item, should be constructed to find out how well pupils have learned the things they were taught.

Examples 15, 16, and 17 are typical essay questions written by classroom teachers.

Example 15. Compare and contrast the North and South in the Civil War. Support your views.

Example 16. Describe what happened to art during the Renaissance.

Example 17. Explain why third graders should study science.

In each of these questions, the pupil's task is not clearly defined. When pupils encounter broad essay questions such as these they have little idea of what the teacher is looking for. Lack of clarity may lead to a poor grade because they guessed wrong about the teacher's intent. Often, knowing the teacher's expectations is practically impossible. Essay questions that are hastily drafted the night before testing tend to be general and all-inclusive, with little attention given to the specific information and thought processes the questions should elicit from pupils. This practice is unfair to pupils and produces test results that do not reflect pupils' achievement. It is good practice for teachers to create a scoring guide at the same time they are constructing essay items. A scoring guide will both clarify the teacher's intent and provide guidance to pupils regarding the focus of the essay.

In order to determine whether pupils have learned what was taught, most essay questions must be narrowed to focus pupils on the teacher's areas of interest. Essay questions should have a defined purpose related to assessing some aspect of instruction. Pupils should be informed about the anticipated nature and scope of their answer. While essay questions should provide the pupil freedom to select, organize, state, and defend positions, they should not afford pupils total freedom to write whatever they want. Obviously, to develop a well-focused essay question the teacher must give consideration to the purpose and scope of the question before he or she can actually write the item.

Below, examples 15, 16, and 17 have been rewritten to more precisely reflect the teacher's intent. Notice how the vague and ambiguous directions ("support your views" and "describe") have been made clearer to pupils in the revised questions. Notice also that the pupils still have latitude to construct their own answers, even though the focus of the essay is narrowed. Scoring will be easier for the teacher.

> What forces led to the outbreak of the Civil War? Indicate in your discussion economic conditions, foreign policies, and social conditions in both the North and the South before the War. Which two factors were most influential in the start of the Civil War? Give two reasons to support your choice of each factor. Your answer will be graded on your discussion of the differences between the North and South at the start of the war and the strength of the arguments you advance to support your choice of the two factors most influential in the start of the war. (30 minutes)

> Compare art during the Renaissance to art prior to the Renaissance in terms of the portrayal of the human figure, use of color, and emphasis on religious themes. Your essay will be judged in terms of the distinctions you identify between the two periods and the explanations you provide to account for the differences.

> Give two reasons why a third grade pupil should study science. What are some things that studying science teaches us? Write your answer in at least five complete sentences.

These essay items could have been rewritten in numerous ways, and these revisions point out the need for focus in essay questions. When pupils approach these revised items, they have a clear sense of what is expected of them; they no longer have to guess the teacher's scope, direction, and intent. Note also that it is much more difficult for the pupil to bluff an answer to the revised items than it is to manufacture a response to the initial, broadly stated ones. The revised items call for answers that are specifically related to instruction and, therefore, test what was taught. In order to write such items, however, the teacher must have a clear sense of what he or she is trying to assess.

To summarize, regardless of the particular type of test item used, pupils should be given a clear idea of what their task is. In the case of multiple-choice items this may mean elaborating a stem in order to clarify the options. In matching items it may involve putting the longer options in the left column. In short-answer or completion items it may mean placing the blank at the end of the statement or specifying precisely the nature of the desired answer. In essay questions it may mean elaborating the question to include information about the scope, direction, and scoring criteria for a desired answer. In all cases, the intent is to allow the pupil to respond validly and efficiently to the items.

Rule 6: Do Not Provide Clues to the Correct Answer

The item-writing rules discussed thus far have all been aimed at problems that inhibit pupils from doing their best. However, the opposite problem arises when test items contain clues that help pupils answer questions correctly even though they do not know the content being tested. Many types of clues appear in items: grammatical clues, implausible option clues, and specific determiner clues. Try to identify the clues in examples 18 and 19.

Example 18. A figure that has eight sides is called an
  A. pentagon
  B. quadrilateral
  C. octagon
  D. ogive

Example 19. As compared to autos of the 1960s, autos in the 1980s
  A. traveling slower
  B. bigger interiors
  C. to use less fuel
  D. contain more safety features
  E. was less constructed in foreign countries

These examples contain grammatical clues to the correct answer. In example 18, using the article "an" at the end of the stem indicates to pupils that the next word must begin with a vowel, so the options "pentagon" and "quadrilateral" cannot be correct. There are two main ways to correct this problem: replace the single article with the combined "a(n)" or get rid of the article altogether by writing the question in the plural form.

Figures that have eight sides are called
  A. pentagons
  B. quadrilaterals
  C. octagons
  D. ogives

In example 19, only option D grammatically fits the item stem. Regardless of pupils' knowledge, they can select the correct answer because of the grammatical clue. Now try to find the clues in examples 20 and 21.

Example 20. Which of the following best describes an electron?
  A. negative particle
  B. neutral particle
  C. positive particle
  D. a voting machine

Example 21. Match the correct phrase in Column A with the term in Column B. Write the <u>letter</u> of the term in Column B on the line in front of the correct phrase in Column A.

Column A	Column B
1. type of flower	A. cobra
2. poisonous snake	B. fission
3. how amoeba reproduce	C. green
4. color of chlorophyll	D. hydrogen
5. chemical element	E. rose

Example 20 contains a clue that is less obvious than those in examples 18 and 19, but which is quite common in multiple-choice items. One of the options is inappropriate or implausible and therefore is immediately dismissed by the pupils. Choice D, "a voting machine" will be dismissed as an unlikely answer by all but the most careless readers. As much as possible, options in test questions should be realistic and at least somewhat plausible choices. A useful rule of thumb to follow is to try to have at least three incorrect (but reasonable) options, or **distractors,** in each multiple-choice item. However, it is not necessary that all multiple-choice items have the same number of response options.

The more choices pupils have, the less likely it is that they can guess the correct answer. Knowing this, teachers sometimes write three or four good options for an item and then add on a fourth or fifth option such as "none of the above" or "all of the above." It is usually better to avoid these options, because it is difficult to write items that are "all" or "none."

Example 21 is a very easy item because the topics to be matched are so different from one another that most of the options in Column B are implausible matches to the statements in Column A. For example, "color of chlorophyll" has only two even remotely possible matches in Column B, "green" and "rose." And how many plausible choices are there in Column B for "how amoeba reproduce?" Matching items should test a single homogeneous subject area such as explorers, states, or presidents. Consider the following matching item that tests pupils' knowledge of a single, homogeneous topic. Note the difference in answering this item compared to example 21.

Match the names of the animals in Column A to their correct classification in Column B. Write the <u>letter</u> of the correct classification on the line in front of each animal name. The choices in Column B may be used more than once.

Column A	Column B
1. alligator	A. amphibian
2. condor	B. bird
3. frog	C. fish
4. porpoise	D. mammal
5. snake	E. reptile
6. salamander	

The revised item is a better test of pupils' knowledge in two ways. First, it does not include the obvious matches and mismatches that occur when many unrelated topics are contained in the same item. The revised version focuses on a single topic, classification of animals into groups. Second, unlike example 21, the revised item has an unequal number of entries in columns A and B. Unequal entries in the two columns of a matching item prevent pupils from getting the last match correct by a process of elimination.

Now look for the clues in examples 22 and 23.

Example 22. Some people think the moon is made of green cheese.   **T.   F.**

Example 23. One should never phrase a test item in the negative.   **T.   F.**

These items contain clues called **specific determiners.** In true-false questions, words such as "always," "never," "all," and "none" tend to appear in statements that are false—very few things in our world happen always or never. Conversely, words like "some," "sometimes," and "may" tend to appear in statements that are true—most things in our world happen sometimes. Thus, in example 22, it is reasonable to assume that *some* people think the moon is made of green cheese, so this question should be marked T. On the other hand, example 23 must be marked F if one can think of even a single situation in which a test item can reasonably be stated in the negative (e.g., Which one of these is *not* an example of democracy?).

There are many types of clues that appear in test items. Often, the nature of the clue is related to a particular type of test item. For example, clues in which the stem does not grammatically match all the options provided occur only in multiple-choice or matching items. Specific determiners occur mainly in true-false items. Nonhomogeneous and implausible options occur in multiple-choice and matching items. Matching, multiple-choice, and completion items are susceptible to clues resulting from improper use of the articles "a" and "an." In all cases, clues serve to artificially improve pupils' test performance.

Box 6.1 provides a list of common item-writing rules that pertain to each of the various item types discussed in this chapter. These rules supplement the more general item-writing principles just considered.

Box 6.1   Suggestions for Preparing Test Items

Multiple-Choice Items
- Set pupils' task in the item stem.
- Include repeated words in the stem.
- Avoid grammatical clues.
- Use positive wording if possible.
- Include only plausible options.
- Avoid using "all of the above" or "none of above."

Matching Items
- Use a homogeneous topic.
- Put longer options in left column.
- Provide clear direction.
- Use unequal numbers of entries in the two columns.

Essay Items
- Use several short-essay questions rather than one long one.

- Provide a clear focus in questions.
- Indicate scoring criteria to pupils.

True-False Items
- Make statements clearly true or false.
- Avoid specific determiners.
- Do not arrange responses in a pattern.
- Do not select textbook sentences.

Completion and Short-Answer Items
- Provide a clear focus for the desired answer.
- Avoid grammatical clues.
- Put blanks at the end of the item.
- Do not select textbook sentences.

Review Items Before Testing

Most of the faults in the previous test items were related less to teachers' lack of sophistication in educational assessment than to their failure to express themselves and their intents clearly. Because the purpose of an achievement test is to provide a fair and representative indication of how well pupils have learned the things they were taught, faulty items are undesirable regardless of whether they inhibit or enhance pupils' test performance. Such items do not provide a fair and representative indication of pupil learning, and thus lower the validity of the assessment.

The simplest way to identify and correct most of the faults shown earlier is to review the items before testing. After writing or selecting the items for a chapter or unit test, a teacher should wait one day and reread them. Proofreading will help identify flaws in the items that can be corrected before test administration. It is also desirable to have a colleague, spouse, or friend review the items critically.

✖ Aligning Instruction with Paper-and-Pencil Assessments

Chapter 4 discussed the importance of aligning objectives with instruction. In this chapter the alignment of instruction and assessments is described. Although these two paths of alignment have been presented independently thus far, it is important to understand that alignment encompasses the links among objectives, instruction, and assessment. Logically, the nature of the objectives should be reflected in the instruction. Similarly, the objectives and instruction should be reflected in the assessments. The examples that follow provide a sense—not exhaustive examples—of alignments between instruction and assessments.

Alignment of Instruction and Assessment: Remembering Factual Knowledge

The main characteristic of remembering factual knowledge is memorizing information of various kinds: dates, names, events, and the like. Instructional strategies linked to remembering factual knowledge include direct instruction, drill and practice, mnemonic devices, and repetition strategies, all ways to help pupils memorize information. When the instructional focus is on memorizing, the assessments should focus on pupil memorization of the factual information taught. Thus, assessment should reflect strategies that assess remembered information. The common assessment approaches for remembering factual knowledge include multiple-choice, true-false, matching, completion, and short-answer items. Following are examples of paper-and-pencil assessment items for remembering factual knowledge.

Multiple Choice

The name of the third president of the United States is
   A. George Washington
   B. John Quincy Adams
   C. Thomas Jefferson
   D. James Monroe

True-False

Ernest Hemingway wrote *The Great Gatsby.*   **T.   F.**

Matching

Draw a line from the inventor to the invention.

Inventor	Invention
Eli Whitney	electric light
Alexander Graham Bell	cotton gin
Thomas Edison	steam engine
Robert Fulton	sewing machine
	telephone

Completion

The name of the man who gave the "I Have A Dream" speech is _____.

Short Answer

What is the chemical formula for sulfuric acid?

Answering each of these items requires pupils to remember factual knowledge. A defining characteristic of remembering factual knowledge is that pupils cannot deduce or figure out the answer. Questions stressing this cognitive process can be answered only from memory.

Alignment of Instruction and Assessment: Understanding Conceptual Knowledge

The task of understanding conceptual knowledge focuses on building connections between new and existing knowledge of concepts and categories. Isolated facts (remembering) become integrated into related concepts (understanding). Instructional activities related to understanding conceptual knowledge are shown in Chapter 4 and include: differentiating between examples and nonexamples of concepts, using diagrams and graphic organizers, questioning, and the rule-example-rule technique. Understanding conceptual knowledge requires the student to go beyond rote memorization to demonstrate an understanding of connections and concepts. The kinds of items used to assess pupils' understanding of conceptual knowledge are similar to those used for remembering factual knowledge, with one very important difference. Understanding conceptual knowledge should require pupils to do more than just remember when answering the assessment item.

It is important to note that if a teacher constructs or selects assessments that are identical to what has been taught in class, he or she is actually assessing remembering factual knowledge, not understanding conceptual knowledge. Thus, to construct items that are intended to assess more than remembering factual knowledge, the teacher should select examples that are *similar* but not identical to what was taught. Assuming that the following items were not directly taught by the teacher, determining the correct response requires more than simply remembering the information provided during instruction.

Multiple Choice

Draw a circle around the letter that does NOT belong with the others.

A   B   E   I   O   U

Which of the following does NOT belong with the others?
   A. red
   B. green
   C. pencil
   D. yellow
   E. orange

Which of the following numbers comes next in this sequence? Circle the correct number.

1   2   4   7   11   16   __

   A. 18
   B. 20
   C. 22
   D. 27

Short Answer

What do the following have in common: pencils, pens, crayons, chalk?
Describe in your own words the relationship between the moon and the tides.
Explain the main theme of Robert Frost's poem "Stopping by Woods on a
     Snowy Evening."
Was the essay we read yesterday an example of a persuasive, informative,
     or biographical essay? Explain your answer.
What would be the best title for this editorial?

Completion

Complete this analogy: President is to country as governor is to ____.
Birch, oak, fir, and willow are all kinds of ____.

Interpretive exercises such as those shown in Figures 6.1 and 6.2 are also excellent ways to assess understanding conceptual knowledge.

Alignment of Instruction and Assessment: Applying Procedural Knowledge

Applying procedural knowledge involves performing the steps in tasks or problems. Writing a sonnet, finding places on a map, cursive writing, constructing a test, drawing a pie chart from given data, reading aloud, constructing a lesson plan, driving a car, and solving simultaneous equations for two unknowns all call for applying procedural knowledge. Each task or problem must be completed by carrying out a number of steps. Instructional strategies for applying procedural knowledge include: flow and sequencing charts, mnemonics, demonstrations, repeated practice, and teacher modeling. It is useful to note the difference between conceptual and procedural knowledge: Conceptual knowledge focuses on understanding and explanation, while procedural knowledge focuses on applying and doing. For example, a pupil may *understand* the process of riding a bicycle (conceptual knowledge), but may not be able to actually carry out the *procedure* of riding the bicycle (procedural knowledge).

Assessing procedural knowledge can involve both pupil products and processes. A product assessment involves a *completed* procedure such as a completed lesson plan, simultaneous equation, or sonnet. A process assessment involves assessment of the various *steps* used to complete an activity, such as the steps for finding places on a map, constructing a lesson plan, or constructing a pie chart. In cases of summative assessment, product assessments are commonly used at the end of instruction to score or grade performance. When the teacher seeks formative assessment information during instruction, process assessment is commonly used to provide feedback to pupils in order to help improve their performance. Thus, in assessing procedural knowledge teachers may assess product or process, according to their instructional and assessment needs. A product assessment does not provide information about why a pupil performed as he or she did, but a process assessment can provide such information.

Short-Answer Products

Write a complex, compound sentence.
Find the lowest common denominator of $\frac{42}{82}$.
Recite the alphabet aloud.
Compute the compound interest for a 3-year loan of $4,000 with an interest rate of 8.00%.
(A short answer process would examine the entire process of these short-answer products, identifying correct and incorrect aspects of each.)

More Complex Processes and Products

Given appropriate materials, carry out the dissection of a frog using the steps discussed yesterday.
Demonstrate the use of the optical scanner.

Carry out a chemistry experiment of your choice to illustrate the steps in
the scientific method.

Write a Shakespearean sonnet.

Apply a set of criteria to assess the quality of a pupil's portfolio.

Two issues need attention when assessing pupils on applying procedural knowledge. First, there are 4 different levels of difficulty in applying
procedural knowledge. Consider the 4 ways applying procedural knowledge can be presented to pupils. (1) A pupil may be given a familiar task
and told the specific procedure to carry out: "Apply this procedure to the
problems we practiced yesterday." (2) A pupil may be given an unfamiliar
problem but told the procedure to use: "Apply this procedure to this new
problem." (3) A pupil may be given a task to apply but not given the procedure to use: "Select an appropriate procedure to apply to this familiar problem." A pupil may be given an unknown task and an unknown procedure:
"Select an appropriate procedure to apply to this unfamiliar problem."
These examples present four levels of increasing difficulty. Teachers should
match their assessments to the appropriate level for their pupils' instruction. Typically, instruction and assessment would begin at the first level
and progress to more advance levels as needed.

Second, there are two approaches to scoring and grading applications
of procedural knowledge. One approach is holistic, providing a single score
or grade for the pupil's response (e.g., "Overall, the pupil's performance on
the procedure is worth a B"). The other approach is analytic, providing a
number of scores for particular aspects of the pupil's response (e.g., "This
pupil merits an A in organization, a B in accuracy of content, a C- in use of
references, and an A- in grammar and content"). Note that to use analytic
scoring the teacher must identify the criteria that will be used to assess
pupils *before* the assessment. Pupils should also be informed of the scoring
criteria to guide their answers. In succeeding chapters we will examine holistic and analytic scoring in more detail.

This section has discussed alignment of instruction and assessment of
the three main process and knowledge pairs: remembering factual knowledge, understanding conceptual knowledge, and applying procedural knowledge. In addition to their own wide use, these three process/knowledge pairs
provide the building blocks for other intended pupil outcomes such as analysis, synthesis, and evaluation. For example, analysis involves breaking down
and examining the important component parts of a whole. We analyze
poems, books, plays, science experiments, facts and opinions, art, and
speeches, etc. If we were analyzing a poem we would first seek the important
aspects of the poem, which would involve applying conceptual knowledge.
That is, our task would be identifying the important aspects of the construct
"poem." Having identified the important components of the poem, we would
apply procedural knowledge to carry out the analysis. Synthesis, on the other
hand, is the opposite of analysis in that it begins with the individual parts
and requires connecting them into a unique, coherent whole. Factual and

conceptual knowledge is needed to identify and integrate the individual parts to be synthesized. Once the pieces are related, procedural knowledge is needed to organize and present the synthesis. Note that syntheses are aimed at producing new, unique products.

Evaluation involves making a judgment about the worth or merit of a product or a process. For example, we can evaluate an essay, an oral speech, a science fair project, a piece of art, a political candidate, an editorial, and the like. Two key aspects of conducting evaluations are understanding conceptual knowledge and applying procedural knowledge. The former is needed to identify the criteria that are appropriate to use in the evaluation. Subsequent to developing the criteria for the evaluation, applying procedural knowledge is employed to carry out and make an evaluative judgment.

It is important to point out that although remembering factual knowledge, understanding conceptual knowledge, and applying procedural knowledge are important in carrying out processes such as analyzing, synthesizing, and evaluation, they are not the only factors required. Analyzing, synthesizing, and evaluating call for more than just these three factors; they imply the development of a unique or novel product and have their own unique characteristics.

Chapter Summary

- The central focus of achievement testing is to obtain a fair and representative indication of what pupils have learned from teachers' instruction.
- Paper-and-pencil tests are composed of two types of test questions: selection (multiple-choice, true-false, and matching) and supply (short-answer, completion, and essay). Each general type can test both higher- and lower- level thinking.
- Selection items can be answered quickly, cover a broad sample of instructional topics, and can be scored objectively. However, they are time-consuming to construct and guessing answers is a problem.
- Supply items can be prepared easily, afford pupils the opportunity to construct their own answers, and are rarely subject to guessing. However, they are difficult and time-consuming to score and tend to cover a limited amount of instructional topics.
- Teachers should try to include higher-level questions in their instruction and in their assessments. The interpretive exercise is a useful way to incorporate higher-level skills into paper-and-pencil assessments.
- When writing or selecting paper-and-pencil test questions, three general guidelines should be followed: cover important topics and behaviors, write clearly and simply, and review items before testing.
- Most of the items in teacher-made and textbook tests are at the recall or memory level because such items are easier to write than higher-level questions. However, if tests are to be valid, they should reflect all the

content and processes taught, both lower and higher level. Tests that do not represent instruction can be invalid, provide a poor indication of pupil learning, and provide little influence in motivating pupils to study.

- Six rules guide item writing: (1) Avoid wording and sentence structure that is ambiguous and confusing; (2) use vocabulary appropriate for the pupils tested; (3) keep test items short and to the point; (4) write items that have one correct answer; (5) give pupils information about the characteristics of the desired answer; and (6) avoid providing clues to test answers.
- Paper-and-pencil test items should be aligned to the teacher's objectives and to the instruction provided.
- Objectives and instruction focused on remembering factual knowledge, understanding conceptual knowledge, and applying procedural knowledge will call for different types of test items.
- Most of the problems encountered in writing paper-and-pencil test items can be overcome by planning in advance for the test by thinking about the nature of the assessment needed, writing or selecting potential test questions, informing pupils of the impending test, and providing meaningful review. Also, reviewing questions before finalizing the test will identify most faults.

Questions for Discussion

1. What are some objectives that are best assessed by supply items? What are some objectives that are best assessed by selection items?
2. How are sizing-up assessment, lesson plans, and instruction related to paper-and-pencil tests of pupil learning?
3. What are the pros and cons of giving pupils choices in answering essay items?
4. What harm could result if a teacher's tests produced invalid information about pupil learning?
5. Are higher-level objectives harder to teach and assess than lower-level ones? Why or why not?

Reflection Exercise

Think back over your school career and consider all the paper-and-pencil tests you have taken. What were the best tests you took? What characteristics made them the best? What were the worst tests you ever took? What made them the worst?

In reflecting on these questions consider not just the test itself, but also the instruction that preceded it, the information you were given about the test, the conditions of administration, the way the test was scored, and the grade you received. What have you learned from your prior experiences that you would avoid when you construct and administer tests to your pupils?

Activities

1. Each of the following eight test items has at least one fault. Read each item, identify the fault(s) in it and rewrite the item to correct the fault(s). When you have finished rewriting the items, organize them into a test to be given to students. Include directions for items and group items of a similar type together.

   1. Robert Fulton, who was born in Scotland and came to the U.S. in 1843, is best known for his invention of the steamboat that he called the Tom Thumb.   **T.   F.**

   2. Minor differences among organisms of the same kind are known as
      A. heredity
      B. variations
      C. adaptation
      D. natural selection

   3. The recall of factual information can best be assessed with a ____ item.
      A. matching
      B. objective
      C. essay
      D. short-answer

   4. Although the experimental research completed, particularly that by Hansmocker, must be considered too equivocal and the assumptions viewed as too restrictive, most testing experts would recommend that the easiest method of significantly improving paper-and-pencil achievement test reliability would be to
      A. increase the size of the group
      B. increase the weighting of items
      C. increase the number of items
      D. increase the amount of testing time

   5. F. Scott Fitzgerald wrote ____.

   6. Boston is the most important city in the Northeast.   True   False

   7. An electric transformer can be used
      A. for storing up electricity
      B. to increase the voltage of alternating current (correct answer)
      C. it converts electrical energy into direct current
      D. alternating current is changed to direct current

   8. The Confederate states were admitted back into the Union shortly after the Civil War.   **T.   F.**

2. Below are five objectives. For each objective write one test item of the type specified in parentheses to assess the objective.

   1. The student can match the symbols of chemical elements to their names.   (matching)
   2. The student can identify the nouns in a sentence that contains more than one noun.   (multiple choice)

3. The student can indicate whether a statement about the U.S. Constitution is true or false.   (true-false)
4. The student can state the name of the Speaker of the House of Representatives.   (short answer)
5. The student can write the correct definition of an adverb. (short answer)

For objectives 4 and 5, describe the minimum answer that would receive full credit.

Review Questions

1. What are the differences between selection and supply items? What are the advantages and disadvantages of each? What are common faults in each type?
2. What are the differences between higher- and lower-level test items?
3. Three guidelines for constructing paper-and-pencil test questions are: (1) cover important topics; (2) write clearly and simply; and (3) review items before testing. How does each of these guidelines lead to improved test questions?
4. What are examples of clues to be avoided in multiple-choice, true-false, completion, and matching items?
5. What is an interpretive exercise and why is it a useful method for assessing higher-level thinking?
6. How do tests of factual knowledge differ from tests of conceptual knowledge?

References

Frisbie, D. A. (1992). The multiple true-false item format: A status review. *Educational Measurement: Issues and Practice, 11* (4), 21–26.

Marso, R. N., & Pigge, F. L. (1989). Elementary classroom teachers' testing needs and proficiencies: Multiple assessments and inservice training priorities. *Educational Review, 13,* 1–17.

Marso, R. N., & Pigge, F. L. (1991). The analysis of teacher-made tests: Testing practices, cognitive demands and item construction errors. *Contemporary Educational Psychology, 16,* 179–286.

Administering, Scoring, and Improving Paper-and-Pencil Tests

Chapter Outline

❖ Assembling the Test
❖ Administer the Test
❖ Issues of Cheating
❖ Scoring Paper-and-Pencil Tests
❖ Posttest Item Analysis: Implications for Validity
❖ Discuss Test Results with Pupils
❖ Testing Pupils with Disabilities

Chapter Objectives

After reading this chapter, the pupil will be able to:

- Define basic terms: holistic scoring, analytic scoring, objectivity
- State basic principles for assembling and administering tests
- Recognize the unacceptability of cheating on tests and identify strategies to reduce cheating
- Distinguish between objective and subjective scoring and holistic and analytic scoring
- Apply methods to improve the objectivity of essay scoring
- Recognize strategies to identify faulty test items
- Identify strategies for testing pupils with disabilities

We have now examined most of the links in the chain of paper-and-pencil achievement testing. We have discussed the importance of providing pupils with good instruction, the decisions teachers must make in planning tests, the instructional review that should precede testing, and the construction or selection of test items that give pupils a fair chance to demonstrate their learning. Four final steps influence the adequacy of achievement tests: (1) assembling and administering the test, (2) understanding and dealing with cheating, (3) scoring the test, and (4) accommodating pupil disabilities in testing. This chapter addresses these topics.

⚔ Assembling the Test

Once test items have been written or selected and reviewed, they must be arranged into a test. If a teacher uses a textbook test, the items will already be arranged and ready for copying. Often teachers cut and paste items from various sources into a single test. In assembling a test, similar types of items should be grouped together and kept separate from other item types. All of the short-answer questions should be together and separate from the multiple-choice, matching, completion, and essay questions. Grouping test items by type avoids the necessity of pupils shifting from one response mode to another as they move from item to item. It also means that a single set of directions can be used for all of the items in that test section, helping pupils cover more items in a given time. Finally, grouping test items makes scoring easier.

Another important consideration in assembling the test is the order in which the item types are presented to pupils. In most tests, selection items come first and supply items come last. Within the supply section, short-answer or completion questions should be placed before essay questions. Supply items are placed at the end of the test so that pupils will not devote a disproportionate amount of time to this part of the test.

When arranging items on a test, remember these commonsense practices.

1.   Leave a common space for pupils to write their name and/or ID number.

2. Little pupils write big, so leave enough space, especially on essay tests, for young pupils to write their answers. Do not cram items together too closely.

3. Do not split a multiple-choice or matching item across two different pages of the test. This can cause unintended errors when pupils flip from one page to the next to read the second half of a matching question or the last two options of a multiple-choice question.

4. Separate multiple-choice options from the stem by beginning the options on a new line.

5. Number test items, especially if pupils must record answers on a separate answer sheet or in a special place on the test.

6. Space items for easy reading and provide enough space for pupils to complete supply items.

7. Proofread or have someone else proofread the test before photocopying.

8. Check the clarity of photocopied tests. Make a few extra copies.

Each section of a test should have directions that focus pupils on what to do, how to respond, and where to place their answers. Lack of clear directions is one of the most common faults in teacher-made tests and often influences test validity. Here are some sample directions.

- Items 1–15 are multiple-choice items. Read each item carefully and write the <u>letter</u> of your answer on the line in front of the question number.
- Use words from the boxes to complete the sentences. Use each word only once.
- Answer each question by writing the correct answer in the space below the question. No answer should be longer than one sentence.
- For items 10 to 15, circle T on F to show your answer.
- Use the chart to help you to answer questions 27–33. Write your answers in the space provided after each question.

Directions such as these at the start of a test section focus pupils by telling them where and how to respond to the questions. To emphasize a point made earlier, it is especially important that each essay question spell out clearly for pupils the scope and characteristics of the desired answer. For older pupils, it is also helpful to indicate the number of points that will be given to each test section so they can make decisions about how to allocate their time.

The test should be reproduced so that each pupil has his or her own copy. Writing the test questions on the blackboard can be time-consuming, create problems for pupils with poor vision, and encourage pupils to look around the room during test taking. Orally reading questions can be used to pace pupils, but this approach places a premium on listening ability and prevents pupils from working at their own pace. This practice should be avoided unless one is assessing listening skills. In most circumstances, giving each pupil his or her own copy is the best way to present the test to pupils.

Box 7.1   Guidelines for Assembling A Test

- Organize the test by item type: selection before supply, essay last.
- Allow sufficient space for written responses, especially for young children's essay items.
- Do not split multiple-choice or matching items across two pages.
- Separate stem from options in multiple-choice questions.
- Number test items.
- Provide clear directions for each section of the test; for older pupils, indicate the value of each section or question.
- Provide enough questions to assure reliability.
- Proofread the test before copying and make extra copies.

Tests that promote valid decisions also need to be reliable—that is, produce consistent scores. Without reliability a test can hardly provide the kind of information on which one would want to base decisions about a pupil's learning. The main factors in attaining reliable achievement tests are (1) the number and representativeness of the items included on the test and (2) the objectivity of scoring. In general, longer tests allow a teacher to look at a larger sample of pupil performance. For example, which of the following spelling tests do you think would produce the more stable and consistent information about a pupil's spelling achievement: test 1, which consists of a single word selected from a 100-word list, or test 2, which contains a sample of 15 words selected from the same 100-word list? Box 7.1 summarizes guidelines for assembling tests.

✎ Administering the Test

Test administration is concerned with the physical and psychological setting in which pupils take the test. The aim is to establish both a physical and psychological setting that permits pupils to show their best performance.

Physical Setting

Pupils should have a quiet, comfortable environment in which to take the test. Interruptions should be minimized; some teachers post a sign on the door indicating that testing is in progress. During testing there is little one can do about interruptions like fire drills or announcements from the classroom "squawkbox." When such interruptions occur, the teacher must make a judgment about whether it is fair for pupils to continue with testing. Obviously a 1-minute interruption from the squawkbox is less disruptive than a 20-minute fire drill, during which pupils may talk to one another about the test. If an interruption is judged sufficiently disruptive to diminish pupils' ability to provide a fair and representative indication of their achievement, testing should be terminated and repeated at another time.

Often interruptions occur when pupils ask questions during testing. A good way to minimize many of these questions is to proofread items and directions prior to administering the test. Occasionally, typographical errors or unclear items are not detected until testing has begun. Usually, a pupil raises his or her hand or approaches the teacher to ask a question or point out a problem. When such situations arise, an announcement should be made to the whole class informing them of the problem (e.g., "Please correct item 17 in the following way," or "Option B in item 29 should be changed to . . . "). In the end, the decision of whether and how to answer pupil questions rests with the individual teacher. Answering questions during testing is appropriate as long as the teacher is consistent in responding to all pupils who ask questions.

Keeping Track of Time

During testing it often helps students if the teacher keeps track of the remaining time with announcements such as "There are 20 minutes left until the test is over." Such reminders can initially be made at 15-minute intervals, then changed to 5-minute intervals near the end of the test. Such reminders are most useful at the middle and high school levels during final exams, which usually take longer than a single class period to administer. In self-contained elementary school classrooms, where testing and instruction are less ruled by the bell schedule, the teacher has discretion regarding when and how to start and end testing.

Psychological Setting

Establishing a productive psychological setting that reduces pupil anxiety and sets a proper atmosphere for testing is as important as providing a comfortable physical environment. Giving pupils good instruction, advance notice of the test, a day or two to prepare for it, and a good chapter or unit review will help diminish pupils' test anxiety. Even so, it is probably impossible to completely allay all test anxiety.

No teacher should precede test administration with a comment like, "This is the most important test you will take this term. Your grade and your future in this course will be determined primarily by how you do on this test." A speech like this will raise pupils' anxiety levels appreciably and hamper their ability to show what they have learned. Conversely, test administration should not be prefaced with remarks such as, "Everybody knows that tests don't mean much; I just give tests because I have to" or "Don't worry about it—it counts very little in your final grade." Describing and treating a test as if it were a trivial interruption in the school day will diminish its ability to motivate pupil study and will interfere with pupils' test performances.

The line between overemphasizing and underemphasizing the importance of a test is hard to define. Pupils should take tests seriously and they should be encouraged to do their best. The appropriate middle ground

---

Box 7.2   Guidelines for Administering a Test

- Provide a quiet, comfortable setting.
- Try to anticipate and avoid questions during the test by using good directions.
- Provide a good psychological setting; provide advance notice, review, and encouragement for pupils to do their best.
- Discourage cheating through seating arrangements, circulating the room, and enforcement of rules and penalties.
- Help pupils keep track of time.

---

between over-and underemphasizing the importance of tests will vary with the age and characteristics of pupils. The more pupils know about the test the more likely their anxiety will be lowered. Good instruction, a thorough review, and prior knowledge of which types of items will be on the test helps pupils relax at test time. Of course, fair, valid test items and no "surprises" such as unannounced tests, unfamiliar item types, and untaught topics will help allay test anxiety. Each teacher must find the middle ground for his or her class, knowing that whatever is done, there will be some pupils who will be very anxious about their performance and some who will not care.

Box 7.2 summarizes important concerns in test administration.

✄ Issues of Cheating

Teachers should be alert to the possibility of cheating on tests, projects, quizzes, and assignments. Unfortunately, cheating is a common occurrence, both in school and in life. Pupils cheat for many reasons: external pressure from teachers or parents; failure to prepare and study for tests; internal pressure from being in an intensively competitive major or course that gives a limited number of high grades; danger of losing a scholarship; and, unfortunately, because "everybody else does it." Some pupils even blame their cheating on the practices of others. For example, some pupils try to justify cheating with excuses like, "No one near me was attempting to cover up their exam paper," "The course material is too difficult," "There's just too much material to learn," or "The instructor gives tests that are unfair."

However, no matter how and why it is done, cheating is an unacceptable, dishonest, and immoral classroom behavior. The argument that says, "So what, everybody does it. It's no big deal," is wrong. It *is* a big deal. Cheating is analogous to lying. When pupils cheat and turn in work or a test under the pretense that they did the work themselves, that is lying and should be recognized and called lying (Summergrad, 1999).

Tables 7.1 and 7.2 provide information about the prevalence of cheating in school as reported by a sample of high school pupils. Table 7.1 shows

TABLE 7.1

Percentage of High School Students Responding "Yes" to the Question "Have You Cheated on a Quiz or Text?"

	Sex		School Type			Community Type		
Year	Male	Female	Public	Private	Parochial	Urban	Suburban	Rural
1993	41.5	39.8	41.2	34.9	41.9	39.1	43.9	38.0
1994	42.2	44.5	44.4	36.0	51.7	45.6	46.2	41.9

Adapted with permission from *Attitudes and Opinions from the Nation's High Achieving Teens: 25th Annual Survey of High Achievers* (pp. 12–15), by Who's Who Among American High School Students, 1994, Lake Forest, IL: Author.

TABLE 7.2

Percentage of High School Students Responding "Never Happens," "Pretty Rare," "Fairly Common," and "Almost Everybody Does It" to the Question "How Common Is Cheating at Your School?"

Year	Never Happens	Pretty Rare	Fairly Common	Almost Everybody Does It
1993	0.5	18.8	70.0	10.1
1994	0.2	10.3	54.8	34.2

Adapted with permission from *Attitudes and Opinions from the Nation's High Achieving Teens: 25th Annual Survey of High Achievers* (pp. 12–15), by Who's Who Among American High School Students, 1994, Lake Forest, IL: Author.

the percentage of high school students who answered "yes" to the question "Have you cheated on a quiz or test?" The table shows that across the board, regardless of gender, type of school, or type of community, large numbers of students admitted cheating. It also shows that the percentage of students replying "yes" to the question increased from 1993 to 1994, in some cases from 5 to 10 percent. There is no reason to think that cheating has diminished in the six years subsequent to 1994. In fact, the likelihood is that cheating has increased.

Table 7.2 shows the frequency of different degrees of cheating as described by a sample of high school students. The table shows that relatively few high school students, less than 20 percent, report that cheating occurs never or rarely in their schools. Conversely, 80 percent and more of the high school students sampled stated that cheating is fairly common or almost always done in their schools. These tables indicate the pervasiveness of cheating in schools.

Types of Cheating

What are the types of cheating pupils use? Cizek (1999) has written a useful and comprehensive book that explores cheating in depth and with understanding. He identifies and gives examples of a very large number of the ways that pupils cheat. The following examples adapted from Cizek (1999) represent a small sample of common ways pupils cheat. He provides many additional and esoteric ways.

1. Looking at another pupil's test paper during a test.
2. Dropping one's paper so that other pupils can cheat off of it.
3. Dropping one's paper and having another pupil pick it up, cheat from it, and re-drop the paper so the original dropper can reclaim his or her paper.
4. Passing an eraser between two pupils who write test information on the eraser.
5. Developing codes such as tapping the floor three times to indicate that a multiple-choice item should be answered "C."
6. Looking at pupils' papers while walking up to the teacher to ask a question about the test.
7. Using crib notes or small pieces of paper to cheat. Crib notes can be hidden in many ingenious places.
8. Switching scratch paper—often allowed by teachers during tests— with one's own scratch paper that contains test answers.
9. Writing test information on the desktop and erasing it after the test; a variation is to write information in allowed reference or textbook pages prior to the test and use the information during the exam.
10. Wearing a tee-shirt with useful test information written on it.
11. Changing answers when teachers allow pupils to grade each other's papers.
12. Using resources forbidden by the teacher in take-home tests or work.

Deterring Cheating

Teachers should monitor test taking in order to deter cheating and to enhance test validity (Slavin, 1994). There are a number of methods that can be used to deter cheating, some relatively easy to apply and others more complicated. Three general approaches that help eliminate or lessen cheating are (1) providing pupils good instruction and information about the test, (2) knowing the common methods of pupil cheating, and (3) observing pupils during testing. Prior to testing, pupils' books and other materials should be out of sight under their desks or elsewhere. Pupils' seats should be spread out in the classroom as much as possible. The author does not permit wearing baseball caps during testing because when the visors are tilted below the eyes, the author cannot see where the pupils' eyes are looking. During testing, the teacher should quietly move about the classroom and observe pupils as they take the test. While observation rarely "catches" a pupil cheating, the presence of the teacher moving about the classroom is a deterrent to cheating.

TABLE 7.3

Students' Perceived Effectiveness of Cheating Prevention Strategies

Rank	Strategy	% Rating Strategy as "Effective" or "Very Effective"
1	Scrambled test forms	81.6
2	Small classes	69.8
3	Using several proctors during examinations	68.4
4	Unique make-up examinations	68.4
5	Using two or more test forms	66.6
6	Providing study guides	54.8
7	Using more essay questions	54.6
8	Making old examinations available for review	52.4
9	Verifying student identity prior to exam	46.9
10	Giving different assignments	42.8
11	Assigning specific topics for term papers	30.2
12	Using specially marked answer booklets	29.5
13	Putting student names on test booklets	28.4
14	Assigning seats for examinations	26.9
15	Checking footnotes in student papers	26.4
16	Give more in-class tests, fewer take-home tests	23.7
17	Permitting only pencils to be brought into exam room	22.7
18	Not allowing anyone to leave during an examination	22.1
19	Give more take-home tests, fewer in-class tests	17.5
20	Provide a telephone hotline to report cheating	16.0

From "Academic Dishonesty and the Perceived Effectiveness of Countermeasures: An Empirical Survey of Cheating at a Major Public University," by R. C. Hollinger & L. Lanza-Kaduce, 1996, *NASPA Journal*, 33(4), p. 301. Copyright © 1996. Reprinted with permission of NASPA, Student Affairs Administrators in Higher Learning.

Table 7.3 shows a variety of strategies to deter cheating and the degree to which pupils report that the strategies are successfull. The fact that scrambled test forms are viewed as the best deterrent to cheating suggests that the main form of cheating is looking at other pupils' test answers. Scrambled forms are most useful in avoiding cheating from other pupils' tests. Note that the list of strategies includes different approaches. Some of the strategies are aimed at stopping cheating by putting up barriers (e.g., scrambled test forms, unique make-up exams, and assigning pupil seats for testing), while others are aimed at providing pupils with good instruction so they will not have to cheat (e.g., providing study guides and making old exams available to pupils). The top eight strategies are all rated over 50 percent effective in preventing cheating.

Many schools and school systems develop honor codes or cheating rules that all pupils are to respect. Such codes or rules spell out in detail what is and is not cheating. Box 7.3 shows a cheating policy from a middle school in California.

Box 7.3   Excerpts from Huntington Middle School Cheating Policy

You are cheating if you:

- Copy, fax, or duplicate assignments that will each be turned in as an "original"
- Exchange assignments by print-out, disk transfer, or modem, then submit as "original"
- Write formulas, codes, key words on your person or objects for use in a test
- Use hidden reference sheets during a test
- Use programmed material in watches or calculators, when prohibited
- Exchange answers with others (either give or receive answers)
- Take someone else's assignment and submit it as your own
- Submit material (written or designed by someone else) without giving the author/artist name and/or source (e.g. plagiarizing, or submitting work created by family, friends, or tutors)
- Take credit for group work, when little contribution was made
- Do not follow additional specific guidelines on cheating as established by department, class, or a certain teacher.

Students caught cheating on any assignment (homework, tests, projects) will be referred to our Assistant Principal. The school-wide citizenship grade will be lowered at least one grade and the parents will be called. Subsequent offenses may result in a "D" or "F" in citizenship, suspension, removal from elected positions and honorary organizations, the inability to participate in school activities, and similar consequences.

From Huntington Middle School Cheating Policy, by H. E. Huntington Middle School, San Marino (CA) Public Schools.

Available: http://www.san-marino.k12.ca.us/~heh/binderreminder/cheatpolic.html. Reprinted with permission.

Reprinted by permission of Gary McGuigan, Principal, Huntington Middle School.

It is the teacher's responsibility to discourage cheating with seating arrangements, careful proctoring, and other activities. If some pupils do cheat, those who do not can be unfairly penalized for their appropriate and ethical behavior, by receiving lower grades and the honors that come from grades. Teachers should discourage cheating and penalize pupils caught doing it, because it is an immoral activity and because it provides an invalid picture of a pupil's achievement. It is, however, important to have strong evidence to support charges of cheating, because pupils have due process rights if accused.

⚔ Scoring Paper-and-Pencil Tests

The product of test administration is a stack of tests that contain information about each pupil's achievement. However, in order to use this information, the teacher must summarize and score it. Scores provide a summary of each pupil's performance on the test. The process of scoring a test involves **measurement**—that is, assigning a number to represent a pupil's performance. In the case of achievement tests, performance on the test items is translated into a score that is used to make decisions about the pupil.

Of course, when pupil achievement is being scored, the same rules should be applied to all tested pupils. For example, if we score Jessica's performance on an achievement test by applying the rule "5 points for every correct answer," then we should score every pupil's performance using the same rule. It would be unfair to give Jessica 5 points for getting an item correct and Ron or Arthur only 2 points for getting the same item correct. Thus, measurement is not only a process of transforming pupils' test performance into numbers, it also requires that common rules be used when assigning those numbers.

The complexity of scoring tests varies with their type. Selection-type items are easiest to score, short-answer and completion items are next easiest, and essays are the most difficult. The reason for this is obvious if one thinks about what a teacher has to do to score each item type. How much time and judgment is involved in scoring each? What precisely does the teacher have to look at to determine whether an item is correct or incorrect? Which type of item requires the most concentration to score? The answers to these questions illustrate the range of ease and difficulty encountered when scoring various item types.

Scoring Selection Items

Pupils respond to selection items by writing, circling, or marking the letter of their response. Scoring selection items is essentially a clerical task in which the teacher compares an answer **key** containing the correct answers to the answers the pupil has given. The number of matches indicates the pupil's score on the test. Before using an answer key, it is a good idea to check to make sure that the key is correct. Similarly, if the test is machine scored, it is good practice for the teacher to hand score a few answer sheets to determine if the machine scoring is accurate.

Scoring selection test items is usually quite **objective**—that is, independent scorers will arrive at the same or very similar scores for a given pupil's test. Conversely, **subjective** scoring means that independent scorers would *not* arrive at the same or similar scores for a given pupil's test. In a subjective test, a pupil's performance depends as much on *who* scores the test as on the pupil's answers. Selection items produce objective scores because there usually is one clearly correct answer to each item, and that answer is identified by a single letter. However, as pupils' responses become more lengthy and complex—as they do with short-answer, completion, and essay items—the judgment of what is a correct or incorrect answer often blurs and scoring becomes more subjective. It has long been known that even when the same person scores the same essay test twice, there is no guarantee that the scores will be the same or similar (Starch and Elliott, 1912, 1913). However, if we are to have confidence in a test score, it is important that the scores be objective.

Scoring Short-Answer and Completion Items

As long as short-answer and completion items are clearly written, focus pupils on their task, and call for a short response such as a word, phrase, date, or number, scoring is not difficult and can be quite objective. However, as items require lengthier responses from pupils, subjectivity of scoring will increase because more and more interpretations of what pupils know or meant to say will have to be made.

No matter how well a teacher has prepared and reviewed test items, he or she never knows how an item will work until *after* it is administered to pupils. Inevitably, there are times when pupil responses to an item reveal that most pupils misinterpreted it, and that the pupils' answers are correct given their interpretation, but incorrect given the teacher's intention. How should such responses be scored? Similarly, if a textbook test contains a few items that were not emphasized in instruction and pupils got them wrong, should adjustments be made in their scores?

How a teacher interprets pupils' unexpected responses or answers to untaught items can influence pupils' test scores and grades greatly. For example, suppose that one item in a 10-item test produces many unexpected responses from pupils. If the teacher simply marks these responses wrong because they do not match the answer key, he or she may be penalizing pupils for his or her own faulty test item. This 10 percent deduction could make a big difference in a pupil's test score or grade.

In reviewing unexpected responses and untaught items, the teacher must decide if wrong answers are the result of faulty items or a lack of pupil learning. Test scores should not automatically be raised simply because many pupils got an item wrong, but the teacher must make a judgment about the likely source of the problem and how it is best handled. At the very least, the problem items should be examined and analyzed.

In the end, scoring decisions rest with the teacher. Teachers must decide who is at fault when pupils misinterpret an item and whether pupils should lose credit for wrong answers on items that were not discussed in class. Two principles should be considered in making such decisions. First, since the test scores should reflect pupils' achievement on the chapter or unit, the scores should deal only with topics that were taught and items that are clearly written. If points are deducted for items not taught or for misinterpreting ambiguous questions, scores will not reflect pupils' true achievement. Second, whatever decision is made regarding the scoring of poor or untaught items, it should be applied uniformly to all pupils.

Three guidelines can help teachers overcome problems of scoring supply items.

1. Prepare an answer key before scoring. Know what you are looking for in pupil responses *before* scoring.
2. Determine how factors such as spelling, grammar, and punctuation—which are usually ancillary to the main focus of the response—will be handled in scoring. Should points be taken off for such factors? Decide before scoring and inform pupils before testing.

3. If pupil responses are technically correct but not initially considered in the scoring guideline, give credit to each unexpected but correct response.

Scoring Essay Items

Essay questions represent the ultimate in scoring complexity because they permit each pupil to construct a unique and lengthy response to the question posed. This means that there is not one definitive answer key that can be applied uniformly to all responses. Interpretation of the responses is necessary. Moreover, the answer to an essay question is presented in a form that contains many distracting factors that contribute to subjective scoring.

Think of an essay answer that you have written. Remember how it looked spread out over the page. Visualize your handwriting and the overall appearance of the written answer. Remember that the essay question was intended to determine how well you understood ideas and information you had been taught. However, the teacher who scored your essay was probably influenced by one or more of the following factors;

- Handwriting
- Writing style, including sentence structure and flow
- Spelling and grammar
- Neatness
- Fatigue of the scorer
- Identity of the pupil
- Location of one's test paper in the pile of test papers

Each of these factors can influence a teacher's reaction to an essay answer, although none of them has anything to do with the actual content of the pupil's response. For example, a pupil whose penmanship is so poor that it forces the teacher to decipher what each scribbled word means will frustrate the teacher and divert attention away from the content of the answer. The essay likely will get a lower score than that of another pupil who provides the same answer in more legible handwriting. A pupil who uses interesting words in a variety of sentence structures to produce an answer that flows smoothly and interestingly from point to point likely will get a better score than a pupil who states the same points in a string of simple declarative sentences. Poor grammar and misspelled words create a negative impression in a teacher's mind. And, neatness does count with teachers.

Scoring essays is a time-consuming and difficult task, so pupil scores may be influenced by how alert the teacher is when the essays are read. The first few essays that are read seem new and fresh and pupils who wrote them tend to get good scores. However, after the teacher has read the same response 15 or more times, familiarity and fatigue set in, and responses similar to the initial ones often get lower scores. Thus, pupils who provide essentially the same answer to an essay question may get different scores depending upon when the scorer read their answer.

Knowledge of who wrote the essay can also influence the scoring process. In almost all essay questions there is at least one point when the teacher must interpret what a pupil was trying to say. Knowledge of who wrote the answer can influence the teacher's interpretation. For example, two pupils, Isobel and Keyshawn, have each written an essay that has some ambiguous statements. The teacher knows that Isobel is an interested, able pupil who always does well on tests and in class discussions. The teacher thinks, "Although Isobel didn't make this point clearly and it's not evident that she understands it, she probably knew the answer even though it didn't come out right. I'll give her the credit." The teacher also knows that Keyshawn generally does poorly in school and remembers his indifference to the topic during a recent class discussion. The teacher thinks, "Since Keyshawn doesn't care about this subject, rarely says anything in class except to disagree with me, and didn't make this point clearly, he probably had no idea of what was correct here. He will get no credit." One way to avoid such biased scoring is to identify papers by number or have pupils put their names on the last page of a test. Notice that knowing the pupil's identity is not a problem in scoring selection items, because there is little interpretation involved in scoring.

Consider the following situation. You are taking an essay examination. All the other pupils have finished and left the room. You are alone with the teacher. As you walk up to turn in your test paper, the teacher says to you, "You have worked hard on this test. I want to reward your effort. Here is the pile of test papers from all the other pupils in the class. When I score them, I shall start with the top paper and work down the pile in order. Because you have worked so hard, I will let you place your test paper anywhere in the pile you wish. Where would you like to place it?" Where would you place it? Could your choice within the stack make a difference in your score? If you think it could, you probably are correct. What does this say about the potential subjectivity of essay tests?

A number of steps can be taken to reduce, if not eliminate, subjectivity in essay scoring. If essay scores are to represent pupils' achievement and be used as a basis for grading or making other decisions about pupils, it is important that a teacher have confidence that the scores are as objective as possible.

Holistic Versus Analytic Scoring

Teachers typically use two approaches to scoring essay questions: holistic scoring and analytic scoring. **Holistic scoring** reflects a teacher's *overall impression* of the whole essay by providing a *single score or grade.* **Analytic scoring,** on the other hand, views the essay as being made up of many components and provides *separate scores* for each component. Thus, an essay that is scored analytically might result in separate scores for accuracy, organization, supporting arguments, and grammar and spelling. Analytic scoring provides detailed feedback that pupils can use to improve different aspects of their essays. Remember from Chapter 5 that Mr. Wysocki provided his pupils with detailed feedback from the practice paragraphs they wrote. Undoubtedly, he used analytic scoring to help his pupils improve. However, attempting to score more than three or four separate features often makes scoring confusing and time-consuming. In both holistic and analytic scoring, the teacher's helpful or encouraging suggestions on pupils' drafts and tests are recommended.

Steps to Ensure Objectivity

Regardless of whether a teacher uses holistic or analytic scoring, certain steps should be followed to ensure that pupils' essays are scored objectively. Although the following suggestions are time-consuming, they are necessary if scores are to be valid for decision making.

1. *Define what constitutes a good answer before administering an essay question.* The less focused an essay question is, the broader the range of pupil responses will be and the more difficult it will be to apply uniform scoring criteria. Including information about the pupil's specific task, the scope of the essay, and the scoring criteria in the essay directions has numerous benefits. First, it helps pupils respond to a precise set of teacher expectations. This in turn will diminish scoring subjectivity. Second, by writing questions that clearly indicate the characteristics of a good answer, the teacher automatically has to confront the issue of scoring. The criteria that focus pupils' responses are also the basic criteria that will be used in scoring the pupils' answers.

2. *Decide and tell pupils how handwriting, punctuation, spelling, and organization will be scored.* Pupils should know in advance what factors will count in scoring the essay.

3. *If possible, score pupils anonymously.* This will help keep the scoring objective by eliminating knowledge and accompanying perceptions of the pupil's effort, ability, interest, and past performance. Each pupil should be scored on the basis of present performance, not in terms of teacher perceptions or past performance.

4. *In tests with multiple essay items, score all pupils' answers to the first question before moving to the second question.* If it is difficult to score a single essay question objectively, it is more difficult to score two or three different essay questions in succession. One must not only contend with the distractions present in each individual essay, but also must shift content orientation and criteria for each question. Scoring all the answers to a single essay question at one time ensures against the "carryover" effect, the tendency to let one's reaction to a pupil's initial essay influence one's perception of succeeding essays written by that same pupil.

5. *Read essay answers a second time after initial scoring.* The best way to check for objectivity in essay scoring is to have a second individual read and score pupils' papers using the same criteria the teacher used to score them. Since this is usually impractical, except when making very important decisions (e.g., awarding a scholarship, selecting for an honor society), an acceptable procedure is for the teacher to reread and, if necessary, rescore a sample of

> ## Box 7.4   Guidelines for Scoring a Test
>
> - Test scores should be based upon topics that were taught and items that are clearly written.
> - Make sure the same rules are used to score all pupils.
> - Be alert for the following distractors that may affect the objectivity of essay scores: writing style, grammar and spelling, neatness, scorer fatigue, prior performance, and carryover effects.
> - Define what constitutes a good answer before administering an essay question.
> - Score all answers to the first essay question before moving on to score the succeeding question.
> - Read essay questions a second time after initial scoring.
> - Carry out posttest review in order to locate faulty test items and when necessary to make scoring adjustments.

the essays before finalizing the scores. Two scorings by the same person, even if done quickly and on only a sample of essays, are better than a single scoring and lead to more objective decision making.

Essay questions permit the assessment of many thought processes that can be assessed in no other way. When such thought processes are part of the instructional objectives and are actively taught to pupils, they should be assessed to obtain a representative picture of pupil learning. Nevertheless, when using essay questions, one must realize the difficulty inherent in scoring them and the dangers of scoring them improperly. A teacher should use essay questions if they are the best way to assess what has been taught, but time should be set aside to score them objectively so that their results can be used with confidence. Box 7.4 summarizes guidelines to follow when scoring tests.

⚔ Posttest Item Test Analysis: Implications for Validity

Even though one has prepared pupils for testing and written or selected appropriate test items, poor test assembly, administration, and scoring can impair test validity. If there are distractions when pupils are taking the test, if the teacher knowingly or unknowingly heightens pupils' anxiety levels immediately before testing, if directions do not make clear to pupils what they are to do, or if scoring, particularly for essay questions, is haphazard and subjective, the validity of achievement tests is reduced. The steps described in the preceding section are intended to produce valid achievement test scores, which can be used with confidence in making decisions about pupil learning.

Although these steps will eliminate most of the common pitfalls found in classroom achievement tests, a teacher never really knows how well test items will work until after they have been administered to pupils. It is all but impossible to anticipate how pupils will react to a given item. Thus, a review of pupil performance after testing in order to identify faulty items is an important final step to ensure the validity of the test results. There are two reasons for performing such posttest reviews: (1) to identify and make scoring adjustments for any items that pupils' answers show were misunderstood or ambiguous and (2) to identify ways to improve items for use on future tests. The following examples illustrate the need for posttest reviewing.

A social studies teacher who taught a unit on the Low Countries (e.g., Belgium, Luxembourg, and Holland) asked the following short answer question.

What are the Low Countries?

She expected that her pupils would respond with the names of the Low Countries even though the item did not ask explicitly for the names. While many students did supply the names, many others responded that the low countries were "a group of countries in Europe that are largely below sea level." How should the teacher treat the responses of this latter group of pupils?

A health teacher wrote the following multiple-choice question.

The main value of a daily exercise program is to
  A. eat less
  B. develop musculature
  C. raise intelligence
  D. keep physically fit

Choice B was keyed as the correct answer, but many students selected D as their answer. What should the teacher do about the pupils who selected option D?

Notice that these problems did not become apparent until *after* the teacher looked over the pupil responses and found unexpected or odd response patterns in a few items: almost everyone missing a particular item; some pupils giving strange or unexpected answers to an item; all of the bright students doing poorly on an item; no consistency in the wrong answers to an item. As these scoring patterns emerge, teachers should inspect pupil responses to determine whether the problem was related to test construction or pupil learning. It is important to emphasize that test scores should not automatically be raised simply because many pupils got an item wrong. In each case, the teacher must make a judgment regarding the source of the problem and how it will be rectified, if at all. Recognize, however, that if problem items are not examined and analyzed, no reasonable decision can be made.

Problems in short-answer and completion items usually become evident when reading pupils' answers. The written responses give a good indication of how pupils understood and interpreted a test item. For example, in the preceding social studies item on the Low Countries, pupils' answers made it clear that the item did not focus students on the names of the Low Countries, and, consequently, produced other responses that were correct but not what the teacher wanted.

Problems in selection items, especially multiple-choice ones, are harder to detect because pupils select rather than construct their own response, which provides little insight into their thinking. To identify problems with multiple-choice items, teachers must view response patterns on the various options provided. This is not hard to do if one is fortunate enough to have a test scoring machine and a computer to analyze the results. Few teachers, however, are so fortunate. So, while it is desirable to review all items in a multiple-choice test, time and resource limitations usually prevent this. It is realistic, however, to expect teachers to review those items that half or more of the pupils answered incorrectly. This is where most, if not all, of the faulty items are likely to be found.

There are many ways that patterns for multiple-choice items can be examined. A number of statistical indices can be calculated to describe each test item (Kubiszyn and Borich, 1999). For example, the **difficulty index** of an item describes the proportion of pupils who answered it correctly. Thus, an item of .70 difficulty (70 percent of the class answered correctly) is easier than one of .40 difficulty (40 percent of the class answered correctly). Items can be ranked in terms of their difficulty to identify pupils' strengths and weaknesses. The **discrimination index** describes how an individual item fares with pupils who scored high and low on the overall test. An item with positive discrimination is one that is more frequently answered correctly by pupils who score high on the test as a whole than by pupils who score low. The use of the difficulty and discrimination indices will be discussed further in Chapter 11.

As noted, most classroom teachers lack the time and resources to perform the numerical analyses required to calculate difficulty and discrimination indices. Therefore they must rely upon simple methods to understand and improve those items that a large proportion of the class answered incorrectly. The following are examples of item response patterns teachers can use to answer the question "What's the problem, if any, with this item?" Each of these patterns indicates a different possible reason why large numbers of pupils might answer incorrectly. In each case, an asterisk indicates the keyed answer.

This first response pattern is typical of multiple-choice items that have two correct or defensible answers, similar to the health item shown previously. Two choices, A and C, were rarely selected. The majority of pupils split themselves almost evenly between options B and D. Only the pupils who marked B, the keyed response, received credit on the item when it was initially scored.

Options	A	*B	C	D
Number of pupils choosing option	2	8	2	8

When the teacher saw that most pupils missed this item, he looked at option D, decided that it was also a correct choice, and decided to give full credit to those who selected D. Remember, the final decision about whether the item or the pupils are at fault rests with the teacher.

The next pattern is one where most pupils select an option other than the keyed one. In the example below, most pupils chose C rather than D, the keyed option. Many times this pattern is simply the result of miskeying on the part of the teacher. In this case the teacher wrote D next to this item when she meant to write C. While miskeying is not always the explanation for such a response pattern, it is a good starting point. If the item was not miskeyed, closer inspection of option C should provide a clue as to why it was chosen so often. If not, pupils should be consulted to explain their answers.

Options	A	B	C	*D
Number of pupils choosing option	2	1	15	2

Finally, consider the following pattern in which all options are selected by about the same number of pupils. Such a pattern may be an indication that pupils are guessing the correct answer. They probably have no idea which option is correct. Faulty wording or untaught material are likely explanations for such a response pattern.

Options	*A	B	C	D
Number of pupils choosing option	5	6	4	5

Posttest reviews using the above strategies can help teachers better understand how well their items are working and why pupils responded as they did. Asking pupils what they were thinking when they answered an item can also produce useful information. While the decision about how to score an item ultimately rests with the classroom teacher, information of the kind described in this section is helpful in making that decision. A posttest review will enhance the validity of the test scores and the decisions made from them.

✂ Discuss Test Results with Pupils

Pupils want information about their test performance. Teachers can provide this information through comments written on papers, tests, or projects that indicate to pupils what they did well and how they might improve. It also is helpful to go over the results of a test with pupils. This is especially useful when the pupils have their marked tests in front of them during the review. The teacher should pay special attention to items that a large proportion of the class got wrong in order to clear up misconceptions and to indicate the nature of the desired answer. For older pupils it also is helpful to explain how the tests were scored and graded. Finally, opportunity should be provided for shy pupils to discuss the test in private with the teacher.

✂ Testing Pupils with Disabilities

In Chapter 3 the history and key features of accommodating pupils with disabilities were described. In that chapter, the focus was on accommodating pupils with disabilities during instruction. In this chapter the focus is on accommodating pupils with disabilities during testing and assessment. There is some overlap between pupil accommodations for instruction and those for assessment, in large part because many disabilities call for the same or similar accommodations for both instruction and testing. In all cases, the purpose of accommodations is to minimize the effect of pupil attributes that are not related to the primary focus of the test. For example, if a pupil has a hearing disability that may interfere with performance on an oral test, the pupil may be provided with a written test. Or, a pupil who is new to the English language may be given the test in his or her own language; if the test must be taken in English the pupil may be given extra time to complete the test. In each of these cases, the idea is to provide an accommodation that will provide the pupil a fair chance to show what he or she knows, unencumbered by the handicap.

Pupil accommodations in testing can be divided into four general categories: modifying the presentation format of the test, modifying the response format of the test, modifying test timing, and modifying test setting. Following are common examples of accommodations in these four areas. The specific accommodations required for a given pupil will be guided by his or her Individual Education Plan (IEP).

Modifying the Presentation Format

- Read directions for each test section; read slowly
- Provide verbal or oral directions as needed
- Present directions as a sequence of steps for the pupil to follow
- Have pupil repeat directions to ensure understanding
- Read test questions aloud
- Spread items over the page; put each sentence on a single line
- Present test in Braille, large print, sign language, native language, or bilingually
- Revise or simplify language level

Modifying the Response Format

- Allow dictionaries, texts, or calculators
- Allow responses in Braille, large print, sign language, native language, or tape recording
- Provide verbal prompts to items
- Provide a scribe to write pupil answers
- Provide examples of expected test responses
- Give pupil an outline for essay items
- Include definitions or formulas for the pupil; allow the use of notes
- Double check pupil's understanding of the items and desired responses
- Make test similar to what was taught during instruction

Modifying Test Timing

- Provide extra time
- Avoid timed tests
- Test over a period of discrete testing sessions
- Give extra breaks during testing
- Allow unlimited time

Modifying Test Setting

- Test in a separate and quiet location
- Seat pupil away from distractions
- Test one-on-one: one pupil, one test administrator

The above four areas include many of the most common accommodations used in classrooms. There are, of course, many other accommodations that can be applied to provide valid assessment of pupils with disabilities, but this list provides a useful beginning for our exploration into this area. The pupil's IEP will guide the teacher in preparing pupils for testing.

One additional issue requires attention. The above accommodations are generally ones that all pupils in a classroom will notice during a test. While it is usually clear that pupils with disabilities are being treated differently from nondisabled pupils, teachers should try not to bring undue attention to pupils with disabilities during testing. For example, teachers could confer privately with pupils with disabilities when setting up needed accommodations. They can make the modified test similar in appearance to the regular test. They can try to be unobtrusive when helping pupils with disabilities during testing and try to monitor all pupils in the same way. The aim of such practices is to be sensitive to embarrassment to pupils with disabilities during testing and avoid it as much as possible.

Pupils with disabilities will increasingly be included in classrooms with their peers who do not have disabilities. This inclusion will have many benefits for all pupils, but will call upon teachers to make accommodations for pupils with disabilities in the construction and administration of assessments.

Chapter Summary

- In assembling items into a test, the various item types should be grouped together, with selection items placed at the start of the test and supply items at the end. Short-answer items should be placed before essay items.
- Each section of the test should have directions that tell pupils what to do, how to respond, and where to place their answers. Older pupils may also be helped by knowing how much each item is worth.
- Each pupil should have his or her own copy of the test.
- A proper physical climate for testing is one in which pupils are comfortable and interruptions are minimized.
- A proper psychological climate is more difficult to attain because some pupils are always more anxious about testing than others. Providing advanced warning of a test, reviewing important objectives, and encouraging pupils to do their best without exerting undo pressure will help set a suitable psychological climate in which pupils can perform their best.
- Cheating is unacceptable and dishonest; it is also common. It is a teacher's responsibility to establish conditions that reduce cheating.
- Cheating can be deterred by scrambling test forms, arranging pupil seating, circulating the classroom during testing, providing study guides,

using more essay items, forbidding pupils to share materials, and enforcing cheating rules and penalties.

- Measurement is a form of scoring in which numbers are assigned to describe pupils' performance.
- An objective test item is one that independent scorers would score the same or similarly. A subjective item is one that independent scorers would not score the same. Factors that contribute to subjectivity include handwriting, style, grammar, and the teacher's perception of the pupil.
- Selection items are easy to score objectively. Supply items become increasingly subjective as pupils are given more freedom to construct their own answers. Essay items are the most subjective kind of item.
- Test scores should be based on the topics that were taught.
- The two principal methods of scoring essay tests are holistic scoring, which produces a single overall score, and analytic scoring, which produces a number of scores corresponding to particular features of the essay (e.g., organization, style, etc.).
- In order to make essay scores objective a teacher should decide what factors constitute a good answer before giving the test; provide those factors in the test item; read all responses to a single essay question before reading responses to other questions; and reread essays a second time to corroborate initial scores.
- After a test is scored, the teacher should review items that show unusual answers or response patterns to determine if the items are faulty. If faulty items are judged to be responsible, a scoring adjustment may be in order.
- It is good practice to conduct a posttest review with pupils in order to (1) help identify any misconceptions, (2) locate faulty test items and make necessary scoring adjustments, and (3) build up a permanent test item file.
- A number of testing accommodations can be provided for pupils with disabilities. The principal types of testing accommodations include modifications of the presentation and response formats of the test and modifications of the test timing and setting.

Questions for Discussion

1. What are some ways that scoring essay questions can be made more objective? What are some consequences of subjective essay scoring?
2. How can a teacher reduce pupils' test anxiety while maintaining their motivation to do well on a test?
3. How should a teacher respond to cheating? Should all forms of cheating be treated in the same way? What cautions should a teacher keep in mind before accusing a pupil of cheating?
4. What learning accommodations would you make in your classroom for a pupil with a physical disability such as cerebral palsy, an affective disability such as emotional outbursts, or a cognitive disability such as extremely short attention span?

Reflection Exercises

1. Imagine that you are a teacher who has just returned a batch of graded essay tests to your pupils. At the end of class, one pupil approaches you and says that he feels he did not receive all the credit he should have on one of the essay questions. He is convinced that he deserves a higher grade than you gave. How would you handle this situation? What steps would you take to reach a resolution? What do you think will be the hardest part of reaching a resolution? Would the situation be any different if the student complained about a matching item? How could you plan in advance for such situations?

2. What can be done to diminish the amount of cheating at all levels of education? Is taking material from the internet and claiming it is one's own work cheating? Is it cheating if parents help their children with homework and projects?

Activities

1. Rewrite the following essay question to make it more focused for pupils. Then state a set of criteria you would use to judge the quality of your pupils' answers.

   Compare the Democratic and Republican Parties.

2. Talk to two teachers about how they deal with and prevent cheating on tests.

3. Talk to a few teachers and find out about the types of disabilities they have in their classes.

Review Questions

1. What is the fundamental purpose of assessing pupils' achievement? What decisions must a teacher make when preparing to assess pupil achievement?
2. How is the validity of an achievement test determined?
3. What are some differences between scoring selection and supply items?
4. What is the difference between objective and subjective scoring? What factors make it difficult to score essay questions objectively? What steps can a teacher take to make essay scoring more objective?
5. What guidelines should be followed in arranging the items in a test?
6. What are some strategies that can be used to limit cheating on tests?
7. How do holistic and analytic scoring differ? When should each be used?
8. What is the relationship among educational objectives, instruction, and achievement testing?
9. What are some examples of pupil accommodations provided during testing?

References

Cizek, G. (1999). *Cheating on Tests: How to do it, detect it, and prevent it.* Mahwah, NJ: Lawrence Erlbaum Associates

Kubiszyn, T., & Borich, G. (1999). *Educational testing and measurement.* Glenview, IL: Scott, Foresman.

Slavin, R. (1994). *Educational Psychology: Theory and Practice,* 4th ed., Boston: Allyn and Bacon.

Starch, D., & Elliott, E. (1912). Reliability of the grading of high-school work in English. *School Review, 20,* 442–457.

Starch, D., & Elliott, E. (1913). Reliability of grading work in mathematics. *School Review, 21,* 254–259.

Summergrad, D. (1999). Calling it what it is. *Education Week,* August 4, p. 46.

Performance Assessment

Chapter Outline

❖ Performance Assessment in Schools
    and Classrooms

❖ Developing Performance Assessments

❖ Validity and Reliability of Performance
    Assessments

Chapter Objectives

After reading this chapter, the pupil will be able to:

- Define basic terms: checklist, rating scale, rubric, performance criteria
- Contrast performance processes and performance products
- Contrast performance assessment with other assessment types
- Write well-stated performance criteria
- Apply different scoring approaches for performance assessments
- Identify strategies to improve the validity and reliability of classroom performance assessments

The following examples describe common classroom assessment practices. How could the validity of these practices be improved?

> Ms. Landers taught her ninth grade science class a unit on microscopes. She taught her pupils how to set up, focus, and use a microscope. Each pupil used a microscope to identify and draw pictures of three or four objects on glass slides. At the end of the unit, she tested the pupils' achievement by giving a paper-and-pencil test that asked them to label parts of a diagrammed microscope and answer multiple-choice questions about the history of the microscope.
>
> In Mr. Cleaver's third grade class, oral reading skills are strongly emphasized, and he devotes a great deal of energy to helping pupils use proper phrasing, vocal expression, and clear pronunciation when they read aloud. All of the tests that Mr. Cleaver uses to grade his pupils' reading achievement are paper-and-pencil tests that assess pupils' paragraph comprehension and word recognition.
>
> Mrs. Wilkes included a unit on cardiopulmonary resuscitation (CPR) in her eleventh grade health class. Pupils were introduced to CPR and shown a movie on how to perform it. An emergency medical technician from the local fire department came to class with a practice dummy and instructed each pupil on the technique using the dummy as an imaginary victim. Mrs. Wilkes tested her pupils' achievement on the unit with a 25-item true-false test on CPR technique.

These examples illustrate an important limitation of many paper-and-pencil tests: they allow teachers to assess some, but not all, important school learning outcomes. In each of these three classrooms, the teacher relied solely on tests that measured *knowledge of performance*, (remember factual knowledge) but not ability to actually *perform the skill* (apply procedural knowledge).

There are many classroom assessment situations for which valid assessment requires that teachers gather formal information about pupils' performances or products. Teachers collect pupil products such as written stories, paintings, lab reports, and science fair projects, as well as performances such as giving a speech, holding a pencil, typing, and cooperating in groups. Generally, products produce tangible outcomes—things you can hold in your hand—while performances are things you observe or listen to. Table 8.1 contrasts the selection and supply items discussed in Chapter 6 with typical examples of performance and product assessments.

Assessments in which pupils carry out an activity or produce a product in order to demonstrate their learning are called **performance assess-**

TABLE 8.1

Examples of Four Assessment Approaches

Selection	Supply	Product	Performance
Multiple choice	Completion	Essay, story, or poem	Musical, dance, or dramatic performance
True-false	Label a diagram	Research report	Science lab demonstration
Matching	Short answer	Writing portfolio	Typing test
	Concept map	Diary or journal	Athletic competition
		Science fair project	Debate
		Art exhibit or portfolio	Oral presentation
			Cooperation in groups

Source: From *If Minds Matter: A Forward to the Future*, Volume Two, edited by Arthur L. Costa, James Bellanca, and Robin Fogarty. ©1992 IRI/Skylight Publishing Inc. Reprinted by permission of Skylight Professional Development. www/skylightedu.com

ments. (They also may be called alternative or authentic assessments.) Performance assessments permit pupils to show what they can do in real situations (Wiggins, 1992). The difference between describing how a skill should be performed and actually knowing how to perform it is an important distinction in classroom assessment. Teachers recognize this distinction, as the following comments illustrate.

> I want my pupils to learn to do math for its own intrinsic value, but also because math is so essential for everyday life. Making change, balancing checkbooks, doing a budget, and many other practical, real - world activities require that pupils know how to use their math knowledge.
>
> The kids need to learn to get along in groups, be respectful of others' property, and wait their turns. I don't want kids to be able to recite classroom rules, I want them to practice them. These behaviors are just as important for kids to learn in school as reading, writing, and math.
>
> Just because they can write a list of steps they would follow to ensure laboratory safety does not mean that in a given situation they could actually demonstrate that knowledge.

Some types of paper-and-pencil test items can be used to provide information about the thinking processes that underlie pupils' performance. For example, a math problem in which pupils have to show their work provides insight into the mental processes used to solve the problem. An essay question can show pupils' organizational skills, thought processes, and application of capitalization and punctuation rules. These two forms of paper-and-pencil test items can assess what pupils can do as opposed to the majority of paper-and-pencil test questions that reveal what pupils know. With most selection and supply questions, the teacher observes the *result* of the pupil's intellectual process, but not the thinking process that produced the result. If the pupil gets a multiple-choice, true-false, matching, or completion item correct, the teacher *assumes* that the pupil must have followed the correct process, but there is little direct evidence to support this assumption, since the only evidence of the pupil's thought process is a circled letter or a single written word. On the other hand, essays and other extended response items provide a product that shows how pupils think about and construct their responses. They permit the teacher to see the logic of arguments, the manner in which the response is organized, and the basis of conclusions drawn by the pupil (Bartz, Anderson-Robinson, and Hillman, 1994). Thus, paper-and-pencil assessments like essays, stories, reports, or "show-your-work" problems are important forms of performance assessments. Table 8.2 shows some of the differences between objective test items, essay questions, oral questions, and performance assessments.

Chapter 2 discussed how teachers observe their pupils' performance in order to size them up and also to obtain information about the moment-to-moment success of their instruction. Such observations are primarily in-

TABLE 8.2

Comparison of Various Types of Assessments

	Objective Test	Essay Test	Oral Question	Performance Assessment
Purpose	Sample knowledge with maximum efficiency and reliability	Assess thinking skills and/or mastery of how a body of knowledge is structured	Assess knowledge during instruction	Assess ability to translate knowledge and understanding into action
Pupil's Response	Read, evaluate, select	Organize, compose	Oral answer	Plan, construct, and deliver an original response
Major Advantage	Efficiency—can administer many items per unit of testing time	Can measure complex cognitive outcomes	Joins assessment and instruction	Provides rich evidence of performance skills
Influence on Learning	Overemphasis on recall encourages memorization; can encourage thinking skills if properly constructed	Encourages thinking and development of writing skills	Stimulates participation in instruction, provides teacher immediate feedback on effectiveness of teaching	Emphasizes use of available skill and knowledge in relevant problem contexts

Source: Adapted from R. J. Stiggins, "Design and Development of Performance Assessments," *Educational Measurement: Issues and Practice,* 1987, *6*(3), p. 35. Copyright 1987 by the National Council on Measurement in Education. Adapted by permission of the publisher.

formal and spontaneous. In this chapter, we are concerned with assessing more formal, structured performances and products, those that the teacher plans in advance, helps each pupil to perform, and formally assesses. These assessments can take place during normal classroom instruction (e.g., oral reading activities, setting up laboratory equipment) or in some special situation set up to elicit a performance (e.g., giving a speech in an auditorium, demonstrating CPR on a dummy). In either case, the activity is formally structured—the teacher arranges the conditions in which the performance or product is demonstrated and judged. Such assessments permit each pupil to show his or her mastery of the same process or task, something that is impossible with informal observation of spontaneous classroom performance and events.

This chapter describes performance assessment. It discusses the development of performances and outlines the pros and cons of performance assessments. Threats to validity and reliability are identified and suggestions to obtain valid and reliable performance assessments are described. Chapter 9 illustrates varied uses of performance assessments.

⚔ Performance Assessment in Schools and Classrooms

The amount of attention that has recently been focused on performance assessment in states, schools, and classrooms would lead one to believe that performance assessment is new and untried, and that it can solve all the problems of classroom assessment. Neither of these beliefs is true (Madaus and O'Dwyer, 1999). Performance assessment has been used extensively in classrooms for as long as there have been classrooms. Table 8.3 provides examples of five common performance assessments that have long been used in schools.

TABLE 8.3

Five Common Domains of Performance Assessment

Communication Skills	Psychomotor Skills	Athletic Activities	Concept Acquisition	Affective Skills
Writing essays	Holding a pencil	Shooting free throws	Constructing open and closed circuits	Sharing toys
Giving a speech	Setting up lab equipment	Catching a ball	Selecting proper tools for shop tasks	Working in cooperative groups
Pronouncing a foreign language	Using scissors	Hopping	Identifying unknown chemical substances	Obeying school rules
Following spoken directions	Dissecting a frog	Swimming the crawl	Generalizing from experimental data	Maintaining self-control

Many factors account for the growing popularity of performance assessment (Ryan and Miyasaka, 1995; Quality Counts, 1999). First, performance assessment is being proposed or mandated as part of formal statewide assessment programs (see Chapters 3 and 11). For example, the vast majority of states currently assess pupils' writing performance, while 26 states assess such things as speaking and listening skills. (Setting the standard from state to state. *Education week special report*, April 12, 1995, 23–35.) Second, increased classroom emphasis on problem solving, higher-level thinking, and real-world reasoning skills has created a reliance on performance and product assessments to demonstrate pupil learning. Third, performance assessments can provide some pupils who do poorly on selection-type tests an opportunity to show their achievement in alternative ways.

Performance-Oriented Subjects

All schools expect pupils to demonstrate communication skills, so reading, writing, and speaking are perhaps the most common areas of classroom performance assessment. Likewise, simple psychomotor skills such as being able to sit in a chair or hold a pencil, as well as more sophisticated skills such as setting up laboratory equipment or using tools to build a birdhouse, are a fundamental part of school life. Closely related are the athletic performances taught in physical education classes.

There also is a growing emphasis on using performance assessment to determine pupils' understanding of the concepts they are taught and measure their ability to apply procedural knowledge. The argument is that if pupils really grasp a concept or process, they can explain and use it to solve real-life problems. For example, after teaching pupils about money and making change, the teacher may assess learning by having pupils count out the money needed to purchase objects from the classroom "store" or act as storekeeper and make change for other pupils' purchases. Or, rather than giving a multiple-choice test on the chemical reactions that help identify unknown substances, the teacher could give each pupil an unknown substance and have them go through the process of identifying it. These kinds of hands-on demonstrations of concept mastery are growing in popularity.

Teachers also constantly assess pupils' feelings, values, attitudes, and emotions. When a teacher checks the "satisfactory" rating under the category "works hard" or "obeys school rules" on a pupil's report card, the teacher bases this judgment on observations of the pupil's performance. Teachers rely upon observations of pupil performance to collect evidence about important behaviors such as getting along with peers, working independently, following rules, and self-control.

Most teachers recognize the importance of balancing supply and selection assessments with performance and product assessments, as the following comments indicate.

> It's not reasonable to grade reading without including the pupil's oral reading skills or their comprehension of what they read. I always spend some time when it's grading time listening to and rating my pupils' oral reading and comprehension quality.

My kids know that a large part of their grade depends on how well they follow safety procedures and take proper care of the tools they use. They know I'm always on the lookout for times when they don't do these things and that it will count against them if I see them.

I wouldn't want anyone to assess my teaching competence solely on the basis of my students' paper-and-pencil test scores. I would want to be seen interacting with the kids, teaching them, and attending to their needs. Why should I confine my assessments of my pupils solely to paper-and-pencil methods?

Early Childhood and Special Needs Pupils

While performance assessment cuts across subject areas and grade levels, it is heavily used in early childhood and special education settings. Because preschool, kindergarten, and primary school pupils are limited in their communication skills and are still in the process of being socialized into the school culture, much assessment information is obtained by observing their performances and products. Assessment at this age focuses on gross and fine motor development, verbal and auditory acuity, and visual development, as well as social behaviors. Box 8.1 illustrates some of the important early childhood behaviors and skills that teachers assess by performance-based means. These examples provide a sense of how heavily the early childhood curriculum is weighted toward performance outcomes.

Many special needs pupils—especially those who exhibit multiple and severe disabilities in their cognitive, affective, and psychomotor development—are provided instruction focused on self-help skills such as getting dressed, brushing teeth, making a sandwich, and operating a

---

Box 8.1   Early Childhood Behavior Areas

Gross motor development: Roll over, sit erect without toppling over, walk a straight line, throw a ball, jump on one or two feet, skip

Fine motor development: Cut with scissors, trace an object, color in the lines, draw geometric forms (circles, squares, triangles, etc.), penmanship, left-to-right progression in reading and writing, eye-hand coordination

Verbal and auditory acuity: Identify sounds, listen to certain sounds and ignore others (tune out distractions), discriminate between sounds and words that sound alike (e.g., "fix" vs. "fish"), remember numbers in sequence, follow directions, remember the correct order of events, pronounce words and letters

Visual development: Find a letter, number, or object similar to one shown by the teacher; copy a shape; identify shapes and embedded figures; reproduce a design given by the teacher; differentiate objects by size, color, and shape

Social acclimation: Listen to the teacher, follow a time schedule, share, wait one's turn, respect the property of others

vacuum cleaner. Pupils are taught to carry out these performances through many, many repetitions. Observation of pupils as they perform these activities is the main assessment technique special education teachers use to identify performance mastery or areas needing further work.

To summarize, performance assessment gathers evidence about pupils by observing and rating their performance or products. Although appropriate at all grade levels, it is especially useful in subjects that place heavy emphasis on performances or products of some kind, such as art, music, public speaking, shop, foreign language, and physical education. It is also very useful with early childhood and special needs pupils whose lack of basic communication, psychomotor, and social skills forces the teacher to rely upon pupil performances to assess instructional success.

Developing Performance Assessments

A diving competition is an instructive example of a skill that is assessed by a performance assessment. Submitting a written essay describing how to perform various dives or answering a multiple-choice test about diving rules are hardly appropriate ways to assess diving *performance.* Rather, a valid assessment of diving performance requires seeing the diver actually perform. And, to make the assessment reliable, the diver must perform a series of dives, not just one.

Diving judges rate dives using a scale that has 21 possible numerical scores that can be awarded (e.g., 0.0, 0.5, 1.0, . . . 5.5, 6.0, 6.5, . . . 9.0, 9.5, 10.0). They observe a very complicated performance made up of many body movements that together take about 2 seconds to complete. The judges do not have the benefit of slow motion or instant replay to review the performance and they cannot discuss the dive with one another. If their attention strays for even a second, they miss a large portion of the performance. Yet, when the scores are flashed on the scoreboard the judges inevitably are in very close agreement. Rarely do all judges give a dive the exact same score, but rarely is there more than a 1-point difference between any two judges' scores. This is amazing agreement among observers for such a short, complicated performance.

With this example in mind, let's consider the four essential features of all formal performance assessments, whether it be a diving competition, an oral speech, a book report, a typing exercise, a science fair project, or something else. This overview will then be followed by a more extensive discussion of each feature. Briefly, every performance assessment should

- have a clear purpose that identifies the decision to be made from the performance assessment;
- identify observable aspects of the pupil's performance or product that can be judged;
- provide an appropriate setting for eliciting and judging the performance or product; and
- provide a judgment or score to describe performance.

Define the Purpose of Assessment

In a diving competition, the purpose of the assessment is to rank each diver's performance in order to identify the best divers. Each dive receives a score and the highest total score wins the competition. Suppose, however, that dives were being performed during practice, prior to a competition. The diver's coach would observe the practice dives, but the coach's main concern would be not with the overall dive, but with examining the many specific features of each dive that the judges will score during a competition. Consequently, the coach would "score" the practice dive formatively, identifying the diver's strengths and weaknesses for all aspect of each dive. The specific areas in which the diver was weak would likely be emphasized in practice.

Performance assessments are particularly suited to such diagnosis because they can provide information about how a pupil performs each of the specific criteria that make up a more general performance or product. This criterion-by-criterion assessment makes it easy to identify the strong and weak points of a pupil's performance. When the performance criteria are stated in terms of observable pupil behaviors or product characteristics, as they should be, remediation is made easy. Each suggestion for improvement can be described in specific terms—e.g., "report to group project area on time," "wait your turn to speak," "do your share of the group work."

Teachers use performance assessment for many purposes: grading pupils, constructing portfolios of pupil work, diagnosing pupil learning, helping pupils recognize the important steps in a performance or product, providing concrete examples of pupil work for parent conferences. Whatever the purpose of performance assessment, it should be specified at the beginning of the assessment process so that proper performance criteria and scoring procedures can be established.

Identify Performance Criteria

Performance criteria are the specific aspects a pupil should perform to properly carry out a performance or produce a product. They are at the heart of successful performance assessment, yet they are the area in which most problems occur.

When teachers first think about assessing performance, they tend to think in terms of general performances such as oral reading, giving a speech, following safety rules in the laboratory, penmanship, writing a book report, organizing ideas, fingering a keyboard, or getting along with peers. In reality, such performances cannot be assessed until they are broken down into the more specific aspects or characteristics that comprise them. These more narrow aspects and characteristics are the performance criteria that teachers will observe and judge.

Studies show that many classroom teachers lack skill in assessing and are unprepared to assess their pupils, especially on performance assessments (Fager, Plake, and Impara, 1997). Relatively few teachers are required to pass a course in classroom assessment in their teacher preparation. Only

Box 8.2   Examples of Performance Criteria

Working in Groups	Playing the Piano	Writing a Book Report
Reports to group project area on time	Sits upright with feet on floor (or pedal, when necessary)	States the author and title
Starts work on own	Arches fingers on keys	Names and type of the book (fiction, adventure, historical, ets.)
Shares information	Plays without pauses or interruptions	Describes what the book was about in four or more sentences
Contributes ideas	Maintains even tempo	States an opinion of the book
Listens to others	Plays correct notes	Gives three reasons to support the opinion
Waits turn to speak	Holds all note values for indicated duration	Uses correct spelling, punctuation, and capitalization
Follows instructions	Follows score dynamics (forte, crescendo, decrescendo)	
Courteous to other group members	Melody can be heard above other harmonization	
Helps to solve group problems	Phrases according to score (staccato and legato)	
Considers viewpoints of others	Follows score pedal markings	
Carries out share of group-determined activities		
Completes assigned tasks on time		

15 states require that preservice teachers take an assessment course (Stiggins, 1999). Teachers tend to be better at providing interesting tasks and performances for their pupils than they are at identifying the criteria that describe what makes a good task or performance. Often, the first question a teacher asks is "What will we do?" A more appropriate question to ask first, especially with performance assessments, is "What do I want my pupils to learn?" (Arter, 1999).

Box 8.2 shows three sets of criteria for assessing pupils' performance when (1) working in groups, (2) playing the piano, and (3) writing a book report. Criteria such as these focus teachers' instruction and assessments in the same way that diving criteria enable judges to evaluate diving performance. Notice how the performance criteria clearly identify the important aspects of the performance or product being assessed. Well-stated performance criteria are at the heart of successful efforts to instruct and assess performances and products.

In order to define performance criteria, a teacher must first decide if a process or a product will be observed. Will processes such as typing or oral reading be assessed, or will products such as a typed letter or book report be assessed? In the former case, criteria are needed to judge the pupil's actual performance of targeted criteria; in the latter, criteria are needed to judge the end product of those behaviors. In some cases, both process and product can be assessed. For example, a first grade teacher assessed both process and product when she (1) observed a pupil writing to determine how the pupil held the pencil, positioned the paper, and manipulated the pencil and (2) judged the finished, handwritten product to assess how well the pupil formed his letters. Notice that the teacher observed different things according to whether she was interested in the pupil's handwriting *process* or handwriting *product*. It is for this reason that teachers must know what they want to observe before performance criteria can be identified (Marzano, Pickering, and McTighe, 1993).

The key to identifying performance criteria is to break down an overall performance or product into its component parts. It is these parts that will be observed and judged. Consider, for example, a product assessment of eighth graders' written paragraphs. The purpose of the assessment is to judge pupils' ability to write a paragraph on a topic of their choice. In preparing to judge the completed paragraph, a teacher initially listed the following performance criteria:

- First sentence
- Appropriate topic sentence
- Good supporting ideas
- Good vocabulary
- Complete sentences
- Capitalization
- Spelling
- Conclusion
- Handwriting

These performance criteria do identify important areas of a written paragraph, but the areas are vague and poorly stated. What, for example, is meant by "first sentence"? What is an "appropriate" topic sentence or "good" vocabulary? What should be examined in judging "capitalization," "spelling," and "handwriting"? If a teacher cannot answer these questions for him or herself, how can he or she provide suitable examples or instruction for pupils? Performance criteria need to be specific enough to focus the teacher on well-defined characteristics of the performance or product. They must also be specific enough to permit the teacher to convey to pupils, in terms they can understand, the specific features that define the desired performance or product. Once defined, the criteria permit consistent teacher assessments of performance and consistent communication with pupils about their learning.

In general, performance criteria are clearly stated if another teacher at your grade level can understand your performance criteria without you explaining them. Following is a revised version of the performance criteria for a well-organized paragraph. Note the difference in clarity and how the revised version focuses the teacher and students on very specific features of the paragraph—ones that are important and will be assessed. Before assigning the task, the teacher wisely decided to share and explain the performance criteria to the pupils.

- Indents first sentence
- Topic sentence sets main idea of paragraph
- Following sentences support main idea
- Sentences arranged in logical order

- Uses age-appropriate vocabulary
- Writes in complete sentences
- Capitalizes proper nouns and first words in sentences
- Makes no more than three spelling errors
- Conclusion follows logically from prior sentences
- Handwriting is legible

Cautions in Developing Performance Criteria

A few words of caution are appropriate here. First, it is important to understand that the previous example of performance criteria is not the only one that describes the characteristics of a well-written paragraph. Different teachers might identify different criteria that they feel are more important or more suitable for their pupils than some of the ones in our example. Thus, emphasis should not be upon identifying the best or only set of criteria for a performance or product, but rather upon stating criteria that are meaningful, important, and can be understood by the pupils.

Second, it is possible to break down most school performances and products into many very narrow criteria. However, a lengthy list of performance criteria becomes ineffective because teachers rarely have the time to observe and assess a large number of very specific performance criteria for each pupil. Too many criteria make the observation process intrusive, with the teacher hovering over the pupil, rapidly checking off behaviors, and often interfering with a pupil's performance.

Numerous detailed performance criteria are useful only when the observer has the time to carry out in-depth observation of a single pupil. As these conditions are rare in most classrooms, it is counterproductive to spend great amounts of time listing performance criteria that cannot be observed and assessed. For classroom performance assessment to be manageable and meaningful, a balance must be established between specificity and practicality. The key to attaining this balance is to identify the *essential* criteria associated with a performance or product. Six to twelve performance criteria is a manageable number for most classroom teachers to emphasize.

Third, the process of identifying performance criteria is an ongoing one that is rarely completed after the first attempt. Initial performance criteria will need to be revised and clarified based on experience from their use, in order to provide the focus needed for valid and reliable assessment. To aid this process, teachers should think about the performance or product they wish to observe and reflect on its key aspects. They can also examine a few actual products or performances as bases for revising their initial list of criteria.

The following list shows the initial set of performance criteria a teacher wrote to assess pupils' oral reports.

- Speaks clearly and slowly
- Pronounces correctly
- Makes eye contact
- Exhibits good posture when presenting

- Exhibits good effort
- Presents with feeling
- Understands the topic
- Exhibits enthusiastic attitude
- Organizes

Note the lack of specificity in many of the criteria: "slowly," "correctly," "good," "understands," and enthusiastic attitude." These criteria hide more than they reveal about what to observe, making it hard for the teacher both to explain to pupils precisely what is expected of them and to develop assessments that are valid and reliable. After reflecting on and observing a few oral presentations, the teacher revised and sharpened the performance criteria as shown in the following list. Note that the teacher first divided the general performance into three areas (physical expression, vocal expression, and verbal expression) and then identified a few important performance criteria within each of these areas. It is not essential to divide the performance criteria into separate sections, but sometimes it is useful in focusing the teacher and pupils.

I. Physical expression
- Stands straight and faces audience
- Changes facial expression with changes in tone of the report
- Maintains eye contact with audience

II. Vocal expression
- Speaks in a steady, clear voice
- Varies tone to emphasize points
- Speaks loudly enough to be heard by audience
- Paces words in an even flow
- Enunciates each word

III. Verbal expression
- Chooses precise words to convey meaning
- Avoids unnecessary repetition
- States sentences with complete thoughts or ideas
- Organizes information logically
- Summarizes main points at conclusion

Developing Observable Performance Criteria

The value and richness of performance and product assessments depend heavily on identifying performance criteria that can be observed and judged. It is important that the criteria be clear in the teacher's mind and that the pupils be taught the criteria. The following guidelines should prove useful for this purpose.

1. *Select the performance or product to be assessed and either perform it yourself or imagine yourself performing it.* Think to yourself, "What would I have to do in order to complete this task? What steps would I have to follow?" You may also observe pupils performing the task and identify the important elements in their performance. Finally, you can actually carry out the performance yourself, recording and studying your performance or product.

2. *List the important aspects of the performance or product.* What specific behaviors or attributes are most important to the successful completion of the task? What behaviors have been emphasized in instruction? The specific behaviors or attributes identified will become the performance criteria that guide instruction, observation, and assessment. Include the important aspects ones and exclude the irrelevant ones.

3. *Try to limit the number of performance criteria, so they all can be observed during a pupil's performance.* This is less important when one is assessing a product, but even then it is better to assess a limited number of key criteria than a large number that vary widely in their importance. Remember, you will have to observe and judge performance on each of the criteria identified. A good rule of thumb is to limit the number of performance criteria to between six and twelve.

4. *If possible, have groups of teachers think through the important criteria included in a task.* Because all first grade teachers assess oral reading in their classrooms and because the criteria for successful oral reading do not differ much from one first grade classroom to another, a group effort to define performance criteria will likely save time and produce a more complete set of criteria than that produced by any single teacher. Similar group efforts are useful for other common performances or products such as book reports, science fair projects, and the like. When teachers within and across grades in a school utilize similar criteria in instructing and assessing performances and projects, it is reassuring to pupils.

5. *Express the performance criteria in terms of observable pupil behaviors or product characteristics.* The performance criteria should direct attention to things the pupil is doing or characteristics of a product that the pupil has produced. Be specific when stating the performance criteria. For example, do not write "The child works." Instead, write "The child remains focused on the task for at least four minutes." Instead of "organization," write "Information is presented in a logical sequence."

6. *Do not use ambiguous words that cloud the meaning of the performance criteria.* The worst offenders in this regard are adverbs that end in *ly.* Other words to avoid are "good" and "appropriate." Thus, criteria such as "appropriate organization," "speaks correct*ly*," "writes neat*ly*," and "performs graceful*ly*" are ambiguous and leave interpretation of performance up to the observer. The observer's interpretation may vary from time to time and from pupil to pupil, diminishing the fairness and usefulness of the assessment. Instead of "organizes adequately" one might substitute "has an identifiable beginning, middle, and end" or "presents ideas in a logical order." Instead of "speaks correctly," one might substitute "enunciates each word," "can be heard in all parts of the room," or "does not run sentences together." Notice also how useful these more descriptive performance criteria are for explaining to pupils how they can improve their performance. The particular criteria will depend upon the teacher and his or her instruction, but the criteria should be stated in terms of observable behaviors and product characteristics, preferably ones that pupils and other teachers could understand. Review and revise criteria as necessary based upon experience using them.

7. *Arrange the performance criteria in the order in which they are likely to be observed.* This will save time when observing and will maintain primary focus on the performance.

8. *Check for existing performance criteria before defining your own.* The performance criteria associated with giving an oral speech, reading aloud, using a microscope, writing a persuasive paragraph, cutting with scissors, and the like have been listed by many people. No one who reads this book will be the first to try to assess these and most other common school performances. The moral here is that one need not reinvent the wheel every time a wheel is needed. Many sources contain performance criteria for many school skills, and these can and should be used as needed. Box 8.3 summarizes the foregoing guidelines.

Regardless of the particular performance or product assessed, clearly stated performance criteria are critical to the success of both instruction and assessment. The criteria define the important aspects of a performance or product, guide what pupils should be taught, and produce a focus for both the teacher and pupil when assessing performance. Although performance and product assessments are widely used in most classrooms, they are frequently used in the absence of well-articulated performance criteria. If the teacher does not know what makes a good essay response or a good science fair project, how are pupils to be guided during instruction and how are they to be assessed fairly? Clear performance criteria are needed, and the tasks used to teach and assess the desired performance should be aligned to the criteria (McTighe, 1996). Box 8.4 presents basic guidelines for stating good performance criteria.

Box 8.3   Guidelines for Stating Performance Criteria

1. Identify the steps or features of the performance or task to be assessed by imagining yourself performing it, observing pupils performing it, or inspecting finished products.
2. List the important aspects of the performance or product.
3. Try to keep the number of performance criteria small enough so that they can be reasonably observed and judged. Six to twelve criteria is a good range to use.
4. Have teachers think through the criteria as a group.
5. Express the criteria in terms of observable pupil behaviors or product characteristics.
6. Avoid vague and ambiguous words like "correctly," "appropriately," and "good."
7. Arrange the performance criteria in the order in which they are likely to be observed.
8. Check for existing performance assessment instruments to use or modify before constructing your own.

> ## Box 8.4   Suggestions for Stating Performance Criteria
>
> 1. State the essential or important performance criteria
> 2. State performance criteria briefly
> 3. Insure that the performance criteria are linked to instruction
> 4. Include performance criteria that require pupil thinking and interpreting
> 5. State the performance criteria in language appropriate for the pupils
> 6. Show and explain the performance criteria to pupils

Provide a Setting to Elicit and Observe the Performance

Once the performance criteria are defined, a setting in which to observe the performance or product must be selected or established. Depending on the nature of the performance or product, the teacher may observe behaviors as they naturally occur in the classroom or set up a specific situation in which the pupils must perform. There are two considerations in deciding whether to observe naturally occurring behaviors or to set up a more controlled exercise: (1) the frequency with which the performance naturally occurs in the classroom and (2) the seriousness of the decision to be made.

If the performance occurs infrequently during normal classroom activity, it may be more efficient to structure a situation in which pupils must perform the desired behaviors. For example, in the normal flow of classroom activities, pupils rarely have the opportunity to give a planned 5-minute speech, so the teacher should set up an exercise in which each pupil must develop and give a 5-minute speech. Oral reading, on the other hand, occurs frequently enough in many elementary classrooms that performance can be observed as part of the normal flow of reading instruction.

The importance of the decision to be made from a performance assessment also influences the context in which observation takes place. In general, the more important the decision, the more structured the assessment environment should be. A course grade, for example, represents an important decision about a pupil. If performance assessments contribute to grading, evidence should be gathered under structured, formal circumstances so that every pupil has a fair and equal chance to exhibit his or her achievement. The validity of the assessment is likely to be improved when the setting is similar and familiar to all pupils.

Regardless of the nature of the assessment, evidence obtained from a single assessment describes only one example of a pupil's performance. For a variety of reasons such as illness, home problems, or other distractions, pupil performance at a single time may not provide a reliable indication of the pupil's true achievement. To be certain that one has an accurate indication of what a pupil can and cannot do, multiple observations and products are useful. If the different observations produce similar performance, a teacher can have confidence in the evidence and use it in decision making. If different observations contradict one another, more information should be obtained.

Develop a Score to Describe the Performance

The final step in performance assessment is to score pupils' performance. As in previous steps, the nature of the decision to be made influences the judgmental system used. Scoring a performance assessment can be holistic or analytic, just like scoring an essay question. In situations such as group placement, selection, or grading, holistic scoring is most useful. To make such decisions, a teacher seeks to describe an individual's performance using a single, overall score. On the other hand, if the assessment purpose is to diagnose pupil difficulties or certify pupil mastery of each individual performance criterion, then analytic scoring, with a separate score or rating on each performance criterion, is appropriate. In either case, the performance criteria dictate the scoring or rating approach that is adopted.

In most classrooms, the teacher is both the observer and the scorer. In situations where an important decision is to be made, additional observers/scorers may be added. Thus, it is common for performance assessments in athletic, music, debate, and art competitions to have more than a single judge in order to make scoring more fair.

A number of options exist for collecting and recording observations of pupil performance: anecdotal records, checklists, rating scales, and rubrics, and portfolios. The following sections explore these options in detail.

Anecdotal Records

Written accounts of significant, individual pupil events and behaviors the teacher has observed are called **anecdotal records.** Only those observations that have special significance and that cannot be obtained from other classroom assessment methods should be included in an anecdotal record. Figure 8.1 shows an example of an anecdotal record. Notice that it provides information about the learner, the date of observation, the name of the teacher observing, and a factual description of the event.

Most teachers have difficulty identifying particular events or behaviors that merit inclusion in an anecdotal record. What is significant and important in the life of a pupil is not always apparent at the time an event or behavior occurs. From the hundreds of observations made each day, how is

---

PUPIL   *Lynn Gregory*   DATE   *12/3/99*
OBSERVER   *J. Ricketts*

All term Lynn has been quiet and passive, rarely interacting w/classmates in class or on the playground. Today Lynn suddenly "opened up" and wanted continual interaction w/classmates. She could not settle down, kept circulating around the room until she became bothersome to me and her classmates. I tried to settle her down, but was unsuccessful.

FIGURE 8.1   *Anecdotal Record for Lynn Gregory*

a teacher to select the one that might be important enough to write down? It may take many observations over many days to recognize which events really are significant. Moreover, anecdotal records are time-consuming to prepare and need to be written up soon after the event or behavior is observed, while it is fresh in the teacher's mind. This is not always possible. For these reasons, anecdotal records are not extensively used by teachers. This does not mean that teachers do not observe and judge classroom events—we know that they do. It simply means that they seldom write down descriptions of these events.

Checklists

A **checklist** is a written list of performance criteria. As a pupil's performance is observed or product judged, the scorer determines whether the performance or the product meets each performance criterion. If it does, a checkmark is placed next to that criterion, indicating that it was observed; if it does not, the checkmark is omitted. Figure 8.2 shows a completed checklist for Rick Gray's oral presentation. The performance criteria for this checklist were presented on page 239.

Checklists are diagnostic, reusable, and capable of charting pupil progress. They provide a detailed record of pupils' performances, one that can and should be shown to pupils to help them see where improvement is needed. Rick Gray's teacher could sit down with him after his presentation and point out both the criteria on which he performed well and the areas that need to improvement. Because it focuses on specific performances, a checklist provides diagnostic information. The same checklist can be reused, with dirrerent pupils or with the same pupil over time. In fact, using the same checklist more than once is an easy way to obtain information about a pupil's improvement over time.

There are, however, disadvantages associated with checklists. One important disadvantage is that checklists give the teacher only two choices for each criterion: performed or not performed. A checklist provides no middle ground for scoring. Suppose that Rick Gray stood straight and faced the audience most of the time during his oral presentation, or paced his words evenly except in one brief part of the speech when he spoke too quickly and ran his words together. How should his teacher score him on these performance criteria? Should Rick receive a check because he did them most of the time, or should he not receive a check because his performance was flawed? Sometimes this is not an easy choice. A checklist forces the teacher to make an absolute decision for each performance criterion, even though a pupil's performance is somewhere between these extremes.

A second disadvantage of checklists is the difficulty of summarizing a pupil's performance into a single score. We saw how useful checklists can be for diagnosing pupils' strengths and weaknesses. But what if a teacher wants to summarize performance across a number of criteria to arrive at a single score for grading purposes?

One way to summarize Rick's performance into a single score is to translate the number of performance criteria he successfully demonstrated

NAME *Rick Gray*   DATE *Nov. 11, 1998*

   I. Physical Expression

      ✓ A. Stands straight and faces audience

      ____ B. Changes facial expression with changes in tone of the presentation

      ✓ C. Maintains eye contact with audience

   II. Vocal Expression

      ✓ A. Speaks in a steady, clear voice

      ✓ B. Varies tone to emphasize points

      ____ C. Speaks loudly enough to be heard by audience

      ✓ D. Paces words in an even flow

      ____ E. Enunciates each word

   III. Verbal Expression

      ____ A. Chooses precise words to convey meaning

      ✓ B. Avoids unnecessary repetition

      ✓ C. States sentences with complete thoughts or ideas

      ✓ D. Organizes information logically

      ✓ E. Summarizes main points at conclusion

FIGURE 8.2   *Checklist Results for an Oral Presentation*

into a percentage. For example, there were 13 performance criteria on the oral presentation checklist and Rick demonstrated nine of them during his presentation. Assuming each criterion is equally important, Rick's performance translates into a score of 69 percent ($9/13 \times 100 = 69\%$). Thus, Rick demonstrated 69 percent of the desired performance criteria. (In Chapter 10 we will discuss the way scores like Rick's 69 percent are turned into grades.)

A second, and better, way to summarize performance would be for the teacher to set up standards for rating pupils' performance. Suppose Rick's teacher set up the following set of standards:

Excellent	12 or 13	performance criteria shown
Good	9 to 11	performance criteria shown
Fair	5 to 8	performance criteria shown
Poor	5 or less	performance criteria shown

These standards allow the teacher to summarize performance on a scale that goes from excellent to poor. The scale could also go from a grade of A to one of D, depending on the type of scoring the teacher uses. The same standard would be used to summarize each pupil's performance. Rick performed nine of the thirteen criteria, and the teacher's standard indicates that his performance should be classified as "good" or "B." Of course, there are many such standards that can be set up and the one shown is only an example. In establishing standards, it is advisable to keep the summarizing rules as simple as possible.

Rating Scales

Although they are similar to checklists, **rating scales** allow the observer to judge performance along a continuum rather than as a dichotomy. Both checklists and rating scales are based upon a set of performance criteria, and it is common for the same set of performance criteria to be used in both a rating scale and a checklist. However, a checklist gives the observer two categories for judging, while a rating scale gives more than two.

Three of the most common types of rating scales are the numerical, graphic, and descriptive scales. Figure 8.3 shows an example of each of these scales as applied to two specific performance criteria for giving an oral presentation. In numerical scales, a number stands for a point on the rating scale. Thus, in the example, "1" corresponds to the pupil *always* performing the behavior, "2" to the pupil *usually* performing the behavior, and so on. Graphic scales require the rater to mark a position on a line divided into sections based upon a scale. The rater marks an "X" at that point on the line that best describes the pupil's performance. Descriptive rating scales, also called **scoring rubrics,** require the rater to choose among different descriptions of actual performance (Wiggins and McTighe, 1998; Goodrich, 1997). In descriptive rating scales, different descriptions are used to represent different levels of pupil performance. To score, the teacher picks the description that comes closest to the pupil's actual performance. A judgment of the teacher determines the grade.

Regardless of the type of rating scale one chooses, two general rules will improve their use. The first rule is to limit the number of rating categories. There is a tendency to think that the greater the number of rating categories to choose from, the better the rating scale. In practice, this is not the case. Few observers can make reliable discriminations in pupil performance across more than five rating categories. Adding a larger number of categories on a rating scale is likely to make the ratings less, not more, reliable. Stick to three to five well-defined and distinct rating scale points, as shown in Figure 8.3.

The second rule is to use the same rating scale for each performance criterion. This is not usually possible in descriptive rating scales where the descriptions vary with each performance criterion. However, for numerical and graphic scales, it is best to select a single rating scale and use that scale for all performance criteria. Using many different rating categories requires

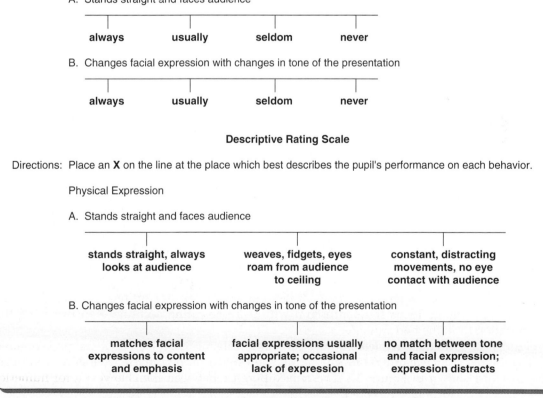

Numerical Rating Scale

Directions: Indicate how often the pupil performs each of these behaviors while giving an oral presentation. For each behavior circle **1** if the pupil **always** performs the behavior, **2** if the pupil **usually** performs the behavior, **3** if the pupil **seldom** performs the behavior, and **4** if the pupil **never** performs the behavior.

Physical Expression

A. Stands straight and faces audience

      1   2   3   4

B. Changes facial expression with changes in tone of the presentation

      1   2   3   4

Graphic Rating Scale

Directions: Place an **X** on the line which shows how often the pupil did each of the behaviors listed while giving an oral presentation.

Physical Expression

A. Stands straight and faces audience

    always   usually   seldom   never

B. Changes facial expression with changes in tone of the presentation

    always   usually   seldom   never

Descriptive Rating Scale

Directions: Place an **X** on the line at the place which best describes the pupil's performance on each behavior.

Physical Expression

A. Stands straight and faces audience

    stands straight, always looks at audience   weaves, fidgets, eyes roam from audience to ceiling   constant, distracting movements, no eye contact with audience

B. Changes facial expression with changes in tone of the presentation

    matches facial expressions to content and emphasis   facial expressions usually appropriate; occasional lack of expression   no match between tone and facial expression; expression distracts

FIGURE 8.3   *Rating Scale Results for an Oral Presentation*

NAME   *Sarah Jackson*   DATE   *Nov. 11, 1999*

Directions: Indicate how often the pupil performs each of these behaviors while giving an oral presentation.
For each behavior **circle 4** if the pupil **always** performs the behavior, **3** if the pupil **usually**
performs the behavior, **2** if the pupil **seldom** performs the behavior, and **1** if the pupil **never**
performs the behavior.

I. Physical Expression

(4) 3 2 1   A. Stands straight and faces audience

4 3 (2) 1   B. Changes facial expression with changes in tone of the presentation

4 (3) 2 1   C. Maintains eye contact with audience

II. Vocal Expression

(4) 3 2 1   A. Speaks in a steady, clear voice

4 (3) 2 1   B. Varies tone to emphasize points

4 3 (2) 1   C. Speaks loudly enough to be heard by audience

4 (3) 2 1   D. Paces words in an even flow

4 3 (2) 1   E. Enunciates each word

III. Verbal Expression

4 3 (2) 1   A. Chooses precise words to convey meaning

4 (3) 2 1   B. Avoids unnecessary repetition

(4) 3 2 1   C. States sentences with complete thoughts or ideas

(4) 3 2 1   D. Organizes information logically

4 (3) 2 1   E. Summarizes main points at conclusion

FIGURE 8.4   *Types of Rating Scales*

the observer to change focus frequently and will decrease rating accuracy by distracting the
rater's attention from the performance.

Figure 8.4 shows the completed numerical rating scale for Sarah Jackson's oral presentation.
Note that the performance criteria for the rating scale shown in Figure 8.4 are identical to those
on the checklist shown in Figure 8.2. The only difference between the checklist and the rating
scale is the way performance is scored.

While rating scales provide more categories for assessing a pupil's performance, and thereby
provide detailed diagnostic information, the multiple rating categories complicate the process of

summarizing performance across criteria to arrive at a pupil's overall score. With a checklist, summarization is reduced to giving credit for check criteria and no credit for uncheck criteria. This cannot be done with a rating scale because performance is judged in terms of *degree,* not presence or absence. A teacher must treat ratings of "always," "usually," "seldom," and "never" differently from each other, or there is no point to having the different rating categories.

Numerical summarization is the most straightforward and commonly used approach to summarizing performance on rating scales. It assigns a point value to each category in the scale and sums the points across the performance criteria. For example, consider Sarah Jackson's ratings in Figure 8.4. To obtain a summary score for Sarah's performance, one can assign 4 points to a rating of "always," 3 points to a rating of "usually," 2 points to a rating of "seldom," and 1 point to a rating of "never." The numbers 4, 3, 2, and 1 match the four possible ratings for each performance criterion, with 4 representing the most desirable response and 1 the least desirable. Thus, high scores indicate good performance. Note that, before summarizing Sarah's performance into a single score, it is important for the teacher to identify areas of weakness so that Sarah can be guided to improve her oral presentations.

Sarah's total score, 39, can be determined by adding the circled numbers. The highest possible score on the rating scale is 52; if a pupil was rated "always" on each performance criterion, the pupil's total score would be 52 (4 points × 13 performance criteria). Thus, Sarah scored 39 out of a possible 52 points. In this manner, a total score can be determined for each pupil rated. This score can be turned into a percentage by dividing it by 52, the total number of points available ($39/52 \times 100 = 75\%$).

Rubrics

Scoring rubrics or descriptive summarization provide a second way to summarize performance on checklists and rating scales. A rubric is a set of clear expectations or criteria used to help teachers and pupils focus on what is valued in a subject, topic, or activity. Scoring rubrics are brief, written descriptions of different levels of pupil performance, based on the performance criteria. They are constructed by combining descriptions of different qualities of performance. Each set of descriptions represents a different level of pupil performance. Rubrics can be used to summarize both pupil performances and products.

The following rubric was used to summarize Sarah Jackson's performance on her oral presentation.

Excellent   Pupil consistently faces audience, stands straight, and maintains eye contact; voice projects well and clearly; pacing and tone variation appropriate; well organized, points logically and completely presented; brief summary at end.

Good   Pupil usually faces audience, stands straight, and makes eye contact; voice projection good, but pace and clarity vary during talk; well organized but repetitive; occasional poor choice of words and incomplete summary.

Fair   Pupil fidgety; some eye contact and facial expression change; uneven voice projection, not heard by all in room, some words slurred; loosely organized, repetitive, contains many incomplete thoughts; little summarization.

Poor   Pupil body movements distracting, little eye contact or voice change; words slurred, speaks in monotone, does not project voice beyond first few rows, no consistent or logical pacing; rambling presentation, little organization with no differentiation between major and minor points; no summary.

Notice that this rubric summarizes the performance criteria into four different levels of performance. In this example, the teacher labeled the four descriptions "excellent," "good," "fair," and "poor." Other teachers might have used other grading terms. In looking at Sarah's numerical ratings and trying to describe her overall performance in terms of the rubric, it is clear that her performance was neither excellent nor poor. Her performance is between good and fair. Sarah's teacher judged that she had more 3's and 4's than 1's and 2's and thus placed her in the "good" rubric category. Note that because teachers cannot separate out single criteria in rubrics, they often have to select a category that best, but not completely, describes the pupil's overall performance.

Rubrics provide a set of guidelines that can help pupils to monitor their own work as well as that of their peers. They can focus teachers on teaching and assessing what is important and valued in pupils' work. They also reduce scoring subjectivity.

Note the difference between checklists and rating scales, which can provide specific diagnostic information about pupil strengths and weaknesses, and scoring rubrics, which summarize overall performance in a general way that provides much less specific diagnostic information.

Rubrics are especially useful for setting pupil achievement targets and for obtaining a summative, single-score representation of pupil performance. They are less useful for diagnostic purposes.

✖ Validity and Reliability of Performance Assessments

Because formal performance assessments are used to make decisions about pupils, it is important that they be valid and reliable. Validity is concerned with whether a teacher's assessments measure the intended results. Reliability is concerned with whether pupils' assessment performances are consistent or dependable. This section first discusses ways teachers can help pupils, prepare for performance assessments and describes some of the problems inherent in judging performance assessment. It then considers steps that can be taken to improve the validity and reliability of performance assessments.

Chapter 7 discussed ways teachers get their pupils ready for assessment. First and foremost, teachers must provide good instruction on whatever objectives or criteria their pupils are expected to learn and demonstrate. Pupils learn to set up and focus microscopes, build bookcases, write book reports, give oral speeches, measure with a ruler, perform musical selections, and speak French the same way they learn to solve simultaneous equations, find countries on a map, write a topic sentence, or balance a chemical equation. They are given instruction and practice. Achievement depends upon pupils being taught the things on which they are being assessed. One of the advantages of performance assessments is their explicit criteria that help teachers focus on aligning instruction and assessment.

In preparing pupils for performance assessment, the teacher should inform and explain the criteria on which they will be judged (Mehrens, Popham, and Ryan, 1998). In many classrooms, teachers and pupils jointly discuss and define criteria for a desired performance or product (Herbert, 1992). This helps pupils to understand what is expected of them by identifying the important dimensions of the performance or product. Another, less interactive way to do this is for the teacher to give pupils a copy of the checklist or rating form that will be used during the performance assessment. If performance criteria are not made clear to pupils, they may perform poorly not because they are incapable but because they were not aware of the teacher's expectations and the criteria for a good performance. In such cases, the performance ratings do not reflect the pupil's true ability to perform, and the grade received could lead to invalid decisions about the pupil.

Scoring performance assessments is a difficult and often time-consuming activity. The limits and difficulties described for scoring essay questions in Chapter 7 are also applicable to performance assessments. The product or process to be scored is complex and often lengthy. Unlike selection items, teachers' interpretation and judgment are necessary for scoring performances and products. Each student will produce or construct a performance or product that is different from those of other students. Consequently, the more criteria to be addressed and the more variation in the products or performances students produce, the more time-consuming and fatiguing scoring becomes (Linn, Baker, and Dunbar, 1991).

Further, like essays, performance assessments are subject to many distractions that may not be relevant to scoring, but may influence the teacher's judgment of the performance assessments (Alleman and Brophy, 1997). For example, teachers' scoring of products such as essays or reports are often influenced by the quality of a pupil's handwriting, neatness, and sentence structure and flow. Sometimes knowing the particular pupil being scored influences the teacher. These and similar factors are not key aspects of the product produced, but they often weigh heavily in scoring. Similarly, when teachers observe pupil performances, they see how their pupils look, watch what they do, and hear what they say. They respond to such observations. They are pleased or annoyed by a pupil's appearance, performance, and attention to the task; they feel sympathy for the pupil who is trying very hard but can't seem to pull off a successful performance. Teachers can rarely be completely dispassionate observers of what their pupils do, because they know their pupils too well and have a set of built-in predispositions for each one. In each case, there are many irrelevant and distracting factors that can influence the teacher's judgments and the validity of performance assessments.

The key to improving rating or scoring skills is to try to eliminate the distracting factors so that the assessment will more closely reflect the pupil's actual performance. In performance assessments, the main source of error is the observer who judges both what is happening during a performance and the quality of the performance. Any distractions or subjectivity that arise during the observation or judging process can introduce error into the assessment, thereby reducing its validity and reliability.

Validity

Validity is concerned with whether the information obtained from an assessment permits the teacher to make a correct decision about a pupil's learning. As discussed previously, failure to instruct pupils on desired performances or the inability to control personal expectations can produce invalid information and decision making. Another factor that can reduce the validity of formal performance assessment is **bias.** When some factor such as race, native language, prior experience, gender, or disability influences the scores of one group differently from those of another (e.g., English speaking and Spanish speaking, prior experience and no prior experience, taught and not taught, hearing disability and no hearing disability) we say the scores are biased (Joint Committee on Standards for Educational and Psychological Testing, 1999). Bias occurs when judgments regarding the performance of one group of pupils are influenced by the inclusion of irrelevant, subjective criteria.

Suppose that oral reading performance was being assessed in a second grade classroom. Suppose also that in the classroom are a group of pupils whose first language is Spanish. The oral reading assessment involved pupils reading aloud from a storybook written in English. When the teacher reviewed her notes on the pupils' performances, she saw that the Spanish-speaking pupils as a group did very poorly. Would the teacher be correct in saying that the Spanish-speaking pupils have poor oral reading skills? Would this be a valid conclusion to draw from the assessment evidence?

A more reasonable interpretation would be that the oral reading assessment was measuring the Spanish-speaking pupils' familiarity with the English language rather than their oral reading performance. How might the English-speaking pupils have performed if the assessment required reading in Spanish? In essence, the assessment provided different information about the two groups (oral reading proficiency versus knowledge of the English language). It would be a misinterpretation of the evidence to conclude that the Spanish-speaking pupils had poorer oral reading skills without taking into account the fact that they were required to read and pronounce unfamiliar English words. The results of the assessment were not valid for the teacher's desired decision about oral reading for the Spanish-speaking pupils.

When an assessment instrument provides information that is irrelevant to the decisions it was intended to help make, the instrument is invalid. Thus, in all forms of assessment, but especially performance assessment, a teacher must select and use procedures, performance criteria, and settings that do not give an unfair advantage to some pupils because of cultural background, language, disability, or gender.

Another source of error that commonly affects the validity of performance assessments is teachers' reliance on mental rather than written record keeping. The longer the interval between an observation and the written scoring, the more likely the teacher is to forget important features of pupil performance.

Teachers' sizing-up perceptions and prior knowledge of their pupils can also influence the objectivity of their performance ratings. Factors such as personality, effort, work habits, cooperation, and the like are all part of a teacher's perceptions of the pupils in his or her class. Often, these prior perceptions influence the rating a pupil is given: the likable, cooperative pupil with the pleasant personality may receive a higher rating than the standoffish, belligerent pupil, even though they performed similarly. Assessing pupils on the basis of their personal characteristics rather than their achievement performance lowers the validity of the assessment. Each of these concerns threatens the validity of teacher interpretations and scores. Note that these concerns are particularly difficult to overcome because of the complexity of performance assessment.

Reliability

Reliability is concerned with the stability and consistency of assessments—e.g., are the results typical of a particular pupil's performance? Hence, the logical way to ensure the reliability of pupil performance is to observe and score two or more performances or products of the same pupil. Doing this, however, is not reasonable in most school settings; once a formal assessment is made, instruction turns to a new topic. Few teachers can afford the class time necessary to obtain multiple pupil assessments on the same topic. This reality raises an important problem with the reliability of performance assessments: they may lack generalizability (Popham, 1995). As noted, performances, products, and portfolios are more complex and fewer in number than selection or short-answer assessments. There are more math items on a multiple-choice test than there are on a performance assessment that requires pupils to show their math work. More short-answer items about factors that led to the Civil War can be asked by a single essay on the same topic. Because of such discrepancies in the quantity of information obtained from particular assessments, the teacher who employs performance assessment sees fewer examples of pupil mastery than the teacher who uses more narrow assessment approaches. The teacher's question them becomes, "How reliable is the limited information I have obtained from pupils?" Does a single essay, a few show-your-work problems, or a portfolio provide enough evidence to be reasonably confident that students would perform similarly on other essays, show-you-work problems, or portfolios? This is the reliability question.

Teachers are put on the horns of a dilemma. Because they want their pupils to learn more than facts and narrow topics, they employ performance assessments to obtain deeper, richer pupil learning. However, by employing an approach that is in-depth and time-consuming, they diminish the reliability of their assessment results. This is a dilemma faced by classroom teachers as well as more general, statewide pupil assessments (Koretz et. al, 1992). Generalizability of performance assessments is not high, and it takes a number of similar performance assessments to obtain high reliability (Brennan and Johnson, 1995; Swanson, Norman, and Linn, 1995). There are few easy ways to overcome the dilemma, so teachers must recognize this limitation but also recognize the importance of providing pupils with performance assessments that assess higher-level learning outcomes. It is better to use evidence from some imperfect performance assessments than it is to make uninformed decisions about pupil achievement on important school outcomes.

Reliability is also affected when performance criteria or rating categories are vague and unclear. This forces the teacher to interpret the criteria, and because interpretations often vary with time and situation, inconsistency can be introduced into the assessment. One way to eliminate much of this inconsistency is to be explicit about the purpose of a performance assessment and to state the performance criteria and rubrics in terms of observable pupil performances. The objectivity of an observation can be enhanced by having several individuals independently observe and rate a pupil's performance. In situations where a group of teachers cooperate in developing criteria for a pupil performance, product, or portfolio, it would not be difficult to have more than one teacher observe or examine a few pupils' products or performances in order to see whether scores are similar across teachers. This is a practice followed in performance assessments such as the College Board English Achievement Essay and in most statewide writing assessments.

The following guidelines can improve the validity and reliability of performance and product assessments.

- Know the purpose of the assessment before beginning.
- Teach and give pupils practice on the performance criteria.
- State the performance criteria in terms of observable behaviors and avoid using adverbs such as "appropriately," "correctly," or "well" in performance criteria because their interpretation may shift from pupil to pupil. Use overt, well-described behaviors that can be seen by an observer and, therefore, are less subject to interpretation. Inform pupils of these criteria and focus instruction on them.
- Select performance criteria that are at an appropriate level of difficulty for the pupils. The criteria used to judge the oral speaking performance of third-year debate pupils should be more detailed than those to judge first-year debate pupils.
- Limit the number of performance criteria to a manageable number. A large number of criteria makes observation difficult and causes errors that reduce the validity of the assessment information.

- Maintain a written record of pupil performance. Checklists, rating scales, and rubrics are the easiest methods of recording pupil performance on important criteria, although more descriptive narratives are often desirable and informative. Tape recordings or videotapes may be used to provide a record of performance, as long as their use does not upset or distract the pupils. If a formal instrument cannot be used to record judgments of pupil performance, then make informal notes of the strong and weak points.
- Be sure the performance assessment is fair to all pupils.

Performance assessment is no different from the other assessment techniques that have been discussed in this text. In all cases, problems can be reduced by following the suggested practices. The next chapter addresses common uses of performance assessments.

Chapter Summary

- Performance assessments require pupils to demonstrate their knowledge by creating an answer, carrying out a process, or producing a product, rather than by selecting an answer. Performance assessments complement paper-and-pencil tests in classroom assessments.
- Performance assessments are useful for determining pupil learning in performance-oriented areas such as communication skills (oral reading, writing, and speaking); psychomotor skills (tracing, cutting with scissors, dissecting); athletic activities (jumping, throwing a ball, swimming); concept acquisition (demonstrating knowledge of concepts by using them to solve real problems); and affective characteristics (cooperation in groups, following rules, self-control)
- Performance assessments have many uses. They can chart pupil performance over time, provide diagnostic information about pupil learning, give pupils ownership over their learning, integrate the instructional and assessment processes, foster pupils' self-assessment of their work, and be assembled into portfolios that show both cumulative evidence of performance and concrete examples of pupils' work. The main disadvantage of performance assessments is the time it takes to prepare for, implement, and score them.
- Successful performance assessment requires a well-defined purpose for assessment; clear, observable performance criteria; an appropriate setting in which to elicit performance; and a scoring or rating method.
- The specific behaviors a pupil should display when carrying out a performance or the characteristics a pupil product should possess are called performance criteria. These criteria define the aspects of a good performance or product. They should be shared with pupils and used as the basis for instruction.
- The key to identifying performance criteria is to break down a performance or product into its component parts, since it is these parts

that will be observed and judged. It is often useful to involve pupils in identifying the criteria of products or performances. This provides them with a sense of involvement in learning and introduces them to important components of the desired performance.

- Try to keep the number of performance criteria small—between 6 and 12—in order to help both teacher and pupil focus on the most important aspects of performance and simplify the observation process. If possible, work collaboratively with other teachers on common assessment areas or performances.

- Avoid using ambiguous words that cloud the meaning of performance criteria (e.g., "adequately," "correctly," "appropriate"); state specifically what should be looked for in the performance or product. The criteria should be stated explicitly, so another teacher could use them independently.

- Performance assessments may be scored and summarized either qualitatively or quantitatively. Anecdotal records, scoring rubrics, and teacher narratives are qualitative descriptions of pupil characteristics and performances. Checklists and rating scales, are quantitative assessments of performances and products.

- Checklists and rating scales are developed from the performance criteria for a performance or product. Checklists provide the observer only two choices in judging each performance criterion: present or absent. Rating scales provide the observer with more than two choices in judging—for example, "always, sometimes, never" or "excellent, good, fair, poor, failure." Rating scales may be numerical, graphic, or descriptive. Performance can be summarized across performance criteria numerically or with a scoring rubric.

- To ensure valid performance assessment, pupils should be instructed on the desired performance criteria before being assessed.

- The validity of performance assessments can be improved by stating performance criteria in observable terms; setting performance criteria at an appropriate difficulty level for pupils; limiting the number of performance criteria to be observed; maintaining a written record of pupil performance; and checking to determine whether extraneous factors (native language, cultural experience) influenced a pupil's performance.

- Reliability can be improved by making multiple observations of performance or by checking for agreement among observers judging the same performance or product and using the same criteria. Making reliable generalizations for performances and products is a concern in performance assessment.

Questions for Discussion

1. Describe some objectives that would be assessed by using performance assessments?

2. How do formal and informal performance assessment differ in terms of pupil characteristics assessed, validity and reliability of the information obtained, and usefulness for teacher decision making?
3. What are the advantages and disadvantages of performance assessments for teachers? For pupils?
4. How should a teacher determine the validity of a performance assessment?
5. Should a teacher tell pupils the specific performance criteria on which they will be judged? Why or why not?
6. What are some examples of how performance assessment can be closely linked to instruction? For example, how can performance assessment be used to involve pupils in the instructional process?

Reflection Exercises

1. Suppose you had to construct a performance assessment to show a superintendent your ability to develop performance criteria and scoring methods for pupils in the grade level you want to teach. What performance or product evidence would you choose? Why would you choose it? Would you choose something different if your prospective employer also wanted to see you administer the performance assessments?
2. What are some instructional strategies that would be important for a teacher to know in order to implement performance assessment?

Activities

1. Construct a performance or product assessment to assess an objective of your choice. Provide the following information.

   - A brief description of the performance or product you will assess and the grade level at which it should be taught
   - A set of at least six clear performance criteria for judging your performance or product
   - One method to score pupil performance
   - A scoring rubric to summarize performance into a single score.

   A two-page document should be sufficient to provide the needed information. Be sure that your performance criteria are clear and specific.
2. Rewrite the following performance criteria for assessing a pupil's poem into clearer form. Remember, you are trying to write performance criteria that most people would understand and interpret the same way.

   - Poem is original
   - Meaningfulness
   - Contains rhymes
   - Proper length
   - Well focused
   - Good title
   - Appropriate vocabulary level

Review Questions

1. How do performance assessments differ from other types of assessment? What are the benefits of using performance assessment?
2. What four steps characterize performance assessment? What happens at each of these steps?
3. Why are performance criteria so important to performance assessment? How do they help the teacher judge pupils' performance and products and also help with planning and instruction?
4. What is the difference between a checklist and a rating scale? When should one use a scoring rubric instead of a checklist or rating scale?
5. What are the main threats to the validity of performance assessments? How can validity be improved?
6. What are the major disadvantages of performance assessment?
7. In what ways is scoring performance assessments similar to scoring essay questions?

References

Arter, J. (1999). Teaching about performance assessment. *Educational Measurement: Issues and Practice, 18*(2), 30–44.

Bartz, D., Anderson-Robinson, S., & Hillman, L. (1994). Performance assessment: Make them show what they know. *Principal, 73,* 11–14.

Brennan, R. L., & Johnson, E. G. (1995). Generalizability of performance assessments. *Educational Measurement: Issues and Practice, 14*(4), 25–27.

Fager, J. J., Plake, B. S., & Impara, J. C. (1997). *Examining teacher educators' knowledge of classroom assessment: A pilot study.* Paper presented at the National Council on Measurement in Education National Conference, Chicago.

Goodrich, H. (1997). Understanding rubrics. *Educational Leadership, 54*(4), 14–17.

Herbert, E. A. (1992). Portfolios invite reflection from both students and staff. *Educational Leadership, 49*(8), 58–61.

Joint Committee on Standards for Educational and Psychological Testing of the American Educational Research Association, the American Psychological Association, and the National Council on Measurement in Education. (1999). *Standards for educational and psychological testing.* Washington, D.C.: American Educational Research Association.

Koretz, D., McCaffrey, D., Klein, S., Bell, R., & Stecher, B. (1992). *Reliability of scores from the 1992 Vermont portfolio assessment program (CSE Technical Report 355).* Los Angeles: RAND Institute on Education and Training/CRESST.

Linn, R., Baker, E., & Dunbar, S. (1991). Complex performance based assessment: Expectations and validation criteria. *Educational Researcher, 20*(8), 15–21.

Madaus, G. F., & O'Dwyer, L. M. (1999). A short history of performance assessment: Lessons learned. *Phi Delta Kappan, 80*(9), 688–695.

Marzano, R., Pickering, D., & McTighe, J. (1993). *Assessing student outcomes: Performance assessment using the dimensions of learning model.* Alexandria, VA: Association for Supervision and Curriculum Development.

McTighe, J. (1996). Performance-based assessment in the classroom: A planning framework. In R. Blum & J. Arter (eds.), *Student performance assessment in an era of restructuring.* Alexandria, VA: Association for Supervision and Curriculum Development.

Mehrens, W. A., Popham, W. J., & Ryan, J. M. (1998). How to prepare students for performance assessments. *Educational Measurement: Issues and Practice, 17*(1), 18–22.

Popham, W. J. (1995). *Classroom assessment.* Boston: Allyn and Bacon.

Ryan, J., & Miyasaka, J. (1995). Current practices in teaching and assessment: What is driving the change? *NAASP Bulletin, 79,* 1–10.

Stiggins, R. (1999). Evaluating classroom assessment training in teacher education programs. *Educational Measurement: Issues and Practice, 18*(1), 23–27.

Swanson, D., Norman, G., & Linn, R. L. (1995). Performance-based assessment: Lessons from the health professions. *Educational Researcher, 24*(5), 5–11, 35.

Wiggins, G. (1992). Creating tests worth taking. *Educational Leadership, 44*(8), 26–33.

Wiggins, G., & McTighe, J. (1998). *Understanding by design.* Alexandria, VA: Association for Supervision and Curriculum Development.

Applications of Performance Assessment

Chapter Outline

❖ Rubrics: Construction and Applications

❖ Types and Examples of Rubrics

❖ Portfolios: Construction and Applications

❖ Developing and Scoring Portfolios

Chapter Objectives

After reading this chapter, the pupil will be able to:

- Identify common characteristics of rubrics
- Perform the steps to prepare and use rubrics
- Construct a rubric from a set of performance criteria
- Describe how portfolios contribute to learning
- Describe different purposes of portfolios
- Suggest ways to score portfolios
- Identify strategies to use when beginning to use portfolios

The preceding chapter described the steps in developing and scoring performance and product assessments. In this chapter we examine some of the applications of performance criteria and assessments that are being used in schools. The examples that follow do not exhaust all the rich and creative ways teachers are implementing performance assessments, but they do suggest the possibilities. In reviewing these applications note especially how critical the identification of clear and coherent performance criteria is to their success.

✂ Rubrics: Construction and Applications

A rubric is a general scoring guide that describes the level at which a pupil performs a process or product. Rubrics have the following common characteristics.

- Rubrics focus on academic areas and performances.
- Rubrics are based on and linked to the teacher's curriculum.
- Rubrics set specific expectations or standards that help pupils focus on and understand what is important in their learning.
- Rubrics help teachers stay focused on what is important and valued work.
- Rubrics are used to assess pupils' products and processes.
- Rubrics are scored using multiple performance levels.
- Rubrics describe what is to be learned, not how to teach.
- Rubrics are descriptive, rarely numerical.
- Rubrics help pupils to monitor and critique their own work.
- Rubrics help eliminate subjectivity in assessments and grading.

As with all performance assessments, rubrics are based on clear and coherent performance criteria. For example, consider the following set of performance criteria developed for a fifth grade book report by one of the author's pupils.

- Tell why you chose the book.
- Describe the main characters of the book.
- Explain the plot of the book in three to five sentences.
- Describe the main place or setting of the book.
- Explain in three sentences how the main characters have changed through the book.
- Write in complete sentences.
- Check spelling, grammar, punctuation, and capitalization.
- Describe whether or not the book was enjoyed and why.

Of course, these criteria could be added to or subtracted from, based on the pupils in a class and what characteristics of a book report the teacher wishes to emphasize. Different teachers might select different performance criteria.

Developing scoring rubrics for processes and products is based on stating levels of the performance criteria that indicate different qualities of pupil performance. For example, the scoring rubric constructed for the fifth grade book report contained three levels of performance labeled "excellent," "good," and "poor." Read each description and note how the authors describe different levels of performance for the criteria.

Excellent: Pupil gives two reasons why the book was chosen; all main characters described in great detail; describes the plot in a logical, step-by-step sequence; gives detailed description of the place in which the book takes place; describes how each main character changed during the book in five sentences; all sentences are complete; no more than a total of five spelling, grammar, punctuation, or capitalization errors; states opinion of the book based on book content.

Good: Pupil gives one reason why the book was chosen; all main characters described, but very briefly; plot described but one main aspect omitted; provides general description of the book setting; briefly describes how most of the main characters changed during the book; a few non-sentences; more than five spelling, grammar, punctuation, or capitalization errors; states opinion of the book but no reference to the book content.

Poor: Pupil fails to state why book was chosen; not all main characters are described; superficial plot description with key aspects omitted; little information about where the book takes place; incorrectly describes changes in the main characters during the book; a few non-sentences; very many spelling, grammar, punctuation, or capitalization errors; no opinion of the book provided.

To score the book report, the teacher would read a pupil's book report, compare it to the three levels, and determine which of the three levels best describes the quality of the pupil's book report. Is it most like the "excellent" description, the "good" description, or the "poor" description? The selected description determines the grade for the pupil's book report. Different rubrics can have different numbers of scoring levels and different descriptions for the levels.

Box 9.1   General Steps in Preparing and Using Rubrics

1. Select a process or product to be taught.
2. State performance criteria for the process or product.
3. Decide on the number of scoring levels for the rubric, usually three to five.
4. State description of performance criteria at the highest level of pupil performance (see "excellent" description of the book report rubric).
5. State descriptions of performance criteria at the remaining scoring levels (for example, the "good" and "poor" levels of the book report rubric).
6. Compare each pupil's performance to each scoring level.
7. Select the scoring level that is closest to a pupil's actual performance or product.
8. Grade the pupil.

Box 9.1 describes the steps used to prepare and use rubrics.

Consider the rubric in Box 9.2 that is used to assess pupils' response journal questions. The rubric has four scoring levels ranging from "excellent" to "poor" performance. After reading the "excellent" scoring level, can you identify the teacher's intended performance criteria? If the criteria are clear you should be able to identify them from the "excellent" rubric.

We can apply the steps in Box 9.1 to the response journal rubric in Box 9.2.

Step 1: Select a performance process or product: journal response questions.

Step 2: Identify performance criteria based on best pupil performance:
  • Answers complete and accurate
  • Answers supported with information from readings
  • Answers include direct quotations
  • Answers show varied and detailed sentences
  • Appropriate spelling, capitals, and punctuation

Step 3: Decide on the number of scoring levels: four.

Step 4: State the description of the performance criteria at the highest level: see the "excellent" category in Box 9.2.

Step 5: State descriptions of criteria at the remaining scoring levels: compare the quality of the "excellent" scoring level to the "good," "needs improvement," and "poor" levels.

Step 6: Compare each pupil's performance to the four scoring levels.

Box 9.2   Scoring Rubric for Fifth Grade Response Journal Questions

3 - Excellent   Answers are very complete and accurate. Most answers are supported with specific information from the reading, including direct quotations. Sentence structure is varied and detailed. Mechanics are generally accurate, including spelling, use of capitals, and appropriate punctuation.

2 - Good   Answers are usually complete and accurate. These answers are supported with specific information from the reading. Sentence structure is varied. Mechanics are generally accurate, including spelling, use of capitals, and appropriate punctuations.

1 - Needs Improvement   Answers are partially to fully accurate. These answers may need to be supported with more specific information from the reading. Sentence structure is varied, with some use of sentence fragments. Mechanics may need improvement, including spelling, use of capitals, and appropriate punctuation.

0 - Poor   Answers are inaccurate or not attempted at all. Sentence structure is frequently incomplete. Mechanics need significant improvement.

Used with Permission of Gwen Airasian

Step 7: Select the scoring level that best describes the level of the pupil's performance on the response journal.

Step 8: Assign grade to pupil.

One important aspect of developing and using rubrics is the construction of scoring levels. The basis for developing good scoring levels depends on the performance criteria and a set of terms that differentiate levels of pupil performance. For example, go back to Box 9.2 and read the four scoring levels. Notice that in each scoring level except the "poor" one, we can see the same aspects of the performance criteria: answers complete and accurate, supported from readings, sentence structure, and mechanics. Even the "poor" level includes three of the four criteria. Note what makes the scoring levels different. It is not the criteria per se. It is the level of performance used to describe each criterion. For example, in the "excellent" level, answers are *very* complete and accurate; in the "good" level, answers are *usually* complete and accurate; in the "needs improvement" level, answers are *partially* accurate; and in the "poor" level, answers are *inaccurate or not attempted*. Try the same analysis with the remaining criteria in Box 9.2

Many common sets of terms are used to describe scoring levels in rubrics. For instance, excellent, good, needs improvement, poor were used in the preceding examples. Other description levels are always, mostly, sometimes, seldom, never; exemplary, competent, inconsistent, lacking; advanced, proficient, basic, in progress; and all, some, few, incomplete. These and many other groups of differentiating labels are used to develop scoring levels.

There are also generic rubrics that can be used to assess a variety of processes and products. Usually, generic rubrics state only the description of the highest level of the scoring rubric. The user must provide his or her own scoring levels to differentiate pupil performance. One example of a description from a generic rubric is "Goes beyond expectation, includes extra information, makes no mistakes, demonstrates exceptional grasp of the topic, understands abstract concepts, and finds links among parts." This generic rubric could be applied to many types of performance assessments.

What descriptions for an average and a poor scoring level might follow from the exemplary generic description? For example, if a particular exemplary description is "goes beyond expectation," what phrasing could be used to describe an average or poor level for "goes beyond expectation"? Two possible "average" examples might be "performs adequately" or "exhibits average expectation." A description of a third, poor level of performance might be stated as "performs inadequately" or "exhibits below average expectation." Now, given the generic exemplary description "makes no mistakes," what average and poor level examples can you identify for the generic example? Scoring rubrics may have only two levels or may use up to six levels, but very rarely does the number of scoring levels exceed four or five. Too many scoring levels makes judging the pupil's appropriate level for grading more difficult and unreliable.

Factors in Using Rubrics

When using rubrics a teacher should inform the pupils about the criteria that will be used to judge their performance or product *before* assessment takes place. Obviously, the teacher should have identified the criteria before the beginning of instruction and assessment. The criteria—and, ideally, specific examples of good and poor performances—should be described and illustrated for the pupils. Pupils should know what makes a good lab report, oral speech, persuasive essay, "show-your-work" math problem, dissection of a frog, analysis of a poem, bar graph, journal response, or any of a thousand other classroom processes and products.

Knowing the criteria of quality performance before assessment leads to a number of benefits for both pupils and teacher. First, knowledge of performance criteria provides information to pupils about what is expected of their work—what characteristics make the work good work. Second, knowledge of the criteria lends focus and structure to pupils' performances and product. They know what is expected of them and thus can concentrate on learning and demonstrating the desired knowledge and behaviors. This, in turn, saves the teacher time in scoring pupils' products or processes because the criteria narrow the breadth of pupil responses.

It is very important to understand that there is a learning curve for mastering the construction and use of rubrics. It takes time to learn to use rubrics well. Trial and error as well as practice for both pupils and teachers are needed to help each gain the most out of rubrics. Start with simple and limited performance criteria and scoring levels—perhaps three or four criteria and two or three scoring levels. Explain the rubric process to the pupils: what rubrics are, why we use them, how they can help improve learning and clarify grading. Practice with the pupils. One approach is to have pupils use a rubric to revise their work before passing it in. A teacher should expect to revise a rubric a few times before he or she and the pupils feel comfortable with it.

Many teachers let pupils help identify the important performance criteria for a classroom process or product. Involving pupils in identifying performance criteria gives them a sense of ownership of the rubric as well as an early preview of the important characteristics of the process or product they will be working on. Some teachers provide pupils with good and poor examples of the process or product they are teaching and ask pupils to identify what makes a good example. In the process of determining what makes good examples, the pupils are also identifying relevant criteria for the process or product. Box 9.3 illustrates the advantages of rubrics for teachers and pupils.

✄ Types and Examples of Rubrics

There are two basic methods of scoring rubrics, holistic and analytic, similar to essay scoring methods. Holistic scoring is used to assess the overall performance of a pupil across all the performance criteria. Previous examples in this chapter exemplify holistic scoring. The teacher selects the description that most closely matches the pupil's overall performance on the process or product. Analytic scoring is used to assess individually each performance criterion stated in the rubric. Each criterion is rated separately using different levels of performance. Figure 9.1 shows an example of holistic scoring for foreign language assessment. There are four scoring levels, each including multiple criteria. The assessor selects the scoring level that best describes the pupil's overall language proficiency.

Box 9.3   Rubrics Aid Teachers and Pupils

Rubrics help teachers by

- specifying criteria to focus instruction;
- specifying criteria to focus pupil assessments;
- increasing the consistency of assessments;
- limiting arguments over grading because of the clear criteria and scoring levels; and
- providing descriptions of pupil performance that are informative to both parents and students.

Rubrics help pupils by

- clarifying the performance tasks that are important;
- pointing out what is important in a process or product;
- allowing them to carry out self-assessment of performance
- providing informative descriptions of performance; and
- providing clearer performance information than traditional letter grades provide.

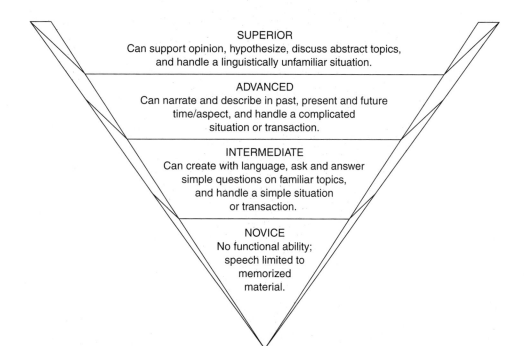

FIGURE 9.1   *An Example of Holistic Scoring* ACTFL Proficiency Levels

Adapted from *Oral Proficiency Interview: Tester Training Manual* (n.p.) by the American Council on the Teaching of Foreign Languages. Copyright 1989 by The American Council on the Teaching of Foreign Languages. Adapted by permission.

Rubrics come in various forms to assess various processes and products. While it is important to illustrate the range of rubrics, a few examples provide a glimpse of their usefulness. Figure 9.2 shows a small portion of a first grade report card that is presented as a rubric. The entire first grade report cards have a number of such rubrics.

Table 9.1 shows a rubric to assess eleventh grade history pupils. There are five scoring levels for each of the two rubrics shown. Can you identify the performance criteria for the two rubrics?

Box 9.4 shows a general four-level persuasive writing rubric that can be used at varied grade levels. Identify the terms in this rubric that are used to differentiate levels of pupil performance (e.g., "clearly," "consistently," "thoroughly maintained," etc.).

Analytic scoring breaks down the general description of a holistic process or product into separate scores for each criterion. For example, consider the persuasive writing rubric in Table 9.4. Unlike a holistic score, analytic scoring would provide a score for each of the five performance criteria. Thus, the teacher might score the criteria in the following manner for the first two performance criteria.

NOT YET—1	2	DEVELOPING—3	4	ACHIEVING—5	EXTENDING
Such as: May demonstrate one or *more* of following:		*Such as:* May demonstrate one or *more* of following:		*Criteria:* Demonstrates *all* of following:	Identifies main ideas. Identifies background knowledge
Identifies the topic but does not identify any details from the book. Cites information incorrectly. Draws only from personal experience rather than from evidence in the book. Identifies details but not topic.		Identifies topic and one (1) detail from the book. Identifies several details, but needs prompting to clearly state the main topic.		Identifies from an informational book: topic of book, two or more supporting details. *Such as:* "This book is about whales. The blue whale is the largest animal on earth. Whales have babies that are born alive—not hatched."	Distinguishes between what s/he already knew and what was just learned. Identifies topic and details of an informational book read by student.

FIGURE 9.2 *Scoring Rubric Used in First Grade Report Card*

Reprinted by permission of the Ann Arbor Public Schools, Ann Arbor, Michigan.

TABLE 9.1

California Assessment Program 1990 History-Social Science Grade 11 Scoring Guide: Group Performance Task

	Level I Minimal Achievement	Level II Rudimentary Achievement	Level III Commendable Achievement	Level IV Superior Achievement	Level V Exceptional Achievement
Communication of Ideas 20	(1–4) Position is vague. Presentation is brief and includes unrelated general statements. Overall view of the problem is not clear. Statements tend to wander or ramble.	(5–9) Presents general and indefinite position. Only minimal organization in presentation. Uses generalities to support position. Emphasizes only one issue. Considers only one aspect of problem.	(8–12) Takes a definite but general position. Presents a somewhat organized argument. Uses general terms with limited evidence that may not be totally accurate. Deals with a limited number of issues. Views problem within a somewhat limited range.	(13–16) Takes a clear position. Presents an organized argument with perhaps only minor errors in the supporting evidence. Deals with the major issues and shows some understanding of relationships. Gives consideration to examination of more than one idea or aspect of the problem.	(17–20) Takes a strong, well-defined position. Presents a well-organized, persuasive argument with accurate supporting evidence. Deals with all significant issues and demonstrates a depth of understanding of important relationships. Examines the problem from several positions.
Knowledge and Use of History 30	(1–6) Reiterates one or two facts without complete accuracy. Deals only briefly and vaguely with concepts or the issues. Barely indicates any previous historical knowledge. Relies heavily on the information provided.	(7–12) Provides only basic facts with only some degree of accuracy. Refers to information to explain at least one issue or concept in general terms. Limited use of previous historical knowledge without complete accuracy. Major reliance on the information provided.	(13–18) Relates only major facts to the basic issues with a fair degree of accuracy. Analyzes information to explain at least one issue or concept with substantive support. Uses general ideas from previous historical knowledge with fair degree of accuracy.	(19–24) Offers accurate analysis of the documents. Provides facts to relate to the major issues involved. Uses previous general historical knowledge to examine issues involved.	(25–30) Offers accurate analysis of the information and issues. Provides a variety of facts to explore major and minor issues and concepts involved. Extensively uses previous historical knowledge to provide an in-depth understanding of the problem and to relate it to past and possible future situations.

Source: © California Department of Education, 1990. Reprinted with permission.

Box 9.4   Generic Rubric to Score Writing to Persuade

When describing observables to incorporate in a rubric to assess student responses to a specific prompt, it is important to address all of the specific criteria that were included in the prompt itself. In addition, we need to consider how skillfully the response was crafted and how effectively it addressed the writer's ability to persuade. To assist you with identifying these factors, the following observables are provided at varying score points.

Students at Level 1:
- Take a position and clearly state their point of view.
- Consistently use facts and/or personal information to develop support for their position.
- Organize details in a logical plan that is thoroughly maintained.
- Consistently enhance what they write by using language purposefully to create sentence variety.
- Incorporate appropriate mechanics (spelling, capitalization, punctuation). Any errors that occur are due to risk-taking.

Students at Level 2:
- Take a position and adequately attempt to clarify their point of view.
- Frequently use facts and/or personal information to develop support for their position.
- Organize details in a logical plan that is adequately maintained.
- Frequently support their position by providing sufficient information.
- Frequently enhance what they write by using language purposefully to create sentence variety.
- Incorporate appropriate mechanics (spelling, capitalization, punctuation). Most errors that occur are due to risk-taking.

Students at Level 3:
- Take a position and make a limited attempt to clarify their point of view.
- Generally use facts and/or personal information which may or may not support their position.
- Organize details in a plan that may or may not be adequately maintained.
- May or may not support their position by providing sufficient information.
- May or may not attend to mechanics (spelling, capitalization, punctuation).

Student at Level 4:
- Usually provide a position and limited information to support the position.
- Minimally organize details that include some support for the position.
- Seldom take their audience into consideration.
- Occasionally choose vocabulary that sufficiently supports the position.
- Seldom enhance what they write by varying sentence structure and incorporating appropriate mechanics (spelling, capitalization, punctuation).

| Take a position and clearly state their point of view | Completely
Generally
Partially
Not at all |

| Consistently uses facts and/or personal information to develop support for their position | Extensively
Partially
Rarely |

Note that analytic scoring can use letters (A, B, C, etc), numbers (4, 3, 2, 1), and descriptions as in the examples above.

Write analytic scoring forms for the remaining three performance criteria.

Table 9.2 shows the State of Kentucky's holistic scoring approach for judging performance assessments of writing. Note that the performance criteria are listed in the left section of the Table. There are six main scoring criteria, ranging from purpose/audience to correctness. On the right side of the table is the holistic scoring guide with four scoring levels ranging from novice to distinguished. The rubric scoring levels each include a set of six criteria, one for each of the six main scoring criteria. This table shows the link between performance criteria and their integration into holistic scoring rubrics.

✂ Portfolios: Construction and Applications

An important addition to the growing use of classroom performance assessments is portfolio assessment. This assessment method is gaining use in schools and classrooms (Mitchell, 1992; O'Neil, 1993; Ryan and Miyasaka, 1995). A **portfolio** is a collection of selected student work. The term *portfolio* derives from the collections that models, photographers, and artists assemble to demonstrate their work. In classroom, portfolios have the same basic purpose: to collect pupil performances to show their work and accomplishments over time. Portfolios do not contain haphazard, unrelated collections of pupil's work. They contain consciously selected examples of work that is intended to show pupil growth and development toward important curriculum goals. Portfolios support instruction and learning and should be related to teachers' objectives.

A portfolio can be made up of many different pupil performances or it can be made up of a single performance. For example, a multifocused writing portfolio might contain writing samples, lists of books read, journal entries about books read, and descriptions of favorite poems. Conversely, a

Kentucky Writing Assessment
Holistic Scoring Guide

Scoring Criteria

Purpose/Audience

The degree to which the writer
- establishes and maintains a purpose
- communicates with the audience
- employs a suitable voice and/or tone

Idea Development/Support

The degree to which the writer provides thoughtful, detailed support to develop main idea(s)

Organization

The degree to which the writer demonstrates
- logical order
- coherence
- transitions/organizational signals

Sentences

The degree to which the writer includes sentences that are
- varied in structure and length
- constructed effectively
- complete and correct

Language

The degree to which the writer exhibits correct and effective
- word choice
- usage

Correctness

The degree to which the writer demonstrates correct
- spelling
- punctuation
- capitalization

Novice
- Limited awareness of audience and/or purpose
- Minimal idea development; limited and/or unrelated details
- Random and/or weak organization
- Incorrect and/or ineffective sentence structure
- Incorrect and/or ineffective language
- Errors in spelling, punctuation, and capitalization are disproportionate to length and complexity

Apprentice
- Some evidence of communicating with an audience for a specific purpose; some lapses in focus
- Unelaborated idea development; unelaborated and/or repetitious details
- Lapses in organization and/or coherence
- Simplistic and/or awkward sentence structure
- Simplistic and/or imprecise language
- Some errors in spelling, punctuation, and capitalization that do not interfere with communication

Proficient
- Focused on a purpose; communicates with an audience; evidence of voice and/or suitable tone
- Depth of idea development supported by elaborated, relevant details
- Logical, coherent organization
- Controlled and varied sentence structure
- Acceptable, effective language
- Few errors in spelling, punctuation, and capitalization relative to length and complexity

Distinguished
- Establishes a purpose and maintains clear focus; strong awareness of audience; evidence of distinctive voice and/or appropriate tone
- Depth and complexity of ideas supported by rich, engaging, and/or pertinent details; evidence of analysis, reflection, insight
- Careful and/or subtle organization
- Variety in sentence structure and length enhances effect
- Precise and/or rich language
- Control of spelling, punctuation, and capitalization

Box 9.5   What Can Go into a Portfolio

Media: Videos, audio tapes, pictures, artwork, computer programs, etc.
Reflections: Plans, statements of goals, self-reflections, journal entries, etc.
Individual work: Tests, journals, logs, homework, essays, etc.
Group work: Cooperative learning sessions, group performances, peer
    reviews, etc.
Work in progress: Rough and final drafts, show-your-work problems,
    science fair projects, etc.

single-focus portfolio might contain multiple pieces of the same process or product, such as a portfolio containing just book reports, just written poems, or just chemistry lab reports. Box 9.5 shows the range of materials that can go into a portfolio.

In one first grade class, pupils developed a reading portfolio. Every third week the pupils read a paragraph or two into their audiotape "portfolio." The teacher monitored pupil improvement over time and pupils could play back their pieces to measure their reading improvement. Also, periodically the pupils' reading portfolios were sent home for the parents to listen to their child's reading improvement—an opportunity parents appreciated.

Portfolios can contribute to instruction and learning in many ways, such as:

- Monitoring pupil progress and improvement over time
- Helping pupils self-evaluate their work
- Providing ongoing assessment of pupil learning
- Helping teachers judge the appropriateness of the curriculum
- Facilitating teacher meetings and conferences with pupils, parents, and both pupils and parents
- Informing teachers about pupils' prior work
- Grading pupils
- Showing pupils' typical work
- Reinforcing the importance of processes and products in learning
- Providing concrete examples of pupil work
- Encouraging pupils to think about what is good performance in varied subject areas
- Providing diagnostic information about pupil performance

- Showing pupils the connections among their processes and products
- Focusing on both the process and final product of learning

Whatever a portfolio's use and contents, it is important that it have a defined, specific purpose that will focus the nature of the information that will be collected in the portfolio. Too often, teachers defer the question of the portfolio's purpose until *after* pupils have collected large amounts of their work in their portfolios. At that time the teacher is likely to be confronted with the question of what to do with all of the pupil information.

Perhaps the greatest contribution that portfolios provide for learning is that they give pupils a chance to revisit and reflect on the products and processes they have produced. For many pupils, life in school is an ongoing sequence of papers, performances, assignments, and productions. Each day a new batch of paperwork is produced and the previous day's productions are tossed away or lost, both mentally and physically. Collecting pieces of pupils' work in a portfolio retains them for subsequent pupil review, reflection, demonstration, and grading. With suitable guidance, pupils can be encouraged to think about and compare their work over time, providing them an opportunity rarely available in the absence of portfolios. For example, pupils might be asked to reflect on questions such as: Which of these portfolio items shows the most improvement and why? Which did you enjoy most and why? From which did you learn the most and why? In what areas have you made the most progress over the year and what was the nature of that progress? Portfolios allow pupils to see their progress and judge their work from the perspectives of time and personal development.

✥ Developing and Scoring Portfolios

Unfortunately, many teachers view portfolios as an undifferentiated collection of pupil performances. However, as noted, there is a great deal more to successful portfolio assessment than simply collecting bunches of pupils' work. Portfolio assessment is a type of performance assessment, and thus depends on the same four elements that all types of performance assessment require: (1) a clear purpose, (2) appropriate performance criteria, (3) a suitable setting, and (4) scoring performance. There are a number of questions that must be answered in developing and assessing portfolios. Box 9.6 lists the main questions that guide classroom use of portfolios.

Box 9.6   Portfolio Questions

1. What is the purpose of the portfolio?
2. What will go into and be removed from the portfolio during its use?
3. Who will select the entries that go into the portfolio: teacher, pupils, or both?
4. How will the portfolio be organized and maintained?
5. How will the portfolio be assessed?

Purpose of Portfolios

The items that go into a portfolio, the criteria used to judge the items, and the frequency with which items are added to or deleted from the portfolio all depend on the portfolio's purpose. If the purpose is to illustrate a pupil's typical work in various school subjects for a parent's night at the pupil's school, the portfolio contents would likely be more wide-ranging than if its purpose is to assess the pupil's improvement in math problem solving over a single marking period. In the latter case, math problems would have to be obtained periodically throughout the marking period and collected in the portfolio. For the "typical work" portfolio for parent's night, a collection of papers from a day or a week of school would suffice to show parents their child's typical performance.

If a portfolio is intended to show a pupil's best work in a subject area, the contents of the portfolio would change as more samples of the pupil's performance became available and as less-good ones were removed. If the purpose is to show improvement over time, earlier performances would have to be retained and new pieces added. If the purpose is to let pupils reflect on their own work, the teacher would need to prepare prompts or questions that could provide focus to the pupils' reflections: What is your best work? In what areas have you shown the most progress? Which was the hardest piece in your portfolio? Such questions help pupils reflect on their learning and growth and it is very useful to provide such prompts for pupils.

Given the many and varied uses of portfolios, purpose is a crucial issue to consider and define in carrying out portfolio assessment. It is important to determine the purpose and general guidelines for the pieces that will go into the portfolio *before* starting the portfolio assessment. It is also critical that all pieces going into a portfolio be dated, especially in portfolios that aim to assess pupil growth or development. Without recorded dates for each portfolio entry, it may be impossible to assess growth and improvement.

In order to promote pupils' ownership of their portfolios, it is useful to allow pupils to choose at least some of the pieces that will go into their portfolios. Some teachers develop portfolios that contain two types of pieces, those required by the teacher and those selected by the pupil. It is also important that all pupil portfolio selections are accompanied by a brief written explanation of why the pupil feels that a piece belongs in her or his portfolio. This will encourage the pupil to reflect on the characteristics of the piece and why it belongs in the portfolio.

Performance Criteria

Performance criteria are needed to assess the individual pieces that make up a portfolio. Without such criteria, assessment cannot be consistent within and across portfolios. The nature and process of identifying performance criteria for portfolios is the same as that for checklists, rating scales, and rubrics. Depending on the type of performance contained in a portfolio, many of the performance criteria discussed earlier in this chapter can be used to assess individual portfolio pieces.

If pupil portfolios are required for all teachers in a grade or if portfolios are to be passed on to the next year's teacher, it is advisable for all affected teachers to cooperate in formulating a common set of performance criteria. Cooperative teacher practice is useful because it involves groups of teachers in the process of identifying important performance criteria. It also helps produce common instructional emphases within and between grades and fosters discussion and sharing of materials among teachers (Herbert, 1992). It is reassuring for pupils as they pass through the grade levels to have some consistency in both instruction and teacher expectations.

It is valuable to allow pupils to help identify performance criteria used for assessing the contents of a portfolio. Helping to identify performance criteria can give pupils a sense of ownership over their performance and help them think through the nature of the portfolio pieces they will produce. Beginning a lesson with joint teacher and pupil discussion of what makes a good book report, oral reading, science lab, or sonnet is a useful way to initiate instruction and get the pupils thinking about the characteristics of the process or product they will have to develop. Such discussions serve both an instructional and an assessment function for pupils and teacher.

There is another very important reason why performance criteria are needed for portfolio assessment. The processes or products that will make up a portfolio should, like all forms of assessment, be related to the instruction provided to pupils. Performance criteria are like the teacher's objectives, identifying the important outcomes pupils need to learn. Without explicit criteria, instruction may not provide all the experiences necessary to carry out the desired learning, thereby reducing the validity of the portfolio. Of course, once stated, performance criteria can always be amended and extended. Often, after examining the first few pieces in pupils' portfolios, the teacher recognizes the need to add to, delete, or modify the initial criteria. In such cases, changes in the criteria should be made to facilitate pupil learning.

Setting

In addition to a clear purpose and well-developed performance criteria, portfolio assessments must take into account the setting in which pupils' performances will be gathered. While many portfolio pieces can be gathered by the teacher in the classroom, others pieces cannot. When portfolios include oral speaking, science experiments, artistic productions, and psychomotor activities, special equipment or arrangements may be needed to properly collect the desired pupil performance. Many teachers underestimate the time it takes to collect the processes and products that make up portfolios and the management and record keeping needed to maintain them. Checking, managing, maintaining, and assessing pupil portfolios is time-consuming but important.

An important dimension of using portfolios is the logistics of collecting and maintaining pupil portfolios. Portfolios require space. They have to be stored in a safe but accessible place. A system has to be established for pupils to add or subtract pieces of their portfolios. Can pupils go to their portfolio at any time or will the teacher set aside special times when all pupils deal with their portfolios? If the portfolio is intended to show growth, how will the order of the entries be kept in sequence? Maintaining portfolios requires time and organization. Materials such as envelopes, crates, tape recorders, and the like will be needed for assembling and storing pupil portfolios.

Scoring Criteria

Scoring portfolios can be quite a time-consuming task. Not only does each individual portfolio piece have to be assessed, but the summarized pieces must also be assessed to provide an overall portfolio performance. Depending on the complexity and variety of the contents of the portfolio, assessing may require considerable time and attention to detail, further increasing assessment time.

Consider the difference in managing and scoring portfolios that contain varied processes or products as compared to portfolios that contain examples of a single process or product. The multifocused portfolio provides a wide range of pupil performance, but at a substantial logistical and scoring cost to the teacher. The single-focus portfolio does not provide the breadth of varied pupil performances of the multifocused portfolio, but can be managed and scored considerably more quickly.

When the purpose of a portfolio is to provide descriptive information about pupil performance for a parent-teacher night or to pass pupil information on to the next year's teacher, no scoring or summarization of the portfolio contents will be necessary. The contents themselves provide the desired information. However, when the purpose of a portfolio is to diagnose, track improvement, assess the success of instruction, encourage pupils to reflect on their work, or grade pupils, some form of summarization or scoring of the portfolio pieces is required. Generally, before summarizing or grading a pupil's portfolio it is important for the teacher and the pupil to discuss the contents of the portfolio. In fact it is an excellent instructional activity for the teacher to discuss and critique portfolios with the pupils. Periodic teacher-pupil conferences can identify strengths and weaknesses in a portfolio, and allow the teacher to ask questions about the portfolio and make suggestions or comments about the pupil's progress. Without such conferences, much of the instructional aspects of portfolios are lost.

Individual portfolio pieces are typically scored using methods we have discussed: checklists, rating scales, and rubrics. Thus, each story, tape recording, lab report, handwriting sample, persuasive essay, or cooperative group product can be judged by organizing the performance criteria into a checklist, rating scale, or rubric. For example, if the portfolio is intended to collect information about pupils' mathematics problem solving and if the performance criteria are (1) selects correct solution method, (2) draws and labels diagrams, (3) shows work leading to solution, and (4) gets correct answer, each individual portfolio piece might be assessed in one of the three ways shown in Table 9.3.

The checklist in Table 9.3 would require a yes or no choice for each criterion. The teacher might summarize performance on the four criteria by determining that four yes responses is an A or excellent for the overall piece; three, a B or good; two, a C or poor; and one or none, a D or failure.

The rating scale shown in Table 9.3 could be scored and summarized by giving each possible response a score. For example, "quickly" or "completely" could be a score of 3; "slowly" or "partially," a 2; and "not at all," a one. If a pupil was rated "quickly," "completely," "partially," and "slowly" on the four performance criteria, the pupil would have a total score of 10 points ($3 + 3 + 2 + 2 = 10$). The highest score possible is 12 and the lowest is 4. The teacher could set up a scoring scale based on the possible scores. For example, scores between 12 and 10 might be excellent or A; 9 to 8, good or B; 7 to 6, fair or C; and 5 to 4, poor or D.

The rubric shown in Table 9.3 would be scored by the teacher comparing a pupil's performance across the four criteria and selecting a rubric scoring level that comes closest to the pupil's performance.

Choose a story from your writing folder that you wish to rewrite. Answer the following questions.

I chose this story because

The best feature of this story is

The things that need improvement in this story are

Rewrite the story, making the improvements you believe are needed. Do your best work. After you have finished rewriting, judge what you have written. Circle the number that describes your story.

Spelling, grammar, punctuation
   1 = few capitals, many misspellings, incorrect punctuation
   2 = some errors in spelling, grammar, and punctuation
   3 = almost no errors in spelling, grammar, and punctuation

Organization
   1 = story switches topics, contains unneeded ideas, and is hard to follow
   2 = story usually stays focused on a single topic or idea
   3 = story is focused on a single topic or idea and is easy to follow

Word Usage
   1 = mostly simple words used, few descriptive words included
   2 = some imaginative and descriptive words used, but only in some parts
   3 = imaginative and descriptive words used throughout

Language and Details
   1 = simple sentence structure used throughout; few details included
   2 = mix of sentence structures in some places; details in some parts
   3 = varied sentence structures and details provided throughout

Story Line
   1 = no central problem or goal; little action or plot development
   2 = story problem or goal stated; story lacks action and development
   3 = story problem or goal stated; plot developed; keeps readers' interest

FIGURE 9.3   *Self-Assessment Exercise*

Of course, the teacher does not always have to be the one who assesses the portfolio pieces. It is desirable and instructive to allow pupils to self-assess some of their portfolio pieces in order to give them practice in critiquing their own work in terms of the performance criteria. Figure 9.3 shows a self-assessment sheet used to encourage pupils to reflect on and re-

TABLE 9.3

Assessing Individual Portfolio Pieces

Checklist

Selects correct solution method	Yes	No
Draws and labels diagrams	Yes	No
Shows work leading to solution	Yes	No
Gets correct answer	Yes	No

Rating Scale

Selects correct solution method	quickly	slowly	not at all
Draws and labels diagrams	completely	partially	not at all
Shows work leading to solution	completely	partially	not at all
Gets correct answer	quickly	slowly	not at all

Rubric

Selects correct solution method; draws complete, labeled diagrams;
shows all work; gets correct answer

Selects correct solution method; draws complete but poorly labeled diagrams;
shows partial work; gets partially correct answer

Selects incorrect solution method; neither draws nor labels diagrams;
shows very little work; gets incorrect answer

vise their work. Note that the performance criteria and options guide the pupils' reflection and revisions. Also notice how the teacher let the pupils select the piece to be examined and revised, but asked them to describe why they chose their particular pieces from their writing portfolios and what the strong and weak points were. The teacher should identify and set bounds for what pupils can include in their portfolio in order to focus them on the objectives they are intended to learn. After rewriting the piece, the pupil rated the revised piece using the five simple rubrics.

Consider how much more pupil involvement in the writing process portfolios provide, compared to when an assignment is given, passed in to the teacher, graded, returned to the pupil, and soon forgotten. Note also how this kind of assessment encourages pupil reflection and learning. Even without formal instruments such as those shown in Table 9.3, it is useful for teachers to develop questions that will focus pupils' reflection on their portfolio pieces (e.g., Which piece was most difficult and why? Which shows your best work and why? Which are you most proud of and why?).

The purpose of assessing an entire portfolio, as opposed to the individual pieces, is usually summative—to assign a grade. Such holistic portfolio assessment requires the development of a set of summarizing criteria. For example, improvement in writing might be judged by comparing a pupil's early pieces to later pieces in terms of these performance criteria: (1) number of spelling, capitalization, and punctuation errors, (2) variety of sentence structures used, (3) use of supporting detail, (4) appropriateness of detail to purpose, (5) ability to emphasize and summarize main ideas, (6) link and flow between paragraphs, and (7) personal involvement in written pieces. An alternative approach might be for the teacher to rate earlier written pieces using a general scoring rubric and compare the level of early performances to later performances using the same rubric.

Different portfolios with different purposes require different summarizing criteria. For example, how would you summarize a portfolio containing a number of tape recordings of a pupil's Spanish pronunciation or a portfolio made up of poems a pupil wrote as part of a poetry unit? What criteria would you use to judge *overall* progress or performance?

The contents of a portfolio can also be reported in terms of a summarizing narrative, as illustrated in Figure 9.4. The top portion of the narrative shows a history of the portfolio contents, including the date each piece was produced, the literary genre, the topic addressed, the reason the piece was written, its length, and the number of drafts produced. The bottom part of the narrative shows the teacher's summary of the pupil's performance, including both descriptions and supporting illustrations. Such narratives are useful in describing a pupil's portfolio, but they are quite time-consuming to construct.

It is instructive to compare two different portfolios, one fairly narrow and the other more broad, in order to work through the differences in portfolios of different breadth. Table 9.4 describes two portfolios. Work through the four steps for developing performance assessments and imagine that you have to apply the four steps to each portfolio. Would there be differences between the two portfolios? How might the differences influence the selection of criteria, the setting in which the portfolio pieces will be collected, and the strategy for evaluating the individual performance criteria and the portfolio as a whole for each portfolio? Notice that both portfolios focus on writing, although the breadth of the portfolios differ.

To summarize, assessments of processes, products, and portfolios broaden considerably the information teachers can gather about pupil achievement. Moreover, they involve pupils in their own learning in a deeper, more reflective manner than most paper-and-pencil assessments. Box 9.7 provides some advice for getting started with portfolio assessment.

Date	Genre	Topic	Reason	Length	Drafts
9/??	Self-Reflection	Thinking About Your Writing	Requested	1 page	1 draft
10/17	Narrative/Dramatic	Personal Monologue	Important	1 page	2 drafts
1/16	Response to Literature	On *The Lord of the Flies*	Unsatisfying	1 page	4 drafts
2/??	Self-Reflection	Response to Parent Comments	Requested	1 page	1 draft
2/28	Narrative/Dramatic	"The Tell-Tale Heart"	Free Pick	3 pages	2 drafts
5/22	Response to Literature	On *Animal Farm*	Satisfying	5 pages	2 drafts
6/??	Self-Reflection	Final Reflection	Requested	2 pages	1 draft

As a writer, Barry shows substantial growth from the beginning of the year in his first personal monologue to his last piece, a response to *Animal Farm.* Initially, Barry seems to have little control over the flow and transition of his ideas. His points are not tied together, he jumps around in his thinking, and he lacks specificity in his ideas. By January, when Barry writes his response to *The Lord of the Flies,* he begins a coherent argument about the differences between Ralph's group and Jack's tribe, although he ends with the unsupported assertions that he would have preferred to be "marooned on a desert island" with Ralph. Barry includes three reasons for his comparison, hinges his reasons with transition words, but more impressively, connects his introductory paragraph with a transition sentence to the body of his essay. In the revisions of this essay, Barry makes primarily word and sentence level changes, adds paragraph formatting, and generally improves the local coherence of the piece.

By the end of February when he writes his narrative response to Poe's "The Tell-Tale Heart," Barry displays a concern for making his writing interesting. "I like the idea that there are so many twists in the story that I really think makes it interesting." He makes surface level spelling changes, deletes a sentence, and replaces details, although not always successfully (e.g., "fine satin sheets and brass bed," is replaced with the summary description "extravagant furniture"). Overall, it is an effective piece of writing showing Barry's understanding of narrative form and his ability to manipulate twists of plot in order to create an engaging story.

Barry's last selection in his portfolio is an exceptional five-page, typed essay on Orwell's *Animal Farm.* The writing is highly organized around the theme of scapegoating. Using supporting details from the novel and contemporary examples from politics and sports, Barry creates a compelling and believable argument. The effective intertextuality and the multiple perspectives Barry brings to this essay result largely from an exceptional revision process. Not only does he attempt to correct his standard conventions and improve his word choices, he also revises successfully to the point of moving around whole clumps of text and adding sections that significantly reshape the piece. This pattern of revision shows the control Barry has gained over his writing.

In Barry's final reflection he describes his development, showing an awareness of such issues as organizing and connecting ideas, choosing appropriate words and details, and making his writing accessible to his readers. "I had many gaps in my writing. One problem was that I would skip from one idea to the next and it would not be clear what was going on in the piece. . . . Now, I have put in more details so you don't have to think as much as you would. I also perfect my transitions and my paragraph form. . . . My reading . . . has improved my vocabulary and it helped me organize my writing so it sounds its best and makes the most sense possible. . . . There are many mistakes I have made throughout the year, but I have at least learned from all of them." I agree with him.

FIGURE 9.4 *Narrative Description of Pupil's Writing Portfolio*

SOURCE: P. A. Moss, et al., "Portfolios, Accountability, and an Interpretive Approach to Validity," *Educational Measurement: Issues and Practice,* 1992, *11*(3), p. 18. Copyright 1992 by the National Council on Measurement in Education. Reprinted by permission of the publisher.

TABLE 9.4

Two Portfolios

	Portfolio 1	Portfolio 2
Purpose	Assess persuasive writing	Grade writing for a marking period
Portfolio Contents	Samples of persuasive writing	Samples of persuasive and creative writing, reports on books read, and summaries of the main ideas of poems
Number of Portfolio Pieces	5 persuasive writing pieces	4 persuasive pieces, 4 creative pieces, 3 book reports, and 5 poems

Box 9.7   Starting Portfolio Assessment

1. Begin slowly. Start with a manageable portfolio exercise that
   - is focused on one specific process or product;
   - will take no more than a month or marking term to complete; and
   - will require relatively few portfolio pieces.
2. Think through the entire process of portfolio assessment, envisioning the process; identify the main questions that guide portfolios.
3. Develop clear but limited performance criteria; know what you want the pupils to learn and experience for the portfolio development and assessment before starting the portfolio process.
4. Identify how pupils will be involved in the selection, review, reflection, and assessment of the portfolio process. The main advantages of portfolios are lost if pupils cannot revisit their work or have some ownership in the process.
5. Devise a simple rubric to assess the portfolio contents.
6. Initially, both you and the pupils will struggle to understand and master the portfolio approach. This is natural. Give it a fair trial, because the benefits for both teacher and pupils are substantial.
7. Do not be afraid to experiment with portfolios to find the procedures and approaches that work best for you and your pupils.

Chapter Summary

- A rubric is a scoring guide that describes the level at which a pupil performs on a process or product.
- As with all performance assessments, rubrics are based on clear and coherent performance criteria.
- The general steps in preparing and using rubrics are (1) select a performance that will be taught; (2) state performance criteria; (3) decide on the number of scoring levels; (4) develop and describe the highest level of performance; (5) state descriptions of the remaining scoring levels; (6) compare each pupil's performance to each scoring level; (7) select the scoring level closest to the pupil's performance; and (8) grade pupil performance.
- Portfolios are collections of pupils' work that show change and progress over time. Portfolios may contain pupil products (essays, paintings, lab reports) or pupil performances (reading aloud, foreign language pronunciation, using a microscope).
- The basis for developing good scoring levels depends on the performance criteria and the terms used to differentiate pupil performance.
- Inform pupils about the criteria before assessing; knowing the criteria of a quality performance before assessment helps pupils perform their best.
- There are two basic scoring methods for rubrics, holistic scoring and analytic scoring.
- A portfolio is a collection of pupil work on a process or product; portfolio pieces are consciously selected to aid assessment.
- Portfolios have many uses: focusing instruction on important performance activities; reinforcing the point that performances are important school outcomes; providing parents, pupils, and teachers with a perspective on pupil improvement; diagnosing weaknesses; allowing pupils to revisit, reflect on, and assess their work over time; grading pupils; and integrating instruction with assessment.
- The greatest contribution of portfolios is that they allow pupils to revisit their work over time.
- There are many types of portfolios, ranging from portfolios used in parent's night at school to long-range portfolios used as part of pupils' graduation from high school.
- In order to promote pupils' ownership of their portfolios it is useful to permit them to select some of the pieces for the portfolios themselves.
- If portfolios are required for all pupils in a grade, it is advisable for the affected teachers to cooperate in identifying important criteria.
- An important concern in using portfolios is the considerable time and attention it takes to maintain pupil portfolios.

- Begin portfolio assessment slowly: select a single process or product to teach; limit the portfolio to no longer than a month or a marking period; and collect only five or so pieces for the portfolio. Also, be patient—you and your pupils will both be learning as you go. Make changes that seem best for you and your pupils, and do not abandon the idea of incorporating portfolios without trying at least twice.

Questions for Discussion

1. What are the merits of rubrics as opposed to checklists and rating scales?
2. Under what circumstances would portfolios be most useful in carrying out instruction?
3. In what ways can rubrics and portfolios be related to instruction?
4. What can pupils and teachers learn from portfolios that they cannot learn without portfolios?

Reflection Exercise

List the advantages and disadvantages of portfolio assessment.

Activities

1. Follow the steps in Box 9.1 to develop a rubric. State four scoring levels for the rubric.
2. Devise a holistic scoring approach for each of the portfolios in Table 9.4.

Review Questions

1. What are the main uses of rubrics?
2. How are rubrics constructed?
3. How would a holistic rubric differ from an analytic rubric?
4. How should portfolios be linked to instruction?
5. What role should pupils have in developing and contributing to their portfolios?

References

Herbert, E. A. (1992). Portfolios invite reflection—From both students and staff. *Educational Leadership, 49* (8), 58–61.

Mitchell, R. (1992). *Testing for learning.* New York: The Free Press.

O'Neil, J. (1993). The promise of portfolios. *ASCD Update, 35* (7), 1–5.

Ryan, J., & Miyasaka, J. (1995). Current practices in teaching and assessment: What is driving the change? *NAASP Bulletin, 79,* 1–10.

Grading Pupil Performance

Chapter Outline

❖ Grading: Its Rationale and Difficulties

❖ Grading as Judgment

❖ Grading: Four Standards of Comparison

❖ Grading for Cooperative Learning and Pupils with Disabilities

❖ Selecting Pupil Performances for Grading

❖ Summarizing Varied Types of Assessment

❖ Assigning Grades to Pupils: Two Approaches

❖ Other Methods of Reporting Pupil Progress

Chapter Objectives

After reading this chapter, the pupil will be able to:

- Define basic terms: norm-referenced, criterion-referenced, grading curve
- Contrast the characteristics of norm- and criterion-referenced grading
- Identify principles of grading and explain their importance
- Describe approaches for grading cooperative learning and pupils with disabilities
- State strategies for conducting effective parent-teacher conferences

We have seen that teachers use a variety of techniques to gather information about their pupils' learning. But teachers must do more than just gather pupils' performances, they also must make judgments about their quality. The process of judging the quality of a pupil's performance is called **grading.** It is the process that translates test scores and descriptive assessment information into marks or letters that indicate the quality of each pupil's learning and performance. Assigning **grades** to pupils is an exceptionally important professional responsibility, one a teacher carries out many times during the school year and one that has important consequences for pupils. Grades are the most common and important forms of classroom assessments that most pupils and parents experience.

Teachers assign grades to single assessments and to groups of assessments. When a pupil says, "I got a B on my book report," or "I got an A on my chemistry test," the pupil is talking about a grade on a single assessment. Report card grades, on the other hand, represent a pupil's performance across a variety of assessments that were completed during a term or grading period. Some people refer to the former process as "assigning grades" and the latter as "assigning marks," but the basic processes are similar, so we shall use the term "grading." Hence, grading is the process of judging the quality of a single assessment or multiple assessments over time.

In order to judge the quality of a pupil's performance, it must be compared to something or someone. There is no grading without comparison. When a teacher grades, he or she is making a judgment about the quality of a pupil's performance by comparing it to some standard of good performance. Suppose that Jamal got a score of 95 on a test. His score *describes* his performance—95 points. But does 95 indicate excellent, average, or poor achievement? This is the grading question—what is Jamal's performance worth? In order to answer this question, we need more than just Jamal's test score. For example, we might want to know how many items were on Jamal's test and how much each item counted. A score of 95 does not provide this information. It would probably make a difference in the way Jamal's performance was judged if he got 95 out of 200 items right as opposed to 95 out of 100 items right. Or, we might like to know how Jamal did in relation to the other pupils in the class. A score of 95 does not tell us this.

It would make a difference in grading to know whether Jamal's score was the highest or the lowest in the class. Finally, one might like to know whether Jamal's 95 represents an improvement or a decline compared to his previous test scores. A score of 95 does not tell us this. Some form of comparison is needed to assign a grade.

✕ Grading: Its Rationale and Difficulties

The purpose of this chapter is to outline the questions teachers face when grading and to provide guidelines to help answer these questions. While the main focus is on the process of assigning report card grades in academic subjects, the principles discussed are also appropriate for grading single tests or assessments. A logical place to begin discussion is with the question "Why grade?"

Why Grade?

The simplest and perhaps most compelling reason that classroom teachers grade their pupils is because they have to. All teachers grade, and grading is one type of official assessment that school teachers are required to carry out. Virtually all school systems demand that classroom teachers make periodic judgments about their pupils' performance.

The form of these written judgments varies from one school system to another and from one grade level to another. Some schools require teachers to record pupil performance in the form of letter grades (e.g., A, A−, B+, B, B−, C+ . . .); some in the form of achievement categories (e.g., excellent, good, fair, poor); some in the form of numerical grades (e.g., 100–90, 89–80, . . .); some in the form of pass-fail; some in the form of a checklist of specific skills or objectives that are graded individually; and some in the form of teachers' written narratives describing pupils' accomplishments and weaknesses. The most widely used systems are letter grades, which are the main grading system in upper elementary, middle, and high schools; and skill-based or objective-based ratings, which are used mainly in kindergarten and the primary grades (Friedman and Frisbie, 1993).

Some school systems also require teachers to write comments about each pupil's performance on the report card, while others require teachers to grade performance in both academic subjects and social adjustment areas. There are many different varieties of grading forms, and Figures 10.1, 10.2, and 10.3 show three examples. Often, there are heated debates over the form of the report cards used in a school district, with some parents wanting the product-oriented A, B, C, D, and F grades and others wanting the more process-oriented checklist (Olson, 1995). Regardless of the particular system or report form used, grades are always based on teacher judgments.

STOUGHTON PUBLIC SCHOOLS
Pupil Progress Report - Grades 1, 2 and 3
Anthony L. Sarno, Jr., Superintendent of Schools

NAME_____ GRADE_____ SCHOOL YEAR_____

SCHOOL _____ HOMEROOM TEACHER_____

KEY	
C Commendable	✓ denotes an area of weakness
S Satisfactory	M denotes modified program
N Needs Improvement	+ or - may be used to modify S

ATTENDANCE RECORD

TERM	I	II	III	IV	TOTAL
ABSENT					
TARDY					
DISMISSED					

	1	2	3	4		1	2	3	4
READING **GRADE**					**SCIENCE (grade 3 only)** **GRADE**				
Effort					Effort				
Connects literature with other experiences					Uses science process skills				
Learns and applies vocabulary					Understands concepts and ideas				
Comprehends teacher read selections					**ART** **GRADE**				
Understands story structure					Effort				
Uses word attack skills					Conduct				
Applies appropriate reading strategies and skills					Understands concepts and ideas				
Reads with fluency					**COMPUTERS** **GRADE**				
Reads with understanding					Effort				
Makes good use of independent reading time					Conduct				
LANGUAGE **GRADE**					Understands concepts and ideas				
Effort					**MUSIC** **GRADE**				
Organizes and expresses ideas orally					Effort				
Expresses ideas through writing					Conduct				
Develops and organizes ideas in written work					Understands concepts and ideas				
Writes with correct usage and mechanics					**PHYSICAL EDUCATION** **GRADE**				
Edits and revises as necessary					Effort				
SPELLING **GRADE**					Conduct				
Effort					Understands concepts and ideas				
Masters assigned spelling words					**WORK HABITS** **GRADE**				
Spells correctly in written work					Listens attentively				
HANDWRITING **GRADE**					Works cooperatively in a group				
Effort					Participates in class				
Forms letters correctly					Completes homework				
Writes neatly and legibly					Completes work independently				
MATHEMATICS **GRADE**					Uses time efficiently				
Effort					Has a positive attitude toward learning				
Understands concepts					Follows directions				
Masters basic facts					Seeks help when needed				
Works with accuracy					Organizes work and materials				
Interprets information to solve problems					Uses study skills				
SOCIAL STUDIES (grade 3 only) GRADE					**CONDUCT** **GRADE**				
Effort					Follows classroom rules				
Demonstrates geographic awareness					Follows school rules				
Understands cultural similarities and differences					Demonstrates self control				
Understands historical concepts and ideas					Accepts responsibility				
					Respects rights, opinions and property of others				

FIGURE 10.1 *Example of an Elementary School Report Card*

SOURCE: Pupil Progress Report from the Stoughton Public Schools System, Stoughton, MA. Reprinted by permission.

COMMENTS

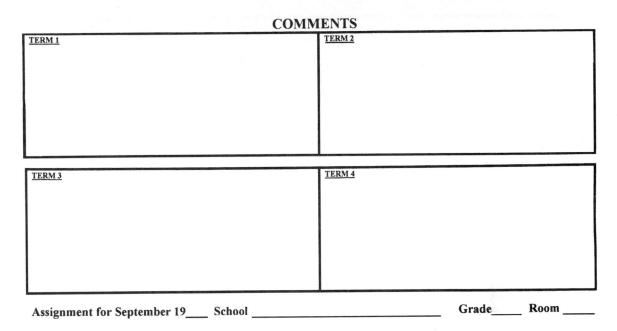

Assignment for September 19____   School _____   **Grade_____   Room _____**

FIGURE 10.1   *Continued*

Figure 10.1 shows a report card for an early elementary school in which pupils are graded in academic and social adjustment areas using a grading system based on the designations "commendable," "satisfactory (with options for + or −)," and "needs improvement." Figure 10.2 shows a high school report card based solely on academic performance using an A through F system. Figure 10.3 shows part of a process-oriented kindergarten report card in which a judgment is made about many individual performances pupils are expected to master. Pupils are scored in terms of Good (G), Satisfactory (S), Needs improvement (I) and Not expected at this time (N).

The purpose of all grades is to communicate information about a pupil's academic performance. The aim of grading is to provide meaningful information about pupil performance to pupils, parents, and others. Within this general purpose are four more specific grading purposes: administrative, informational, motivational, and guidance. Administratively, grades help determine such things as a pupil's rank in class, credits for graduation, and suitability for promotion to the next level. Informationally, grades are used to inform parents, pupils, and others about a pupil's academic performance. Grades represent the teacher's summary judgment about how well pupils have mastered the content and processes taught in a subject area during a particular term or grading period. Because report card grades are given only four or five times a year, the information they convey is limited to summary judgments. Grades rarely provide diagnostic information

SEMESTER 1 1997 - 1998

STUDENT NAME		YEAR OF GRAD	STUDENT I.D.	TELEPHONE	HOME ROOM	PREV. CREDITS 62.00

SEMESTER SCHOLARSHIP REPORT

NO.	COURSE		TEACHER	1ST GRADE	1ST MISSED	2ND GRADE	2ND MISSED	EXAM	FINAL GRADE	CREDITS EARNED
11	HEALTH	34	Mr. Fleagle	A	1	A–		B	A–	1.00
133	ENGLISH	30	Mr. Turcotte	B	2	B+		B	B+	2.50
221	AP EUR HIS	30	Mrs. Golden	B	1	B+		B	B	2.50
321	GEOMETRY	30	Ms. Franklin	B	2	C+		C+	B–	2.50
433	PHYSICS	31	Mr. Wind	B–		B	1	B–	B	3.00
737	INTRO LAW	34	Mr. Tarot	B+	1	A–	2	B+	A–	2.50
	MERITS			100		100				

CREDITS TO DATE   76.00

ATTENDANCE	THIS GRADING PER.	TOTAL THIS YEAR
DAYS ABSENT	0	0
TIMES TARDY	0	0
TIMES DISMISSED	1	1

ATTENDANCE IS RECORDED AS OF 01-19-98

NATICK HIGH SCHOOL
15 WEST STREET
NATICK, MASS. 01760

GUIDANCE COUNSELOR
TELEPHONE

PARENT / STUDENT
PLEASE SEE REVERSE SIDE FOR EXPLANATION OF GRADES

FIGURE 10.2 *Example of a High School Report Card*

SOURCE: Natick High School Report Card Form. Reprinted by permission of Natick Public Schools, Natick, Massachusetts.

FIGURE 10.3 *Kindergarten Report Card*

SOURCE: Reprinted by permission of Our Lady of Lourdes School, Jamaica Plain, MA.

KINDERGARTEN PROGRESS REPORT

Our Lady of Lourdes School
54 Brookside Avenue
Jamaica Plain, MA 02130
542-6136

Student's Name _____
Teacher's Name _____

School Year 19 ___ - 19 ___

EVALUATION KEY
G - Good   S - Satisfactory
I - Needs Improvement
N - Not expected at this time

ATTENDANCE

	D	M	J
Absent			
Tardy			

READING READINESS

	D	M	J
Recognizes own name			
Knows alphabet in sequence			
Recognizes upper case letters			
Recognizes lower case letters			
Associates sounds with letters			
Is able to blend sounds into words			
Works from left to right			
Shows interest in books/stories			

LANGUAGE DEVELOPMENT

ORAL

	D	M	J
Speaks clearly			
Expresses ideas and feelings well			
Shares ideas and feelings well			
Uses adequate vocabulary			
Speaks in complete sentences			
Tells story in sequence			

WRITTEN

	D	M	J
Can print full name			
Prints alphabet			

MATH READINESS

	D	M	J
Can count in order			
Recognizes numbers to 10			
Recognizes numbers above 10			
Writes numbers clearly			
Applies knowledge of numbers			
Identifies basic shapes			
Understands math items			
Visually discriminates among likenesses and differences			

PHYSICAL DEVELOPMENT

SMALL MUSCLE

	D	M	J
Dresses self			
Buttons			
Zips			
Laces			
Controls pencil well			
Can cut well			
Colors neatly			
Pastes neatly			

LARGE MUSCLE

	D	M	J
Runs and jumps well			
Can catch, bounce, and throw ball			
Shows partiality to left or right			

DEVELOPMENT IN ART AND MUSIC

	D	M	J
Is eager to explore art materials			
Is imaginative with art materials			
Identifies colors, shapes and sizes			
Shows enthusiasm for music			
Enjoys singing			

RELIGIOUS DEVELOPMENT

	D	M	J
Is learning to pray and talk to God			
Is learning about God and His creation			

SOCIAL DEVELOPMENT

	D	M	J
Accepts responsibility			
Respects others' property			
Respects others' feelings			
Respects authority			
Works well with others			
Plays well with others			
Listens when others talk			

WORK HABITS

	D	M	J
Observes rules and regulations			
Listens carefully			
Follows directions			
Has good attention span			
Completes activities promptly			
Works well independently			
Uses materials correctly			
Takes care of materials			
Cleans up after work period			
Finishes what has been started			
Values own work			
Is observant			

PERSONAL

	D	M	J
Knows full name			
Knows address			
Knows phone number			
Knows age and birthday			

about pupil accomplishments and shortcomings. Teachers recognize this limitation (Hubelbank, 1994), but it does not diminish the importance of grades for pupils and parents. Grades are important, but bear in mind that grades are only one means of communicating with pupils and parents. Other methods such as parent conferences can provide more detailed information about school progress, and will be described later in this chapter.

Grades are also used to motivate pupils to study. A high grade is a reward for learning. This motivational aspect of grading is, however, a two-edged sword. Pupil motivation may be enhanced when grades are high, but may be diminished when grades are lower than expected or when the same pupils continually get low grades. Moreover, it is not desirable to have students study solely to get a good grade, so teachers should try to balance grading rewards with other kinds of rewards.

Lastly, grades are used for guidance. They help the pupil, parent, teacher, and counselor choose appropriate courses and course levels for the pupil. They help identify pupils who may be in need of special services and they provide information to colleges about the pupil's academic performance in high school.

Grades are used in schools for many reasons, and while there are periodic calls to abolish grades, it is difficult to envision schools in which judgments about pupils' performance would not be made by teachers and communicated to various interested parties. The basis on which teacher judgments are made may change, the format in which the grades are reported may be altered, and the judgments may no longer be called "grades," but the basic process of teachers judging and communicating information about pupil performance—that is, "grading"—will still go on.

Grades in whatever form are potent symbols in our society, symbols that are taken very seriously by teachers, pupils, parents, and the public at large. Regardless of your personal feelings about the value and usefulness of grades and grading, it is necessary to take the grading process seriously. That means you should devise a grading system for your pupils that (1) is fair to your pupils and (2) delivers the message about pupil performance you wish to convey. Teachers have a responsibility to be objective and fair in assigning grades and should never use grades to punish or reward pupils the teacher likes or dislikes.

The Difficulty of Grading

Grading can be a very difficult task for teachers for four reasons: (1) few teachers have had formal instruction in how to grade their pupils (Brookhart, 1999; Slavin, 1994); (2) school districts and principals provide little guidance to teachers regarding specific grading policies and expectations (Hubelbank, 1994); (3) teachers know that grades are taken seriously by parents and pupils and that the grades a pupil gets will be scrutinized and often challenged; and (4) the knowledge of each pupil's needs and characteristics that teachers must have to provide good instruction is difficult to ignore when the teacher is called upon to be a dispassionate, objective dispenser of grades.

Teachers inevitably face the dilemma of what constitutes fairness in grading. Must a teacher always be steadfast to the institution that expects dispassionate grading, or can fairness include consideration of a pupil's unique needs, circumstances, and problems? Which is the greater misuse of power, to ignore or to take into account individual pupil circumstances when grading? The special helping relationship that teachers have with their pupils makes it difficult for teachers to judge them on a solely objective or dispassionate basis (Brookhart, 1992; Hubelbank, 1994). This is especially so for grading, because the judgments made about pupils are public, taken very seriously, have real consequences for pupils, and can influence the pupil's educational, occupational, or home status.

The following remarks indicate some of the ambivalence teachers feel about grading.

> Report card time is always difficult for me. My pupils take grades seriously and talk about them with each other, even though I warn them not to. They're young (fourth graders) and some let their grades define their self-images, so grades can have a negative effect on some. Still, I guess it doesn't do a kid much good to let him think everything's great in his schoolwork when it really isn't . . . but putting it down on a report card makes it final and permanent. You know you can't make everyone happy when you grade and that some hopes will be dashed. One thing's for sure. I agonize over the grades I give.
>
> The first report card of the year is always the toughest because it sets up future expectations for the child and his or her parents.
>
> At the high school level where I teach, grades are given more "by the book" than I think they are in the elementary school. Here we don't get to know our students as well as elementary school teachers and so we can be more objective when grading. I have to admit though, that I do recognize differences in pupil interest, effort, and politeness that probably influence my grades a little bit.
>
> Sitting in judgment of students is always difficult, but report card grades are especially so for me. Subject matter grades are supposed to reflect only academic performance, so some good and desirable qualities of students get left out. Yet parents and many kids take these incomplete indicators very, very seriously. I try to cover each student's good, nonacademic qualities in my written report card comments. Another reason report card grades are so difficult for me is because my grade is the first one in which students receive letter grades in subject areas. Every time I give a report card grade, I am aware that I'm setting expectations for the student, the student's parents, and future teachers.

These comments indicate that grading is a difficult, time-consuming process that demands considerable mental and emotional energy from teachers because grades have important consequences for pupils and others. Grading is further complicated by the fact that there are no uniformly accepted strategies for assigning grades. Grading systems are not comparable from school to school nor from teacher to teacher, so each teacher must find his or her own answer to the many questions associated with the grading process. Table 10.1 summarizes both the purposes of grading and some of the more difficult considerations teachers face when assigning grades to their pupils.

TABLE 10.1

The Purposes and Difficulties of Grading

Purposes	Difficulties
Informational: Communicate pupils' subject matter achievement **Administrative:** Make decisions about graduation, grade promotion, class standing, etc. **Motivational:** Raise pupils' academic efforts **Guidance:** Help choose appropriate courses, course levels, and services	Teacher's dual role: judgmental, disciplinarian relationship versus helping relationship Preventing pupil's personal circumstances, characteristics, and needs from distorting judgment regarding academic achievement Judgmental, subjective nature of grading; evidence always inconclusive Lack of formal training in grading Lack of universally accepted strategies for grading

✷ Grading as Judgment

The single most important characteristic of the grading process is its dependence upon teacher judgments. Ultimately, all grades are based on judgment. Although there are general guidelines to help develop a classroom grading system, all such systems rely on teacher judgment because the teacher knows the pupils and their accomplishments better than anyone else does. Consequently, in assigning grades, teachers are granted considerable discretion and autonomy—no one else can or should make grading judgments for a teacher's pupils.

Teacher judgments are dependent upon two characteristics: (1) information about the person being judged (e.g., test scores, book reports, performance assessments) and (2) a basis of comparison that can be used to translate that information into grading judgments (e.g., what level of performance is worth an A, B, C, D, or F). Information provides the basis for judgment, but note that judgment is different from mere guessing. Guessing is what one does when there is no information or evidence to help make a judgment: "I have no information, so I'll just have to guess." To *judge* implies that the teacher has some evidence to consider in making the judgment. Thus, a teacher gathers evidence of various kinds to help make judgments and decisions about pupil learning. Without this evidence, the teacher's grades would be guesses, not judgments.

But judgment also implies uncertainty, especially in the classroom setting. When there is complete certainty, there is no need for a teacher to judge. For example, when teachers state "Gerhard is a boy," "Svetlana's parents are divorced," or "Sigmund got the highest score on the math test," they are stating facts, not making judgments. Judgment, then, falls between guessing and certainty. It is based upon evidence, but the evidence is rarely conclusive or complete, and because of this uncertainty teachers are required to make a judgment. Using greater amounts of information can reduce, but rarely eliminate, the need for teacher judgment. It is because assessment evidence is always incomplete that teachers must be concerned about the validity and reliability of judgments made from the evidence.

To summarize, the goal of grading is to obtain enough valid evidence about pupil accomplishments to make a grading judgment that is fair, communicates the level of a pupil's academic performance, and can be supported with evidence. Because grades are important public judgments, they should be based mainly on formal evidence such as tests, projects, and performance assessments. The concreteness of these evidence types not only helps the teacher to be objective in awarding grades, but also can help to explain or defend a grade that is challenged. Bearing this in mind, there are three main factors teachers must confront to make a **grading system:**

- Against what standard shall I compare my pupils' performance?
- What aspects of pupil performance shall I include in my grades?
- How should different kinds of evidence be weighted in assigning grades?

Embedded in these three questions are other questions that all teachers must address when grading. Unfortunately, few school districts have explicit grading policies that tell a teacher how to answer these questions. Most districts have particular grading formats teachers must use (A, B, C, . . .; good, satisfactory, poor, etc.), but teachers must work out the specific details of their grading systems for themselves. They must answer questions such as What level of performance is A work and what is D work? What is the difference between good and satisfactory performance? and Should pupils be failed if they're trying? Even if a teacher does not consciously ask such questions when grading, he or she must implicitly answer them, because grades cannot be assigned without confronting these issues.

✻ Grading: Four Standards of Comparison

A grade is a judgment about the quality of a pupil's performance. As noted earlier, it is impossible to judge performance in the abstract. Comparison must be involved. Recall the difficulty we had in judging how good Jamal's test score of 95 was when that was our only piece of information. We needed to seek additional information that would allow us to compare Jamal's performance to some standard of goodness or quality. Thus, without comparison, there can be no grading.

Many bases of comparison can be used to assign grades to pupils (Frisbie and Waltman, 1992). Those most commonly used in classroom grading compare a pupil's performance to

- the performance of other pupils,
- predefined standards of good and poor performance,

- the pupil's own ability level, or
- the pupil's prior performance (improvement).

The vast majority of teachers use one of the first two comparisons in assigning grades to their pupils (Brookhart, 1999; Friedman and Frisbie, 1993). This is just as well, since for technical and substantive reasons, the comparisons based on ability or improvement are not recommended.

Comparison with Other Pupils

Assigning grades to pupils based upon a comparison with other pupils in the class is referred to as **norm-referenced grading.** Other names for this type of grading are "relative grading" and "grading on the curve." A high grade means that a pupil scored higher than most of his or her classmates, while a low grade means the opposite. When a teacher says things like "Garth is smarter than Omar," "Rowanda works harder in social studies than Tiffany and Tamika," and "Maria completes her math worksheets faster than anyone else in the class," the teacher is making norm-referenced comparisons.

In norm-referenced grading, not all pupils can get the top grade, no matter how well they perform. The system is designed to ensure that there is a distribution of grades across the various grading categories. Notice that in norm-referenced grading, the grade a pupil gets provides no indication of how well or poorly the pupil performed. Pupils get A grades for having higher scores than their classmates. If a pupil answered only 40 out of 100 test questions correctly, but was the highest scorer in the class, he or she would receive an A grade in norm-referenced grading, in spite of answering only 40 items correctly. The opposite is true at the other end of the scoring range: a pupil may answer 97 out of 100 questions correctly but get a C because most other pupils in the class got 98's, 99's, and 100's. Compared to classmates, a score of 97 falls in the middle of the group, even though, in absolute terms, it is very high performance.

Norm-referenced grading is based on grading on the curve. Teachers establish a **grading curve** that defines what percentage of the pupils can get A's, B's, C's, etc. This curve, which varies from teacher to teacher and is established before an assessment is given, sets up quotas for each grade. Following are two examples of grading curves.

A	Top 20% of pupils	A	Top 10% of pupils
B	Next 30% of pupils	B	Next 40% of pupils
C	Next 30% of pupils	C	Next 45% of pupils
D	Next 10% of pupils	D	Last 5% of pupils
F	Last 10% of pupils		

If the curve on the left were applied to grading a chapter or unit test, the teacher would administer the test, score it, and arrange the pupils in order of their scores from highest to lowest. The highest scoring 20 percent of the pupils (including ties) would get an A grade; the next 30 percent, a B grade; the next 30 percent, a C grade; and so on. If the same curve were to be applied when giving report card grades, the teacher would first have to summarize the varied information about pupil performance that was gathered over the entire term. The summary score for each pupil would be arranged in order from highest to lowest, and the percentages in the curve would be applied to allocate grades.

There is no single best grading curve that should be used in every norm-referenced grading situation. Some teachers give mostly A's and B's, while others give mainly C's. Some teachers do not believe in giving pupils F's, while others give many F's. Teacher discretion determines the nature of the grading curve. However, if a teacher's curve gives too many high grades to mediocre pupils, pupils will not respect it. If it is too difficult even for bright, hardworking pupils to get an A, they will give up. In the end, one seeks a grading curve that is fair to the pupils and that represents academic standards that the teacher feels are appropriate and realistic for the pupils.

The type of comparison that is used to assign grades to pupils can influence their effort and attitude. For example, norm-referenced grading tends to undermine the learning and effort of pupils who repeatedly score near the bottom of the class, since they continually receive poor grades. Norm-referenced grading poses a lesser threat to the top pupils in the class, although it can spur competition among pupils for the high grades. Competitive, norm-referenced approaches that make a pupil's success or failure dependent on the performance of classmates can also reduce pupil cooperation and interdependence, because success for one pupil reduces the chance of success for other pupils.

Comparison to Predefined Standards

Instead of grading by comparing one pupil to others, a teacher can compare a pupil's performance to preestablished performance standards. **Performance standards** define the level or score that a pupil must attain to receive a particular grade. All pupils who reach a given level get the same grade, regardless of how many pupils reach that level. The test for a driver's license is a simple, pass-fail example of performance standards. In many states, the driver's test contains two parts, a written section covering knowledge of the rules of the road and a performance section in which the applicant must actually drive an automobile around local roads. (Notice how paper-and-pencil tests *and* performance assessments are combined in driver's tests to make certain the all-important knowledge and skills of safe driving are assessed. This is a good example to keep in mind for your own classroom assessments.)

The written portion of the driver's test usually contains 20 multiple-choice items that must be passed before the performance portion is attempted. The written test is administered to groups of applicants in much the same way paper-and-pencil tests are administered in schools. In most states, passing the test depends upon getting 70 percent of the items correct. In this case, 70 percent is the performance standard. Whether any single applicant passes or fails depends only on how he or she compares to the performance standard of 70 percent. Passing has nothing whatsoever to do with how other applicants taking the test perform, because applicants' scores are not compared to one another. They are compared to the predetermined 70 percent performance standard. In this system it is possible for all or none of the applicants to pass.

Grading that compares a pupil's achievement to predefined performance standards is called **criterion-referenced grading** or absolute grading. As in the driver's test, each pupil is graded on the basis of his or her own performance. Since pupils are not compared to one another and do not compete for a limited percentage of high grades, it is possible for all students to get high or low grades on a test. Criterion-referenced grading is the most commonly used grading system in schools. The criteria used to determine performance standards can be either performance-based or percentage-based.

Performance-Based Criteria

There are two types of performance-based standards that can be used in criterion-referenced grading. One type spells out in detail the specific learning pupils must demonstrate in order to receive a particular grade. For example, in some classrooms teachers utilize contract grading in which the pupil and teacher negotiate the quality and amount of work the pupil must satisfactorily complete in order to receive a particular grade. If the pupil meets the negotiated performance standard by the end of the semester, he or she receives the promised grade. Alternatively, a more narrow performance standard could be set up to grade each pupil who must give an oral speech. The teacher would observe the speech, concentrating on the specific activities listed in the oral speech performance standards. At the end of the speech, the teacher would refer to the performance standards or rubric and assign a grade to each pupil. A sample rubric based on preset performance standards for an oral speech is presented below. Again, notice that each pupil's grade depends upon how he or she performs in comparison to the standard, not in comparison to other pupils.

A   Pupil consistently faces audience, stands straight, and maintains eye contact; projects voice well and clearly; pacing and tone variation appropriate; well-organized points logically and completely presented; brief summary at end.

B   Pupil usually faces audience, stands straight, and makes eye contact; voice projection good, but pace and clarity vary during talk; well organized but repetitive; occasional poor choice of words; incomplete summary.

C   Pupil fidgety; some eye contact and facial expression change; uneven voice projection, not heard by all in room, some words slurred; loosely organized, repetitive, contains many incomplete thoughts; poor summary.

D   Pupil body movements distracting, little eye contact or voice change; words slurred, speaks in monotone, does not project voice beyond first few rows, no consistent or logical pacing; rambling presentation, little organization with no differentiation between major and minor points; no summary.

Percentage-Based Criteria

A second, more common type of criterion-referenced standard uses cutoff scores based on the percentage of items answered correctly. In the case of report card grading, an overall percentage of mastery across many individual assessments is used. The following cutoff percentages comprise perhaps the most widely used standard of this type.

90 to 100 percent of items correct = A
80 to 89 percent of items correct = B
70 to 79 percent of items correct = C
60 to 69 percent of items correct = D
less than 60 percent of items correct = F

Any pupil who scores within one of the above performance standards will receive the corresponding grade. There is no limit on the number of pupils who can receive a particular grade and the teacher does not know what the distribution of grades will be until after the tests are scored and graded. Note that this is not the case in the norm-referenced approach.

Many teachers use percentage-based cutoff scores other than those shown here; some use 85 percent and higher as the cutoff for an A grade and readjust the cutoffs for the remaining grades accordingly. Others refuse to flunk a pupil unless he or she gets less than half (50 percent) of the items incorrect. Like the curve in norm-referenced grading, the grading standards that are used in criterion-referenced grading are based upon a teacher's judgment about what is suitable and fair for his or her class. Standards should be reasonable given the ability of the class and the nature of the subject matter, and they should be academically honest and challenging for the pupils.

Interpreting and Adjusting Grades

A criterion-referenced grading system is intended to indicate how much a pupil has learned of the things that were taught. Grades based on poor instruction, invalid assessments, or assessments that fail to cover the full range of what pupils were taught will convey an incorrect message about pupil learning. Of course, good instruction and valid instruments that fully assess what pupils have been taught should always be used, regardless of the grading approach. However, the focus on content mastery in criterion-referenced grading makes it especially crucial that teachers provide good instruction and develop assessments that are fair and that cover the full range of objectives taught.

In criterion-referenced grading, getting an invalid or unclear test item wrong can have major implications for pupil grades. Suppose that two out of ten items on a teacher's test were not taught to pupils and as a consequence many pupils answered these two items incorrectly. The highest score these students could get would be 80 percent. If they made no other mistakes and were being graded on performance standards in which

80 percent or higher is a B grade, the highest grade these pupils could receive would be a B, even though the two items that they got wrong were
not their fault.

Thus, before using assessment information to grade pupils, the quality
of that information should be considered. Grades are only as meaningful as
the information on which they are based. If grades are assigned subjectively, if scoring criteria change at random from pupil to pupil, if there are
no established grading criteria, or if the teacher's attention wanders during
scoring, grades will not accurately reflect pupil achievement. If unit tests
are unfair to pupils or do not test a representative sample of what was
taught, the scores pupils attain will not be valid indicators of their achievement. It is important for teachers to examine assessment results that are unusual or unexpected. Typically, unexpectedly low results provoke teachers'
concern and attention. Teachers ask themselves, "Do these low scores indicate a problem with the test or instruction, or a problem with the effort
pupils put into preparing for the test?" and "How should this result be handled in grading?"

Suppose a teacher's test produced lower than usual scores for most
pupils. When he compared the test items to what he had taught, he found
that the test contained items on a section of the unit he had not taught.
Thus, the match between the unit test and classroom instruction was not
good. Pupils were being penalized because his instruction failed to cover
many concepts included in the test. Thus, to use these scores would provide
a distorted picture of his pupils' actual achievement, and this, in turn,
would reduce the validity of their grades.

To avoid this, the teacher decided to change the pupils' scores on the
test to better reflect their achievement. He estimated that about 20 percent
of the items on the test were from the section he had not taught. After determining that most pupils had done poorly on these items, so he decided to
increase each pupil's test score by 20 percentage points to adjust for the invalid items. He correctly reasoned that the increased scores would provide
a better indication than the original scores of what pupils had learned *from
the instruction provided.*

It is important to reiterate the critical need to make such adjustments
when a criterion-referenced grading approach is being used. It is also important to note that the teacher adjusted the low scores on the test only *after*
reexamining both the test and his instruction. He did not raise the scores to
make the pupils feel better about themselves, to have them like him more,
or for other, similar reasons. In this instance the test scores were raised so
that they would provide a more valid indication of how well pupils learned
from the instruction. It made his grades better reflect the pupils' subject
matter mastery. However, scores should not be raised simply because they
are low or because the teacher is disappointed with them.

Regardless of whether one employs a norm- or a criterion-referenced
grading system, the grading curve or performance standards should be determined before assessment is carried out. Doing this helps teachers to think
about expected performance and allows them to inform pupils of what will

TABLE 10.2

Comparison of Norm-Referenced and Criterion-Referenced Grading

	Norm-Referenced	Criterion-Referenced
Comparison Made	Pupil to other pupils	Pupil to predefined criteria
Method of Comparison	Grading curve; percentage of pupils who can get each grade	Standard of performance; scores pupils must achieve to get a given grade
What Grade Describes	Pupil's performance compared to others in the class	Pupil's percentage mastery of course objectives
Availability of a Particular Grade	Limited by grading curve	No limit on grade availability

be needed to get high grades. When properly defined, a grading system tells pupils what constitutes high and low achievement. However, judgments are sometimes incorrect and need to be adjusted. Consequently, once established, performance standards and grading curves need not be set in stone. If a standard or grading curve turns out to be inappropriate or unfair for some reason, it can and should be changed before grades are assigned. While changes in performance standards or grading curves should not be made frivolously, it is better to make changes than to award grades that are incorrect and invalid. Usually, increased experience with a class helps a teacher arrive at a set of standards or a grading curve that is appropriate and fair. The discretion lies with the classroom teacher to make changes in grading curves and standards when the teacher judges them to be invalid for some reason. Teacher discretion is at the heart of good grading.

Having made this point, it must also be emphasized that fairness to pupils does not mean selecting standards or curves to ensure that everyone gets high grades. Lowering standards or grading curves to guarantee high grades discourages pupil effort and diminishes the validity of the grades. Fairness means fully assessing what pupils were taught, using assessment procedures appropriate to the grade level and type of instruction used, and establishing performance standards or grading curves that are realistic if pupils work hard. These are the teacher's responsibilities in integrating instruction, assessment, and grading. Table 10.2 compares the main features of norm- and criterion-referenced grading.

Comparison to a Pupil's Ability

Teachers frequently make remarks like "Dwayne is not working up to his ability," "Maurice is not doing as well as he can," or "Jaklyn continues to achieve much higher than I expected she would." When teachers make such statements, they are comparing a pupil's actual performance to the performance they expect, based on their judgment of the pupil's ability. The terms "overachiever" and "underachiever" are used to describe pupils who do better or worse than teacher judgments of what they should be doing. Many teachers assign grades by comparing a pupil's actual performance to their perception of the pupil's ability level (Hubelbank, 1994).

In this grading approach, pupils with high ability who do excellent work would receive high grades, as would pupils with low ability whom the teacher believed were achieving "up to their potential." Even though the actual performance of the low-ability pupils may be well below that of the high-ability, high-achieving pupils, each group would receive the same grade if each were perceived to be achieving up to their ability. Conversely, pupils with high ability who were perceived by their teacher to be under-achieving—that is, performing below what the teacher thinks they are capable of performing—would receive low grades. An argument that is advanced in defense of this grading approach is that it motivates pupils to do their best and get the most from their ability. It also punishes lazy pupils who do not work up to their perceived ability.

However, grading based on pupil ability is not recommended for a number of reasons (Frisbie and Waltman, 1992; Kubiszyn and Borich, 1999). First, the approach depends on the teacher having an accurate perception of each pupil's ability. In reality, teachers rarely know enough about their pupils to permit valid and precise assessments of their abilities. Teachers do have a general sense of pupils' abilities from their sizing-up assessments and the pupils' classroom performance, but this information is too imprecise to use as a baseline for grading. Formal tests designed to measure ability are rarely precise enough to accurately predict a pupil's capacity for learning. Even for experts, it is all but impossible to make valid predictions about what a pupil of a certain general ability level is capable of achieving in any specific subject area.

Second, teachers often have a difficult time differentiating a pupil's ability from other pupil characteristics such as self-assurance, motivation, or responsiveness. This is especially problematic in light of recent constructivist thinking that pupils have numerous types of abilities or intelligences, not just one (Gardner, 1995; Sternberg, 1997). Given these multiple abilities or intelligences that help pupils learn and perform in different modalities (e.g., oral, visual, written, etc.), which ones should a teacher focus on to judge a pupil's ability?

Third, grades comparing performance against expectations are confusing to people outside the classroom, especially parents. For example, a high-ability pupil who attained 80 percent mastery of the instruction might receive a C grade if perceived to be underachieving, while a low-ability pupil who attained 60 percent mastery might receive an A grade for exceeding expectations. An outsider viewing these two grades would probably think that the low-ability pupil mastered more of the course, because that pupil got the higher grade. In short, there is little correlation between grades and student mastery of course content in ability-based grading systems.

These reasons argue strongly against the use of a grading system that compares actual to predicted achievement. Some report cards do allow separate judgments about pupil achievement and ability. The teacher can record a subject matter grade based on the pupil's actual achievement, and then, in a separate place on the report card, indicate if he or she thinks the pupil is working up to expectations. Usually, the teacher writes comments or checks boxes to show whether the pupil "needs improvement," "is improving," or "is doing best" relative to his or her ability. Even in this approach, teachers must be cautious about putting too much faith in their estimates of pupil ability and potential.

Comparison to Pupil Improvement

Basing grades on pupil improvement over time creates problems similar to those of grading estimates of pupil ability. Pupil improvement is determined by comparing a pupil's early performance to his or her later performance. Pupils who show the most progress or growth get the high grades and those who show little progress or growth get the low grades. An obvious difficulty with this approach is that pupils who do well early in the grading period have little opportunity to improve, and thus have little chance to get good grades. Low scorers at the start of the term have the best chance to show improvement, and thus tend to get high grades. It is not surprising that students graded on improvement quickly realize that it is in their best interests to do poorly on the early tests. They "play dumb" so early performance will be low and improvement can be shown easily.

Also, like comparing actual to predicted performance, grading on the basis of improvement causes problems with grade interpretation. A pupil who improves from very low achievement to moderate achievement may get an A, while a pupil who had high achievement at the start and therefore improved little may get a B or a C, when in fact, the latter pupil has mastered considerably more of the subject matter than the pupil who got the A grade.

Some teachers recognize this difficulty and propose the following solution: Give the pupils who achieve highly throughout the term an A grade for their high performance, but also give A grades to pupils who improve their performance a great deal over time. While this suggestion overcomes the problem noted above, it creates a new problem. In essence, these teachers are proposing to use two very different grading systems, one based on high achievement and the other on high pupil improvement. This approach provides rewards for both groups of pupils, but confuses the meaning of their grades, since the grades can mean two different things, achievement or improvement. Thus, grading systems based on improvement and ability, and grading systems based on combinations of these two, are not recommended. Grades can convey a consistent, understandable message only if the same approach is applied to all pupils.

⚹ Grading for Cooperative Learning and Pupils with Disabilities

Grading in Cooperative Learning

Classrooms at all levels of education are increasingly emphasizing group-based or cooperative learning strategies. In cooperative learning, small groups of two to six pupils are presented with a task or problem situation that they must solve together. While the problem given in a cooperative group can be posed in virtually any subject area, the main purpose of cooperative learning is to have pupils learn to work together to arrive at a single, group-generated solution.

In grading cooperative learning, teachers are usually concerned with assessing three important outcomes: (1) the interactive, cooperative processes that go on within the group, (2) the quality of the group's solution, and (3) each member's contribution to and understanding of that solution. While the assessment of the group processes is important, assessment of subject matter learning is equally important. However, conducting assessment of each individual group member is difficult because the group turns in a single, cooperatively reached product. At issue is how a teacher should assign individual pupil grades on the basis of a single group production.

The most common grading practice in cooperative learning is to assign a single grade to a group's solution and to give that grade to each group member. The difficulty with such a strategy is that it assumes equal contributions and understanding on the part of each group member. Both the pupil who contributed and learned a great deal and the pupil who contributed and learned very little receive the same grade. On the other hand, to push too hard for individual pupil solutions and contributions can destroy many of the benefits of cooperative problem solving. Thus, for many teachers, grading in cooperative learning situations creates problems not encountered in grading individual pupil performance.

There is no single acceptable solution to these problems. Many teachers see no difficulty in assuming equal contributions and learning from each group member and give identical grades to all of them. Other teachers mingle assessment of the group process with assessment of the group product, relying on their observations and interactions with pupils to provide them with an indication of the contribution and comprehension of each group member. Teachers then adjust individual grades according to their observations of pupil participation, contribution, and understanding. Still other teachers let the pupils self-assess their own contribution and understanding by grading themselves. This approach is less than ideal because pupils' self-assessments will often be based as much on their self-perceptions and self-confidence as on their actual contribution and learning.

Another strategy that has some advantages over the preceding ones combines group and individual grades. All members of the group get the same grade for their single, group-based solution or product. Subsequently, the teacher requires each pupil to individually answer or perform follow-up or application activities related to the group problem or task. The purpose of these follow-up activities is to determine how well each pupil understands and can apply the group solution in solving similar types of problems. This approach blends both participation and contribution with subject matter learning in a way that helps the teacher know what each pupil has learned.

Grading Pupils with Disabilities

In Chapters 3 and 7 the issues of instructing and assessing pupils with disabilities were discussed. We saw that more and more pupils with disabling conditions are being integrated or "included" into regular education classrooms. While it is recognized that disabling conditions often prevent pupils from performing at a level similar to their nondisabled classmates in some areas, it is perceived that the intellectual and social benefits of inclusion warrant placing pupils who have disabilities with their nondisabled peers. However, because of the disparities in academic performance that often occur between some disabled and nondisabled pupils, grading can present classroom teachers with a variety of concerns. In fact, one of the questions asked most frequently by classroom teachers is "How should I assign grades to my included pupils with disabilities?"

Embedded in this single question is a host of other questions. For example, who should be responsible for grading an included pupil: the classroom teacher, a special education teacher, or these two in combination? Should the same standards be used to assess pupils with and without disabilities? How should an included pupil's Individual Education Plan enter into the grading process? What is the best way to report the performance of pupils with disabilities? These and many other questions face the classroom teacher who must grade pupils with disabilities.

Here we will examine issues associated with grading pupils with disabilities placed in regular classrooms. We will consider a variety of ways in which such grading can be done and the limitations of these methods. We will also identify the primary problem that confronts teachers who must grade pupils with disabilities and suggest how that grading can be made more manageable and informative.

Consider the question of who should be responsible for grading pupils with disabilities. The answer to this question depends on the extent of a pupil's inclusion in regular classrooms. Different pupils with different disabilities often spend different amounts of time in regular classrooms—from full-time inclusion, to part-time inclusion for instruction in particular subject areas, to no inclusion at all. Generally, the teacher who delivers the instruction in a subject area should be responsible for grading a student in that subject area. Thus, fully included pupils with disabilities should be graded by the regular classroom teacher, as should partially included students who take particular courses from a classroom teacher. Subject areas taught by special education teachers in separate education classrooms should be graded by the special education teacher. Our focus here is on the issues related to grading pupils with disabilities who are included part- or full-time in a regular classroom.

The main problem teachers face in grading pupils with disabilities is the often large disparity in their achievement compared to the achievement of nondisabled pupils. While it is important to understand that not all disabilities hamper a pupil's ability to achieve at a level comparable to nondisabled peers, many disabilities do. Two questions teachers often ask are "Should grading standards be the same for all pupils in my class?" and "How can I take into account a pupil's disability when I assign grades to my class?"

If a teacher applies the same grading standard to all pupils, many of the pupils with disabilities will receive low grades. If the teacher uses different standards for pupils with and without disabilities, the same grade will mean different things depending on which grading standard was applied to a given pupil. Notice that this is a problem whether a norm-referenced or criterion-referenced grading system is used. However, it is especially a problem for pupils with disabilities in criterion-referenced grading where the performance standards are rigid and inflexible (Polloway et al., 1994). The problem is heightened because pupils who are moved from special education classrooms to regular classrooms previously were graded on standards different than those used in regular classrooms (Valdes, Williamson, and Wagner, 1990), thereby creating more confusion about the meaning of a grade.

Many alternative grading strategies have been adopted to grade pupils with disabilities (Salend, 1990). All of the approaches are based on the objectives in a pupil's Individual Education Plan, since these represent the instruction given and the desired pupil outcomes. Most of the approaches are based on a set of standards unique to each pupil, so that a pupil is compared to her- or himself in some way. Following are explanations of some of these alternative strategies.

- **Contract grading:** The teacher and the pupil jointly determine the type and quality of work a pupil will complete in order to receive a particular grade. The contract spells out what amount of work at what level of quality is needed for a pupil to receive an A, B, C, etc. Different pupils have different contracts with different terms.
- **IEP-based grading:** Pupils are graded on the percentage of objectives in their IEP that they complete in a term or marking period. The grading standards would be criterion-referenced with different percentages of completion resulting in different grades (i.e., 80 percent or more completion is an A, 70 to 79 percent completion is a B, and so on). This approach is similar to grading a pupil based on her or his improvement over time.
- **Multiple grading:** The pupil receives different grades for different performances rather than a single, overall grade. For example, a pupil could receive separate grades for effort, participation, achievement, and progress. Such an approach allows the teacher to make some

distinctions in the pupil's overall performance and to show areas of strength and weakness. A similar approach is to adjust grading weights for different pupils by, for example, counting effort or projects more than test results. Report cards that are similar in form to checklists or rating scales also permit more detailed descriptions of pupil performances.

- **Level-based grading:** Pupils are given grades that indicate both their achievement level and curriculum level. For example, a pupil who shows B-level achievement in an accelerated curriculum can be graded B(1), while a pupil who shows B-level achievement in a below grade level curriculum can be graded B(3). The number in parentheses represents the level of the curriculum a pupil is performing in. This is another way of representing a pupil's ability level in a grade.
- **Narrative grading:** The teacher does not assign a grade per se, but provides a substantial written or oral description of the pupil's performance, achievements, strengths, and weaknesses based upon his or her observations and assessments of the pupil. Note that this is an informative, but time-consuming, grading approach.

A survey of non–special education teachers (Bursuck et al., 1996) indicates that classroom teachers utilize many of these strategies in grading pupils *both* with and without disabilities. The survey also showed that teachers use some strategies more than others in grading pupils with disabilities. Among the commonly used strategies are grading on the basis of improvement in IEP objectives; awarding separate grades for process (effort, participation) and achievement (test results); weighting pupil process more than product in grading; and using contract grading. For pupils with disabilities, teachers were less likely to change their grading standards, pass pupils just for high effort, or pass them no matter what their performance. Note that while all of the above strategies are used by teachers, none of these strategies avoid the grading problems of measuring improvement, determining ability, and applying differing grading standards.

The main problem most teachers face in grading classes that contain pupils both with and without disabilities is the inability of any single type of grade to convey the many important messages to the many different audiences interested in grades.

The most common grading system used in schools is the A, B, C, D, and F letter grade system (Polloway et al., 1994; Friedman and Frisbie, 1993). This system limits the information that can be conveyed in a grade because all a teacher can record for a pupil's grade is a single letter, perhaps with a plus or minus added. A, B, C, D, F grading conveys little of the specifics of what the student can or cannot do and has or has not learned. Letter grades create particular problems for teachers who want to take a pupil's disability into account when awarding a grade. As noted previously, regardless of whether teachers use a norm- or criterion-referenced grading system, many pupils with disabilities are likely to receive low grades. On the one hand, if teachers raise a grade because of a pupil's disability, they are constrained to do it within the letter grading system. This means that although a pupil with a disability performed less well than another pupil, both pupils were given the same grade. People who see the two grades will assume that they represent the same achievement. However, if teachers do not take the disability into account, many pupils with disabilities will continually receive low grades. This is the teacher's grading dilemma.

Reporting systems that allow teachers to provide more information about a pupil's grade than a single letter or number can help teachers with this dilemma. Systems such as the level-based and narrative grading approaches allow the teacher to provide important information about the meaning of the pupil's performance. The ability to describe pupils' specific learning outcomes, the grade level of pupil performance, the amount of improvement, the weight given to effort and achievement, the availability of an aide for a pupil, or other pertinent factors related to pupil performance helps teachers when grading pupils with disabilities. Employing such information takes a pupil's disability into account in their grades and also provides the desired perspective on the meaning of the grades.

✸ Selecting Pupil Performances for Grading

Once the comparative basis for assigning grades is decided on, it is necessary to select the particular pupil performances and products that will be used to award grades. If a teacher is grading a single test or a project, there is obviously only one performance to be considered. If a teacher is assigning report card grades, many formal and informal performances could be considered.

The quantity and the nature of the assessment information available to a teacher varies depending on the grade level and subject area. For example, assigning a term grade in spelling simply involves combining the results of each pupil's performance on the Friday spelling tests. In American history or social studies, however, a teacher may have information from quizzes, tests, homework, projects, reports, portfolios, and worksheets. High school math teachers have homework papers, quizzes, portfolios, and test results to consider in assigning grades, while English teachers have tests, reports, homework, quizzes, portfolios, projects, and class discussion to consider. In addition to these formal indicators of achievement, teachers also have informal perceptions of pupils' effort, interest, motivation, helpfulness, and behavior. Each teacher must decide which of all the available information will be used in determining report card grades. This decision is critical, because the performances that are included define what the grade really means. Two questions teachers have to ask about grading are (1) What do I want my grades to convey about pupil performance? and (2) Do the assessments I've included in the grade reflect what I want to convey? Note that it is not necessary or even desirable for teachers to include all available pupil information when assigning grades.

Academic Achievement

Grades are usually viewed as an indication of how much pupils have learned from instruction. Formal assessments of pupils' achievement of the course objectives should be the major component of subject matter grades. Note that the more valid the assessments used in grading, the more valid the resulting grades (Brookhart, 1999). However, effort, behavior, interest, motivation, and the like should *not* be a major part of subject matter grades. These pupil characteristics focus on pupil processes, not pupil learning. To judge pupil learning, we are interested in the *results* of effort, motivation, and interest as evidence of formal assessments.

To give an A grade to a pupil who is academically marginal but very industrious and congenial, would be misleading to the pupil, parents, and others who would interpret the grade as indicating high achievement. Pupils who work hard, are cooperative, and show great motivation and interest are desirable to have in class and deserve to be rewarded, but subject matter grades are not the proper arena for such rewards. Finally, grades should not be heavily weighted toward pupil behavior, interest, and attendance, and should not be used to punish pupils for behavioral problems or late work (Hills, 1991).

Formal, subject matter assessments such as teacher-made and textbook tests, papers, quizzes, homework, projects, worksheets, portfolios, and the like are the best types of evidence to use in assigning report card grades. They are suitable in two respects. First, they provide information about pupils' academic performance, which is what grades are intended to describe. Second, being tangible products of pupils' work, they can be used to explain or defend a grade if the need arises. It is defensible to say to a pupil, "I gave a C grade because when I compared your test scores, projects, and homework assignments in this marking period to my grading standards, you performed at a C level." It is indefensible to say, "I gave a C grade because I had a strong *sense* that you were not working as hard as you could and because I have a negative *general perception* of your daily class performance." This rationale would be difficult to defend or explain to pupils, parents, or principals.

Because formal assessments of pupil achievement should be accorded major weight in assigning grades, it is important to stress that grades will be only as good as the instruction and formal assessments on which they are based. Grading as a process cannot be separated from the quality of the instruction and assessment information teachers collect prior to grading. Just as good instruction can be undermined by invalid assessment, good grading can be undermined by poorly constructed, invalid, and unreliable assessments. Irrelevant, invalid evidence about pupil achievement will produce irrelevant, invalid grades. The guidelines for constructing valid assessments described in Chapters 5 through 9 should underlie the assessments teachers construct and use in their grades.

As the culminating step in the process of assessing pupils' academic achievement, grading should be based upon a varied assortment of valid and reliable evidence. A general rule of grading is to draw on several different types of information rather than a single type, because this gives pupils more opportunity to show what they can do. Also, since most subject areas require pupils to remember, understand, and apply, varied procedures are needed to assess all-important outcomes of instruction.

If subject matter grades were assigned by computers, it would be easy to grade solely on formal assessments of pupil achievement. We could program the computer and it would provide the grades. But teachers are not computers and teachers know a great deal more about their pupils than any computer ever could. Teachers know their pupils as whole persons, not one-dimensional scores or achievers. Teachers understand pupils' home backgrounds and know the effects grades will have on pupils and their parents. Because of this, teachers rarely can be completely objective and dispassionate dispensers of report card grades, as the following excerpts illustrate.

> Peter works harder than any pupil in my class, but he cannot seem to overcome his lack of ability. No one tries harder yet his tests and projects are all failures. But I just can't in good conscience give Peter a failing grade because he tries so hard and an F would destroy him.

> Brianne had a terrible term. Her test scores dropped off, her attention during instruction was poor, and she failed to complete many homework assignments. The reason for these behaviors is in her home situation. Her father left the home, her mother had to find a job, and Brianne had to assume most of the household and babysitting responsibilities because she is the oldest child. How can I not take this into account when I grade her this term?

> Jermaine is the ultimate itch: constant motion, inattention, socializing around the classroom at inappropriate times. He drives me crazy. However, his classwork is well done and on time. When I sit down to grade him, I have to refrain from saying "OK Jermaine, now I'm going to get you for being such a distraction." I have a hard time separating his academic performance from his classroom behavior.

Affective Performances

Although affective characteristics should not be major factors in report card grades, the fact that teachers do have perceptions of their pupils' affective characteristics means that they often enter into grading decisions. A common situation in which pupil motivation, interest, and effort enter into grades is when they are used to give borderline pupils the benefit of the doubt. When a teacher awards a B+ to a pupil whose academic performance places her between a B and a B+ grade, but who is motivated, participates in class, and works diligently, the teacher is taking into account more than just formal assessments of achievement. Teachers often nudge the grades given to conscientious, participating pupils upward in order to keep them motivated. Strictly speaking, such adjustments distort the intended meaning of a grade, but most teachers do make them based upon their knowledge of particular pupil characteristics and needs. Grading is a human judgmental process, and it is virtually inevitable that such teacher adjustments will be made.

These borderline decisions usually operate for the benefit of the pupil and the psychic comfort of the teacher. However, a teacher should guard against allowing effort, motivation, interest, or personality to become the dominant factors in grades. If that happens, grades are distorted, providing little useful information about the pupil's academic achievement. Although few teachers can ignore nonacademic evidence like pupils' ability, effort, and improvement when they grade, most correctly use such evidence as a basis for adjustments in pupils' grades, not as the central determiner of grades (Brookhart, 1992; Griswold and Griswold, 1992; Nava and Loyd, 1992).

To summarize, we have seen that teachers must decide what standards of comparison to use in assigning grades. This means deciding upon either a norm-referenced or a criterion-referenced standard. Once this decision has been made, the teacher must establish a grading curve in the norm-referenced approach or a set of performance standards in the criterion-referenced approach. Next, the teacher must determine what performances will be included in the grade. Because grades are mainly intended to convey information about pupils' subject matter mastery, rather than their personal qualities, grades should be based primarily upon formal assessments of pupil achievement. Although, teachers' subjective perceptions and insights inevitably influence the grading process to some extent, they should not be allowed to greatly distort the subject matter grade.

✕ Summarizing Varied Types of Assessment

Report card grades require teachers to summarize each pupil's performance on the many individual assessments gathered during the marking period. In some subject areas, summarization across a term is easy and straightforward. Suppose Ms. Fogarty is getting ready to assign report card grades in spelling. To do this she would refer to her grade book of her pupils' scores on each of the weekly spelling tests given during the grading period. It is very important that teachers maintain such grade books and that they be carefully guarded to ensure confidentiality of pupil grades. It is recommended that teachers keep two copies of the grade book, one kept in the classroom and one kept at home. A lost grade book can place a teacher in great difficulty when trying to give grades by reconstructing the contents of the lost grade book.

Figure 10.4 shows part of a teacher's actual grade book for the first 5 weeks of term two in a fifth grade geography class. The pupils' names have been removed for privacy. At the bottom of the figure is a list of all the assessments the pupils were expected to complete. Each pupil is assigned a grade for each of the assessments. Grades that have an empty circle indicate that the pupil has not yet turned in that assessment. Assessment topics that have no grades listed for all pupils, such as "Around World in 26 Letters," indicate assessments that are in process but not completed.

At the end of term, teachers must synthesize each pupil's assessments. Calculating each pupil's overall performance has been made easier with the

Subject: Geography, Section 02	Assign.	Weekly Geo #8 (10)	Current Event — Oct	Pictontious Quiz (9)	Weekly Geo #9 (14)	Around World in 26 letters (25)	Current Event — Nov	Mystery Post Card	American Squares	Weekly Geo #10 (18)	Sec 2 Quiz (10) P26-30	Weekly Geo #11 (15) — Sit Report	December Cities	Around World in 20 cards	Weekly Geo #12 (11)	
(check marks)		√	√	√	√		√			√	√	√ √ (Term 2)		√	√	
(assignment #)		1	2	3	4		5			6	7	8		9	10	
(weeks / days)		1st week M T W T F			2nd week M T W T F			3rd week M T W T F			4th week M T W T F			5th week M T W T F		
Students	1	70	12	79	99	ı	91	ı	√+	81	60	47	√	80	82	85
	2	50	15	79	12	ı	90	ı	√+	100	60	86	√+	100	91	100
	3	40	82	47	O	ı	74	ı		O	80	40	ı	80	64	55
	4	70	76	89	86	ı	82	ı	√+	93	80	79	√+	90	99	100
	5	54	84	47	(88) 88	ı	67	ı-10	(39)	39		62		55	(96)	80
	6	60	91	84	100	ı	85	ı	√+	91	70	87	√	100	100	95
	7	49	67	47	O	ı	(55)	ı	√+	59	40	58	√		(98)	80
	8	70	94	89	100	ı	86	ı	√+	92	40	93	√+	97	100	
	9	69	68	100	83	ı	88	ı	√+	89	80	87	√+		100	90
	10	(30)	73	74	100	ı	99	ı	√+	0	20	73		80	77	80
	11	39	73	47	98	ı	(62)		√+	90	70	46		70	100	80
	12	70	76	89	92	ı	78	ı	√+	88	70	67	√	80	99	100
	13															
	14	68	62	79	81	ab	69	ı	√+	31	ab	59	√	70	94	80
	15	63	79	74	98	ı	79	ı	√+	77	80	60	√	95	99	
	16	59	34 60	58	92	ı	75	ı-10	(√)	86	100	67	ı		82	80
	17	(71)	87	100	85	ı	95	ı-10		89	100	59	√+	100	100	75
	18	80	79	100	83	ı	74	ı-10	√+	6	100	53	√+	95	80	95
	19															
	20															
	21															
	22															
	23															
	24															
	25															
	26															
	27															
	28															
	29															
	30															
	31															
	32															
	33															
	34															
	35															

FIGURE 10.4   *Fifth Grade Teacher's Rank Book*

use of spreadsheets and varied computer grading programs. The convenience of computer grading depends on the teacher keeping accurate assessment data to synthesize. Table 10.3 shows the results of a computer grading program. Again, pupil names have been removed for privacy. The scores for each assessment are shown in the columns numbered 1 to 13. The average of each pupil's assessments is shown on the left of the table under "Average." Scores shown in bold in the "Average" column indicate pupils who have not completed all the term assessments. Note that synthesizing pupils'

TABLE 10.3

Computer Grading Program
1999–00 Term 1 Geography

Average	13	12	11	10	9	8	7	6	5	4	3	2	1
85.40	95	95	100	100	83	49	35	91	91	96	88	88	88
92.20	95	95	88	100	87	100	80	90	91	100	88	95	94
85.16		95		80	58	88	85	94	82	89	50	85	94
94.40	95	95	100	100	82	88	85	98	100	100	88	95	94
86.53	92	92	88	90	75	98	80	83	55	100	100	85	94
95.40	95	95	100	100	92	98	85	100	87	96	94	95	94
74.93	85	95	88	65	82	88	25	76	36	71	88	85	88
94.87	95	95	100	100	92	100	85	92	100	100	94	92	94
91.33	95	95	100	100	88	88	85	83	87	100	94	95	94
77.67	95	88	100	90	87	63	85	45	64	82	88	88	100
77.60	95	95	87	50	58	87	95	63	73	100	56	85	94
89.13	95	95	100	90	83	75	80	89	73	96	88	95	100
80.13	95	92	74	90	81	67	70	75	60	71	88	95	94
82.13	95	95	100	70	83	100	60	65	64	100	88	82	100
75.01		85	100	70	49	56	40	72	73	100	63	85	94
89.24	95	95	99	100	81	99	85	72	91	100	88		100
90.40	95	100	100	80	91	100	75	80	96	100	100	88	91

term performance as shown does *not* produce pupil grades. The teacher must still apply grading standards to the scores to determine pupil grades.

Returning to Ms. Fogarty's task of assigning report card grades for spelling, suppose there were 11 spelling tests for each pupil, each scored on the basis of 100 points. Ms. Fogarty must summarize the scores for each pupil and use the resulting number to assign a report card grade. This is a relatively easy task for her, since each test was scored on the basis of 100 total points and each test was worth the same amount. She would sum each pupil's score on the 11 tests and calculate the mean or average score.

Let us assume that Ms. Fogarty decided to assign spelling grades using a criterion-referenced approach with the following performance standards: 100 to 90 = A, 89 to 80 = B, 79 to 70 = C, and below 70 = D. She also decided not to flunk any pupils in the first term and not to award plusses and minuses, but instead to use only A, B, C, and D as possible grades. It is important to recognize that not all teachers would have made the same decisions as Ms. Fogarty. Some might have used a norm-referenced grading system, selected different performance standards, or made adjustments based on effort and motivation. There is no best way to assign grades in all classrooms; we can only discuss the topic in terms of examples that allow us to look at basic issues that should be considered in all grading situations. In this example, Ms. Fogarty would compare each pupil's spelling average to the performance standards and then award the corresponding letter grade: all pupils whose average scores were between 90 and 100 would be given an A, all between 80 and 89 a B, and so on.

This example provides a basic frame of reference for understanding the grading process. It shows how standards come into play in allocating grades, how formal assessment evidence is recorded in a marking book, and how individual scores are summarized to provide a summary of pupil performance for report card purposes. However, most grading situations are not as simple as this example. Consider the more typical example of Ms. Fogarty's marking book for social studies, shown in Figure 10.5.

Notice two important differences between the information Ms. Fogarty has available to grade social studies and the information that was available in the spelling example. In spelling, the only formal assessments were the weekly spelling tests. In social studies, Ms. Fogarty has collected many different kinds of assessment information. Four homework assignments, two quiz results, four unit test results, and two projects make up the information Ms. Fogarty can use to assign grades in social studies. In spelling, all test re-

---

SOCIAL STUD.

TERM # 1

	HW #1	HW #2	HW #3	HW #4	quiz	quiz	test unit 1	test unit 2	test unit 3	test unit 4	proj. explor Amer	proj. colon.
Aston, J.	✓	✓	✓	✓-	85	90	80	85	50	80	B+	B
Babcock, W.	✓	✓	✓	✓-	90	90	85	80	60	80	B	B
Cannata, T.	✓	✓-	✓	✓	80	75	70	70	45	75	C-	C
Farmer, P.	✓+	✓+	✓+	✓	100	95	90	85	70	95	A-	A-
Foster, C.	✓+	✓+	✓	✓	90	80	85	90	65	80	B	B+
Gonzales, E.	✓	✓-	✓-	✓-	70	75	60	70	55	70	C	B-
Grodsky, F.	✓-	✓-	✓-	✓-	65	65	65	60	35	60	C	C
Martin, J.	✓	✓	✓	✓	80	90	70	85	65	85	C	B
Picardi, O.	✓	✓	✓	✓	75	80	85	75	65	80	B	B-
Ross, O.	✓+	✓	✓	✓	85	80	90	90	75	95	A	A-
Sachar, S.	✓-	✓	✓	✓+	80	85	75	80	40	80	B+	B
Saja, J.	✓	✓	✓	✓	75	80	85	85	50	80	B	B+
Stamos, G.	✓	✓+	✓+	✓	70	60	75	85	50	70	B-	B
Whalem, W.	✓	✓	✓	✓	70	70	50	60	60	70	B-	B-
Yeh, T.	✓+	✓+	✓+	✓+	95	100	95	95	75	95	A	A-

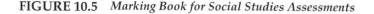

FIGURE 10.5 *Marking Book for Social Studies Assessments*

sults were expressed numerically, on a scale of 0 to 100. In social studies, different grading formats are used for different assessments: homework assignments are rated ✓+, ✓, ✓−, quizzes and tests are recorded on a scale of 0 to 100; and the two projects are recorded as letter grades. Grading social studies will be a more complicated process than grading spelling.

Despite their differences, both grading processes start out with the same concerns. First, what standard of comparison will be used to award grades? Second, what specific performances will be included in the grade? Let us assume that, in social studies, Ms. Fogarty wishes to use a criterion-referenced grading approach and that she wishes to use plusses and minuses. With this decision made, she must next determine which of the four different kinds of assessment information available to her will be included in the grade. She must not only decide which of these to include, but how much each kind of information will count in determining the grades. For example, should a project count as much as a unit test? Should two quizzes count as much as one unit test or four homework assignments? These are questions all teachers face when they try to combine different kinds of assessment information into a single indicator. The following sections contain suggestions for answering such questions.

What Should Be Included in a Grade?

Figure 10.5 shows a marking book page with four different formal indicators of Ms. Fogarty's pupils' academic performance: homework, quizzes, unit tests, and projects. In addition to these formal indicators, Ms. Fogarty also has many informal, unrecorded perceptions about each pupil's effort, participation in class, interest, behavior, and home situation. Should all the formal and informal information be included in her pupils' grades?

Almost all teachers would include the unit tests and the project results in determining their pupils' grades. These are formal, summative indicators of pupil achievement that should be reflected in the grade a pupil receives. Most teachers rightly assign grades based mainly on formal assessments. Many teachers would also include quiz results and homework, although there would be less unanimity among teachers on this point. Some teachers regard quizzes and homework as practice activities that are more closely tied to instruction than to assessment. Other teachers view homework and quizzes as indicators of how well pupils have learned their daily lessons and thus include them as part of the pupil's grade. Others would not count homework because it is never clear who actually does the work. As with most grading issues, the final decision is the classroom teacher's.

Let us assume that Ms. Fogarty has decided to include three types of formal assessment information in her pupils' social studies grades: tests, projects, and quizzes. Let us also assume that she has decided not to include a formal rating of each pupil's effort, participation, interest, and behavior. Having decided what pupil performances will be included, she now must determine whether each kind of information will count equally or whether some kinds should be weighted more heavily than others.

Selecting Weights for Assessment Information

An immediate concern in summarizing pupil performance on different kinds of evidence is how each should be weighted. In general, teachers should give the more important types of pupil performance—such as tests, projects, and portfolios—more weight than short quizzes or homework assignments, since the former provide a more complete, integrated and valid view of pupils' subject matter learning. Ms. Fogarty decided that unit tests and projects should count equally and that both should count more than quiz results. She was fairly certain that she had used valid tests that reflected the important aspects of her instruction and that the projects assigned required pupils to integrate their knowledge about the topic. Thus, she was confident in using tests and projects as the main components of her social studies grade. Finally, she decided that the two quizzes would count as much as one unit test.

Although many teachers do not count homework directly in determining grades, they often warn pupils that if more than three or four homework assignments are not turned in, their report card grade will be lowered. Used this way, homework becomes more an indicator of effort or cooperation than of subject matter mastery. This lowers the validity and clarity of the grade. Some teachers do not actually compute pupil homework averages, but rely instead on an informal "sense" or "intuition" of how a pupil has performed. Although timesaving, this practice allows subjective factors such as the pupil's behavior or interest in the subject matter to influence the teacher's judgment. Neither lowering pupil grades for missed homework assignments nor determining grades on the basis of an informal "sense" of pupil performance is recommended.

Regardless of how a teacher weights each kind of assessment information, it is strongly suggested that the weightings be simple. It is better to weight some things twice as much as others than to weight some five times as much and others seven times as much. In most instances, the final grades arrived at using a simple weighting scheme will not differ greatly from those arrived at using a more complex, cumbersome weighting scheme.

After deciding on her weightings for quizzes, unit tests, and projects, Ms. Fogarty identified seven pieces of information that she would combine to determine her pupils' report card grades in social studies:

- One overall assessment of quiz results
- Four scores from the unit tests
- Two project grades

In the final weightings, quiz results count one-seventh of the grade, unit tests count four-sevenths of the grade, and projects count two-sevenths of the grade. Ms. Fogarty next had to combine the available information according to the selected weights.

Combining Different Assessment Information

Figure 10.5 shows that pupil performance on different assessments often is represented in different ways. Somehow Ms. Fogarty must combine the selected scoring formats into a single summary score that includes performance on tests, projects, and quizzes. Some of the information shown in Figure 10.5 will have to be changed into another format, preferably a numerical one. This means that the project letter grades will have to be converted into numerical scores on a scale of 0 to 100 percent, so that they will correspond to the scores for the quizzes and unit tests.

It is important to stress that all performance indicators should be expressed in terms of the same scale, so that they can be combined meaningfully. For example, suppose a teacher gave two tests, one with 50 items and one with 100 items, and that the teacher wanted each test to count equally in determining a pupil's grade. Now suppose that two pupils, Terence and Marcus, each got a perfect score on one of the tests and a zero score on the other: Marcus got his perfect score on the 50-item test and Terence got his on the 100-item test. Because the tests are to count equally, one would think that the pupils' grades should be the same regardless of the number of items on each test. However, if the teacher calculates the average performance for Marcus and Terence using the *number* of items they got right across both tests, the resulting averages will be quite different: Marcus's average would be 25 (50 + 0)/2 = 25) and Terence's average would be 50 (0 + 100)/2 = 50). Terence would get a higher grade than Marcus, even though they each attained a perfect score on one test and a zero score on another and the tests were to count equally. Clearly, combining raw scores or number of items correct and finding their average does not give equal weight to each test.

The problem in the preceding example is that the teacher did not take into account the difference in the number of items on the two tests—the teacher did not put the two tests on the same scale before computing an average. If the teacher had changed the scores from number of items correct to percentage of items correct *before* averaging, Marcus and Terence would have had the same overall performance [Marcus = (100 + 0)/2 = 50; Terence = (0 + 100)/2 = 50]. Or if the teacher had expressed performance on both tests in terms of the 100-point test, the averages would have been the same, since Marcus's perfect score on a 50-item test would be worth 100 points on a 100 point scale. Once again, if scores are not expressed in a common scale, pupil performance will be distorted and grades will not reflect actual achievement.

Returning to Ms. Fogarty's grading task, a way must be found to express project performance on a scale that corresponds to the 0 to 100 percent scale used for quizzes and unit tests. She decided that for project grades, the following scale would be used to assign numerical scores to the projects: 95 = A, 92 = A–, 88 = B+, 85 = B, 82 = B–, 78 = C+, 75 = C, 72 = C–, 68 = D+, 65 = D, 62 = D–, less than 60 = F. If, for example, a pupil got a B– on one of the projects, that pupil's numerical score on the project would be 82. When Ms. Fogarty applied these values to the projects, she ended up with the information shown in Table 10.4. It is important to note that Ms. Fogarty's is not the only way that the different scores could be put on the same scale, nor is it without limitations. It is, however, one way she could accomplish her task with a method she felt comfortable using. With this task completed, Ms. Fogarty has to confront one additional issue prior to computing grades.

TABLE 10.4

Social Studies Assessment Scores Placed on the Same Scale
Social Studies, Term 1

	Quiz 1	Quiz 2	Test 1	Test 2	Test 3	Test 4	Proj. 1	Proj. 2
Aston, J.	85	90	80	85	50	80	88	85
Babcock, W.	90	90	85	80	60	80	85	85
Cannata, T.	80	75	70	70	45	70	72	70
Farmer, P.	100	95	90	85	70	95	92	92
Foster, C.	90	80	85	90	65	80	85	88
Gonzales, E.	70	75	60	70	55	70	75	82
Grodsky, F.	65	65	65	60	35	60	75	75
Martin, J.	80	90	70	85	65	85	75	85
Picardi, O.	75	80	85	75	65	80	85	82
Ross, O.	85	80	90	90	75	95	95	92
Sachar, S.	80	85	75	80	40	80	88	85
Saja, J.	75	80	85	85	50	80	85	88
Stamos, G.	70	60	75	85	50	70	82	85
Whalem, W.	70	70	50	60	60	70	82	82
Yeh, T.	95	100	95	95	75	95	95	92

Validity of Assessment Information

Before combining assessment information into a grade, the quality of that information must be considered. Grades will be only as meaningful as the information on which they are based. If the project grades were assigned subjectively, with no clear criteria in mind and with shifting teacher attention during scoring, they will not accurately reflect pupil achievement. If the unit tests were unfair to pupils or did not test a representative sample of what was taught, the scores pupils attained will not be valid indications of their achievement. In this regard, Ms. Fogarty should examine the results of the unit 3 test, since they were much lower than scores on the other unit tests. Do these scores indicate a problem with the test or a problem with the effort pupils put into preparing for the test? How should this result be handled in grading? These questions have to be answered before information can be combined and used for grading.

Ms. Fogarty noticed the poor performance on the unit 3 test when she scored the test, and no doubt asked herself why the scores were so low. Normally, questions about the match between an assessment instrument and the things pupils were taught occur *before* an assessment instrument is used. Sometimes, however, mismatches are overlooked or do not become apparent until after the instrument is administered and scored. Unexpectedly low scores typically provoke teachers' concern and attention; rarely do unexpectedly high scores provoke the same reaction. The reason for this discrepancy in teacher reaction is that most teachers probably assume that unexpectedly low scores are the result of a faulty assessment instrument, while unexpectedly high scores are the result of their superior teaching.

Ms. Fogarty looked over the items in the unit 3 test, which was a textbook test, and compared the items to the topics and skills she had taught in that unit. She found that one section of the unit that she had decided not to teach contributed a large number of test items that she had failed to remove. Thus, the match between the unit test and classroom instruction was not good. Pupils were being penalized because her instruction had failed to cover many concepts included in the test. Thus, to use these unit 3 scores would provide a distorted picture of her pupils' actual achievement, and this, in turn, would reduce the validity of their grades.

To avoid this, Ms. Fogarty decided to change the pupils' scores on the unit 3 test to better reflect their achievement. She estimated that about 20 to 25 percent of the items on the test were from the section she had not taught. She checked and saw that most pupils had done poorly on these items, so she decided to increase each pupil's unit 3 score by 20 percentage points. She correctly reasoned that the increased scores would provide a better indication of what pupils had learned *from the instruction provided* than would the original scores. Adjusting each pupil's unit 3 score places all of the assessment information on a common scale that ranges from 0 to 100 and indicates the percentage of mastery by each pupil on each assessment.

It is important to point out that Ms. Fogarty adjusted the low scores on the unit 3 test only after reexamining both the test and her instruction. She did not raise the scores to make the pupils feel better about themselves, to have them like her more, or for other, similar reasons. The test scores were raised so that they would provide a more valid indication of how well pupils learned from their instruction. It made her grades better reflect her pupils' subject matter mastery. Low assessment scores should not be raised simply because they are low or because the teacher is disappointed with them.

Computing Pupils' Overall Scores

Having decided on score equivalents for the project assessments and having adjusted scores on the unit 3 test to correct the partial mismatch between instruction and assessment, Ms. Fogarty is ready to compute her pupils' social studies grades. To do this, she must (1) give each kind of assessment information the weight she decided on; (2) sum the scores; and (3) divide by 7, which is the number of assessment items she is using to grade (one overall quiz score, four unit test scores, and two project scores). This computation will provide an average social studies score for each pupil's marking period. Table 10.5 shows the seven components to be included in each pupil's grade, their total, and their average. To make her task simpler, Ms. Fogarty decided that all fractions would be rounded off to the nearest whole number.

TABLE 10.5

Computation of Pupils' Social Studies Grades
Social Studies, Term 1

	Quizzes	Test 1	Test 2	Test 3	Test 4	Proj. 1	Proj. 2	Total Score	Average
Aston, J.	88	80	85	70	80	88	85	576	82
Babcock, W.	90	85	80	80	80	85	85	585	84
Cannata, T.	78	70	70	65	70	72	70	495	71
Farmer, P.	98	90	85	90	95	92	92	642	92
Foster, C.	85	85	90	85	80	85	88	598	85
Gonzales, E.	73	60	70	75	70	75	82	505	72
Grodsky, F.	65	65	60	55	60	75	75	455	65
Martin, J.	85	70	85	85	85	75	85	570	81
Picardi, O.	78	85	75	85	80	85	82	570	81
Ross, O.	83	90	90	95	95	95	92	640	91
Sachar, S.	83	75	80	60	80	88	85	551	79
Saja, J.	78	85	85	70	80	85	88	571	82
Stamos, G.	65	75	85	70	70	82	85	532	76
Whalem, W.	70	50	60	80	70	82	82	494	71
Yeh, T.	98	95	95	95	95	95	92	665	95

Strictly speaking, the actual weight that a particular assessment carries in determining a grade depends on the spread of scores on that assessment compared to the spread of scores on other assessments (Frisbie and Waltman, 1992). The greater the spread of scores on an assessment, the greater the influence that assessment will have on the final grade when averaged with other assessments. Fairly simple and straightforward techniques are available for equalizing the influence of assessments whose scores are widely spread. However, this is not a major problem with most classroom assessments, because they are similar in format, given to the same group of pupils, cover topics taught in instruction, and are scored in the same way. Under these conditions, the spread of scores on different assessments will usually be close enough so that adjustments need not be made. Table 10.5 shows that the difference between the highest and lowest score on each of the seven assessments is 33 for the quiz score; 45, 35, 40, and 35 for the four unit tests; and 23 and 22 for the two projects. These ranges are similar enough to permit the seven components to be added and averaged to determine an overall pupil score.

Table 10.5 shows the final average of each pupil after each piece of assessment information was weighted in the way Ms. Fogarty chose. Consider J. Aston's scores in Table 10.5. This pupil received a total quiz score of 88, based upon the average of two quizzes rounded off to a whole number. The four test scores–with 20 points added to the unit 3 score—are as shown in the table. The two project grades are expressed in terms of the numerical equivalents Ms. Fogarty selected. Adding these scores gives a total score of 576, which, when divided by 7 (for the seven pieces of information that were combined), gives an average performance of 82. The average for each pupil gives an indication of the proportion of social studies objectives each pupil achieved in the marking period. Notice that this interpretation is only appropriate if Ms. Fogarty's various assessments are scored in terms of percentage mastery and if they are a fair and representative assessment of the things that were taught. Ms. Fogarty can now apply her performance standards to award pupils' grades.

⋊ Assigning Grades to Pupils: Two Approaches

A Criterion-Referenced Example

Ms. Fogarty decided to assign grades based on a criterion-referenced approach because she felt that this approach gave each pupil a chance to get a good grade if he or she mastered what was taught. The performance standards Ms. Fogarty adopted for her social studies grades follow:

A = 94 or higher	C = 74 to 76
A– = 90 to 93	C– = 70 to 73
B+ = 87 to 89	D+ = 67 to 69
B = 84 to 86	D = 64 to 66
B– = 80 to 83	D– = 60 to 63
C+ = 77 to 79	F = less than 60

This is a widely used criterion-referenced grading standard.

Looking at the overall semester averages as shown in Table 10.5, Ms. Fogarty can apply her performance standards to award grades. It is at this juncture that she is likely to consider pupils' nonacademic characteristics. For example, she may say to herself, "This pupil has worked so hard this term despite an unsettled home situation that it's amazing she was able to focus on her schoolwork at all" or "There is so little positive reinforcement in this kid's life right now that a failing grade would absolutely crush him, even though his performance has been very poor." In short, Ms. Fogarty, like most teachers, is aware of her responsibility to grade pupils primarily on their academic performance, but allows herself some room for small individual adjustments. Opinions will always differ about making such grading adjustments, as the following excerpts show.

> I grade strictly by the numbers. I calculate each pupil's average and assign grades based strictly on that average. A 79.4 average is not an 80 average, and thus will get a C+. This is the only way I can be fair to all pupils.
>
> I calculate the averages based on tests and assignments just like the books say to. But when it comes time to assign the grade, I know I'm not grading an average, I'm grading a kid I know and spend time with every day. I know how the kid has behaved, how much effort has been put into my class, and what effect a high or low grade will have on him or her. I

know about the pressure the kid gets from parents and what reaction they will have to a particular grade. If I didn't know about these things, grading would be much easier.

When Ms. Fogarty applied her performance standards to her class averages, her grades were as follows:

Name	Average	Grade	Name	Average	Grade
Aston, J.	82	B–	Picardi, O.	81	B–
Babcock, W.	84	B	Ross, O.	91	A–
Cannata, T.	71	C–	Sachar, S.	79	C+
Farmer, P.	92	A–	Saja, J.	82	B–
Foster, C.	85	B	Stamos, G.	76	C
Gonzales, E.	72	C–	Whalem, W.	71	C–
Grodsky, F.	65	D	Yeh, T.	95	A
Martin, J.	81	B–			

Notice that some pupils such as S. Sachar and G. Stamos are within one point of the performance standard for the next higher grade. It is for pupils who are close to reaching the next higher grade that teacher judgments about nonacademic characteristics usually enter into grading.

To summarize, Ms. Fogarty had to make many decisions to arrive at these grades. She had to decide whether to use a norm-referenced or a criterion-referenced grading approach. Having selected the criterion-referenced approach, she had to decide on performance standards for awarding grades. Next she had to decide upon the kinds of assessment information that would be included in her grades and how to weight each kind. Because some of the information she wished to include was expressed as percentage scores out of 100 and other information was expressed as letter grades, Ms. Fogarty had to decide how to put all assessment scores on the same scale. Then she had to decide whether to adjust any scores because of faulty instruments. Finally, she had to decide whether to base her grades solely on the pupils' average academic performance or to alter them slightly because of affective or personal characteristics, (Borich, 1996; Tombari & Borich, 1999). Different teachers with different classes and in different schools likely would have made different decisions than Ms. Fogarty, but they all would have had to confront the same issues. Box 10.1 summarizes the steps in the grading process.

A Norm-Referenced Example

To complete this example, consider how Ms. Fogarty would have assigned grades if she had chosen a norm-referenced grading approach. In this case, she would have decided in advance upon a grading curve that identified the percentage of pupils whom she wanted to receive each grade. Suppose she used a norm-referenced curve that gave the top 20 percent of the pupils an A, the next 20 percent a B, the next 40 percent a C, and the last 20 percent a D.

To assign grades using this norm-referenced curve, Ms. Fogarty must first arrange the pupils from highest to lowest average score. This ordering for Ms. Fogarty's class is shown on page 327.

Box 10.1   Steps in the Grading Process

- Select a standard of comparison (norm-referenced or criterion-referenced).
- Select types of performances (tests, projects, etc.).
- Assign weights for each type of performance.
- Record the number of points earned out of the total possible points for *each individual performance* graded.
- Total the points earned for *each type of performance* and divide this by the total number of possible points. This gives a percentage for each type of performance.
- Multiply each of these percentages by the weights assigned.
- Sum the totals and apply the chosen standard of comparison to the totals.
- Review the grades and make adjustments if necessary.

Name	Score	Name	Score
Yeh, T.	95	Saja, J.	82
Farmer, P.	92	Sachar, S.	79
Ross, O.	91	Stamos, G.	76
Foster, C.	85	Gonzales, E.	72
Babcock, W.	84	Cannata, T.	71
Aston, J.	82	Whalem, W.	71
Martin, J.	81	Grodsky, F.	65
Picardi, O.	81		

Because there are 15 pupils in the class, 20 percent of the class is three pupils. Thus, T. Yeh, P. Farmer, and O. Ross, the three highest-scoring pupils, received A grades. The next 20 percent of the pupils—C. Foster, W. Babcock, and J. Aston—got B grades. The next 40 percent of the class (six pupils) got C grades. Finally, the last 20 percent of the class—T. Cannata, W. Whalem, and F. Grodsky—received D grades. In assigning grades by the norm-referenced approach it is important to bear in mind that two pupils who attain the same score must receive the same grade, regardless of the curve being used. Notice the differences in the grade distributions under the norm-referenced and the criterion-referenced approaches. Remember that these differences are mainly the result of decisions made about the grading curve or performance standards that are used. Regardless of the method of grading adopted, it is extremely important for the teacher to be able to explain the grading process to pupils, parents, and administrators. Box 10.2 lists the guidelines for grading.

✄ Other Methods of Reporting Pupil Progress

Report card grades are the most common way that pupils and their parents are kept informed of how things are going in the classroom. But the functionality of grades is limited because they are usually provided infrequently, provide little *specific* information about how a pupil is performing,

---

Box 10.2   Guidelines for Grading

- The chosen grading system is consistent with the purpose of grading.
- Data for grading is gathered throughout the grading period.
- Varied pieces of data are collected (tests, projects, quizzes, etc.).
- Students are informed about the system used to grade them.
- The grading system separates subject matter achievements from nonacademic performance (effort, motivation, etc.). Nonacademic performance is evaluated independently of subject matter performance.
- Grading is based on valid and reliable assessment evidence.
- Important evidence of achievement is weighted more than less-important evidence (e.g., tests weighted more than quizzes).
- The grading system is applied consistently across all pupils.

Box 10.3   Options for Parent-Teacher Communication

- Report cards
- Weekly or monthly progress reports
- Parents' nights
- School visitation days
- Parent-teacher conferences
- Phone calls
- Letters
- Class or school newsletter
- Papers and work products

---

and rarely include information about the teacher's perceptions of a pupil's effort, motivation, cooperation, and classroom demeanor. Moreover, since report card grades usually reflect pupil performance on a variety of assessment tasks, it is quite possible for two pupils to receive the same grade but have performed very differently on the assessments used to determine the grade. Because of these limitations, other approaches for reporting pupils' school progress also are needed and used by teachers. Box 10.3 lists the many ways teachers can communicate and interact with parents. Each of these forms of communication can provide important supplementary information that rounds out the picture of a pupil's life at school.

Parent-Teacher Conferences

Parent-teacher conferences allow flexible, two-way communication, unlike the one-way communication that grades provide. The nature of the communication differs as well. Conferences permit discussion, elaboration, and explanation of pupil performance. The teacher can get information from the parents about their concerns and perceptions of their child's school experience. Information can also be obtained about special problems the pupil is having, from physical and emotional problems to problems of classroom adjustment. Parents can inform the teacher of their concerns and ask questions about their child's classroom behavior and about the curriculum being taught. Preschool teachers or those who teach the last grade of elementary or middle school will often be asked by parents to recommend the type of school, teacher, or academic program that is most suitable for their child. Certainly a parent-teacher conference can address a broader range of issues and concerns than a report card grade can.

Moreover, parents learn a great deal about their children's performance from parent-teacher conferences. A study by Shepard and Bliem (1995) on a sample of elementary school parents examined the usefulness of report cards, parent-teacher discussions, standardized tests, and graded examples of pupils' schoolwork for parents' understanding of their child's progress in school. Ninety-four percent of the parents indicated that discussions with teachers were useful or very useful in understanding their child's progress, and 90 percent also said that receiving graded examples of their child's work was useful or very useful. Only 76 percent of the parents felt that report cards were useful or very useful for informing them about their child's school progress. Thirty-six percent cited standardized tests as being useful or very useful for informing them about progress. Parents look for information beyond report cards to indicate how their children are performing in school.

It is natural for teachers to feel somewhat uneasy at the prospect of a conference with parents. The teacher will want to be respected by the parents, will not want a confrontational experience, and may have to tell parents some unpleasant things about their child. Because the teacher will have certain things he or she wants the parents to know and because there is always an element of uncertainty about the way the conference will go, it is recommended that the teacher prepare an agenda of the things he or she wants to cover. Parents will probably do this also. For example, most teachers will want to provide a description of the pupil's academic and social classroom performance. The teacher will also want to ask the parents questions such as "Does your child act this way at home?" "What does he say about the work load in school?" Certainly the teacher will want to give parents the opportunity to ask questions. Parents are most likely to ask questions such as "What are my child's current levels in reading and math?" "How is my child's behavior in class?" "Does she get along with her classmates?" or "Why did my son get a C– in math?" Finally, the teacher, in conjunction with the parents, may want to plan a course of action to help the pupil. The course agreed upon should contain actions on the part of the teacher, the parent, and the pupil. A teacher may want a counselor or administrator to attend the conference if it is likely to be confrontational.

Planning conferences is necessary to accomplish such agendas. The teacher will want to gather samples of the pupil's work—perhaps in a portfolio—and identify (with examples) particular behavioral or attitudinal issues that should be raised. If there is a major existing or potential problem, the teacher ought to look over the pupil's permanent record file in the school office to see whether the problem surfaced in other grades. All of this preparation should be done before the conference.

Finally, the teacher will want to locate a comfortable, private spot to hold the conference. Usually this means before or after school in the teacher's classroom, when pupils are not present. If this is the case, provide suitable, adult-sized chairs for the parents. The author is a veteran of many elementary school conferences in which the teacher sat comfortably behind his or her desk and the author was scrunched down in a primary-sized pupil chair, knees near his chin, trying to act dignified and carry on a productive conference. Conferences work better when they are private and undisturbed, and when all parties are comfortably situated.

The following tips can help the actual parent-teacher conference proceed successfully. Set a proper tone. This means making parents feel welcome, maintaining a positive attitude, and remembering that a pupil is not "their" concern or "your" concern, but a mutual concern. If possible, find out what parents want to know about before the conference so that you can prepare for their questions. Don't do all the talking; be a good listener and use the conference to find out about parents' perceptions and concerns. Talk in terms parents will understand; avoid educational jargon, such as "discovery learning," "rubrics," "higher-order thinking skills," or "prosocial behavior," that confuses rather than clarifies discussion. Concrete examples help when explaining things to parents. Providing examples of pupil work from portfolios, performance assessments, and scoring rubrics can help parents understand classroom expectations and pupil performance.

Be frank with parents, but convey both the pupil's strengths and weaknesses. Do not hold back unpleasant information because you think the parents will become confrontational. The aim of parent-teacher conferences is for each party to understand and help the pupil. It is the teacher's responsibility to raise issues with parents that will help the pupil, even though discussion of those issues might be unpleasant. If you do not know the answer to a question, do not bluff. Tell the parents you do not know the answer, then research it after the conference and follow up by relaying it to the parents.

Further, do not talk about other pupils or colleagues by name or by implication. Never belittle colleagues or the principal in front of parents, no matter what your feelings. Saying things like "Last year's teacher did not prepare Rosalie well in math" or "Teachers get so little support for their ideas from the principal" is inappropriate. Regardless of whether the statements are true, it is not professional to discuss such issues with parents. Do not compare a child to other pupils by name or show parents other pupils' work, test scores, or grades. Teachers are professionals and they have an obligation to act professionally. This means being truthful with parents, not demeaning colleagues in front of parents, concentrating discussion only on the parents' child, and not discussing information from the conference with other teachers. These guidelines are appropriate for all forms of parent-teacher interaction.

Box 10.4   Guidelines for Parent-Teacher Conferences

1. Plan in advance of the conference by gathering samples of the pupil's work and identifying issues to discuss with parents; find out what parents want to know before the conference, if possible.
2. Identify a private, comfortable place for the conference.
3. Set a proper tone by
   a. remembering that the pupil is of mutual concern to you and the parents;
   b. listening to the parents' perspectives and concerns;
   c. avoiding educational jargon, yet giving concrete examples; and
   d. being frank with parents when conveying the pupil's strengths and weaknesses.
4. Admit to not knowing the answer to a question and be willing to find out; do not try to bluff parents.
5. Do not talk about or belittle other colleagues or pupils by name or implication; do not compare one pupil to another by name.
6. If a remedial action is agreed to, plan the action jointly with parents and make each party responsible for part of the plan.
7. Orally review and summarize decisions and planned actions at the end of the conference.
8. Write summary notes of the conference.

If a course of remedial action for the pupil seems appropriate, plan the action jointly with the parents. Make both parties responsible for implementing the plan: "I will try to do these things with Janessa in class, and you will try to do these other things with her at home." Finally, summarize the conference before the parents leave. Review the main points and any decisions or courses of action that have been agreed upon.

Parent-teacher conferences can be very useful to both teachers and parents if planned and conducted successfully. They allow the teacher to supplement his or her information about the pupil and the parents to obtain a broader understanding of their child's school performance. The main drawback to parent-teacher conferences is that they are time-consuming, although many school districts are beginning to set aside a day or two in the school calendar specifically for parent conferencing. Box 10.4 summarizes the above guidelines for holding an effective parent-teacher conference.

Other Reporting Methods

A common method of informing parents about their child's school performance is to either send examples of school work home or to collect it in a portfolio to be examined during a parent-teacher conference or school open house. Periodic newsletters, often written and assembled by pupils, can be sent home. If a teacher has developed or selected a scoring rubric, a copy of the rubric with the pupil's level of performance circled can be used to provide information about an area of the pupil's learning.

Letters and phone calls to parents are used mainly to inform parents of a special problem that has occurred and, as such, are used quite infrequently by teachers. Regular written or phone communication between a teacher and a parent is very rare and occurs only if the parent specifically requests frequent written progress reports and the teacher agrees to provide them. Certainly, from a time-efficiency viewpoint, phone calls are better than writing letters to parents. If you do write to parents, it is extremely important that your letter be free of spelling and grammatical errors. Few things can create a poorer impression in a parent's mind than a misspelled, grammatically incorrect letter from their child's teacher.

Chapter Summary

- The process of judging the quality of a pupil's performance is called grading. The single most important characteristic of the grading process is its dependence on teacher judgment, which is always subjective to some degree.
- Grading is a difficult task for teachers because they have had little formal instruction in grading; they have to make judgments based on incomplete evidence; they have conflicting classroom roles; they must not allow pupils' personal characteristics and circumstances to distort subject matter judgments; and there is no single, universally accepted grading strategy.
- In grading, the teacher's prime aims are to be fair to all pupils and to reflect pupils' subject matter learning.
- The main purpose of report card grades is to communicate information about pupil achievement. Grades serve administrative, informational, motivational, and guidance functions.
- All grades represent a comparison of pupil performance to some standard of excellence or quality.
- Norm-referenced grades compare a pupil's performance to that of other pupils in the class. Pupils with the highest scores receive the designated number of high grades as defined by the grading curve.
- Criterion-referenced grades compare a pupil's performance to a predefined standard of mastery. There is no limit on the number of pupils who can receive a particular grade.
- Basing grades on comparisons of a pupil's performance to the pupil's ability or record of improvement is not recommended.
- After selecting the comparative basis for grading, the teacher next must decide which pupil performances will be considered in awarding grades. For subject matter grades it is recommended that pupil performances that demonstrate subject matter mastery be included in the grade. Effort, motivation, participation, and behavior should not be major parts of subject mastery grades.

- Grading requires teachers to summarize many different types of information into a single score. More important types of pupil performance such as tests and projects should be weighted most heavily in arriving at a grade.
- In order to summarize various types of information, each type must be expressed in the same way and on the same scale, usually a percentage scale.
- Before combining information into a grade, the quality of each piece of selected assessment information should be reviewed and adjustments made if invalid assessments are found. Grades will be only as valid as the assessment information on which they are based.
- Grading information should be expanded and supplemented by other means of parent-teacher communication, such as conferences, parents' nights, progress reports, and papers and projects sent home.

Questions for Discussion

1. What are the purposes of giving grades to pupils? How well do different grading formats meet these purposes?
2. What are a teacher's responsibilities to pupils when assigning grades on a paper, test, or project? What additional responsibilities to pupils do teachers have when they assign report card grades?
3. Is the task of assigning report card grades the same for elementary and high school teachers? How might the process of assigning grades differ at the two levels?
4. How can the information on report cards be supplemented and made more informative for parents and pupils?
5. What are possible ways, both good and bad, that grades can impact pupils? What can be done to lessen the detrimental impact of grades?

Reflection Exercises

1. Suppose that you were asked to develop the ideal report card for a school. What would the report card look like? What would be its major strengths and major weaknesses?
2. Five approaches to grading pupils with disabilities were described in this chapter. Which one of the five would you feel most comfortable about using in your own classroom? Why? Which one of the five would you feel least comfortable using? Why?
3. (To be answered after the activity presented in the following section is completed.) What are the strengths and weaknesses of the grading system you have developed?

Activity

Table 10A contains information that a teacher accumulated about her pupils during a marking period. Use this information to assign a report card grade to each pupil. Answer the questions that follow the table.

TABLE 10A

Grading Activity

Student	Test 1	2	3	4	Project	Class Participation	General Effort	Quizzes and Homework	Behavior	Pupil's Ability (Estimate)
Malcolm	40	60	55	100	A–	Good	G	G	G	M
Gretchen	90	95	45	85	A	Excellent	Ex	Ex	Ex	H
Charles	70	65	20	30	C	Excellent	G	P	P	M
Thomas	85	80	50	85	B–	Poor	P	G	P	H
Jack	70	70	15	65	D	Good	Ex	P	Ex	L
Susan	45	75	45	100	C	Excellent	Ex	G	G	M
Maya	75	80	45	75	B–	Good	G	G	G	M
Maria	70	75	30	70	A	Excellent	G	G	G	M
Oscar	80	90	45	85	C	Poor	P	P	P	M
Angelina	30	40	10	40	D–	Poor	Ex	P	Ex	L
James	60	60	15	45	D	Poor	P	P	P	H

1. Will you use a norm-referenced or a criterion-referenced grading approach? Why?
2. Will you include all the information in the table in determining a grade or only some of the information? State what you will and will not include and explain why?
3. Will all the pieces of information you have decided to include count equally, or will some things count more than others?
4. How will you take into account the fact that pupil performance on different pieces of information is represented differently (e.g., percentages, letter grades, excellent-good-poor, high-middle-low)?
5. What, if anything, will you do about test 3?
6. How will you summarize the different pieces of information into a single score or rating?
7. What will be your grading curve (norm-referenced) or performance standards (criterion-referenced) for awarding grades?
8. What grade would each pupil receive?
9. In what ways is this exercise artificial? That is, would there be a difference between the way you graded these pupils and the way a teacher who had actually taught them for the marking period would grade them?

10. If you graded the pupils in a norm-referenced way, go back and regrade using a criterion-referenced approach. If you graded the pupils in a criterion-referenced approach, go back and regrade using a norm-referenced approach.
11. Complete Reflection Exercise 3.

Review Questions

1. What are grades and why are they important? Why do schools and teachers give grades?
2. What questions must a teacher answer in order to carry out the grading process? What teacher judgments must be made in the grading process? Why is there no single best way to assign grades to pupils?
3. In what way is all grading based on comparison? What common methods of comparison are used in grading and how do they differ? What is the difference between norm- and criterion-referenced grading? Which method would you use and why?
4. What are advantages and disadvantages of norm- and criterion-referenced grading? What are the advantages and disadvantages of grading accommodations made for pupils with disabilities?
5. Why should grades be determined mostly by the academic performances of pupils, rather than other information a teacher has about pupils?
6. What information should a teacher provide students about the grading process?

References

Borich, G. D. (1996). *Effective teaching methods.* Englewood Cliffs, NJ: Prentice Hall.

Brookhart, S. M. (1992). *Teachers' grading practices: Meaning and values.* Paper presented at the annual meeting of the American Educational Research Association, San Francisco.

Brookhart, S. M. (1999). Teaching about communicating assessment results and grading. *Educational Measurement: Issues and Practice, 18*(1), 5–13.

Bursuck, W. D., Polloway, E. A., Plante, L., Epstien, M. H., Jayanthi, M., & McConeghy, J. (1996). Report card grading adaptations: A national survey of classroom practices. *Exceptional Children, 62*(4), 301–318.

Friedman, S. J., & Frisbie, D. A. (1993). *The validity of report cards as indicators of student performance.* Paper presented at the annual meeting of the National Council on Measurement in Education, Atlanta.

Frisbie, D. A., & Waltman, K. K. (1992). Developing a personal grading plan. *Educational Measurement: Issues and Practice, 11*(3), 35–42.

Gardner, H. (1995). *Frames of mind: The theory of multiple intelligence.* New York: Basic Books.

Griswold, P. A., & Griswold, M. M. (1992). *The grading contingency: Graders' beliefs and expectations and the assessment ingredients.* Paper presented at the annual meeting of the American Educational Research Association, San Francisco.

Hills, J. R. (1991). Apathy concerning grading and testing. *Phi Delta Kappan, 72*(7), 540–545.

Hubelbank, J. H. (1994). *Meaning of elementary school teachers' grades.* Unpublished dissertation, Boston College, Chestnut Hill, MA.

Kubiszyn, T., & Borich, G. (1999). *Educational testing and measurement.* New York: John Wiley & Sons, Inc.

Nava, F. J., & Loyd, B. (1992). *The effect of student characteristics on the grading process.* Paper presented at the annual meeting of the National Council on Measurement in Education, San Francisco.

Olson, L. (1995). Cards on the table. *Education Week,* June 14, 23–28.

Polloway, E. A., Epstein, M. H., Bursuck, W. D., Roderique, T. W., McConeghy, J. L., & Jayanthi, M. (1994). Classroom grading: A national survey of politics. *Remedial and Special Education, 15*(3), 162–170.

Salend, S. J. (1990). *Effective mainstreaming.* New York: Macmillan.

Shepard, L., & Bliem, C. (1995). Parents' thinking about standardized tests and performance assessment. *Educational Researcher, 24,* 25–32.

Slavin, R. E. (1994). *Educational psychology,* 4th ed. Boston: Allyn and Bacon.

Sternberg, R. (1997). What does it mean to be smart? *Educational Leadership, 54*(6), 20–24.

Tombari, M., & Borich, G. (1999). *Authentic assessment in the classroom.* Upper Saddle River, NJ: Prentice Hall.

Valdes, K. A., Williamson, C. L., & Wagner, M. M. (1990). *The national longitudinal transition study of special education students,* Vol. 1. Menlo Park, CA: SRI International.

Standardized
Achievement Tests

Chapter Outline

❖ Teachers' Perceptions of Standardized Tests
❖ Commercial Achievement Tests
❖ Administering Commercial Achievement Tests
❖ Interpreting Commercial Achievement Test Scores
❖ Three Examples of Test Interpretation
❖ The Validity of Commercial Achievement Tests
❖ Reporting Standardized Test Results to Parents
❖ Statewide Assessments

Chapter Objectives

After reading this chapter, the pupil will be able to:

- Define commercial and statewide testing terms
- State differences between teacher-made, commercial, and statewide tests in terms of objectives, construction, and scoring
- Interpret commercial achievement test results
- Identify factors that influence the validity and reliability of commercial and statewide achievement tests
- Explain how statewide assessments are scored

With the exception of statewide assessments, the types of formal assessment discussed in this text are ones that are selected and controlled by the classroom teacher. The teacher decides who to assess, when to assess, what to assess, how to assess, how to score, and how to use the results of the assessments. These teacher-based assessments and decisions are the fundamental ingredients in the teaching-learning process.

However, teachers do not control all of the assessments used in their classrooms. Two types of standardized assessments are commonly administered in most classrooms. A **standardized assessment** is one that is (1) designed to be used in many classrooms and schools, and (2) administered, scored, and interpreted in the same way no matter when or where it is administered. These assessments, which are not under the direct control of the classroom teacher or the day-to-day work of teachers and pupils, include commercially published national achievement tests and statewide achievement tests.

Commercially published national standardized achievement tests will be called **commercial achievement tests** hereafter. They are constructed and sold to school systems by private testing companies. The following are among the most widely used of these tests.

California Achievement Tests
Comprehensive Tests of Basic Skills
Terra Nova
Iowa Tests of Basic Skills
Metropolitan Achievement Tests
Sequential Tests of Educational Progress
SRA Achievement Series
Stanford Achievement Tests

Most schools administer at least one commercial achievement test to pupils in varied grades each year. Decisions about the use of and grades to be tested by the commercial tests are made by individual school systems or by the state board of education. Classroom teachers have little or no say in test selection. Commercial achievement tests have three main purposes: (1) to compare the performance of local pupils to that of similar pupils nationally; (2) to provide developmental information about pupil achievement over time; and (3) to identify areas of pupil strengths and weaknesses.

Statewide achievement tests are a more recent phenomenon and, as their name suggests, are mandated by a state legislature or board of education for use within that state (Airasian, 1993). Pupil's test performances are compared to statewide performance standards to help make decisions about whether pupils will be allowed to graduate from high school, be promoted to the next grade level, or be assigned to remedial instruction. Other statewide tests are used to assess individual teachers and entire schools.

Commercial and statewide achievement tests are similar in that both are standardized, are intended for use in many different classrooms, assess content that is not selected by classroom teachers, and are administered infrequently during the school year. They also differ from each other in some ways. Commercial achievement tests are given at the discretion of the local school district, whereas local districts are often mandated to give the statewide achievement tests. The purposes of the tests also differ. Commercial achievement tests are intended to compare the performance of pupils in a particular classroom, school, or district to the performance of similar pupils nationwide. Statewide tests are intended to determine whether an individual pupil or a school as a whole has achieved a minimum level of acceptable performance on objectives defined by the state. Table 11.1 compares teacher-made, commercial, and statewide achievement tests on a number of important dimensions.

Table 11.1 shows that teacher-made tests focus on the instructional objectives specific to a particular classroom, while commercial or statewide tests tend to be based on objectives that may or may not be common to most classrooms. The type of test item found on teacher-made tests varies at the teacher's discretion, while most commercial tests are composed mainly of multiple-choice items, although these tests have begun to include more open-ended, performance-based items. Statewide assessments generally include both multiple-choice items and performance-based exercises. Finally, teacher-made tests provide information about the performance of pupils in the teacher's classroom, while commercial achievement tests provide information about how a pupil compares to peers nationwide and statewide tests indicate mastery or nonmastery of objectives defined by state authorities.

This chapter is about standardized commercial and statewide achievement tests. It describes their construction, administration, scoring, and interpretation, as well as important cautions that should be exercised in their use. Before beginning that discussion, however, it is instructive to consider how teachers view commercial and statewide tests.

❧ Teachers' Perceptions of Standardized Tests

Teachers have mixed reactions about both commercial and statewide achievement tests. The following comments provide a sense of the main issues of teachers' concerns.

TABLE 11.1

Comparison of Teacher-Made, Commercial, and State-Mandated Achievement Tests

	Teacher-Made	Commercial	Statewide
Content and/ or Objectives	Specific to class instruction; picked or developed by the teacher; narrow range of content tested, usually one unit or chapter of instruction in a subject	Topics commonly taught in many schools across the nation; broad range of content covering a year of instruction in a subject	Topics commonly taught or desired to be taught in schools of a state or district; broad range of content covered in a subject area, often covering many years of instruction in a subject
Item Construction	Written or selected by the classroom teacher	Professional item writers	Professional item writers
Item Type	Various types	Mainly multiple-choice items	Multiple-choice and performance items
Item Selection	Teacher picks or writes items as needed for test	Many items written and then screened and tried out on pupils before best items chosen for test	Many items written and then screened; best items chosen for test
Scoring	Teacher	Machine	Machine and scorers
Scores Reported	Number correct, percent correct	Percentile rank, stanine, grade equivalent scores	Usually pass-fail for individuals; percent or proportion of mastery for groups
Interpreting Scores	Norm- or criterion-referenced, depending on classroom teacher's preference	Norm-referenced and developmental	Criterion-referenced

Test Content

The tests are inappropriate for my class because our curriculum doesn't cover some of the test content. I vary my instruction from the textbook, introducing enrichment material and omitting certain text sections. A lot of what I teach is on the standardized tests, but the match between the test content and what I teach is by no means exact.

The test is so short and the content so general that one gets only a superficial view of how well pupils have learned from my instruction.

Classroom Time

These tests are just one more thing to do in an already crowded day. They take time away from instruction and are another intrusion on the dwindling instructional time I have. Some of the tests take almost a week to administer.

Receiving Results

The tests have to be sent away for scoring. I have to wait six to eight weeks to get results back. When I do, I rarely get the information in a form I can use and rarely get guidance to help me interpret what all the numbers mean.

In my school we test kids at the start of the year on a lot of material that hasn't been taught yet. When the results come back in late October or November, I look them over, but I really don't find much use for them.

Parental Concern

If a test has a separate answer sheet it's taken much more seriously by kids and their parents than if it doesn't. Parents put so much emphasis on the commercial achievement tests. They're so concerned about how their child compares to kids across the country. I dread sitting down with parents during a conference and trying to explain why Mary or Mark was above or, more problematically, below their expectations.

Many parents put more faith in a 50 or 100 item standardized test than in my judgment based upon months of observing their child in school. An outside-the-classroom source of information is given more credence than "good old, I'm here every day with your child, Mrs. Barber." These tests are treated like the good housekeeping seal of approval of a kid's learning. Too much emphasis is placed on these short, general, one-shot standardized tests.

Teaching to the Test

My principal puts a great deal of emphasis on our school's performance on the statewide basic skills tests. He's very concerned about how we do compared to neighboring schools when the results are published in the local paper. There is a subtle, and sometimes not so subtle, pressure to help pupils do well on the tests so the school will look good. The emphasis is to include test topics in our curriculum and to give those topics more instructional time.

Using Test Results

Its hard to know what to do with the commercial test results. They give a sense of how pupils are doing, but they mainly corroborate what I already know about the pupils. Occasionally a pupil will perform very differently than I expected and this forces me to look more carefully at my initial impression of the pupil. But for the most part, I don't need a standardized test to tell me how my pupils are doing.

Two years ago we started testing students in the Spring. I like this much better than testing them in the Fall. I now look forward to seeing the test results so I can compare them to my students' results from last year to see if they've improved. It's sort of like my report card for the year. I can also use the results in making suggestions to next year's teacher about the class.

The state tests really aren't for the classroom teacher. They're more for administrators and curriculum planners. The teacher has little say in the construction or use of these tests, other than to implement a policy or recommendation made by the state legislature or school administrators.

These comments illustrate a number of points about the role that external, standardized tests play in classrooms. First, neither commercial nor statewide tests are viewed by teachers as being very important in the day-to-day functioning of the classroom. Second, teachers do not see many direct, instructional uses for the results they get back from such tests, although they do use them in parent conferences, to corroborate their initial perceptions of pupils, and to judge the success of their instruction at the end of the year. Third, teachers suggest that there is some pressure, particularly in the case of statewide tests, to alter classroom instruction to fit the test content (Canner et al., 1991; Smith and Rottenberg, 1991). With these teacher perceptions in mind, we can begin consideration of commercial achievement tests.

⚔ Commercial Achievement Tests

There are two key points to remember about commercial achievement tests: (1) they are usually norm-referenced and (2) their main function is to compare each pupil's performance to that of a national group of similar pupils. Comments like "Martin scored higher than 87 percent of seventh graders nationwide in math," "Maria is in the third grade, but her grade equivalent score on the standardized test was sixth grade, third month," "Kerry scored above average in science compared to eighth graders in the United States," and "Compared to second graders across the country, Winston was in the bottom quarter in reading" refer to the results of commercial achievement tests. Each of these descriptions compares a pupil's test performance to that of a group of similar pupils from across the country. The ability to provide comparisons of pupil achievement beyond the confines of a single classroom is the primary reason that commercial achievement tests are used in schools and followed so closely by parents. Other types of tests do not allow for national comparisons.

The most commonly used commercial achievement tests are published in the form of test batteries. A **test battery** is a collection of tests in many different subject areas that are administered as a group. Rather than constructing one test for math, a totally separate test for reading, and yet another for science, most commercial test publishers construct a single test battery that contains tests in many different subject areas. For example, the Iowa Tests of Basic Skills battery for the fifth grade is made up of the following subject tests, or, as they are commonly called, **subtests:** vocabulary, reading, spelling, capitalization, punctuation, usage and expression, visual materials, reference materials, math concepts, math problems, math computation, social studies, and science. The entire battery consists of 458 items that take just over 5 hours to administer. The main advantage of a test battery such as the Iowa Tests of Basic Skills is that its broad content coverage in many subject areas provides a general picture of a pupil's school performance. It also can show whether a pupil's score on one subtest is similar to scores on others (Ebel and Frisbie, 1991).

Test Construction

Because the information obtained from a commercial achievement test differs from that obtained from a teacher-made or textbook test, it should not

CONSTRUCTING ACHIEVEMENT TESTS

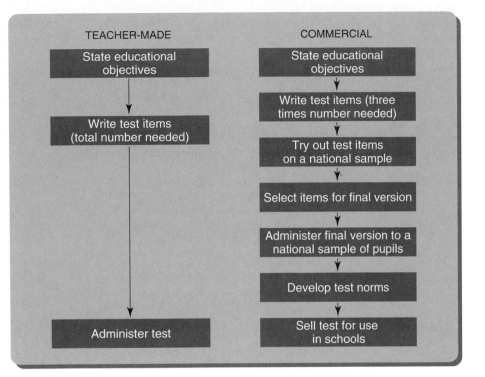

FIGURE 11.1   *Steps in Constructing Teacher-Made and Commercial Achievement Tests*

be surprising to learn that the commercial test is constructed differently from the teacher-made or textbook achievement test. A well-constructed commercial achievement test has three main characteristics: (1) it is carefully constructed, with item tryouts, analysis, and revisions before the final version of the test is completed; (2) there are explicit directions and procedures for administering and scoring the test; and (3) score interpretation is based on the test having been administered to a carefully selected sample of pupils from across the nation. The performance of this national sample or **norm group** is what other pupils are compared to when they take the test. Figure 11.1 compares the steps in constructing a teacher-made achievement test with the steps in constructing a commercial achievement test.

Choosing Objectives

Teacher-made and commercial achievement tests both start with the educational objectives to be tested. For the teacher-made test, the objectives are those that the classroom teacher will emphasize during instruction. The commercial test constructor, on the other hand, wants to identify objectives that are nationally taught in *all* classrooms at a particular grade level. Unless such common objectives are selected, the commercial test constructor will not be able to obtain information to provide national averages for the test. Objectives that are taught in most classrooms are found by examining widely used textbooks and state curriculum guidelines. Those topics and skills that are common across textbooks and guidelines are selected for inclusion in the test.

> The first step was to review curriculum guides and commonly used textbooks to identify skills that should be measured. . . (CTB/McGraw-Hill, 1986a, p. 5)
>
> The Stanford series is designed to reflect what is being taught in schools throughout the country. In order to insure that the test content would be valid in this sense, a thorough analysis of curriculum materials was undertaken. The most widely used textbook series in the various subject areas were studied along with syllabuses, state guidelines, and research literature pertaining to children's vocabulary and concept development at successive ages and grades. (The Psychological Corporation, 1984, p. 1-1)

The basic idea is to construct a test that all teachers or local school administrators can look at and say, "Yes, we cover these topics in our school." Teachers who do not use a popular text or who supplement their instruction with a great deal of new and unusual topics are likely to find that a commercial test will not assess many of the things they have taught.

Writing and Reviewing Items

Once the objectives to be assessed are identified, the commercial test publisher, like the classroom teacher, must construct or select test items. Unlike the classroom teacher, who writes only as many items as are needed for a test, the commercial test publisher writes two or three times more items than will be needed on the final test.

> . . . sufficient numbers of items measuring each objective were written to allow for the production of twice as many complete test forms . . . as were actually needed. This was done so that items that did not function well in the classroom could be eliminated without adversely affecting the balance of content. (The Psychological Corporation, 1984, p. 1-1)

To make scoring easy and to provide detailed analyses of pupil performance, items on commercial achievement tests are largely multiple choice, although more test publishers are also including some open-ended items in their tests. The items go through several cycles of review and revision before being accepted for use in the test. Curriculum specialists study the items to be sure that they assess the intended objectives. Test construction specialists review them to be sure they are well written and without ambiguity or clues. Other groups review the items to determine whether they are biased in favor of particular pupil groups. At the end of this stage of test construction, a large selection of items that have been screened by many groups are available to the test publisher.

Each item and subtest was reviewed and edited for content, style, and appropriateness for measuring the stated objective, as well as for ethnic, · cultural, racial, and sex bias. (The Psychological Corporation, 1984, p. 1-1)

Item Tryout

All the items written are tried out, and the more valid and reliable ones are selected for the final version of the test. Because no test constructor, whether a classroom teacher or a commercial publisher, knows how well the test items will work until they are actually tried out on a group of pupils, commercial test publishers administer their items to a sample of pupils similar to those for whom the final version of the test is intended. The test publisher knows that some of the items will not work well and will have to be discarded. The trial test items look like the final test form and are administered by classroom teachers, so that the administrative situation during the tryout will be as similar as possible to the way that the final, published tests will be administered.

> In order to empirically determine the behavior and characteristics of test items, it is necessary to conduct item tryout studies. . . . A national item tryout study was conducted for the ITBS (Iowa Tests of Basic Skills). The sample included 47,000 students in 38 states. . . . (Riverside Publishing Company, 1986, p. 8)
>
> The National Item Analysis Program was conducted in order to determine the appropriateness of the item types and objectives, the difficulty and sensitivity of the items, the grade progression of difficulty, the effectiveness of the options, and the reactions of pupils and teachers to the clarity, format, and content of the test. The program took place in April, 1980, with approximately 100,000 students from 50 school systems across the country participating [about 10,000 per grade]. (The Psychological Corporation, 1984, p. 2-1)

There are two reasons why commercial achievement test constructors try out test items before finalizing the test. First, the test constructor wants to make sure that all the items are clearly written and understood by pupils. By examining pupil responses after the tryout, unclear or misunderstood items can be identified and then revised or discarded. Second, test items that will insure a spread of scores among the pupils who take the test must be selected. After the tryout, the statistical properties of each item are analyzed to insure that the final test contains items that will differentiate among test takers and allow the norm-referenced comparisons that are desired in national standardized achievement tests.

Two important indices for judging test items are difficulty and discrimination (see Chapter 7 and Appendix B). The **difficulty index** of a test item indicates the proportion of test takers who answered the item correctly. Thus, a difficulty of 90 means that 90 percent of the pupils answered the item correctly, while an item with a difficulty of 15 was answered correctly by only 15 percent of the test takers. The **discrimination index** of an item indicates how well pupils who scored high on the test as a whole scored on a particular item. A test item that discriminates between test takers is one that high scorers on the total test get correct and low scorers on the total test get incorrect.

The commercial test constructor seeks to differentiate pupils in terms of their performance. The test constructor is not likely to select items that all pupils got right or wrong in the tryout for the final test. Such items do not help differentiate high from low scorers. To accomplish the desired differentiation among pupils, the test must contain mainly items that will spread out pupils' scores. Only then will the test differentiate pupils across the entire scoring range and permit the desired norm-referenced comparisons among test takers. A few easy items will be included at the beginning of the test so as not to discourage pupils at the start of testing. A few difficult items will be placed at the end of the test to challenge the very able pupils.

The preceding steps accomplish three important aims: (1) they identify test objectives that reflect what teachers across the nation are teaching; (2) they produce test items that assess these objectives; and (3) they identify a final group of items that will produce the desired norm-referenced comparisons among test takers. The final version of the test, as well as the test directions, answer sheets, and time limits, must then be "normed."

Norming the Test

In order to provide information that allows comparison of an individual pupil's performance to that of a national sample of similar pupils, the final version of the test must be given to a sample of pupils from across the country. This process is called "norming the test," and the pupils who provide the national sample are called the **norm group. Norms** describe the performance of a national sample of pupils who took the test.

Suppose that a commercial test publisher needed to norm the final version of a commercial achievement test for fifth graders. To do this, the test publisher would need to obtain information about how fifth graders across the country perform on the test. The publisher would (1) select a representative sample of fifth grade pupils from across the country; (2) administer the test to this sample; (3) score the test; and (4) use the scores of the sample to represent the performance of all fifth graders across the country. Assuming the sample of fifth graders was well chosen, the scores made by the sample group would provide a good indication of how fifth graders nationwide would perform on the test. Obviously, the quality and representativeness of the sample of fifth graders selected has a great influence on how much confidence a teacher can have in the comparisons made between a pupil and the "national average." The development of norms is a critical aspect of constructing commercial tests. Commercial test publishers strive to select samples that are representative of the group for whom a test is being normed.

> A test is standardized nationally by administering it under the same conditions to a national sample of students. The students tested become a norm or comparison group against which future individual scores can be compared. . . . The sample should be carefully selected to be representative of the national population with respect to ability and

achievement. The sample should be large enough to represent the many diverse elements in the population; . . . Sampling units should be selected primarily on the basis of school district size, region of the country, and socioeconomic characteristics. Procedures should be included for obtaining a proportional balance among public and non-public schools. (Riverside Publishing Company, 1986, p. 11)

Four criteria are used to judge the adequacy of standardized test norms: sample size, representativeness, recentness, and description of procedures. Other things being equal, a large sample of pupils in the norm group is preferable to a small sample; we would prefer a norming sample of 50,000 fifth graders to one of 10,000 fifth graders. But size alone does not guarantee representativeness. If the 50,000 pupils in the norming group were all from private schools in the same state, the sample would not provide a good representation of the performance of pupils nationwide. The norming group should be representative of the national group for whom the test is intended.

School curricula change over time. New topics are added and others are dropped. Thus, it is important that commercial achievement tests be reviewed and renormed about every 7 to 9 years in order to keep up with these changes. If today's curriculum is different from that followed when a standardized test was first normed 10 years ago, it is unfair and invalid to compare today's pupils to a 10-year-old norm group that was taught a different curriculum.

The final criterion for judging the adequacy of standardized test norms is the quality of the procedures used to produce the norms. The more clear and detailed the description of the procedures followed in test construction, the better the test user can judge the appropriateness of the test for his or her needs. To describe their procedures, commercial test publishers provide manuals to accompany their tests. A technical manual provides information about the construction of the test, including objective selection, item writing and review, item tryout, and norming. A teacher manual provides a description of the topics tested as well as guidelines for appropriately interpreting and using the test results. These manuals should be accessible to classroom teachers to help them understand and use the test results meaningfully. Another source of information about published tests is the *Mental Measurement Yearbooks,* which are produced every few years and which provide reviews of published tests written by experts in the field of assessment.

✂ Administering Commercial Achievement Tests

Once a commercial test is normed, it is ready to be sold to local school districts. Selection of a particular test is usually based on the judgment of a district administrator or a joint administrator-teacher committee. Selection of a test leads to other decisions. In what grades will pupils be tested? Will all subtests of the achievement battery be administered? What types of score reports are needed? Should pupils be tested at the start of the school year or at the end of the year? Different school systems answer these questions differently. Whatever the ultimate decisions, it is usually the classroom teacher who is given the task of administering the tests.

A standardized test is meant to be administered to all pupils under the same conditions whenever and wherever it is given. The reason for standardizing test conditions is to allow valid comparisons between the scores of local pupils and those of the national norm group. If local pupils take the test under conditions different than those of the national norm group, comparisons of their performance to the norm group will be invalid and misleading. For example, it would not be fair to compare the performance of a pupil who was given 40 minutes to complete a test to that of others who were given only 30 minutes. Similarly, it would not be fair to compare the performance of a pupil who received coaching during testing to the performance of pupils who did not. Thus, all commercial achievement tests come with very specific and detailed directions for administration.

The directions spell out in great detail how a teacher should prepare for testing, how the room should be set up, what to do while the pupils are taking the test, how to distribute the tests and answer sheets, and how to time the tests. In addition, the directions suggest ways to prepare pupils for taking the test. The directions provide an actual script that the teacher is expected to read word for word when administering the test. Every teacher who administers a commercial achievement test is expected to use its accompanying directions and script without deviation. If the conditions of administration vary from the directions provided by the test publisher, comparisons with the norm group may be invalid.

❈ Interpreting Commercial Achievement Test Scores

Four to eight weeks after administration, commercial test results are returned to the school. Remember that the tests are usually norm-referenced and compare a pupil's performance to that of a large national group of similar pupils. The most common comparisons made are those of a pupil against a national norm group in the same grade. However, these are not the only comparisons that can be made from a commercial achievement test.

A school district also might wish to compare its pupils to a narrower sample than nationwide pupils in the same grade. For example, suppose your school district is an urban one that serves a large, multiracial, multiethnic population. What you might really like to learn from the test is how pupils in your school district compare to a national sample drawn from school districts with similar characteristics. Most commercial test publishers can provide such a comparison.

Or, suppose your school district is in an affluent suburban area. Past experience has shown that when pupils in your district are compared to a representative national sample, they generally perform very well. What you would really like to know is how pupils in your district perform when compared to similar pupils in other affluent suburban areas. This is the group your pupils will compete with for admission to prestigious colleges. Once again, commercial test publishers can usually provide such a comparison.

Sometimes school districts are interested in comparing a pupil's performance to other pupils in the same grade in that school district. Test publishers can also provide information about how any pupil in the local district compares to all other pupils in the same grade in that district. Norms confined to pupils in a specific school district are called **local norms.** Although national norms are the most commonly used and reported, most commercial test publishers can provide more specific standardized test norms according to geographic location, type of community (rural, suburban, urban), type of school (public, private), and particular school system. Note that a pupil's test performance will appear quite different depending on the norm group he or she is compared to.

Commercial achievement tests provide the classroom teacher with many different kinds of scores. In interpreting these tests, the number of items a pupil got correct, called the **raw score,** is *not* useful in itself. The teacher needs to know how that raw score compares to the norm group. Special types of scores provide this information (see Appendix B). Because there are so many types of scores to compare, discussion here will be confined to the three most common types: percentile rank, stanine, and grade equivalent scores. The teacher or class guide manual that accompanies a test will provide the desired explanations to questions about the meaning and interpretation of scores not discussed here.

Percentile Rank Scores

Probably the most commonly used commercial standardized test score is the **percentile rank.** Percentile ranks range from 1 to 99 and indicate what percentage of the norm group the pupil scored above. If Felix, a seventh grader, had a percentile rank of 91 on a standardized science test, we can say that he scored higher on the test than 91 percent of the national sample of seventh grade pupils who made up the norm group. If Arieh had a percentile rank of 23 in reading, we can say that he scored higher on the reading test than 23 percent of the pupils in the norm group. Percentiles do not refer to the percentage of items a pupil answered correctly; they refer to the percentage of pupils in the norm group who scored *below* a given pupil.

The composition of the norm group influences the comparison that can be made. For example, it is quite possible for Felix to achieve at the 91st percentile rank in science when compared to seventh graders nationally, but only at the 60th percentile rank when compared to seventh graders in his own school district. It is also important to keep in mind that when local norms are used, half of the pupils in the school district *must* be below average. The norm-referenced nature of commercial standardized tests produce a spread of scores from higher to lower.

One of the advantages of standardized achievement test batteries is that each subtest is normed on a single group. This allows the teacher to compare a pupil's performance across many subtests and to identify areas of relative strength and weakness.

TABLE 11.2

Approximate Percentile Ranks Corresponding to Stanine Scores

Stanine Score	Approximate Percentile Rank
9	96 or higher
8	89–95
7	77–88
6	60–76
5	40–59
4	23–39
3	11–22
2	4–10
1	Below 4

Stanine Scores

The **stanine** is a second type of standardized commercial test score. Stanines are 9-point scales, with a stanine of 1 representing the lowest performance and a stanine of 9 the highest. These nine numbers are the only possible stanine scores a pupil can receive. Like a percentile rank, stanines are designed to indicate a pupil's performance in comparison to a larger norming sample. Table 11.2 shows the approximate relationship between percentile ranks and stanines.

Although there is comparability between stanine scores and percentile rank scores, many teachers group stanines to provide general categories of achievement, with stanine scores of 1, 2, and 3 considered below average; 4, 5, and 6 considered average; and 7, 8, and 9 considered above average. While stanines are not as precise as percentile ranks, they are easy to work with and interpret, which is a major reason for their increasing popularity with teachers. As with a pupil's percentile ranks, a pupil's stanine in one subject can be compared to his or her stanine in other subjects in the same test battery to identify areas of strength and weakness.

Grade Equivalent Scores

While stanines and percentile ranks provide information about a pupil's standing compared to the norm group in a particular grade level, other types of standardized test scores seek to identify a pupil's developmental progression across grade levels. The most common developmental scale is the **grade equivalent score,** which represents pupils' achievement in terms of a scale based on year and month in school. A grade equivalent score of 7.5 stands for seventh grade, fifth month of school. A grade equivalent score of 11.0 stands for the beginning of the eleventh grade. On some tests, the decimal point is omitted in grade equivalent scores, in which case a grade equivalent score of 43 stands for fourth grade, third month, and a score of 108 stands for tenth grade, eighth month.

Grade equivalent scores are easily misinterpreted. A scoring scale that is organized in terms of grade and month in school is so familiar to most test users that it can seduce them into making incorrect interpretations of scores. Consider Luisa, who took a standardized achievement test battery at the start of the fifth grade. When her teacher received the results he saw that Luisa's grade equivalent score in mathematics was 7.5. What does this score indicate about Luisa's mathematics achievement?

If we asked 100 teachers to explain what they believed Luisa's grade equivalent score in math meant, the great majority of them would give one of the following *incorrect* intepretations.

- Luisa does as well in mathematics as a seventh grader in the fifth month of school.
- Luisa can do the mathematics work of a seventh grader.
- Luisa's score indicates that she can succeed in a seventh grade mathematics curriculum.

In fact, except under very rare conditions, each of these interpretations is incorrect or unsubstantiated. Remember, Luisa took a *fifth grade* mathematics test, which contains mathematics items commonly taught in the fifth grade. Luisa did not take a seventh grade mathematics test, so we have no way of knowing how she would do on seventh grade math material. Certainly she wouldn't have had the benefit of math normally taught in the sixth grade. All we know is how Luisa performed on a fifth grade test, and this tells us nothing about how she might perform on higher grade-level tests. If a common test had been given to fifth and seventh grade pupils, we might be able to say how Luisa performed in comparison to seventh graders, but this is rarely done.

If all of the preceding interpretations are inappropriate, what is the correct interpretation of Luisa's grade equivalent score of 7.5? The most appropriate interpretation is that *compared to other fifth graders*. Luisa is well above the national average in fifth grade mathematics. Developmentally, she is ahead of the "typical" fifth grader in mathematics achievement. Caution must be exercised when interpreting grade equivalent scores more than one grade level above or below that of the test taker. Commercial test publishers warn against misinterpretations of grade equivalent scores in their manuals, but unfortunately, classroom teachers rarely have access to these manuals. One test publisher includes the following very appropriate and useful caution regarding grade equivalent scores in the Test Coordinator's Handbook.

> Grade equivalents are not appropriate for placing students in school grades corresponding to the test scores. A second grade student who scores above 4.0 in reading should not be advanced to the fourth grade reading class as a result of the test score alone. This score of 4.0 is a good indication that the student reads considerably better than the average second grade student. However, if this student had taken a reading test designed for the fourth grade, it is possible that he or she would not have scored at 4.0. Because

TABLE 11.3

Comparison of Three Common Standardized Test Scores

	Percentile Rank	Stanine	Grade Equivalent Score
Format of Score	Percentage	Whole number	Grade and month in school
Possible Scores	1 to 99 in whole numbers	1 to 9 in whole numbers	Prekindergarten to 12.9 in monthly increments
Interpretation	Percent of pupils a given pupil did better than	1 to 3 below average; 4 to 6 average; 7 to 9 above average	Above average, average, below average compared to pupils in the same grade
Special Issues	Small differences often overinterpreted	General index of pupil achievement	Frequently misinterpreted and misunderstood

> misinterpretation can easily result if thorough explanation does not accompany the score, it is strongly recommended that grade equivalents not be used in reporting a student's scores to parents or other persons with no training in testing. (CTB/McGraw-Hill, 1986a, p. 88)

Another use of the grade equivalent score is to assess a pupil's academic development over time. The change in a pupil's grade equivalent score over time is often used as an indication of whether the pupil is making "normal progress" in his or her learning. For example, if a pupil's grade equivalent score is 8.2 when tested in the eighth grade, one might expect the pupil's grade equivalent to be around 9.2 if tested at the same time in the ninth grade. However, it is important to recognize that development is an irregular process, which may jump ahead greatly at certain times, but remain static at others. Thus, small deviations from so-called normal growth of one grade equivalent per year should not be interpreted as representing a problem. Table 11.3 compares the characteristics of percentile rank, stanine, and grade equivalent scores.

Three Examples of Test Interpretation

Although many types of standardized test scores can be provided by test publishers, the percentile rank, stanine, and grade equivalent are the most used. Given the preceding discussion, we are now ready to examine some specific examples of how commercial achievement tests are reported to classroom teachers.

Example 1: Pupil Performance Report

Figure 11.2 shows Brian Elliott's test results on the Metropolitan Achievement Tests battery. The extreme top of the report tells us that Brian was administered both the Metropolitan Achievement Tests and the Otis-Lennon School Ability Test, which is a test of general ability, not of achievement in specific school subjects. The top of the form tells us also that Brian's teacher is Ms. or Mr. Smith, his school is the Lakeside Elementary School, and that the Lakeside school is in the Newtown school district.

The middle portion at the top of the form tells us that Brian is in the fourth grade and that he took the Metropolitan in May, 1993. This is near the end of the school year, which has an important bearing on the national norming group against which Brian's performance is compared. Suppose that Brian took the test in October, at the beginning of the school year. How would his performance in October probably compare to his performance in May? In October, Brian was just starting the fourth grade and had not had much instruction on fourth grade objectives. By May, Brian had 9 months of instruction on fourth grade objectives, so it is likely that he would test higher in May than he would have tested in October. The time of the year that a pupil takes a commercial achievement test makes a considerable difference in his or her performance level; the more instruction the pupil has had, the higher his or her scores should be.

Commercial achievement test constructors recognize this fact and take it into account when they norm their tests. They develop different norms for tests in both the fall and the spring, so that pupils who are tested in the fall can be compared to the fall norming group and pupils who take the test in the spring can be compared to the spring norming group. At the top of Brian's report form under "Norms" is the entry "Spring," which means that Brian, who was tested in May, was compared to a national sample of fourth graders who were tested in the spring.

Finally, the top of the form describes the level and form of the test Brian took. This information usually is not critical to interpreting the test results. The **level** of a test describes the grade level for which the test is intended. On the Metropolitan Achievement Tests the level called "Elem 2" is intended for the fourth grade. The **form** of the test refers to the version of the test administered. Often standardized test constructors will produce two interchangeable versions of a test to allow schools that wish to test more than once a year to use a different but equivalent version of the test each time.

Below this general information are Brian's actual test results. First, marked by the circled *A*, is a list of all the subtests that make up the Metropolitan Achievement Tests battery and the number of items in each. The subtest list starts with total reading and ends with thinking skills. Each of these subtests assesses performance in a distinct curriculum area. Subtest results can be grouped to provide additional scores. For example, the total reading score is made up of the combined performance on the vocabulary and reading comprehension subtests. What three subtests are combined to

METROPOLITAN ACHIEVEMENT TESTS
SEVENTH EDITION WITH OTIS-LENNON SCHOOL ABILITY TEST, SIXTH EDITION

TEACHER: SMITH

SCHOOL: LAKESIDE ELEMENTARY GRADE: 04

DISTRICT: NEWTOWN

TEST DATE: 05/93

1992 NORMS: SPRING

MAT/ NATIONAL LEVEL: ELEM 2 FORM: S

OLSAT NATIONAL ELEM 2

INDIVIDUAL REPORT FOR Brian Elliott

AGE 09 YRS 10 MOS

TESTS	NO. OF ITEMS	RAW SCORE	SCALED SCORE	NATL PR-S	NATL NCE	GRADE EQUIV	ACC RANGE
Total Reading	85	66	632	68-6	59.9	5.9	MIDDLE
Vocabulary	30	27	667	90-8	77.0	8.4	HIGH
Reading Comp. (A)	55	39	618	53-5	51.6	5.0	MIDDLE
Total Mathematics	64	43	602	55-5	52.6	5.1	MIDDLE
Concepts & Problem Solving	40	29	617	68-6	59.9	6.0	MIDDLE
Procedures	24	14	579	37-4	43.0	4.3	LOW
Language	54	33	609	51-5	50.5	4.8	MIDDLE
Prewriting	15	10	606	47-5	48.4	4.7	MIDDLE
Composing	15	8	602	43-5	46.3	4.5	LOW
Editing	24	15	614	56-5	53.2	5.3	LOW
Science	35	25	628	65-6	58.1	5.9	MIDDLE
Social Studies	35	25	630	69-6	60.4	6.0	MIDDLE
Research Skills	36	29	635	73-6	62.9	6.5	MIDDLE
Thinking Skills	83	56	615	61-6	55.9	5.7	LOW
Basic Battery	203	142	617	60-6	55.3	5.4	MIDDLE
Complete Battery	273	192	619	62-6	56.4	5.5	MIDDLE

NATIONAL GRADE PERCENTILE BANDS: 1 10 30 50 70 90 99

OTIS-LENNON SCHOOL ABILITY TEST		RAW SCORE	SAI	AGE PR-S	AGE NCE	SCALED SCORE	NATL GRADE PR-S	NATL GRADE NCE
Total	72	49	112	77-7	65.6	632	81-7	68.5
Verbal	36	25	114	81-7	68.5	637	85-7	71.8
Nonverbal	36	24	109	71-6	61.7	627	76-6	64.9

FIGURE 11.2 *Standardized Test Report for an Individual Pupil*

make the total language score? The basic battery total includes all subtests except science and social studies, while the complete battery total includes these two subtests. Finally, below the Metropolitan scores, are the scores on the Otis-Lennon School Ability Test.

What kind of information is provided about Brian's performance on the Metropolitan subtests? The section marked with a circled *B* lists raw scores; scaled scores (a developmental score used to measure year-to-year growth in pupil performance); national percentile ranks and national stanines (NATL PR-S); national normal curve equivalents (NATL NCE), a score similar to the percentile rank; grade equivalent scores; and an achievement-ability comparison labeled ACC. The raw score tells how many items Brian got correct on each subtest. He got 27 of the 30 items on the vocabulary subtest and 29 of the 40 items on the concepts and problem solving subtest correct. Because different subtests have different numbers of test items, raw scores are *not* useful in interpreting or comparing pupil performance on the subtests. Also, since scaled scores are difficult to interpret and normal curve equivalents are replaceable by percentile ranks in most cases, we shall not describe them here. More detailed information about these and other standardized test scores can be found in the interpretive guides for teachers that are available for most commercial achievement tests.

The score column labeled "NATL PR-S" shows Brian's national percentile rank and corresponding stanine score on each subtest. How should Brian's performance of 56-5 on the editing subtest be interpreted? Brian's percentile rank of 56 means that he scored higher than 56 percent of the fourth grade national norm group on the editing subtest. His stanine score of 5 places him in the middle of the stanine scores and indicates that his performance is average compared to fourth graders nationwide. Interpret Brian's national percentile rank and stanine on the vocabulary subtest.

Compare Brian's performance in reading comprehension and composing. In terms of percentile rank, Brian did better in reading comprehension (53rd percentile rank) than in composing (43rd percentile rank), but in terms of stanines, Brian's performance on the two subtests was the same (stanine 5). The apparent difference in the percentile rank and stanine scores illustrates two points. First, the stanine score provides a more general indication of performance than the percentile rank. Second, and more important, fairly large differences in percentile ranks, especially near the middle of the percentile rank scale, are not different when expressed as stanines.

Many teachers and parents forget that all test scores contain some unreliability. No test score, not even one from a published standardized test, can be assumed to provide an exact, error-free assessment of a pupil's performance. Unfortunately, people who ignore this fact mistakenly treat small differences in percentile ranks (up to eight or so percentile ranks) as indicative of meaningful difference in performance. Sometimes answering only one or two more items correctly can change a pupil's score by eight to ten percentile ranks, yet not alter a pupil's stanine score. This fact should caution Brian's teacher to not read too much into the percentile rank differences in these two areas. The stanine score, though more inclusive than the percentile rank, reminds us that although Brian's percentile ranks differed on the two subtests, his performance did not differ when expressed in terms of stanines.

Note that standardized test batteries like Brian's are not only useful for comparing a pupil's performance to that of similar pupils nationwide; they are also useful for identifying areas of pupil strength and weakness. Thus, Brian's teacher can see that although Brian is average in most subtests (stanines of 4, 5, or 6), he is weaker in math procedures (37-4) than he is in vocabulary (90-8). The use of standardized tests to identify areas of pupils' strengths and weaknesses is more important from an instructional viewpoint than information about how pupils rank compared to a national sample of pupils in the same grade.

Consider Brian's grade equivalent scores. Brian is a fourth grader who took the Metropolitan Achievement Tests in the ninth month of the school year. If he had performed the same on a subtest as the average of fourth graders in the spring norming group for the Metropolitan, his grade equivalent scores on that subtest would have been 4.9, since that is the score given to average performance for fourth graders who take the test in May. Looking at Brian's grade equivalent scores in Figure 11.2 shows that, in most areas, he scored at the fourth-, fifth-, or sixth grade level. In general, Brian is average to a bit above average in comparison to the national norm group. He got more answers correct on the fourth grade tests than did the average fourth grader in the norm group. This is basically the same as the information provided by Brian's percentile ranks and stanines. As with percentile ranks, small differences in grade equivalent scores (4 to 6 months) should not be overinterpreted or used as the primary basis for decision making about pupils.

The achievement-ability comparison (ACC) shown in Figure 11.2 is provided by many test publishers when the school testing program includes both a standardized achievement test and a standardized ability test. In essence, the comparison tries to provide information about how a pupil performs on the achievement test compared to a national sample of pupils who have a similar ability level. Problems associated with interpreting and using the achievement-ability comparison in a meaningful way are similar to those raised in the discussion of grading pupils based on their ability in Chapter 10: (1) there are problems in accurately assessing ability; (2) the error in the two tests used in the comparison increases the imprecision of the decision; (3) information about an achievement-ability comparison is difficult to translate into meaningful, instructionally-related practices; (4) the information may label a pupil or influence a teacher's expectations for the pupil; and (5) there are many different types of ability that affect learning in addition to paper-and-pencil tests (Gardner, 1995). For these reasons, achievement-ability comparisons can be misleading and should be interpreted and used with extreme caution.

The area marked with a circled C in Figure 11.2 shows the national percentile bands for Brian's performance on each subtest. Presenting Brian's performance in this way is useful, not only because it provides a graphic contrast to the numerical scores, but also because it reminds the test user about the unreliability in all test scores. In essence, the **percentile bands** tell us that no score is error-free, so it is wrong to treat a score as if it were precise and infallible. It is best to think of a score not as a single number, but as a range of numbers, any one of which could be the pupil's true performance on an error-free test. Thus, looking at the percentile bands, it is more appropriate to say that Brian's true performance on the total reading subtest falls somewhere between about the 62nd and 80th percentile rank, not exactly and precisely the 68th percentile. His true performance on the math procedures subtest is best interpreted to be between a percentile rank of about 22 and 45, rather than exactly 37. Thinking of test performance in terms of a range of scores prevents overinterpretation of test results based on small score differences. Even if percentile bands are not provided, it is important to think of all types of test scores as representing a range of performance, not a single point.

What does all of this information tell about how Brian performs in his fourth grade classroom? By itself, it tells very little. However, in conjunction with the teacher's own classroom observations and assessments, commercial achievement test results can be useful. Commercial achievement tests provide information about (1) how a pupil compares to a national sample of pupils in the same grade, (2) the pupil's areas of relative strength and weakness in important subject areas, and (3) the pupil's developmental level. The tests do not tell how the pupil does in the day-to-day activities in his or her own classroom. If Brian is in a class of low achievers, he may perform very well in class, much better than would be expected on the basis of his standardized test scores. If he is in a class of high achievers, he may perform much lower than his standardized test scores would suggest. In either case, commercial achievement tests scores should *not* be interpreted without also considering information about the pupil's daily classroom performance.

Sometimes commercial test publishers provide information on pupils' performance on specific skill areas within a subtest. For example, the vocabulary subtest can be broken down into smaller skills such as synonyms, antonyms, and hyphenation. Or, a science subtest could be broken down into life science, physical science, earth science, and research skills. The classroom teacher can use this information to identify more specific areas where a pupil or the class has difficulty.

However, one caution should be noted in using this skill area information. In most cases, any single skill area will be assessed by a small number of items. A small number of items cannot be relied upon to provide reliable enough information for curriculum planning or decision making. Rather, teachers should follow up the skill area information with additional information collected on their own.

Example 2: Class Performance Report

Figure 11.3 shows the overall class performance for Mr. or Ms. Ness's fourth grade on the Iowa Tests of Basic Skills. The subtests of the Iowa are

Iowa Tests of Basic Skills

Service 9:
Report of Class Averages

Class/Group: NESS
Building: WEBER
Building Code: 304
System: DALEN COMMUNITY
Norms: SPRING 1992
Order No. 000-A33-76044-00-001

Grade: 4
Form: K
Test Date: 03/93
Page: 40

| | | READING | | | LANGUAGE | | | | | MATHEMATICS | | | | SOURCES OF INFO. | | | | |
AVERAGES	ITBS:	VOCAB-ULARY	COMPRE-HENSION	TOTAL	SPELL-ING	CAPITAL-IZATION	PUNC-TUATION	USAGE/EXPRESS	TOTAL	CON-CEPTS/ESTIM.	PROBS/DATA INTERP.	TOTAL	CORE TOTAL	SOCIAL STUD-IES	SCI-ENCE	MAPS & DIA-GRAMS	REF. MATLS	TOTAL	COM-POSITE	MATH COMPU-TATION
	N	24	24	24	24	24	24	24	24	24	24	24	24	24	24	24	24	24	24	24
	SS	2030	224.3	213.6	214.5	255.7	249.2	227.8	236.9	214.5	21.64	21.55	221.9	221.3	228.5	219.0	227.0	223.0	223.0	213.9
GE OF AVG SS		5.0	6.5	5.8	5.9	9.3	8.7	6.9	7.6	6.1	6.0	6.0	6.4	6.2	6.9	6.1	6.8	6.3	6.4	5.9
	NCE	54.2	67.1	62.5	62.8	78.7	76.6	65.4	75.4	65.5	61.8	63.8	68.8	66.4	69.2	61.8	71.2	67.1	69.8	66.0
PR OF AVG SS: NATL STUDENT NORMS		58	78	72	74	91	88	77	88	77	72	74	81	78	81	74	84	79	82	78

N TESTED= 27

SS=Standard Score, GE=Grade Equivalent, NCE=Normal Curve Equivalent, NPR=Nat'l%ile Rank

THE RIVERSIDE
PUBLISHING COMPANY
a Houghton Mifflin Company

FIGURE 11.3 *Standardized Test Report for a Class*

listed across the second line of the figure, beginning with vocabulary and ending with math computation. Four different scores are reported: the standard score (SS), the average grade equivalent score (GE), the average normal curve equivalent (NCE), and the average national percentile rank (NPR). Mr. or Ms. Ness can obtain a general picture of the performance of the class as a whole by examining the national percentile ranks.

The percentile ranks indicate the combined class average on each of the subtests of the Iowa in comparison to the national fourth grade norm. The composite score at the far right of Figure 11.3 shows that class performance across all the subtests in the battery had a percentile rank of 82. This indicates that summing across all subtests, the typical pupil in the class did better than 82 percent of similar students across the nation. Overall, the average national percentile ranks indicate that the class is somewhat above the national average on the various subtests. In most cases the class performed better than 70 to 80 percent of similar fourth graders nationwide. Note that the grade equivalent scores across the many subtests are also higher than the 4.3 one would expect of fourth graders tested in the third month of the fourth grade. This indicates that the pupils in this class answered more items correctly on the fourth grade test than did their peers nationally. Remember, grade equivalent scores do not indicate the grade level a pupil is achieving at or the grade she should be placed in. Figure 11.3 also shows that compared to most other subject areas, the class is relatively weak in vocabulary. This is something the teacher may wish to investigate further.

Example 3: Summary Report for Parents

Figure 11.4 shows a California Achievement Tests report that is sent home to parents after testing to help them understand their child's performance. All commercial achievement test publishers can provide similar forms. The section marked with a boxed *A* provides parents with a general introduction to the test and its purposes. The section marked *B* shows Ken Allen's percentile ranks on the total reading, total language, and total math tests, as well as his performance on the total battery. The areas labeled "below average," "average," and "above average" give parents a general indication of how Ken did compared to his national fifth grade peers.

The right third of the figure (labeled *C,* and *D*) provides more detailed information about Ken's performance. The four boxes contain, respectively, percentile ranks for the subtests that made up the total reading, total language, total math, and remaining battery subtests. Thus, for example, Ken's percentile ranks in vocabulary and comprehension, the two subtests that make up total reading, were 47 and 68. He scored higher than 47 and 68 percent of fifth graders nationally on vocabulary and comprehension, respectively. The boxes also show areas of Ken's strength and weakness on the skills that make up the reading, language, and math tests. This information is similar to the skill area information described in the discussion of Figure 11.2 and should be treated with the same caution. Teachers should

CAT/5 Home Report

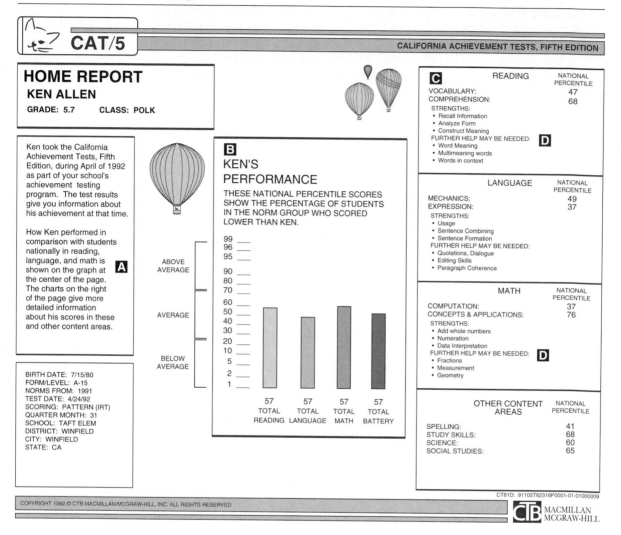

FIGURE 11.4   *Parent Report Form*

SOURCE: Reproduced from the California Achievement Tests, 5th Edition, by permission of the publisher, CTB/McGraw-Hill, a division of McGraw-Hill School Publishing Company. Copyright © 1992 by McGraw-Hill School Publishing Company. All rights reserved.

be prepared to answer parents' questions about the information contained in such home reports.

Commercial test publishers can provide scores and information additional to that described in the preceding sections, but Figures 11.2, 11.3, and 11.4 show the basic types of information that are returned to classroom teachers and parents as part of a school district's commercial achievement testing program. Each test publisher presents the results in slightly different formats, but the basic information and its interpretation do not vary much from publisher to publisher. The variety of forms and pupil analyses that are available from a commercial test publisher can be found in the manual that accompanies the test.

⚔ The Validity of Commercial Achievement Tests

A great deal of time, expertise, and expense are put into the construction of commercial achievement tests. The most widely used tests are technically strong, with well-written items, an attractive format, statistically sophisticated test norms, and reliable pupil scores. More care, concern, and expertise are put into producing a standardized achievement test than are put into constructing a teacher-made or textbook test.

Nonetheless, it is still appropriate to raise the issue of whether a commercial achievement test provides the information needed to make valid decisions about a pupil's achievement. Teacher-made and textbook achievement tests are judged in terms of whether they provide a fair assessment of how well pupils have learned the things they were taught. Commercial achievement tests are also judged on this basis, as well as on how well they compare a pupil's achievement to that of similar pupils nationwide. Regardless of the test, if it does not provide the desired information about pupil achievement it is not valid and therefore not useful for decision making.

Four issues influence the validity of commercial achievement tests: (1) the appropriateness of the content and objectives tested; (2) the representativeness of the norming sample; (3) the conditions under which the test is administered; and (4) misinterpretations of test results. This section examines these issues and their potential effect on the validity of standardized achievement tests.

Coverage of Objectives Taught

Commercial tests are not constructed to assess each classroom teacher's unique instructional objectives. Rather, they seek to assess a set of core objectives that most classroom teachers cover in their instruction. By selecting a common set of objectives, commercial test constructors seek to ensure that most pupils will have had exposure to what is tested.

While most classroom teachers will find the objectives tested in commercial achievement tests to be relevant to their instruction, few teachers will find all the topics they teach included in commercial tests. Teachers whose classroom instruction deviates greatly from the text or who consistently introduce novel materials and concepts often find that the topics covered by the commercial tests are quite different from those they have been teaching.

The time of year that testing takes place and the teacher's instructional focus also influence pupils' opportunities to learn the content being tested. Finally, virtually all commercial achievement tests rely heavily on multiple-choice test items. Restricting items to the multiple-choice format means that some topics or objectives may be tested differently than the way they were taught or tested in the classroom. For example, to assess spelling, most teachers give a weekly spelling test in which pupils have to spell each word correctly when it is said aloud by the teacher. In commercial achievement tests, spelling is assessed by presenting pupils with four or five words and asking them to identify the one that is spelled incorrectly. This is not the way pupils are taught spelling. These factors can reduce the match between the content of a commercial achievement test and the content of classroom instruction, thus lowering validity.

It is the responsibility of each local school district and each classroom teacher to determine if the content on a national achievement test is appropriate for pupils in that district or classroom. The objectives a test assesses are best identified by inspecting the actual test items. If, after inspecting the items, the test content appears quite different from what pupils are taught, judgments about pupils' achievement may not be valid and should be made with caution.

Test Norms

Commercial test publishers strive to obtain norming samples that are representative of national groups of pupils. However, there are important factors that can undermine the appropriateness of test norms and thereby test validity: (1) norms go out of date; (2) the curriculum in a subject area changes; (3) textbooks are revised and new instructional materials appear; and (4) the same test is administered in a school district over many years so teachers and pupils become familiar with its content and items. The relevance and representativeness of commercial test norms are dependent upon these factors and can influence the validity of test interpretations. Inappropriate or out-of-date test norms reduce the validity of comparisons and decisions made from standardized achievement tests. While there is no hard and fast period within which standardized achievement test norms should be revised, 7 to 9 years is a generally accepted time period used by the publishers of the most widely used standardized tests. Obviously, the older the test norms, the less representative they will be of instructional content and national pupil performance. Specific information about test-norming procedures and the age of the norms should be provided in the publisher's test manual.

Test Administration

Earlier it was emphasized that valid interpretations of pupils' standardized test performance is dependent on the pupils having taken the test under the conditions mandated by the test publisher. Deviations from the test administration directions, such as allowing pupils more time than specified, helping pupils while they are taking the test, coaching pupils before the test on the specific items they will be asked, and generally not following the directions provided, all reduce the validity of the test results and the decisions based on those results. It is imperative that administration directions be followed closely if valid test scores are to result.

Of course, pupils who require accommodations in testing should be provided with the appropriate resources as illustrated in Chapter 7. Typically, when the scores of pupils who receive accommodations are reported, they are flagged to indicate that the test was not taken under standard conditions. While this is generally an appropriate practice, the mere flagging of a pupil's score may lead to bias or discounting performance on the part of the test interpreter or user (Heaney and Pullin, 1998).

Interpreting Commercial Test Results

There are two common problems in interpreting commercial test scores: misinterpretation and overinterpretation. Because the types of scores that are used to describe pupil performance on commercial achievement tests are different from those teachers commonly use, the likelihood of misinterpretation is heightened. The most common misinterpretations involve the percentile rank, which is mistaken for the percentage of items a pupil answered correctly, and the grade equivalent score, which is mistakenly thought to indicate the grade level at which a pupil is performing in a subject area. Percentile ranks indicate the percentage of pupils in the norm group that the pupil scored above. Grade equivalent scores provide an indication of how well a pupil did, compared to other pupils in his or her grade, on a test built around objectives taught in that grade.

The main problem, however, in interpreting commercial achievement test scores is overinterpretation, not misinterpretation. Because commercial tests are constructed by professionals, tried out on nationwide samples of pupils, and provide numerical indices that describe a pupil's performance compared to pupils nationwide, there is a widespread belief that they give precise, scientifically accurate descriptions of pupils' achievement. Certainly parents and the public at large put more faith in commercial test results than in teacher-made assessments gathered over time in the day-to-day classroom setting. Teachers too often put undue faith in the precision of commercial achievement tests. Think about the 50 or so items that are contained in the typical subtest and compare that information (gathered only once) to the information a teacher accumulates through daily instruction and assessment of pupils. Doesn't such heavy reliance on commercial test scores seem unjustified or misplaced? One test publisher, in describing how teachers should present commercial achievement test results to parents during conferences, points out a limitation that all test users should bear in mind.

> It should be emphasized to parents that test scores represent achievement in basic skills areas at only one particular time and must be reviewed together with the student's actual classroom work and other factors. Parents should also understand that the test measures the basic content skills that are most common to curricula throughout the country. It cannot possibly measure, nor should it attempt to measure, the full curriculum of a particular classroom, school, or district. (CTB/McGraw-Hill, 1986b, p. 100)

Even when there are no problems with content, norms, and administration, commercial test scores still are overinterpreted. For example, it is common for teachers and parents to treat small differences in commercial test scores as if they were significant and indicated real performance differences between pupils. A percentile rank difference of 6 to 8 points or a 2- to 5-month grade equivalent difference between pupils rarely indicates important differences in their achievement or development. There is sufficient error in any test score—whether commercial or teacher-made—to make small scoring differences unreliable indicators of real differences between pupils. Commercial achievement test constructors try to defeat overinterpretation of small score differences by warning against them in their test manuals and by presenting scores as percentile or stanine bands (see Figure 11.2), but they are not always successful. In short, teachers should guard against treating small score differences as if they were meaningful.

Overinterpretation also occurs when teachers put too much faith in achievement-ability comparisons. These comparisons provide at best a general indication of how a pupil performs relative to other pupils of similar ability. Before a teacher acts on commercial test information of this type, he or she should reflect on personal knowledge about the pupil's work habits, personality, and achievement gained by daily exposure to the pupil in the classroom.

Finally, the smaller the number of items that make up a test score, the less reliable its results and the less trustworthy its score. This can be a particular problem in commercial achievement tests that include a few performance-based, open-ended items. While performance-based items can assess areas not tested by multiple-choice items, one must interpret performance-based items cautiously because there are relatively few such items. Normally, the subtest scores on commercial test batteries are quite reliable and consistent. However, when a subtest is broken down into specific topics or skill areas and a separate score given for each, caution must be exercised in interpreting and using the scores. While such information may provide a basis for further exploration of pupil performance, it should be reviewed critically because of the very few items on which it is typically based.

While commercial achievement tests can give teachers useful assessment information that they cannot gather for themselves, such information should be used in conjunction with information gathered from teacher assessments. For the most part, the information from commercial achievement tests will corroborate perceptions the teacher has already formed about pupils. When the two types of evidence do not corroborate each other, the teacher should look again at his or her perceptions to be sure the pupil is not being misjudged.

❧ Reporting Standardized Test Results to Parents

Often, teachers are expected to provide information to parents about pupils' performance on standardized tests. This may occur during a parent-teacher conference or by a written description sent to the parent. Explanation is easier done with a copy of the pupil's test results in hand or included in the mailing. Some useful guidelines for reporting to parents follow.

- Remember that the parent is not likely to be a testing expert and will basically want to know how the pupil performed.
- Start with some general information about the test and its purpose.
- Distinguish between a commercial standardized test and a classroom test or assessment.
- It is not necessary to tell parents all you know about standardized tests; your task is to get your message across in simple, understandable terms.
- Make your interpretations brief but accurate; you don't have to interpret every bit of information in the test report.
- Pick one or two subject areas such as math and reading, and one of the standardized scores (stanines or percentile ranks, but not grade equivalents because they are difficult to explain), and take the parent through the two subjects.
- Identify the pupil's strengths and weaknesses based on the test results; describe the pupil's overall performance.
- Do not patronize the parent; avoid comments like "You probably don't understand all of this," or "I understand that this is difficult for a parent."
- Be careful of stressing terms such as "error in testing," "flaws or imprecision in the tests," and "unreliability." Such remarks undermine the test information. It is better to say, "No single test can give an exact indication of performance," or, "Although these tests are generally accurate, they can vary from time to time."
- Remember that standardized tests are "one-shot" assessments and should be interpreted in the context of the pupil's general classroom performance to fully understand the pupil's achievement.

To summarize, commercial achievement test batteries can be used to compare an individual pupil's performance to that of a larger group of pupils beyond the local classroom or district, usually a national sample of pupils in the same grade. They can also provide information about a pupil's areas of strength and weakness. Because such comparisons are sought, commercial achievement test constructors must go through a complicated test construction process to develop their tests. They must identify content and objectives that are commonly taught at a particular grade level in classrooms across the country. Then they must write and try out items that assess these common objectives. From this trial assessment a final set of items is selected based upon content appropriateness and a desired statistical range. The final version of the test, with its directions, answer sheets, and test booklets, is then administered to a large sample of pupils who are thought to represent pupils across the country. The purpose of this test "norming" is to provide information about the performance of a national sample of pupils against which the performance of future test takers can be compared.

Pupil performance on commercial achievement tests is described mainly through scores that indicate how a pupil compares to other pupils. The most commonly used scores are (1) percentile ranks, which describe what percentage of the norming sample the pupil scored above; (2) stanines, which scoring on a scale of 1 to 9, roughly divide pupils into below average, average, and above average categories; and (3) grade equivalent scores, which are developmentally-based scores indicating how well a pupil compares to a national sample of peers in his or her grade. Other kinds of scores are sometimes provided with commercial tests, but they are less used than these three.

Commercial achievement test results should be interpreted in conjunction with what teachers know about pupils from their own classroom assessments. Further, interpretations of commercial test results should be based on knowledge of the test objectives, the representativeness and age of the test norms, and the conditions under which the test was administered to pupils. A mismatch between test and classroom objectives, old or nonrepresentative norms, or not following prescribed administrative conditions can reduce the validity of decisions based on the test results. Finally, test users must be cautious about assuming that commercial test scores are error-free. Small score differences should not be overinterpreted, because they rarely indicate meaningful performance differences.

✄ Statewide Assessments

Statewide standards were introduced in Chapter 3. Examples of statewide standards from a variety of states and in a variety of subject areas were illustrated. We saw that different states assess different subject areas and different standards. We also saw that different states provided varying support materials such as example assessments and instructional strategies to help pupils and teachers. The use of statewide assessments has been common in the United States for many years.

In prior decades statewide assessments stood alone, largely divorced from the teaching-learning process. Their main purpose was to provide a snapshot view of how pupils across a state were performing in particular subject areas, usually reading and math. In most cases, the tests were not tied to a specific set of state standards required to be taught in all state classrooms. The focus was on obtaining a general portrait of achievement at the school or district level, not at the individual pupil level.

In the past decade, the focus and emphasis of statewide assessment has greatly changed. There has been a much more active and concerted effort in most states to link state-endorsed standards to classroom instruction and assessment. Most states have identified standards (also called "content standards" or "curriculum frameworks") that pupils statewide are expected to achieve in various subject areas. These standards are at the heart of statewide educational reform. They are used to guide activities such as teachers' instructional emphases, textbook selection, and assessment methods. Instruction and assessment are coordinated to reflect the state standards. Teachers are strongly encouraged to incorporate these standards into their curricula, and in many states statewide achievement tests that reflect the standards are administered to pupils.

At present, 48 states have defined or are in the process of defining state standards in a variety of school subject areas. Thirty-two states have developed or are developing statewide assessment programs to supplement the standards. Thirty states now link or plan to link their state standards to the statewide testing program (Olson, 1995). There is significant activity among states to define state standards, develop statewide assessment programs, and link the standards to assessment.

In many of these states, the state assessments have important consequences for teachers, schools, and pupils. In some states, teachers and schools are rated based on their pupils' performance on state standards and assessments. Schools that have a history of poor pupil performance on the assessments, can be put on probation or closed. In a few states, teachers and schools whose pupils perform very well on the state assessments are rewarded with merit pay. In many states, pupils can be placed in remedial programs, held back from promotion, or denied a high school diploma if they perform poorly on statewide assessments. Box 11.1 indicates the growing prevalence and broad range of uses of statewide standards and assessments.

Box 11.1

Prevalence and Uses of Statewide Standards and Assessments

- Forty-eight states have statewide assessments of varied form.
- Sixteen states place state sanctions on schools chronically failing on statewide assessments.
- Fourteen states provide monetary rewards for improved assessment scores.
- The most common statewide standards and performance assessments are in the subject areas of writing (42 states) and various performance assessments (34 states); only 13 states use solely multiple-choice items in statewide assessments.
- The subjects most commonly assessed are English/language arts (48 states), math (47 states), writing (42 states), and science (36 states).
- Nineteen states use statewide assessments to evaluate school performance; eight more states plan to evaluate schools.
- Ten states can remove principals of failing schools; 16 states permit taking over failing schools.
- Currently, 19 states, and seven more in the future, will link high school graduation to statewide assessments.
- Six states link grade promotion to statewide assessments.

Source: Assembled from *Education Week,* volume XVIII, No. 17, January 11, 1999, Quality Counts '99.

Construction of Statewide Assessments

Most statewide assessments are criterion-referenced and are constructed in the following manner. First, the state standards are determined by statewide curriculum committees made up of teachers, administrators, parents, professional assessment developers, business people, and other concerned citizens. Their task is to identify important standards and skills in the subject areas that pupils will be expected to learn. The list of standards need not be confined to ones that are presently taught in schools. In fact, one way to influence the direction of curriculum and assessment is to develop and assess new content topics.

Once the standards are identified, assessment items are written or selected. Because performance is often reported for each individual standard, many items must be written to obtain stable, reliable scores. The items are then reviewed to determine whether they assess the intended standards, are culturally unbiased, and are at an appropriate language level for the intended pupils. Items are then assembled into tests.

When the purpose of statewide assessment is to provide information about achievement at the school or school district level, it is not necessary for every pupil in the school or district to answer every assessment. For school or district reporting purposes, the amount of information gathered can be maximized and the amount of testing time minimized by having each pupil answer only some of the questions. Suppose a curriculum committee identified 20 science standards that it felt seventh graders statewide should know. Suppose also that 10 tests items were written to assess each of the 20 objectives, thus producing a total of 200 seventh grade science items. Rather than giving each seventh grade pupil a 200-item test, the items could be divided into four tests of 50 items each. All four tests would then be administered at random to seventh graders in each school or district in the state, but each pupil would be required to take only one of the tests. Summing the results of all four tests would give a good estimate of school or district performance on all 20 seventh grade science objectives. It is important to recognize, however, that if the purpose of the state assessment is to make decisions about each *individual* pupil, it is necessary to give all pupils the same set of assessments. Otherwise individual pupils cannot be compared.

The format of statewide assessments differs considerably from that of a commercial achievement test. As noted previously, commercial achievement tests are comprised mainly of multiple-choice items. State assessments tend to use a broader mix of assessment types. In 42 states, statewide assessment includes a pupil writing sample of some type. Thirty-four states include performance assessments in their statewide assessments. Most statewide assessments also include a few open-ended questions that require pupils to briefly state and defend their answers. Performance assessments in oral reading, cooperative problem solving, or science experiments are included in some state assessments. Six states include pupil portfolios as part of the information collected in the statewide assessment program (Olson, 1999).

Scoring Statewide Assessments

Scoring on statewide assessments is usually criterion-referenced; predetermined standards are established and the performance of a school or an individual pupil is compared to the standards. Two types of criterion-referenced standards are used in statewide scoring: percentage and performance (see Chapter 10). In percentage scoring, passing the test is based on obtaining a given percentage of the test items correct. The percentage or percentages selected are often called the **cut score** or scores. For example, if a state defines mastery as a cut score of 70 percent or above on a statewide assessment, pupils who correctly answer 70 percent or more would pass the test. Pupils scoring below 70 percent would not pass. The Massachusetts statewide tests use four cut scores to differentiate pupil performance: Advanced, Proficient, Needs Improvement, and Failing. Each cut score is based on predefined score ranges that define pupils' performance on the statewide tests. Percentage scoring is used mainly for selection-type items.

Performance scoring is used to score assessments that require pupils to write essays, perform a process, or present a portfolio. Percentage scoring is difficult and cumbersome to implement for scoring such complex performances, so performances and portfolios are typically scored using rubrics. Box 11.2 shows a rubric that is used to score the quality of third graders' writing for personal expression in the Maryland statewide assessment program. There are four criteria associated with writing for personal expression: development, organization, focus on audience, and language. The rubric contains four levels of performance, labeled 3 to 0. Scorers read a third grader's essay and assign it to one of the categories depending on which category best describes the quality of the pupil's writing. A class, school, or district with many 1's and 0's would be alerted to the need to re-examine its curriculum to determine why many pupils did poorly. Note that the statewide results do not dictate changes in curriculum, but they do provide information that can help in deciding whether or not instruction in an area needs to be revised.

An Example of Statewide Assessment

One of the most highly developed and pervasive statewide assessment programs has been proposed in North Carolina (North Carolina Department of Public Instruction, 1992). While the program is not yet fully implemented, it provides an example of how states are using assessment to assess and improve schools. The North Carolina statewide assessment program is linked to the statewide Standard Course of Study, which is the state curriculum that defines what pupils are to know and do in school subjects at all grade levels. All statewide assessments are constructed to match closely the Standard Course of Study. Note that in addition to the assessments mandated by the state, local school districts may also administer additional commercial achievement test batteries of their choice. The features of the North Carolina statewide assessment program are outlined below.

Box 11.2

Scoring Rubric: Writing to Express Personal Ideas

3 points

- *Development:* consistently develops ideas into a complete, well-developed whole.
- *Organization:* sequences in a logical and effective manner.
- *Focus on Audience:* anticipates and answers the audience's needs and questions.
- *Language:* consistently uses language that enhances the writing.

2 points

- *Development:* partially develops the ideas and does not provide a complete, well-developed whole.
- *Organization:* purposely orders ideas for reader to follow.
- *Focus on Audience:* usually anticipates and answers the audience's needs and questions.
- *Language:* frequently uses language to enhance the writing.

1 point

- *Development:* rarely develops ideas and produces poorly-developed and incomplete ideas.
- *Organization:* usually orders ideas but some interruptions in the flow.
- *Focus on Audience:* occasionally anticipates and answers the audience's needs and questions.
- *Language:* sometimes uses language that enhances the writing.

0 points

- *Development:* no development of ideas into a complete whole.
- *Organization:* rarely evidences logical ordering of ideas.
- *Focus on Audience:* does not anticipate and answer the audience's needs and questions.
- *Language:* fails to use language that enhances the writing.

  Blank—no written response
  Focus—did not answer the stated question
  Unreadable—writing is illegible, writing not comprehensible

- Grades 1 and 2: Assessment in the first two grades will be by portfolios of pupils' work. The samples of pupil work can be reviewed by parents and teachers to determine pupil progress toward the designated goals.
- Grades 3 through 8: Three different mandated assessments are administered in these grades.

1. The North Carolina End-of-Grade (EOG) Tests will be administered at the end of each school year to assess mastery of grade-level knowledge and skills. Pupils will be tested annually in five subject areas: reading, writing, mathematics, science, and social studies.
2. Minimum Skills Diagnostic Tests (MSDT) will be given at the end of the year in grades 3, 6, and 8 to pupils who score below the state-designated passing score on the End-of-Grade Tests and who show other forms of difficulty with school work. The primary purpose of the Minimum Skills Diagnostic Tests is to identify a pupil's strengths and weaknesses so proper instruction and remediation can be planned. The MSDT is administered in reading, mathematics, and language.
3. North Carolina Competency Tests (NCCT) are administered to pupils in grade 8 in the subjects of reading, mathematics, and writing. Pupils in grade 8 who score below the cutoff score for the tests will be retested each year until they reach the minimum passing score in all three subjects. Obtaining a passing score on all three tests is necessary to receive a high school diploma.

- Grades 9 through 12: Two types of mandated assessment are carried out at these grades.
    1. North Carolina Competency Tests (NCCT) are administered yearly to those pupils who failed to attain the minimum passing score in reading, mathematics, and writing in grade 8.
    2. North Carolina End-of-Course (EOC) Tests are administered at the end of each course in the following subject areas: algebra I and II, geometry, biology, physical science, physics, chemistry, U.S. history, economic/legal/political systems, English I and II. Tests in other courses are planned in the future.

The North Carolina state assessment program is more extensive than most other statewide programs, mainly because very few other states have specific end-of-course or end-of-grade tests to determine pupil and school-wide progress. North Carolina is, however, one of a growing number of states that links statewide standards in subject areas to its statewide assessment program. In other respects, the North Carolina assessments are different to those in other states. Table 11.4 presents a sample of four different statewide assessment programs.

The four programs give an idea of the differences between states. All of the states shown have defined learning outcomes and standards for pupils in the state. The grade levels and the subject areas tested vary across states, as does the type of item or performance used to collect evidence of pupil learning. Some of the states have a fully developed statewide assessment program, while others are still in the process of constructing theirs. All of the states except Nebraska tie testing to statewide standards and use statewide assessment to make important decisions about pupils or schools.

TABLE 11.4

State-Based Testing in Four States

State	Name of Standards	Assessment
Louisiana	State curriculum guides	State curriculum guides apply to all grades, but are usually grouped by elementary, secondary, and high school levels. The state curriculum guides are mandatory. State-based assessment is focused on the curriculum guides. Grades 3, 5, and 7 pupils take criterion-referenced tests. High school pupils take tests in math, language arts, writing, science, and social studies. Material for all the tests comes from the state curriculum guides. Pupils must pass the high school subject tests to graduate.
Maryland	Maryland learning outcomes	Learning outcomes describe pupil learning in grades 3, 5, 8, and high school. Learning outcomes are mandatory and tied to state-based assessments. Criterion-referenced tests in grades 3, 5, and 8 in math, reading, science, social studies, and writing/language usage are administered. High school tests are being developed. Schools that do not make adequate progress toward state performance standards face possible reconstitution. The standards may be tied to high school graduation in the future.
Nevada	Courses of study	The courses of study identify what pupils are to learn in grades K, 3, 6, 8, 9, 10, 11, and 12. The courses of study are mandatory. A state-based writing assessment and a norm-referenced commercial test are administered to pupils. A state-based high school graduation test in reading, writing, and math is given.
Nebraska	Curriculum frameworks	The state department of education is developing curriculum standards for student learning in grades pre-K to 5, 6 to 8, and 9 to 12. Nebraska is a strong local control state so the frameworks are voluntary for schools and districts. There is no state-based assessment.

Source: Adapted from Olson. Setting the standards from state to state. *Education Week,* April 12, 1995, 23–35.

Maryland relies on its testing programs to help identify schools and districts that are not performing well. Louisiana and Nevada use statewide assessment results to decide which pupils will receive a high school diploma.

Most statewide assessment programs share the following common features.

- A sizable amount of assessment is required.
- Part of the assessment includes performance/portfolio-based information.
- Decisions about performance are made by comparing a pupil's score to a predetermined, statewide passing score.
- The assessments have important implications for pupils and schools.

- Because poor performance on the assessment can affect pupils' opportunities, teachers must decide how much emphasis they will devote to preparing pupils for the tests.
- Combining performance across pupils provides information that can be used for district, school, or teacher accountability.

Although teachers have relatively little influence over statewide assessment programs, the programs can and do influence teachers considerably. State assessments—especially those with important consequences for schools, teachers, or pupils—increase the pressure on school districts and teachers to revise their curricula to better match the state standards and assessments. In fact, one of the main reasons for statewide standards and aligned statewide assessments is to standardize the objectives and instructional emphases across a state.

Additional pressure is put on teachers because performance on state-based tests is usually reported in newspapers. Parents and school administrators follow state-based test scores with the same intensity that they follow baseball pennant races and the Dow Jones Averages. This interest produces pressure on schools and districts to "look good" relative to other schools and districts in the state. In Massachusetts, for example, state assessment results are reported on a district-by-district basis, but also in smaller groupings composed of districts of similar size, location, and socioeconomic status. A district's results are reported along with the results of similar districts in its group. The publication of these results always creates pressure on the low-scoring districts to improve their performance. Parents pressure administrators who then pressure teachers to respond to the low performance, usually by rearranging the curriculum to spend more time on tested topics. This pressure is magnified when comparisons are also made among the individual schools within a given school district. A general rule that describes the impact of assessment on instruction is: Whenever the results of an assessment have important consequences for pupils, teachers, or school districts, the assessment will be taken seriously and there will be pressure to incorporate the assessed objectives into the school curriculum.

Statewide assessment is a fact of teaching life in many states. Teachers cannot ignore such tests and the objectives they emphasize; they must find a viable balance between the demands of the state assessments and the needs of their pupils.

While the focus here is on classroom assessments, it is useful to note another consequence of the standards movement. In addition to assessing pupils, a number of states have begun developing and using standards and assessments to determine whether beginning teachers will receive state certification. In Massachusetts, for example, candidates who want to obtain teacher certification must take and pass assessments in reading, writing, and in a content area. The assessments are scored using criterion-referencing and all candidates must pass all three assessments, although they can retake the test to pass a section that was previously failed. Find out about teacher certification in your state by contacting your state Department of Education.

Chapter Summary

- Two important types of standardized achievement tests are (1) commercial norm-referenced tests and (2) state-based criterion-referenced tests. Commercial, norm-referenced tests provide information about how a pupil's achievement compares to that of similar pupils nationwide, while statewide tests usually provide criterion-referenced information about a pupil's or school's performance in relation to statewide achievement standards.

- Standardized assessment instruments must be administered, scored, and interpreted in the same way no matter where or when they are used. Otherwise, valid interpretations of their scores are difficult to make.

- Although teachers have little voice in the selection and scoring of either commercial or statewide tests, pressures are often exerted on them to ensure that their pupils do well on such tests.

- Commerical norm-referenced tests are constructed and scored differently than teacher-made classroom assessments. Commercial assessments are constructed by (1) identifying objectives that are common to most classrooms at a given grade level; (2) writing two to three times more items than are needed on the final test; (3) trying out the items to identify ones that will spread out the scores of test takers; (4) selecting items for the final version of the test; (5) trying out the final version on a large norm group of pupils from across the country; and (6) using the performance of the norm group as a baseline against which to compare the performance of individual pupils who take the test.

- Four criteria are used to judge the adequacy of commercial standardized test norms: sample size, representativeness, recency, and description of procedures.

- Commercial standardized achievement tests usually come in the form of a test battery containing subtests in a variety of subject matter areas. Scores are provided for each subtest and a composite score is provided for the overall test.

- In order to make valid interpretations from norm-referenced tests, it is important that the test's directions be strictly followed.

- Unlike teacher-made tests, norm-referenced commercial tests are not interpreted in terms of number or percentage of items correct. Instead, special comparative scores are used to represent pupil performance. The most commonly used scores are: (1) the percentile rank, which indicates the percentage of similar pupils nationwide a given pupil scored above; (2) the stanine, which uses the scores 1 to 9 to indicate whether a pupil is below average (stanines 1, 2, or 3), average (stanines 4, 5, and 6), or above average (stanines 7, 8, and 9) compared to similar pupils nationwide; and (3) the grade equivalent score, which is a developmental score that indicates whether a pupil is above, below, or at the level of similar pupils in his or her grade.

- A pupil's test performance may appear quite different depending on the norm group he or she is being compared to: a representative national sample, a sample of pupils in a similar type of school district, or a sample of pupils in the local district.

- Caution should be exerted when interpreting small differences in norm-referenced test scores, especially percentile ranks and grade equivalent scores. Because all tests have some degree of error in them, it is best to think of a score not as a single number, but as a range of numbers, any one of which might indicate the pupil's true performance. Small differences in test scores are not usually significant.

- Interpretation and use of norm-referenced achievement tests should be guided by a number of concerns, such as how well the tested content matches classroom instruction, how the information agrees or disagrees with the teacher's own perceptions of pupils, the recency of the test norms, the extent to which administrative directions were followed, and the understanding that no score is exact or infallible.

- Commercial achievement tests provide useful comparative information that teachers cannot get for themselves. However, teachers should always use such information in conjunction with their other teacher assessments when making decisions about pupils. Usually, the two types of information corroborate each other.

- Statewide tests are usually based upon statewide standards or objectives that identify what pupils are expected to learn in the school subjects they take. Individual pupils and schools as well as entire districts are the objects of statewide tests. School and district-wide tests assess curriculum mastery by groups of pupils, while pupil-centered tests are used to make decisions about whether a pupil will graduate from high school, be promoted to the next grade, or be placed in a remedial class. Both are scored in terms of statewide criterion-referenced standards called cut scores.

- The standards, test formats, subject areas tested, scoring approaches, and uses of test results vary considerably from state to state.

- Because the results of statewide tests are important and are usually made public, they can create pressures on teachers to emphasize only tested objectives. Teachers inevitably must weigh the extent to which they will incorporate tested content into their instruction.

Questions for Discussion

1. Are standardized tests fair to all students? Why or why not? What student characteristics might influence performance on a standardized test? Would these same characteristics influence performance on a teacher-made test? Why?

2. What can a teacher do to help make students less anxious about taking standardized tests? Would the same actions help students when they take teacher-made tests?

3. If you could select only one scoring format from a commercial standardized test to explain to parents, which would you choose? Why? What limitations would your choice have?

4. What factors should influence the use of commercial test results by classroom teachers?
5. What are some of the reasons why many states have adopted statewide standardized testing programs for all schools in the state?

Reflection Exercises

1. Why do students, parents, and school administrators put so much emphasis on commercial and state-based test results?
2. How might a statewide testing program such as that used in North Carolina influence classroom instruction for the better and for the worse?
3. How influential have commercial achievement tests been in your life? Do you think your life would have been much different if you never had taken one?

Activities

1. Read the commercial achievement test report for Nicole Kovitz, a fourth grade student. Your task is to write a one-page letter to Nicole's parent explaining the results of her test performance. The following suggestions should guide your letter.

   - Nicole's parent will receive a copy of the test report sheet.
   - Nicole's parent is not a standardized testing expert and basically will want to know how his/her daughter performed.
   - You should start with some information about the test and its purpose.
   - You should describe the information in the test report sheet.
   - You should interpret the information about Nicole's performance.
   - What are Nicole's strengths and weaknesses? How can the parent see these on the test report form?
   - Describe Nicole's overall performance to the parent.
   - Indicate what the parent should do if she/he has questions.

   Your letter will be judged on the accuracy of the information about Nicole's performance you convey to the parent and the extent to which you make the information understandable to the parent. You do not have to convey every bit of information in the test report. You must identify which information is most important and convey it in a way that a parent could understand. A letter full of technical terms will not do. Remember, the parent can always arrange to visit you in school if more information is desired.

Iowa Tests of Basic Skills

Student:	KOVITZ, NICOLE	Level:	10
I.D. No.:		Form:	K
Class/Group:	NESS	Grade:	4
Building:	WEBER	Test Date:	03/93
Bldg. Code:	304	Norms:	SPRING 1992
System:	DALEN COMMUNITY	Page:	359
Order No.:	000-A33-76044-00-001		

SS = Standard Score
GE = Grade Equivalent
NS = Nat'l Sta9

NCE = Normal Curve Equvalent
NPR = Nat'l %ile Rank (▬▬)
N Att. = Number Attempted

THE RIVERSIDE
PUBLISHING COMPANY
a Houghton Mifflin Company

Tests	Scores					National Percentile Rank
	SS	GE	NS	NCE	NPR	
Vocabulary	187	4.0	4	40	31	
Reading	208	5.4	6	57	63	
Reading Total	198	4.6	5	50	49	
Spelling	222	6.5	7	70	82	
Capitalization	215	5.9	6	60	69	
Punctuation	222	6.5	6	63	74	
Usage & Expression	189	4.0	4	43	37	
Language Total	212	5.6	6	59	66	
Math Concepts & Estimation	207	5.3	6	59	66	
Math Probs & Data Interp.	200	4.8	5	51	53	
Math Total	204	5.2	5	55	59	
Core Total	205	5.1	5	54	58	
Social Studies	227	6.8	7	70	83	
Science	193	4.2	5	46	42	
Maps & Diagrams	174	3.0	3	30	17	
Reference Materials	251	8.9	9	88	96	
Sources of Info. Total	212	5.6	6	60	68	
Composite	208	5.3	6	57	62	
Math Computation	210	5.6	6	63	72	

2. Find a website that contains statewide standards. Select a state to examine. List the website address, the subject area you will examine, and the grade you will focus on. Now, complete the following exercises:

- Do the standards described apply to each school year or to groups of years (e.g., grades 1 to 4)?
- State three standards.
- Identify if there are benchmarks (standards to be taught and assessed), the kind of items used to assess the standards, and the implication of the standards for instruction (e.g., Are the standards very general or very specific? Are they appropriate for the age group who will be tested?).
- Write two paragraphs describing your perspective on statewide standards and assessment.

Review Questions

1. What is a standardized test? What information can a commercial standardized test provide a teacher that a teacher-made or textbook test cannot? What is a test battery? What are subtests? How does the construction of a commercial standardized achievement test differ from that of a teacher-made achievement test?
2. What are test norms? What information do they provide a teacher about a pupil's performance? How are the following norms interpreted: percentile rank, stanine, and grade equivalent score? How do test norms differ from raw scores? Why are norms used instead of raw scores?
3. What are fall and spring norms? Why do commercial standardized tests provide them?
4. What factors should teachers consider when they try to interpret their pupils' commercial standardized test scores? That is, what factors influence the results of standardized tests and thus should be considered when interpreting scores?
5. What are the differences in construction and use between commercial and statewide standardized tests?

References

Airasian, P. W. (1993). Policy-driven assessment or assessment-driven policy? *Measurement and Evaluation in Counseling and Development* (26), 22–30.

Canner, J., Fisher, T., Fremer, J., Haladyna, T., Hall, J., Mehrens, W., Perlman, C., Roeber, E., & Sandifer, P. (1991). *Regaining trust: Enhancing the credibility of school testing programs.* Xeroxed National Council on Measurement in Education Task Force.

CTB/McGraw-Hill. (1986a). *California achievement tests forms E and F: Test coordinator's handbook.* Monterey, CA: CTB/McGraw-Hill.

CTB/McGraw-Hill. (1986b). *California achievement tests forms E and F: Class management guide.* Monterey, CA: CTB/McGraw-Hill.

Ebel, R. E., & Frisbie, D. A. (1991). *Essentials of educational measurement.* Englewood Cliffs, NJ: Prentice Hall.

Gardner, H. (1995). *Frames of mind: The theory of multiple intelligences.* New York: Basic Books.

Heaney, K. J., & Pullin, D. C. (1998). Accommodations and flags: Admission testing and the rights of individuals with disabilities. *Educational Assessment, 5*(2), 71–93.

North Carolina Department of Public Instruction (1992). Quick reference for parents and teachers: Testing at various grade levels. *Parent Involvement,* September-October.

Olson, L. (1995). Standards times 50. *Education Week,* April 12, 14–20.

Olson, L. (1999). In search of better assessments. *Education Week,* January 11, 17–20.

The Psychological Corporation. (1984). *Stanford achievement test technical review manual.* New York: The Psychological Corporation.

Riverside Publishing Co. (1986). *Iowa tests of basic skills: Preliminary technical summary.* Chicago: Riverside Publishing Co.

Smith, M. L., & Rottenberg, C. (1991). Unintended consequences of external testing in elementary schools. *Educational Measurement: Issues and Practice, 10*(4), 7–11.

Teacher Self-Assessment

Chapter Outline
❖ Need for Teacher Self-Assessment
❖ Informal and Formal Approaches
❖ Self-Assessment Examples
❖ Classroom Assessment: Summing Up
❖ Final Thoughts

Chapter Objectives

After reading this chapter, the pupil will be able to:

- Explain the purpose and advantages of teacher self-assessment
- Construct a self-assessment tool
- Apply principles to guide appropriate interpretation of classroom assessment information

Thus far we have examined many features of classroom assessment: types of assessment, times at which assessment occurs, formal and informal ways to collect assessment information, and methods of constructing and grading assessments. We have explored the assessment of pupils, classroom climate, learning, instruction, textbooks, lesson plans, and standardized tests. These topics have all been discussed from the perspective of how teachers assess them in their classrooms. In spite of the variety of assessment topics addressed, there is one very important type of classroom assessment that has yet to be discussed: how teachers assess themselves and their own teaching practice.

Teacher self-assessment focuses on the assessments teachers make about the adequacy and effectiveness of *their own* knowledge, performance, beliefs, or effects so that they can understand and improve their teaching (Airasian and Gullickson, 1994a). Teacher self-assessment occurs when a teacher asks questions like What do I believe about education, teaching, and learning and to what extent are these beliefs reflected in what I do in my teaching? How much do I know about educational innovations, methods, and strategies and in which areas of knowledge do I need strengthening? How well do I carry out the many demands of planning, delivering, and assessing instruction? and How much do I know about the effects of my beliefs, knowledge, and practices on my pupils' learning? Other approaches such as "reflective practice," "teacher research," "action research," "analysis of practice," and "self-understanding" are similar to teacher self-assessment in that they all recognize and emphasize the teacher's professional responsibility to continually examine and improve her or his own classroom practice. Teacher self-assessment is a type of formative assessment of the teacher by the teacher and for the teacher.

✸ Need for Teacher Self-Assessment

Teachers should carry out self-assessment for many reasons (Airasian and Gullickson, 1997; McColsky and Egelson, 1993). First, as noted, it is a teacher's professional responsibility to examine, refine, and broaden his or her practice on a continuing basis. Second, self-assessment focuses on the classroom level where teachers have their greatest expertise and their greatest effects on pupils. Third, it recognizes that the most successful improvements occur when individuals change themselves and their own practice, rather than when change is mandated by others. Fourth, it makes teachers aware of the strengths and weaknesses of their practice, encouraging continual change and improvement, and thereby discouraging unexamined and unchanging classroom practices. Fifth, it treats the teacher as a professional who has a personal responsibility for improvement and it gives the teacher a "voice" or a stake in his or her practice. Sixth, if planned in advance, it can encourage and develop interactions and learning among groups of teachers.

There are many levels at which teachers can assess their own practice, ranging from broad assessments focused on the social and political consequences of their teaching on pupils to more narrow assessments such as how well they have followed guidelines for implementing cooperative learning groups or scoring rubrics (Valli, 1992). In this discussion, the focus will be on the more narrow aspects of teaching practice, rather than upon more general, sociocultural aspects. Further, focus will also be on formal methods of self-assessment rather than on informal ones.

✖ Informal and Formal Approaches

Informal Approaches

Before examining formal approaches to teacher self-assessment, it is necessary to say something about the importance of informal teacher self-assessments. By far, the majority of teachers' self-assessments are informal, spontaneous ones that occur during the ebb and flow of normal classroom activities. During instruction teachers do two things: teach and assess their teaching. While engaged in the process of teaching, a teacher is also asking her or himself many questions about what is going on: "Did I make that explanation clear?" "Should I give another example?" "Am I going too fast?" "Am I holding their interest?" Questions such as these are self-assessment questions focused on the teacher's need to determine how things are going and what adjustments are needed. Those of you who have taught or are in the process of doing a teaching practicum know how many questions teachers ask about themselves and their own instruction while they are teaching. Note that because these questions occur *during* instruction, while the teacher is engaged with the class, it is difficult for the teacher to rely upon formal evidence gathering to provide answers. The teacher must provide on-the-spot answers to these questions while maintaining the flow of instruction. The teacher cannot stop, think carefully, or collect formal information, so the teacher usually relies on the looks on pupils' faces, their apparent interest, or their questions to determine how things are going. Such informal, spontaneously occurring self-assessments have been termed "reflections in action" because they happen during the action of teaching (Schon, 1983).

While extremely common and important in all classrooms, informal, spontaneous teacher self-assessments have some limitations as a means to help teachers understand and improve their practice (Airasian and Gullickson, 1994b; Farnham-Diggory, 1994; Elbaz, 1990). While instructing, a teacher has little time to think carefully about any particular self-assessment question, which often means that decisions are made on the basis of the teacher's intuition or "gut level" feelings rather than thoughtful reflection. Also, teachers pose a large number of self-assessment questions during instruction. These questions are so intertwined with the activities of instruction that, after instruction is completed, teachers rarely remember them or the situations that prompted them. Often, teachers are not aware of the fact that they are self-assessing. Finally, most self-assessments are prompted by what is happening during instruction, which means that many other important aspects of teaching (test construction, lesson planning, sizing-up decisions, etc.) are ignored or rarely exposed to self-assessment. Thus, while all teachers carry out multiple, spontaneous self-assessments during instruction, these assessments are not particularly helpful in changing or improving teacher practice in the long run.

Formal Approaches

Not all teacher self-assessments are based on spontaneously occurring instructional events. Other self-assessments take place out of the immediacy of practice, when the teacher is not in front of the class and therefore has more opportunity to contemplate and assess his or her practices, beliefs, and effects. These self-assessments are called "reflections on action" (Schon, 1983). Self-assessment based on reflection on action is a conscious, rather than tacit, process, and it is a process that the teacher controls, not a spontaneously occurring one. The ability to revisit issues or events of practice permits lengthy, conscious reflection and leads to an awareness of one's practice that is not possible from reflection in action. Without a good awareness of practice, self-assessments are difficult to perform and, if performed, subject to many biases (Airasian and Gullickson, 1995).

Here are some common teacher self-assessment questions that cannot be easily answered using informal observation of pupils during instruction. In fact, most of these questions would not even arise if teachers confined their self-assessments strictly to events and issues arising while instructing pupils. Imagine you are a teacher. How would you go about answering these questions?

- What is the proportion of negative and positive feedback I give to my pupils?
- What proportion of the items on my last test were lower-level items and what proportion were higher-level items?
- How much are pupils learning from my homework assignments?
- How often this week did I end my lessons with a summary of important points?
- Do I give pupils of all ability levels an equal chance to participate in class discussions and questioning periods?

If you really wanted to answer these questions, you would need to do more than make a "gut level" or intuitive judgment about your practice. To answer each of these questions you would need to obtain a clear awareness of your current practice by setting up a plan to collect formal evidence that would inform your answers. What kinds of evidence would you collect, and from whom?

Teachers who understand the importance of awareness of practice as a critical basis for self-assessment often supplement their self-assessments with various types of formal evidence. This approach is highly recommended because it provides assessment information that supplements teachers' reflections and thereby leads to better assessments. There are many types of formal procedures that teachers use to collect information for self-assessment. Box 12.1 lists eight of the most common ones, with a brief description of each.

Box 12.1

Eight Methods for Performing Formal Teacher Self-Assessment

1. **Self-assessment questionnaires** are designed to be completed by the teacher to allow her or him to assess performance in a particular area of teaching.
2. **Audio or video recordings** allow the teacher to record a sample of classroom performance for subsequent analysis by the teacher and/or peers. Microteaching is an example of this method.
3. **Student feedback** can be similar to self-assessment questionnaires except that pupils, not the teacher, complete the questionnaire. Teacher-made questionnaires or pupils' journals/logs are examples of this method.
4. **Teacher portfolios** are self-prepared collections that provide information about a teacher's practice and the changes it undergoes over time. A portfolio can include many different types of information, including many of the methods described in this table. For example, a portfolio could contain a group of videotapes, self-assessment questionnaires, or student feedback reports that the teacher can examine to carry out self-assessment.
5. **Student performance data** include pupils' tests, products, and performances. Review of pupils' work can inform one about the success of one's instruction and areas in which pupils need additional help.
6. **External or peer observation** involves having a peer or colleague observe, assess, and provide information about one's strengths and weaknesses in areas such as questioning behavior, lesson organization, and pupil reinforcement.
7. **Journal writing** permits the teacher to keep a written record over time of classroom events and problems that can be reflected upon and examined for the success of different ways to handle problems.
8. **Joint problem solving** involves groups of teachers or peers discussing and sharing common teaching problems, perceptions, and strategies. Exposure to the ideas and practices of colleagues is a potent strategy for teacher reflection and improvement.

Source: Adapted from Airasian and Gullickson, *Teacher self-evaluation tool kit.* 1997.

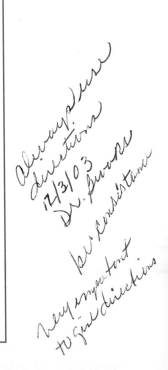

You probably have already been exposed to some of these teacher self-assessment strategies. You may be required to keep a journal of your teaching experiences that allows you to record and analyze particular situations or activities about your teaching, beliefs, or practice. You may have had to complete a microteaching exercise in which you were videotaped while teaching a short lesson. Think about how much you were able to assess and learn about your teaching from watching the tape. Many teachers and prospective teachers have begun to assemble teaching portfolios that contain information about and examples of their educational philosophy, lesson plans, teaching beliefs, classroom practices, and the like. These portfolios provide information both to prospective employers and to the teacher about one's ways of thinking about teaching and one's actual classroom practice. Reviewing a portfolio helps one become more aware of one's teaching beliefs, knowledge, and effects, and thus is a useful self-assessment technique. Peer observation and review is another common self-assessment method experienced by both pre- and in-service teachers. Talking with your peers in class or your cooperating teacher about teaching issues such as grading, discipline, teaching students with disabilities, or interactions with parents offers a good opportunity to compare your practices and beliefs to those of your peers or cooperating teacher. Such comparisons provide a form of self-assessment by making you evaluate your personal practices and beliefs. Note that all of these common self-assessment approaches are based upon providing concrete evidence to the teacher to guide and shape reflection and personal assessment.

The examples of formal teacher self-assessment tools presented in the following sections are adapted from Airasian and Gullickson, 1997 and are used with permission. These examples illustrate the use of teacher and student feedback methods and the use of video or an external observer.

✠ Self-Assessment Examples

Pupil Feedback Example

First, we will examine a simple, widely used self-assessment tool called the "minute survey" or the "minute response." The minute survey is a very flexible and simple strategy to obtain feedback from pupils about many different aspects of classroom activities. To conduct a minute survey, the teacher sets aside 2 or 3 minutes at the end of class to survey pupils about some aspect of the lesson. The teacher asks each pupil to take out a piece of paper (or, for earlier grades to raise their hand or make some other indication) and answer one or two questions about the lesson. For example, the teacher might ask one or two of the following questions.

1. Write two things you learned from today's lesson.
2. Write one question about today's lesson that you would like answered.
3. Would you like to spend more time on today's topic?

4. How confident do you feel about doing the homework based on today's lesson?

5. How well did last night's reading assignment prepare you for today's lesson?

6. Here are two problems similar to the ones we did in class today. Solve the problems.

There are, of course, many other questions a teacher could ask pupils about a lesson, an assignment, a homework exercise, a field trip, a video presentation, or even a test. The information gained from the minute survey can help the teacher assess his or her success during instruction or how well pupils are learning from the instruction. To make the minute survey most informative, three guidelines should be followed. First, let pupils respond anonymously so they will answer honestly. Second, keep the amount of writing small. The minute survey is meant to be completed quickly and hence should focus on only one or two aspects of the lesson. Third, before reading pupils' responses, answer the questions in the way you think most pupils will answer. For example, what do you (the teacher) think will be the two most important things pupils get from your lesson? Answering the questions yourself, before examining the pupils' responses, will provide a comparison to tell you whether you have sized-up the lesson in the same way your pupils have.

Self-Reflection Example

Often, the simple task of rating oneself can lead to reflection about what one really knows or can do and what areas are in need of improvement or better understanding. In carrying out such self-ratings, it is better to rate specific areas of knowledge or practice than it is to rate more general ones. The more specific the statement about knowledge or practice, the easier it is to focus on its improvement. For example, rather than rating one's grading in general, it is better to use the following format. The teacher rates his or her knowledge or skill as high, medium, or low for each of these specific aspects of grading. You might want to try rating yourself.

My understanding of:

the effects my grades have on pupils	H	M	L
biases in my grading practices	H	M	L
the importance of grades to parents	H	M	L
norm- versus criterion-referenced grades	H	M	L
what my grades actually represent	H	M	L
the fairness of my grading system	H	M	L
the way I grade pupils with disabilities	H	M	L

These questions make a teacher think about what he or she is doing in the classroom, and that thinking leads to increased awareness of personal teaching practice. Based on the ratings, a teacher could select one or two of the low rated understandings and work to improve them. In this way, the teacher's practice improves.

Video Recording or External Observer Example

This example focuses on a cooperative learning lesson. The lesson can be assessed either by a teacher videotaping and analyzing pupil activities during the cooperative lesson or by having a colleague observe and critique the lesson. Whether a teacher self-assesses individually or with a colleague, it is very helpful to focus the observation on a specific set of performance criteria. Here are some areas the teacher wanted to self-assess in a cooperative learning lesson.

- Determine the appropriateness of the topic for pupils
- Have materials ready at the start of the lesson
- Explain goals and purposes of the lesson clearly
- Explain procedures for cooperation to pupils
- Make a smooth transition into group activities
- Help each team during the lesson
- Visit each team at least twice
- End the lesson with a summary or directions for continuation

With these areas spelled out, the teacher or observer would examine the teacher's performance for strong and weak points.

There are many sources for additional examples of formal teacher self-assessment instruments and procedures (Airasian and Gullickson, 1995; Arends, 2001; Pollard and Tann, 1993; Haysom, 1985; Angelo and Cross, 1993; Saphier and Gower, 1987; Kremer-Hayon, 1993). At the heart of all such approaches is an emphasis on making teachers aware of their practice. This usually entails more than just reflecting on practice. It demands the examination of some evidence about practice. Before teachers can meaningfully reflect on their practice, they must have an awareness of what that practice is. That is the focus of teacher self-assessment. Without awareness, it is difficult to change or improve. Box 12.2 lists some guidelines to help in getting started with teacher self-assessment. It is hoped that you will employ some of these self-assessment techniques to understand and improve your own classroom practice.

✄ Classroom Assessment: Summing Up

Assessment is not an end in itself. It is a means to an end—classroom decision making. The decision-making process itself is made up of three steps: (1) collecting information, (2) interpreting information, and (3) making a decision based upon the interpretation. The validity of decisions depends upon both the quality of the information collected and the quality of the interpretation. Information is the raw material of classroom decision making, and meaning is added to this raw material when the teacher answers the question "What is this information telling me?" Because the decisions that teachers make can affect both pupils and teachers in important ways, teachers are responsible for the quality of both the assessment information they collect and the interpretations they make from that information.

Box 12.2

*Guidelines for Getting Started
with Self-Assessment*

1. **Start small:** Begin with small self-assessment activities, ones that can be completed easily; choose narrow aspects of teaching to self-assess rather than more global ones.
2. **Use comparisons:** Include a prediction or hypothesis about what a self-assessment will show *before* examining the results of the self-assessment; comparing your initial prediction to actual results will heighten your awareness of your practice.
3. **Vary strategies:** Because no single self-assessment approach is useful for all important questions of practice, vary the self-assessment approach to fit the method or areas of practice being examined.
4. **Provide anonymity:** When obtaining self-assessment information from pupils, protect their anonymity; this will make them feel more secure and allow them to give honest information to you.
5. **Work with colleagues:** Teachers have many of the same concerns about practice and can learn much from their fellow teachers; working collaboratively on self-assessment provides many mutual benefits and learning experiences.

Collecting Assessment Information

Good decisions are based upon good information, and three factors determine the quality of assessment information:

1. The conditions under which information is collected, including the physical and emotional context during assessment, the opportunity provided to pupils to show their typical behavior, and the quality of instruction provided prior to assessing achievement
2. The quality of the instruments used to collect the information, including factors such as the clarity of test items or performance criteria, the relationship of an assessment procedure to the characteristic being assessed, and the appropriateness of the language level of items
3. The objectivity of the information, including unbiased scoring

If efforts are not made to minimize such pitfalls, the assessment information that teachers rely on in their decision making will be seriously flawed. Consider, for example, the things that can lower the validity and reliability of the report card grades a teacher assigns.

- Portions of a teacher's achievement tests might assess things the pupils were not taught. (validity lowered)
- The items a teacher writes might be ambiguous, poorly written, or too complex for the pupils. (validity lowered)

- The sample of behavior observed might be too small to provide information about the pupils' typical behavior. (reliability lowered)
- Scoring of the assessment information might be careless and subjective. (validity and reliability lowered)
- Informal information about pupil interest, motivation, and attitude might be based on inappropriate indicators. (validity lowered)

Most teachers will interpret whatever information they have as if it were valid and reliable. If it is not, decisions will be faulty, and the grades will not be a valid indication of pupil learning. The same is true for all other teacher decisions.

Interpreting Assessment Information: Five Guidelines

The second step in decision making is interpreting the available assessment information. It is not until information is interpreted that decisions about classroom organization, discipline, planning, teaching, learning, and grading can be made. Although it is not reasonable to expect teachers to always interpret information correctly, it is reasonable to expect them to improve their interpretations as a result of conscientious practice.

Teachers are most likely to misinterpret assessment information early in the school year, when a pupil's behavior changes abruptly, or when new information about the pupil becomes available. In general, the less a teacher knows about a pupil, the more interpretation is required, and the more likely that subsequent interpretations will tend to be based upon earlier ones.

Box 12.3 presents five general principles that should guide interpretation of classroom assessment information. These principles cut across all assessment purposes and types that have been discussed. The following section describes these principles in greater detail.

1. *Assessment information describes pupils' learned behaviors and their present status.* The behaviors and performances observed during assessment represent what pupils have learned to do, think, feel, and say. For a variety of reasons (cultural, societal, economic, familial, etc.), some pupils learn more, retain more, and have more opportunities to learn than others. Whatever the cause of these learning differences, the information classroom assessment provides tells only about what pupils have learned to do.

Assessment also describes how pupils currently perform, not necessarily how they will perform in the future. Pupils can change. They can have sudden developmental spurts, become more interested in some things and less interested in others, and reach a point when they "bloom" academically after many years of poor performance or "hit the wall" and experience a decline in academic performance. Thus, when teachers or parents use words like *potential* and *capacity* to describe pupils, they are making assumptions that assessments do not always support. Discussion of a pupil's "capacity" suggests a fixed amount of ability, interest, or motivation that places a limit on a pupil's performance. Assessments cannot gauge such limits, and interpretations along these lines should be avoided. Interpreta-

Box 12.3

Principles for Interpreting Assessment Information

- Assessment information describes pupils' learned behaviors and present status.
- Assessment information provides an estimate, not an exact indication, of pupil performance.
- Single assessments are a poor basis for making important decisions about pupils.
- Assessments do not always provide valid information.
- Assessment information describes performance; it does not explain the reasons for it.

tions focused on "potential" and "capacity" can be especially damaging to poor or disadvantaged pupils who often have had fewer opportunities to learn than other pupils, but who often perform quite well given proper opportunity and practice.

But isn't assessment information used to predict pupil success and adjustment? Aren't scores on the SAT and the ACT used by college admissions officers to predict pupils' performance in college? Don't the grades pupils receive in one school year often predict the grades they receive in future years? Aren't pupils in the lowest first grade reading group usually still in that group at the end of elementary school? Although these examples seem to suggest that assessments can provide information about pupils' potential or capacity, such a conclusion is faulty.

The chief reason that many pupils maintain the same subject grades or reading group placement over time has less to do with their "potential" or "capacity" than with the stability of their school and classroom environment. If we take a pupil at the start of first grade, place him or her in the lowest reading group, and provide objectives and instruction that are less challenging than those for other groups, we should not be surprised if the pupil fails to move out of that reading group by the end of the school year. This is an example of the self-fulfilling prophecy that was described in Chapter 2. It suggests that the reason assessments often remain stable over time has more to do with the nature of classroom expectations and instruction than with our ability to assess pupils' potential or capacity. Thus, assessment information should be interpreted as indicating a pupil's current level of performance, which can change.

2. *Assessment information provides an estimate, not an exact indication, of performance.* Under no condition should assessment information be treated as if it were infallible or exact. There are always numerous sources of error that can influence pupils' performances. A single observation or test result has

limited meaning and provides, at best, an approximation of a pupil's performance. Commercial achievement test publishers explicitly recognize this fact and use score bands to indicate the range of scores within which the pupil's true performance is likely to fall if tested many times. In all assessments, small differences or changes in pupils' performances should not be interpreted as real or significant. Placing Marcie in the top reading group and Jake in the middle reading group based upon a 3- or 4- point test score difference in reading performance is an overinterpretation of the assessment information.

Although informal assessments are rarely expressed numerically, they too are best treated as estimates of pupil performance. Individual assessments should always be interpreted with the above cautions in mind. The larger the sample of behavior obtained and the more varied the assessments used, the more confident a teacher can be when interpreting the information. In all cases, however, it is best to interpret assessments as if they provided an estimate of performance, not an exact indication of it.

3. *Single assessments are a poor basis for making important decisions about pupils.* Many teacher decisions can substantially affect the lives and opportunities of pupils. Consequently, such decisions should not be based on a single assessment. Also, a by-product of single-assessment decision making is the tendency to ignore additional information about pupils that might contribute to improving the validity of important decisions.

Unfortunately, in our fast-paced, bureaucratic world there is strong pressure to rely upon the results of a single assessment when making decisions. The growing use of scores from state-based tests to determine who will be promoted, receive a high school diploma, and require remedial education is one example of this pressure. Using a single score or rating seems objective and fair to people who do not understand the limitations of assessment information. Although reliance on single assessments makes decision making quicker and easier than collecting more broadly based information, it also increases the likelihood of making invalid decisions. Most teachers are sensitive to this danger and collect varied kinds of assessment information before making a grading, promotion, or placement decision about a pupil.

4. *Assessments do not always provide valid information.* Validity pertains to the interpretations that are made from assessment information. It deals with whether or not the information being collected is pertinent to the characteristics the teacher wishes to assess. Consequently, before interpreting assessment information, the classroom teacher should understand precisely what characteristic is being assessed. It is important to know this because pupils are often described in terms of the general characteristics teachers think they have assessed, not in terms of the actual behaviors that were observed. Thus, they describe a pupil as "unmotivated" as a result of receiving messy homework papers from that pupil. Or, they classify a pupil as a "poor learner" as a result of doing poorly on a classroom "achievement" test that was badly constructed and covered material not taught. Because the behavior actually observed is quickly replaced by more global labels like "unmotivated," "poor learner," "unintelligent," "self-confident," and "hard worker," it is very important that assessment information be a valid indicator of the desired pupil characteristic. Otherwise, improper interpretations and incorrect labeling will result.

5. *Assessment information describes performance; it does not explain the reasons for it.* An assessment describes pupil performance at a particular point in time: Jack was observed hitting Paul, Lisa performed poorly on the math test, Bart's oral speech was not well prepared, Ed acted out in class all day, Mary's astronomy project was the best in the class. When teachers observe pupils, they usually interpret their observations in terms of underlying causes that they use to explain what they have seen. Jack hit Paul because he is aggressive. Lisa performed poorly on the math test because she is lazy. Bart has no interest in public speaking. Ed acted out because he is a defiant, spiteful child. Mary did the best work because she is the most motivated pupil in the astronomy class. Such interpretations of pupil behavior are typical, but often they are also incorrect and incomplete.

It is rarely possible to determine with reasonable certainty why pupils performed as they did just by examining the assessment itself. In order to explain pupil performance, teachers must look beyond the immediate assessment information. Did Paul provoke Jack into hitting him? Did Paul hit Jack first? Were they just horsing around? Was Lisa up all night working on a term paper? Did her grandmother recently die? The answers to these questions are not to be found in the original assessment information; new information must be collected to answer them. Teachers must be cautious when interpreting explanations of pupil performance, because more often than not, failure to look beyond the assessment information at hand leads to incorrect interpretations about pupils and their characteristics.

This caution is especially appropriate for minority pupils who have poor English fluency, limited out-of-school opportunities, or cultural behaviors that are different from those of the majority group. When a pupil is confronted by an unfamiliar language, new situations, or expectations that are alien to his or her culture, the underlying causes of that pupil's performance may be very different from those that underlie performance among majority group pupils. Teachers must be sensitive to such differences when interpreting pupils' performances. Box 12.4 lists some specific do's and don'ts for interpreting assessment information.

⚙ Final Thoughts

Assessment is a chain of many links that imposes numerous responsibilities on teachers because it is such an integral part of what goes on in classrooms. It is not expected that teachers will always assess correctly, interpret information appropriately, and decide infallibly. However, it is expected that teachers will recognize their responsibilities in these areas and strive to carry them out as best they can. Remember, how teachers collect, interpret, and use assessment information has many important consequences for their pupils.

Box 12.4

Guidelines for Interpreting Assessment Information

- **Do** base interpretations on multiple sources of evidence.
- **Do** recognize the cultural and educational factors that influence and explain pupil performance.
- **Do** determine whether the information collected provides a valid description of pupils' characteristics.
- **Do** recognize that any single assessment provides an estimate of a pupil's present status, which can change with changes in the environment.
- **Do** consider contextual factors that might provide alternative explanations for pupil behavior or performance.
- **Don't** use assessment results to draw conclusions about a pupil's capacity or potential.
- **Don't** treat small score or rating differences as if they were meaningful and important; scores and ratings that are similar, though not identical, should be treated the same.
- **Don't** rely upon a single assessment when making a decision that has important consequences for pupils.
- **Don't** confuse information provided by an assessment with explanations of what caused the performance; explanations must be sought outside the bounds of the original assessment information.
- **Don't** uncritically assume that an assessment procedure provides valid information about the desired characteristic.

An analogy is an appropriate way to conclude. The automobile is a useful tool that enables us to accomplish a great many activities. When operated properly and with an understanding of its dangers and limitations, it saves much time and energy. However, if operated carelessly and improperly, the automobile also has the potential to inflict serious injury. When it was time for you to apply for your driver's license, your parents were apprehensive about the prospect of your driving. They knew the advantages of obtaining a license, but they also knew the dangers. They did not deny you the privilege of driving despite the dangers, but they probably explained to you both its benefits and its dangers. They also no doubt impressed on you the responsibility that accompanies being in control of an automobile. They said, "Get your license, drive, and take full advantage of the many benefits an automobile provides. But also be aware of the consequences of its misuse and of your responsibilities as a driver." The same advice is appropriate for your use of classroom assessment.

Chapter Summary

- Teacher self-assessment is concerned with the assessments teachers make about the adequacy and effectiveness of their own knowledge, performance, beliefs, or effects so that they can understand and improve their teaching.
- Teacher self-assessment represents a teacher's responsibility to examine, refine, and improve his or her teaching practice. Self-assessment focuses on classroom practice in an attempt to make teachers aware of the strengths and weaknesses of their practice.
- The majority of teacher self-assessment occurs during instruction, when teachers respond to spontaneous events by informally making decisions about their instructional performance and pupils' learning on the basis of informal observations. The fleeting nature of self-assessments made during instruction limits the usefulness of these informal self-assessments for improving teachers' practice.
- Formal teacher self-assessment occurs outside of the immediacy of practice when the teacher has time to reflect on the strengths and weaknesses of practice. Formal teacher self-assessments also examine a broader range of teacher practice than do the informal, spontaneous self-assessments that occur during teaching.
- There are eight general approaches to formal teacher self-assessment: self-assessment questionnaires, audio or video recordings, student feedback, teacher portfolios, student performance data, external or peer observation, journal writing, and joint problem solving.
- Assessment decision making is composed of three steps: collecting assessment information, interpreting assessment information, and making decisions based on the interpretations.
- There are five guidelines for interpreting assessment information: (1) assessment information describes pupils' learned behaviors and their present status; (2) assessment information provides an estimate, not an exact indication, of performance; (3) single assessments are a poor basis for making important decisions about pupils; (4) assessments do not always provide valid information; and (5) assessment information describes performance, it does not explain the reasons for it.

Questions for Discussion

1. In what ways can teacher self-assessment improve teaching? What areas of teaching do you think would be easiest to self-assess? Why?
2. What advantages do you think teacher self-assessment would have over the more typical procedure of principal observation and evaluation of a teacher's teaching?
3. What are the consequences for pupils if teachers ignore the five guidelines for interpreting assessment information? Think of at least two consequences for each principle.

Reflection Exercise

One of the guidelines for interpreting assessment information states "Assessment information describes pupils' learned behaviors and their present status." Reflect on what this principle means for interpreting pupils' performance on an assessment. If information describes only learned behaviors and present status, what reasonable interpretations can you make about high and low scorers? Are all behaviors learned? Does present status predict future status, and if so, how does that fact affect interpretations of assessment information? How would the application of these principles influence the contents of the letter you wrote to Nicole Kovitz's parent for Activity 1 in Chapter 11?

Activity

Select one of the eight self-assessment strategies described in the chapter and perform a self-assessment of some aspect of teaching. Write the strategy selected, how it was used, the aspect of teaching that you self-assessed, and what you found out about yourself. Did you identify any areas that could be improved or changed for the better?

Review Questions

1. What is teacher self-assessment and how does it help teachers improve their practice?
2. What are the differences between informal and formal teacher self-assessment? What are the advantages and disadvantages of each in helping teachers understand and improve their practice?
3. What strategies are available to carry out teacher self-assessment?
4. What three steps make up the process of assessment decision making?
5. What five guidelines are pertinent when interpreting assessment information?

References

Airasian, P. W., & Gullickson, A. R. (1994a). Examination of teacher self-assessment. *Journal of Personnel Evaluation in Education, 8,* 195–203.

Airasian, P. W., & Gullickson, A. R. (1994b). Teacher self-assessment: Potential and barriers. *Kappa Delta Pi Record, 31*(1) 6–9.

Airasian, P. W., & Gullickson, A. R. (1997). *Teacher self-evaluation tool kit.* Thousand Oaks, CA: Corwin Press.

Angelo, T. A., & Cross, K. P. (1993). *Classroom assessment techniques: A handbook for college teachers.* San Francisco: Jossey-Bass.

Arends, R. I. (2001). *Learning to teach,* 5th ed. New York: McGraw-Hill, Inc.

Elbaz, F. (1990). Knowledge and discourse: The evolution of research on teacher thinking. In C. Day, M. Pope, & P. Denicolo (eds.), *Insights into teachers' thinking and practice* (pp. 15–42). London: The Falmer Press.

Farnham-Diggory, S. (1994). Paradigms of knowledge and instruction, *Review of Educational Research, 64*(3), 463–477.

Haysom, J. (1985). Inquiring into the teaching process: Towards self-evaluation and professional development. In *Research in education series,* Volume 12. Toronto: The Ontario Institute for Studies in Education Press.

Kremer-Hayon, L. (1993). *Teacher self-evaluation: Teachers in their own mirrors.* Boston: Kluwer Academic Publishers.

McColsky, W., & Egelson, P. (1993). *Designing teacher evaluation systems that support professional growth.* Greensboro, NC: Southeastern Regional Vision for Education (SERVE).

Pollard, A., & Tann, S. (1993). *Reflective teaching in the primary school,* 2nd ed. London: Cassell Educational Limited.

Saphier, J., & Gower, R. (1987). *The skillful teacher.* Carlisle, MA: Research for Better Teaching, Inc.

Schon, D. A. (1983). *The reflective practitioner: How professionals think in action.* New York: Basic Books.

Valli, L. (1992). *Reflective teacher education: Cases and critiques.* Albany, NY: State University of New York Press.

Appendix A
Standards for Teacher Competence in Educational Assessment of Students

The professional education associations began working in 1987 to develop standards for teacher competence in student assessment out of concern that the potential educational benefits of student assessments be fully realized. The Committee[1] appointed to this project completed its work in 1990 following reviews of earlier drafts by members of the measurement, teaching, and teacher preparation and certification communities. Parallel committees of affected associations are encouraged to develop similar statements of qualifications for school administrators, counselors, testing directors, supervisors, and other educators in the near future. These statements are intended to guide the preservice and inservice preparation of educators, the accreditation of preparation programs, and the future certification of all educators.[2]

A standard is defined here as a principle generally accepted by the professional associations responsible for this document. Assessment is defined as the process of obtaining information that is used to make educational decisions about students, to give feedback to the student about his or her progress, strengths, and weaknesses, to judge instructional effectiveness and curricular adequacy, and to inform policy. The various assessment techniques include, but are not limited to, formal and informal observation, qualitative analysis of pupil performance and products, paper-and-pencil tests, oral questioning, and analysis of student records. The assessment competencies included here are the knowledge and skills critical to a teacher's role as educator. It is understood that there are many competencies beyond assessment competencies which teachers must possess.

By establishing standards for teacher competence in student assessment, the associations subscribe to the view that student assessment is an essential part of teaching and that good teaching cannot exist without good student assessment. Training to develop the competencies covered in the standards should be an integral part of preservice preparation. Further, such assessment training should be widely available to practicing teachers through staff development programs at the district and building levels.

Standards developed by the American Federation of Teachers, the National Council on Measurement in Education, and the National Education Association. Copyright © 1990 by the National Council on Measurement in Education. Reprinted by permission of the publisher.

The standards are intended for use as:

- A guide for teacher educators as they design and approve programs for teacher preparation
- A self-assessment guide for teachers in identifying their needs for professional development in student assessment
- A guide for workshop instructors as they design professional development experiences for in-service teachers
- An impetus for educational measurement specialists and teacher trainers to conceptualize student assessment and teacher training in student assessment more broadly than has been the case in the past

The standards should be incorporated into future teacher training and certification programs. Teachers who have not had the preparation these standards imply should have the opportunity and support to develop these competencies before the standards enter into the evaluation of these teachers.

Approach Used to Develop the Standards

The members of the associations that supported this work are professional educators involved in teaching, teacher education, and student assessment. Members of these associations are concerned about the inadequacy with which teachers are prepared for assessing the educational progress of their students, and thus sought to address this concern effectively. A committee named by the associations first met in September 1987 and affirmed its commitment to defining standards for teacher preparation in student assessment. The committee then undertook a review of the research literature to identify needs in student assessment, current levels of teacher training in student assessment, areas of teacher activities requiring competence in using student assessments, and current levels of teacher competence in student assessment.

The members of the committee used their collective experience and expertise to formulate and then revise statements of important assessment competencies. Drafts of these competencies went through several revisions by the committee before the standards were released for public review. Comments by reviewers from each of the associations were then used to prepare a final statement.

Scope of a Teacher's Professional Role and Responsibilities for Student Assessment

There are seven standards in this document. In recognizing the critical need to revitalize classroom assessment, some standards focus on classroom-based competencies. Because of teachers' growing roles in education and policy decisions beyond the classroom, other standards address assessment competencies underlying teacher participation in decisions related to assessment at the school, district, state, and national levels.

The scope of a teacher's professional role and responsibilities for student assessment may be described in terms of the following activities. These activities imply that teachers need competence in student assessment and sufficient time and resources to complete them in a professional manner:

- **Activities Occurring Prior to Instruction.** (a) Understanding students' cultural backgrounds, interests, skills, and abilities as they apply across a range of learning domains and/or subject areas; (b) understanding students' motivations and their interests in specific class content; (c) clarifying and articulating the performance outcomes expected of pupils; and (d) planning instruction for individuals or groups of students
- **Activities Occurring During Instruction.** (a) Monitoring pupil progress toward instructional goals; (b) identifying gains and difficulties pupils are experiencing in learning and performing; (c) adjusting instruction; (d) giving contingent, specific, and credible praise and feedback; (e) motivating students to learn; and (f) judging the extent of pupil attainment of instructional outcomes
- **Activities Occurring After the Appropriate Instructional Segment (e.g., Lesson, Class, Semester, Grade).** (a) Describing the extent to which each pupil has attained both short- and long-term instructional goals; (b) communicating strengths and weaknesses based on assessment results to students, and parents or guardians; (c) recording and reporting assessment results for school-level analysis, evaluation, and decision-making; (d) analyzing assessment information gathered before and during instruction to understand each student's progress to date and to inform future instructional planning; (e) evaluating the effectiveness of instruction; and (f) evaluating the effectiveness of the curriculum and materials in use
- **Activities Associated with a Teacher's Involvement in School Building and School District Decision-Making.** (a) Serving on a school or district committee examining the school's and district's strengths and weaknesses in the development of its students; (b) working on the development or selection of assessment methods for school building or school district use; (c) evaluating school district curriculum; and (d) other related activities
- **Activities Associated with a Teacher's Involvement in a Wider Community of Educators.** (a) Serving on a state committee asked to develop learning goals and associated assessment methods; (b) participating in reviews of the appropriateness of district, state, or national student goals and associated assessment methods; and (c) interpreting the results of state and national student assessment programs

Each standard that follows is an expectation for assessment knowledge or skill that a teacher should possess in order to perform well in the five areas just described. As a set, the standards call on teachers to demonstrate skill at selecting, developing, applying, using, communicating, and evaluating student assessment information and student assessment practices. A brief rationale and illustrative behaviors follow each standard.

The standards represent a conceptual framework or scaffolding from which specific skills can be derived. Work to make these standards operational will be needed even after they have been published. It is also expected that experience in the application of these standards should lead to their improvement and further development.

1. Teachers should be skilled in choosing assessment methods appropriate for instructional decisions. Skills in choosing appropriate, useful, administratively convenient, technically adequate, and fair assessment methods are prerequisite to good use of information to support instructional decisions. Teachers need to be well-acquainted with the kinds of information provided by a broad range of assessment alternatives and their strengths and weaknesses. In particular, they should be familiar with criteria for evaluating and selecting assessment methods in light of instructional plans.

Teachers who meet this standard will have the conceptual and application skills that follow. They will be able to use the concepts of assessment error and validity when developing or selecting their approaches to classroom assessment of students. They will understand how valid assessment data can support instructional activities such as providing appropriate feedback to students, diagnosing group and individual learning needs, planning for individualized educational programs, motivating students, and evaluating instructional procedures. They will understand how invalid information can affect instructional decisions about students. They will also be able to use and evaluate assessment options available to them, considering among other things, the cultural, social, economic, and language backgrounds of students. They will be aware that different assessment approaches can be incompatible with certain instructional goals and may impact quite differently on their teaching.

Teachers will know, for each assessment approach they use, its appropriateness for making decisions about their pupils. Moreover, teachers will know of where to find information about and/or reviews of various assessment methods. Assessment options are diverse and include text- and curriculum-embedded questions and tests, standardized criterion-referenced and norm-referenced tests, oral questioning, spontaneous and structured performance assessments, portfolios, exhibitions, demonstrations, rating scales, writing samples, paper-and-pencil tests, seatwork and homework, peer- and self-assessments, student records, observations, questionnaires, interviews, projects, products, and others' opinions.

2. Teachers should be skilled in developing assessment methods appropriate for instructional decisions. While teachers often use published or other external assessment tools, the bulk of the assessment information they use for decision-making comes from approaches they create and implement. Indeed, the assessment demands of the classroom go well beyond readily available instruments.

Teachers who meet this standard will have the conceptual and application skills that follow. Teachers will be skilled in planning the collection of information that facilitates the decisions they will make. They will know and follow appropriate principles for developing and using assessment methods in their teaching, avoiding common pitfalls in student assessment. Such techniques may include several of the options listed at the end of the first standard. The teacher will select the techniques which are appropriate to the intent of the teacher's instruction.

Teachers meeting this standard will also be skilled in using student data to analyze the quality of each assessment technique they use. Since most teachers do not have access to assessment specialists, they must be prepared to do these analyses themselves.

3. Teachers should be skilled in administering, scoring, and interpreting the results of both externally-produced and teacher-produced assessment methods. It is not enough that teachers are able to select and develop good assessment methods; they must also be able to apply them properly. Teachers should be skilled in administering, scoring, and interpreting results from diverse assessment methods.

Teachers who meet this standard will have the conceptual and application skills that follow. They will be skilled in interpreting informal and formal teacher-produced assessment results, including pupils' performances in class and on homework assignments. Teachers will be able to use guides for scoring essay questions and projects, stencils for scoring response-choice questions, and scales for rating performance assessments. They will be able to use these in ways that produce consistent results.

Teachers will be able to administer standardized achievement tests and be able to interpret the commonly reported scores: percentile ranks, percentile band scores; standard scores, and grade equivalents. They will have a conceptual understanding of the summary indexes commonly reported with assessment results: measures of central tendency, dispersion, relationships, reliability, and errors of measurement.

Teachers will be able to apply these concepts of score and summary indexes in ways that enhance their use of the assessments that they develop. They will be able to analyze assessment results to identify pupils' strengths and errors. If they get inconsistent results, they will seek other explanations for the discrepancy or other data to attempt to resolve the uncertainty before arriving at a decision. They will be able to use assessment methods in ways that encourage students' educational development and that do not inappropriately increase students' anxiety levels.

4. Teachers should be skilled in using assessment results when making decisions about individual students, planning teaching, developing curriculum, and school improvements. Assessment results are used to make educational decisions at several levels: in the classroom about students, in the community about a school and a school district, and in society, generally, about the purposes and outcomes of the educational enterprise. Teachers play a vital role when participating in decision making at each of these levels and must be able to use assessment results effectively.

Teachers who meet this standard will have the conceptual and application skills that follow. They will be able to use accumulated assessment information to organize a sound instructional plan for facilitating students' educational development. When using assessment results to plan and/or evaluate instruction and curriculum, teachers will interpret the results correctly and avoid common misinterpretations, such as basing decisions on scores that lack curriculum validity. They will be informed about the results of local, regional, state, and national assessment and about their appropriate use for pupil, classroom, school, district, state, and national educational improvement.

5. Teachers should be skilled in developing valid pupil grading procedures which use pupil assessments. Grading students is an important part of professional practice for teachers. Grading is defined as indicating both a student's level of performance and a teacher's valuing of that performance. The principles for using assessments to obtain valid grades are known and teachers should employ them.

Teachers who meet this standard will have the conceptual and application skills that follow. They will be able to devise, implement, and explain a procedure for developing grades composed of marks from various assignments, projects, in-class activities, quizzes, tests, and/or other assessments that they may use. Teachers will understand and be able to articulate why the grades they assign are rational, justified, and fair, acknowledging that such grades reflect their preferences and judgments. Teachers will be able to recognize and to avoid faulty grading procedures such as using grades as punishment. They will be able to evaluate and to modify their grading procedures in order to improve the validity of the interpretations made from them about students' attainments.

6. Teachers should be skilled in communicating assessment results to students, parents, other lay audiences, and other educators. Teachers must routinely report assessment results to students and to parents or guardians. In addition, they are frequently asked to report or to discuss assessment results with other educators and with diverse lay audiences. If the results are not communicated effectively, they may be misused or not used. To communicate effectively with others on matters of student assessment, teachers must be able to use assessment terminology appropriately and must be able to articulate the meaning, limitations, and implications of assessment results. Furthermore, teachers will sometimes be in a position that will require them to defend their own assessment procedures and their interpretations of them. At other times, teachers may need to help the public to intepret assessment results appropriately.

Teachers who meet this standard will have the conceptual and application skills that follow. Teachers will understand and be able to give appropriate explanations of how the interpretation of student assessments must be moderated by the student's socio-economic, cultural, language, and other background factors. Teachers will be able to explain that assessment results do not imply that such background factors limit a student's ultimate educational development. They will be able to communicate to students and to their parents or guardians how they may assess the student's educational progress. Teachers will understand and be able to explain the importance of taking measurement errors into account when using assessments to make decisions about individual students. Teachers will be able to explain the limitations of different informal and formal assessment methods. They will be able to explain printed reports of the results of pupil assessments at the classroom, school district, state, and national levels.

7. Teachers should be skilled in recognizing unethical, illegal, and otherwise inappropriate assessment methods and uses of assessment information. Fairness, the rights of all concerned, and professional ethical behavior must undergird all student assessment activities, from the initial planning for and gathering of information to the interpretation, use, and communication of the results. Teachers must be well-versed in their own ethical and legal responsibilities in assessment. In addition, they should also attempt to have the inappropriate assessment practices of others discontinued whenever they are encountered. Teachers should also participate with the wider educational community in defining the limits of appropriate professional behavior in assessment.

Teachers who meet this standard will have the conceptual and application skills that follow. They will know those laws and case decisions which affect their classroom, school district, and state assessment practices. Teachers will be aware that various assessment procedures can be misused or overused resulting in harmful consequences such as embarassing students, violating a student's right to confidentiality, and inappropriately using students' standardized achievement test scores to measure teaching effectiveness.

Notes

[1]The Committee that developed this statement was appointed by the collaborating professional associations. James R. Sanders (Western Michigan University) chaired the Committee and represented NCME along with John R. Hills (Florida State University) and Anthony J. Nitko (University of Pittsburgh). Jack C. Merwin (University of Minnesota) represented the American Association of Colleges for Teacher Education, Carolyn Trice represented the American Federation of Teachers, and Marcella Dianda and Jeffrey Schneider represented the National Education Association.

[2]The associations invite comments that may be used for improvement of this document. Comments may be sent to: Teacher Standards in Student Assessment, American Federation of Teachers, 555 New Jersey Avenue, NW, Washington, DC 20001; Teacher Standards in Student Assessment, National Council on Measurement in Education, 1230 Seventeenth Street, NW, Washington, DC 20036; or Teacher Standards in Student Assessment, Instruction and Professional Development, National Education Association, 1201 Sixteenth Street, NW, Washington, DC 20036.

Please note that this document is not copyrighted material and that reproduction and dissemination are encouraged.

Appendix B
Statistical Applications for Classroom Assessment

This appendix describes some of the basic statistical information classroom teachers can use in scoring and interpreting their pupils' test performance. It contains a basic introduction to four areas: (1) raw scores and score distributions, (2) the mean and standard deviation, (3) item difficulty and discrimination, and (4) the normal distribution and standardized test scores.

Raw Scores and Score Distributions

A raw score indicates the number of points a pupil got on a test. For example, Joe took a 70-item multiple-choice test and got 42 items correct. If 1 point is given for each correct answer, his raw score is 42. Jemma took a 20-item short-answer test on which each item counted 5 points. She got 17 items correct and thus received a raw score of 85 (17 items × 5 points each). Most frequently, raw scores are converted to percentage scores using the formula: raw score/highest possible score × 100 = percentage score. Thus Joe's percentage score is 60 (42/70 × 100 = 60), and Jemma's percentage score is 85 (85/100 × 100 = 85).

Either raw or percentage scores can be arranged into a **test score distribution** that shows how the class as a whole performed. The raw and percentage scores for a class of 15 pupils who took a math test that had 10 problems worth 5 points each appear in Table B.1.

The performance of this class can be represented by a test score distribution by listing scores from highest to lowest. Test score distributions can be based on either raw scores or percentage scores. To construct a distribution, start by listing the possible scores pupils could have earned. For example, the class above took a 10-item test on which each item counted 5 points. Thus, the only raw scores possible ranged from 50 to 0 in 5-point increments (that is, 50, 45, 40, 35, . . . , 15, 10, 5, 0). Similarly, since percentage scores are based on a 100-point scale, the only percentage scores possible on the 10-item test ranged from 100 to 0 in 10-point increments (that is, 100, 90, 80, . . . , 20, 10, 0). The test score distributions in Table B.2 show how the class did. "Number" indicates the number of pupils who got a particular score; for example, three pupils got a raw score of 50, four got 40, and none got 10.

The two test score distributions show the same information on two different scales. The raw score scale is based on the total number of points on the test, 50, while the percentage score scale is based on a test of 100 total

TABLE B.1

Name	Raw Score (Number Right × 5)	Percentage Score (Raw Score/50 × 100)
Lloyd	25	50
Chris	35	70
Jennifer	50	100
Kristen	40	80
Gail	25	50
Marta	35	70
Marita	40	80
David	40	80
Juan	45	90
Mike	20	40
Ted	30	60
Charles	50	100
Christina	35	70
Heather	40	80
Sara	50	100

TABLE B.2

Raw Score Distribution		Percentage Score Distribution	
Raw Score	Number	Percentage Score	Number
50	3	100	3
45	1	90	1
40	4	80	4
35	3	70	3
30	1	60	1
25	2	50	2
20	1	40	1
15	0	30	0
10	0	20	0
5	0	10	0
0	0	0	0

points. Teachers often transform the raw score distribution into a percentage score distribution to keep all of their tests on a 100-point scale. Recall from Chapter 10 that Ms. Fogarty did this with her tests and quiz scores so there would be comparability across the different tests and quizzes.

Notice also that the above example is intended to be mathematically simple to convey the basic ideas of test score distributions. For practice, redo this example assuming that the pupils' raw scores remained the same but that the test had 12 items worth 5 points each.

TABLE B.3		
Name	**Raw Score**	**Percentage Score**
Lloyd	25	50
Chris	35	70
Jennifer	50	100
Kristen	40	80
Gail	25	50
Marta	35	70
Marita	40	80
David	40	80
Juan	45	90
Mike	20	40
Ted	30	60
Charles	50	100
Christina	35	70
Heather	40	80
Sara	50	100
Sum of scores	560	1120

Summarizing Test Scores

The Mean

Test score distributions are useful, but often teachers want to summarize the information they provide into a single score that represents the performance of the class. There are many ways to summarize scores, but the most common is the **mean.** The mean, also commonly called the **average,** is calculated by adding together each pupil's test score and dividing the total by the number of pupils. One can calculate the mean of either raw scores or percentage scores.

The original raw and percentage scores for our hypothetical class appear in Table B.3. The sums of the raw and percentage scores are shown at the bottom of the table. If these sums are divided by the total number of pupils, 15, the raw and percentage score means are 37.33 and 74.67, respectively. These means provide a single-number description of the class's performance. The mean raw score for the class is 37.33 out of 50, and the mean percentage score is 74.67 out of 100.

Two additional, though less frequently used, indices of a class's average performance are the median and the mode. The **median** is the middle score in the test score distribution, after the scores have been arranged in order from highest to lowest. The **mode** is the score that more pupils got than any other. Medians and modes are best determined after constructing a test score distribution. For example, consider the score distribution in Table B.4.

The median is the middle score in the distribution. Because there are 15 pupils who took the test, the middle score is the eighth from the top.

TABLE B.4

Raw Score	Number
50	3
45	1
40	4
35	3
30	1
25	2
20	1
15	0
10	0
5	0
0	0

Three pupils had raw scores of 50, 1 had a raw score of 45, and 4 had a score of 40. Thus, the eighth score from the top is a 40, and this is the median. Note that if there is an even number of scores in the distribution, the median would be determined by taking the average of the two middle scores. The mode is the score (or scores, as there can be more than one mode) that more pupils received than any other. The distribution shows that the score more pupils got than any other was 40, so the mode is 40. In this case, the median and the mode were the same, although this is not always the case.

The Standard Deviation

Suppose that two classes were tested with the same test and that the mean score in each class was 74. Could we conclude that performance in the two classes was identical? No, we could not, because the mean does not tell us how the two classes' scores are distributed from high to low. Table B.5 compares the scores of pupils in two classes, each of which has a mean of 74. Construct two score distributions to compare the classes. Would you say that the performance in the two classes was identical?

Comparing the performance of the two classes indicates that the pupils in class A performed much more alike than the pupils in class B. The **range,** or the difference between the highest and lowest score, was 6 (77–71) in class A and 48 (98–50) in class B. In other words, pupils in class A were much more similar, or homogeneous, in their performance than were pupils in class B, who were quite heterogeneous. The mean score for each class B, who were quite heterogeneous. The mean score for each class, though the same, does not indicate how similar or dissimilar the scores within the classes were. Note how a sense of the spread of scores could be obtained by examining the score distribution for each class.

Pupil	Class A	Class B
TABLE B.5		
1	72	74
2	76	64
3	74	84
4	75	50
5	73	98
6	74	60
7	77	88
8	71	59
9	72	89
10	76	74
Sum	740	740
Mean	74	74

When we describe a test score distribution, we also must consider the extent to which the scores are spread out around the mean. To find out about this characteristic of scores, we use another statistic called the **standard deviation.** The standard deviation provides information about score variability—that is, how similar or dissimilar a class's test scores are. Usually, test scores are described by both their mean and standard deviation. The mean tells about the average performance of a class, and the standard deviation tells about how homogeneous or heterogeneous scores were within the class.

Mathematically, the standard deviation is represented as

$$\text{Standard deviation} = \sqrt{\frac{\text{sum of } (x^2)}{n}}$$

where x is the difference of a pupil's score from the mean (score minus the mean) and n is the number of pupils who were tested. Calculating the standard deviation for class A's scores would be done as shown in Table B.6, given that the mean score for class A was 74. Adding up the squared difference of each pupil's score from the mean equals 36. Thus, according to the formula, the standard deviation of the scores in class A is equal to the square root of 36 divided by 10 (the number of pupils who were tested), or 3.6. The square root of 3.6 is equal to 1.89, which is the standard deviation for class A. Calculate for yourself the standard deviation for class B, which also has a mean of 74. You should get a standard deviation of 14.81 [square root of (2194/10) = 14.81]. Notice that the larger the standard deviation, the more spread out the scores are around the mean. Although class A and class B had the same mean score, the standard deviation of class B was much larger than that of class A, indicating greater heterogeneity in class B.

TABLE B.6

Pupil	Class A	(Pupil's Score – Mean Score)^2
1	72	$(72-74)^2 = 4$
2	76	$(76-74)^2 = 4$
3	74	$(74-74)^2 = 0$
4	75	$(75-74)^2 = 1$
5	73	$(73-74)^2 = 1$
6	74	$(74-74)^2 = 0$
7	77	$(77-74)^2 = 9$
8	71	$(71-74)^2 = 9$
9	72	$(72-74)^2 = 4$
10	76	$(76-74)^2 = 4$

Item Difficulty and Discrimination

The **difficulty** of a test item is indicated by the percentage of pupils who got the item correct. Thus, if 20 out of 25 pupils in a class answered an item correctly, the difficulty of that item would be $(20/25) \times 100 = 80$ percent. Clearly, the higher the difficulty, the easier the item.

The difficulty of test items is related to the spread of test scores. If all items on a test are very easy, most pupils will get high scores and there will be few differences among pupils. The same is true if all the test items are very difficult, except that all pupils will get low scores. When the difficulty of test items is around 50 percent, meaning that about half the pupils pass and half fail each item, the resulting test scores will be maximally spread out from low to high. This is an important result for the construction of commercial standardized norm-referenced tests, which are intended to compare the relative achievement of pupils. The more pupils' scores differ, the better for making comparisons and distinctions among them. Thus, in standardized norm-referenced test construction, it is necessary to have items that have difficulties in the middle (35 to 65 percent) range to ensure a spread of scores.

In classroom assessment, which is generally *criterion-referenced* and focuses on individual pupil mastery (not differentiation among pupils), item difficulty is not a major concern. Classroom assessment items usually have higher difficulties (that is, are easier) than standardized, norm-referenced test items. This would be expected as long as classroom tests reflect classroom instruction.

Item **discrimination** compares the difference in performance of high and low test scores on an item. An item is said to have *positive discrimination* if more pupils who do well on the test as a whole answer it correctly than pupils who do poorly on the test as a whole. Thus, if 85 percent of the class with the highest overall test scores got an item correct compared to only 55 percent of those with the lowest overall test scores, the item discrimination would be 85 percent – 55 percent = 30 percent. In determining item discrimination, the lower group's percentage is always subtracted from the higher group's. The higher the discrimination, the greater the difference between the high and low test scorers on that item. Notice that it is possible to get *negative discriminations*. For example, if 40 percent of the top scorers and 60 percent of the bottom scorers got the item correct, the discrimination index would be 40 percent – 60 percent = – 20 percent. In such a case, one might want to check the scoring key or look at the options in the item to try to identify the ones that the top group is selecting incorrectly.

Item discrimination, like item difficulty, is important in the construction of commercial standardized tests. It is necessary that each item in such tests have high positive discrimination. While it is also desirable for classroom tests to have items with positive discrimination, it is less important than for commercial tests because classroom tests are usually scored in a criterion-referenced way and their higher item difficulties reduce the differences between high and low scorers.

Normal Distributions

The *normal distribution* is the familiar "bell-shaped" curve shown in Figure B.1. This curve is quite important in commercial standardized achievement testing because norms such as the percentile rank and stanine are derived from it.

The distribution shows the test scores of a large group of pupils who took a standardized test. Along the bottom of the curve are the possible scores on the test, with the lowest possible score at the far left and the highest possible score at the far right. Other possible scores are arranged, in order, between these two extremes. The height of the distribution at any given point represents the number of pupils who got the score that corresponds to that point. Notice that the distribution is highest in the middle and lowest at the two ends, indicating that most test takers score near the middle and very few score at either end.

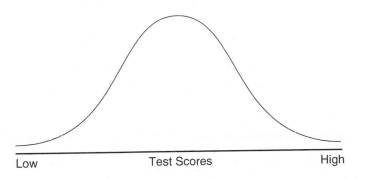

FIGURE B.1   *The Normal Distribution*

The normal distribution has three important properties:

- The mean score is exactly in the middle of the distribution, and half of all scores fall above it and half below it.
- The median and mode scores are the same as the mean.
- The standard deviation divides the normal distribution into sections as follows:

    1. Sixty-eight percent of all the pupils' scores fall between 1 standard deviation below the mean and 1 standard deviation above the mean.
    2. Ninety-five percent of all the pupils' scores fall between 2 standard deviations below the mean and 2 standard deviations above the mean.
    3. Almost 100 percent of all the pupils' scores fall between 3 standard deviations below the mean and 3 standard deviations above the mean.

The following example provides a concrete illustration of these properties and how they are used in obtaining norm-referenced scores on standardized achievement tests. Assume you are a standardized test constructor who has produced a 30-item norm-referenced mathematics computation test for seventh graders. To do this, you followed the steps described in Chapter 11: select common objectives, write items to assess these objectives, and try the items out on many seventh graders to identify the items with moderate difficulties and high discriminations to include on the final test version. You have identified the 30 items for your test and have but one additional step to complete: administering the test to a representative sample of 10,000 seventh graders from across the country in order to develop test norms. These norms will be the comparative scores that will be used to interpret future test takers' performance.

You administer the test to the 10,000 seventh graders who are meant to represent all seventh graders across the country, and you score each pupil's test. You now have 10,000 scores. Because you selected items of moderate difficulty and high discrimination and because you tried out the final version of the test on a large number of seventh graders, the distribution of scores on your test will be similar to the normal curve; many pupils will score near the middle of the score range and few will score very low or very high. Because 10,000 individual scores is a large number to deal with, you decide to summarize them by calculating the mean and standard deviation, using the procedures described previously. Let's assume that when your computer finishes these calculations on the math computation test scores, the mean score is 13 and the standard deviation is 3. You have a normal distribution with a mean score of 13 and a standard deviation of 3. This distribution is shown in Figure B.2.

Notice that the score of 13, which is the mean score for the group, is at the center of the distribution. Note also how the standard deviation has been used to mark off other score points on the distribution. The scores that correspond to 1 standard deviation below the mean, 10 (13 − 3 = 10), and to 1 standard deviation above the mean, 16 (13 + 3 = 16), are shown, along

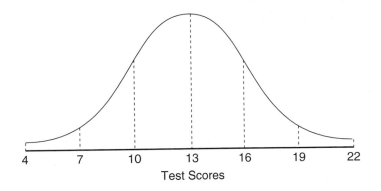

FIGURE B.2   *Normal Distribution with Mean of 13 and Standard Deviation of 3.*

with the scores corresponding to 2 standard deviations below (13 − 6 = 7) and above (13 + 6 = 19) the mean and 3 standard deviations below (13 − 9 = 4) and above (13 + 9 = 22) the mean.

Suppose a pupil got a raw score of 13 items correct on your test. What percent of the 10,000 pupils who represent all seventh graders did she perform better than? If her score was 13, she was exactly at the mean of the norm group and, according to the first property of the normal curve, the mean divides the normal curve into two equal halves. Thus, she performed better than 50 percent of seventh graders in the norm group. Notice how using the normal curve allows one to turn a raw score (13) into a percentile rank (50th) (see Chapter 11).

Suppose another pupil had a raw score of 16 items correct. What is that pupil's percentile rank? To determine this, it is necessary to remember that 68 percent of all the pupils are between the score corresponding to the mean minus 1 standard deviation (10) and the score corresponding to the mean plus 1 standard deviation (16). Because the mean (13) divides the normal curve in half, 34 percent of the students are between the mean (13) and 1 standard deviation below the mean (10), and 34 percent are between the mean (13) and 1 standard deviation above the mean (16). So, if a pupil had a score of 16, she was higher than all the 50 percent of pupils who were below the mean and also higher than the 34 percent who were between the mean (13) and 1 standard deviation above the mean (16). Thus, a raw score of 16 on the math computation test corresponds to a percentile rank of 84 (50 + 34 = 84). The pupil scored higher on the test than 84 percent of the norm group. Now see if you can find the percentile rank that corresponds to a raw score of 10 and a raw score of 19.

The above example was designed to illustrate how the normal curve can be used to change raw scores into the comparative scores that are used to give meaning to standardized norm-referenced test performance. The example did not indicate how to change scores that are not exactly 1, 2, or 3 standard deviations above or below the mean into percentile ranks. Most introductory statistics books provide examples of how to do this, and you should refer to one if you wish further information.

Appendix C
Websites

American Federation of Teachers
http://www.aft.org

This site provides the latest AFT union information, conference information, policy briefs and other publications, and news and information for K–12 teachers, public employees, higher education staff, nurses and health professionals, and paraprofessionals and school-related personnel.

Argus Clearinghouse
http://www.clearinghouse.net

This site includes and extensive research library. The education category contains guides on topics pertaining to the development of knowledge, skill, ability, or character by systematic instruction and schooling.

Ask ERIC
http://ericir.syr.edu/

This site contains an ERIC question and answer service, links to the ERIC Virtual Library and the ERIC database, and information on new and noteworthy contributions to the ERIC database.

Berliner/Biddle Study
http://olam.ed.asu.edu/epaa

Volume 4 of the online scholarly journals *Educational Policy Analysis Archives* contains a full-text review of Berliner and Biddle's book, *The Manufactured Crisis,* as well as a reply to this review by Berliner and Biddle themselves.

Children's Defense Fund
http://www.childrensdefense.org

This site contains news and reports, job information, Internet links, and other publications related to the Children's Defense Fund's mission of ensuring every child a healthy start, a head start, a fair start, a safe start, and a moral start in life and a successful passage to adulthood.

Creating Lesson Plans
http://www.ericsp.org

This site of the ERIC clearinghouse on teaching and teacher education contains an extensive collection of lesson plans for every subject, ideas to help manage and access information for the classroom, and extensive K–12 educational resources. The site includes professional resources, teacher education, digests and publications, and information about becoming a teacher.

CRESST
http://cresst96.cse.ucla.edu/index.htm

The site of the National Center for Research on Evaluation, Standards, and Student Testing (CRESST), which conducts research on important topics related to K–12 educational testing, contains and online library with full-text reports and newsletters, assessment samples, guidebooks, and databases, and a listserve for discussion on relevant topics.

CSTEEP
http://www.csteep.bc.edu/ctest

The Center for the Study of Testing, Evaluation, and Educational Policy (CSTEEP) is an educational research organization with the goals of conducting research on testing and evaluation and public policy studies to improve school assessment practices. The CSTEEP site contains information on current CSTEEP projects and links to useful education sites on the Internet.

Developing Educational Standards
http://www.putwest.boces.org/standards.html#section2

This site contains links to full-text versions of standards by state and subject area, as well as U.S. government standards and standards from other nations. It also provides links to centers, clearinghouse, labs, state-focused groups, newspapers, magazines, and other organizations that deal with or focus on standards.

Education World
http://www.education-world.com

This site is practical and informative resource for teachers that includes suggestions for lesson planning, curriculum guides, related books, articles, and reviews of other Internet resources. The site ranking system is a unique feature that facilitates Internet searches.

Eric Clearinghouse on Assessment
http://ericae.net/

The Eric Clearinghouse on Assessment seeks to provide balanced information concerning educational assessment and resources to encourage responsible test use. It contains links to numerous assessment and evaluation sites on the Internet, as well as full online assessment articles and digests and a test collection database with records on over 10,000 tests and research instruments covering a wide range of subjects and fields.

Eric Clearinghouse on Urban Education
http://eric-web.tc.columbia.edu/

This clearinghouse contains digests, bibliographies, parent guides, abstracts, and other publications on such subjects as equity and cultural diversity, urban teachers, curriculum and instruction, compensatory education, administration and finance, and other subjects that are of interest in urban education. It also contains links to other urban education resources on the Web and to historically black colleges and universities, as well as links to the entire ERIC database.

International Reading Association
http://www.reading.org

This site provides information related to the International Reading Association: conferences, publications, projects, research, and news, as well as an online bookstore and an online membership directory.

Kathy Schrock's Guide for Educators
http://school.discovery.com/schrockguide

This site contains a categorized list of Internet sites found to be useful for enhancing curriculum and teacher professional growth. The site also contains numerous links to subject-related lesson plans, bulletin boards, and a forum for interactive discussion with other educators.

Massachusetts Department of Education
http://www.doe.mass.edu

This website contains information for administrators, teachers, students, parents, and communities regarding the Massachusetts curriculum frameworks, state tests, teacher certification, school reform, educational technology, and more.

National Alliance for Safe Schools
http://www.safeschools.org

Dedicated to the promotion of an orderly educational environment, this site contains NASS news and publications, information on NASS workshops, school security assessments, and links to related sites on the Web.

National Association of Test Directors
http://www.natd.org

The NATD website contains full-text symposium papers, news about the national achievement tests and other issues, and links to Internet assessment and evaluation resources, including general K–12 assessment resources, curriculum standards, the regional education laboratory network, U.S. government resources, professional organizations related to assessment and evaluation, and grant-seeker information available on the Internet.

National Board of Professional Teaching Standards
http://www.nbpts.org

The National Board of Professional Teaching Standards is working to strengthen the teaching profession and to improve student learning in America's schools. The site provides detailed information for educators who are interested in National Board Certification and a discussion forum for teacher candidates.

National Center for Education Statistics
http://nces.ed.gov/pubs98/violence/index.html

This site contains the full research report, "Violence and Discipline Problems in US Public Schools: 1996–97," which was published in March 1998 by the National Center for Education Statistics. The report can be downloaded or viewed as a PDF file.

National Council for Social Studies
http://www.ncss.org

This site contains information of interest to social studies teachers, including the NCSS annual conference and membership information, social studies journals and publications, teaching resources, news for educators, and information about standards and curriculum, as well as Internet links to resources, discussion groups, a bookstore, and local and state organizations.

National Council for Teachers of English
http://www.ncte.org

This site contains useful resources on teaching ideas, teacher talk, standards, public policy, professional development, teacher preparation, journals, grants and awards, jobs, research, NCTE meetings and membership, and various NCTA organizations.

National Council for Teachers of Mathematics
http://www.nctm.org

This site provides information about NCTM membership and meetings, full-text articles and abstracts of articles in NCTM publications, a fax-on-demand service, means for ordering NCTM products, full-text NCTM principles and standards, and online classified job listings and math announcements.

The National Education Association
http://www.nea.org

This site provides the most current NEA information. It includes a variety of articles about current issues in education. The site also contains numerous links to articles and resources concerning education, students, teachers, schools and parents.

National School Safety Center
http://www.nssc1.org

This site presents information related to research on school crime and violence, as well as NSSC services, training programs, school safety studies, resources for parents, and links to other resources.

PBS TeacherSource
http://www.pbs.org/teachersource/

This site provides curriculum materials, recommendations for books, links to other sites, and instructional suggestions for PBS programming and educational services. The site is organized according to content areas.

Study Web
http://www.studyweb.com

The Study Web is a very practical and easily manipulated site that facilitates research on a variety of content-related topics for educators and students. The site contains teaching resources, lesson plans, curriculum ideas, and grade-level appropriate search categories.

in the form of lesson
ɔr discussion groups,

ɔnt information; a
n of performance.

:o inexperienced teach-
,ɔlogy. *Teachers Helping*
to classroom resources.
ducators and even tips

ɔrformance criteria
tivity or product on
ɔupil's performance
that has only two

related to intellectual
ng, memorizing,
d applying.
    Typically a norm-
pupil's score to a
ɔ.

This innovative site is a
m management, organi-
year activities.

ɔledge that
general concepts.
ion that has one

Determining the
ɔ by comparing it to
ɔtery.
ɔances, attitudes,
ɔ learn from
f desired pupil
als, and the
ɔd to teach

ɔnal issues, as well as the
ɔ on education and links
ducational resources. It is
ɔration's education priori-
ɔrtment of Education pro-

ɔre used to
ɔrmance, given

ɔn of online resources made
to facilitate projects, create
ɔformation that encourages
ɔ, promotes professional de-
ɔies.

ɔes what percent of
ɔers answered

ɔroportion of pupils
ɔy.

Glossary

A

Ability   What one has learned over a period of time from both school and nonschool sources; one's general capability for performing tasks.

Achievement   What one has learned from formal instruction, usually in school.

Affective domain   Behaviors related to feelings, emotions, values, attitudes, interests, and personality; nonintellectual behaviors.

Analytic scoring   Essay scoring method in which separate scores are given for specific aspects of the essay (e.g., organization, factual accuracy, and spelling).

Anecdotal record   A short, written report of an individual's behavior in a specific situation or circumstance.

Aptitude   One's capability for performing a particular task or skill; usually involves a narrower skill than ability (e.g., mathematics aptitude or foreign language aptitude).

Assessment   The process of collecting, synthesizing, and interpreting information to aid classroom decision making; includes information gathered about pupils, instruction, and classroom climate.

Average   The number derived by adding up all the test scores and dividing the total by the number of pupils who took the test.

B

Benchmark   A stated level of performance or standard that indicates what pupils should be able to achieve at a given grade level used for comparing pupil performance.

Bias   A situation in which assessment information produces results that give one group an advantage or disadvantage over other groups because of problems in the content, procedures, or interpretations of the assessm[...] distortion or misrepresentatic[...]

C

Checklist   A written list of p[...] associated with a particular ac[...] which an observer marks the [...] on each criterion using a scale[...] choices.

Cognitive domain   Behavior[...] processes like thinking, reason[...] problem solving, analyzing, ar[...]

Commercial achievement test[...] referenced test that compares a[...] national group of similar pupi[...]

Conceptual knowledge   Kno[...] demonstrates understanding o[...]

Convergent question   A ques[...] correct answer.

Criterion-referenced grading[...] quality of a pupil's performanc[...] preestablished standards of ma[...]

Curriculum   The skills, perfor[...] and values pupils are expected[...] schooling; includes statements[...] outcomes, descriptions of mater[...] planned sequence that will be u[...] pupils.

Cut score   A predetermined sc[...] differentiate levels of pupil perf[...] usually in statewide assessment[...]

D

Difficulty   An index that descr[...] a test item that a group of test ta[...] correctly.

Difficulty index   Indicates the [...] who answered a test item correc[...]

Direct indicators   Information or perspectives provided by a firsthand observer or source.

Discrimination index   Indicates the extent to which pupils who get a particular test item correct are also likely to get a high score on the entire test.

Distractor   A wrong choice in a selection test item.

Divergent question   A question that has more than one acceptable answer.

E

Educate   To change the behavior of pupils; to teach pupils to do things they could not previously do.

Educational objectives   Statements that describe a pupil accomplishment that will result from instruction—specifically, the behavior the pupil will learn to perform and the content on which it will be performed.

Evaluation   Judging the quality or goodness of a performance or a course of action.

F

Factual knowledge   Knowledge based on remembering or recalling information.

Form   The particular version of a commercial test that has more than one equivalent version.

Formative assessment   The process of collecting, synthesizing, and interpreting information for the purpose of improving student learning while instruction is taking place; assessment for improvement, not grading.

G

Global objectives   Very broad statements of intended learning that require years to accomplish.

Grade equivalent score   A standardized test score that describes a pupil's performance on a scale based upon grade in school and month in grade; most commonly misinterpreted score; indicates pupil's level of performance relative to pupils in his/her own grade.

Grades   Symbols or numbers used by teachers to represent a pupil's achievement in a subject area.

Grading   The process of judging the quality of a pupil's performance.

Grading curve   The proportion of pupils who can receive each grade in a norm-referenced grading system.

Grading system   The process by which a teacher arrives at the symbol or number that is used to represent a pupil's achievement in a subject area.

Group administered assessments   Tests or assessments taken by more than a single pupil.

H

Holistic scoring   Essay scoring method in which a single score is given to represent the overall quality of the essay across all dimensions.

I

Indirect indicators   Information or perspectives provided by a secondhand observer or source.

Individually administered assessments   Tests or assessments taken by one pupil at a time.

Individual Education Program (IEP)   A special education plan developed for a pupil after extensive assessment of the pupil's special educational needs.

Instruction   The methods and processes by which pupils' behaviors are changed.

Instructional assessment   The collection, synthesis, and interpretation of information needed to make decisions about planning or carrying out instruction.

Instructional objectives   Specific objectives used to plan daily lessons.

Interpretive exercise   A test situation that contains a chart, passage, poem, or other material that the pupil must interpret in order to answer the questions posed.

Items   Questions or problems on an assessment instrument.

K

Key   A list of correct answers for a test.

L

Level   The grade level(s) at which a particular commercial test should be administered to pupils.

Levels of tolerance   The extent to which a teacher can tolerate different noise levels, activities, and pupil behavior.

Local norms   Norms that are confined to pupils in a specific school district.

Logical error   The use of invalid or irrelevant assessment information to judge a pupil's status or performance.

M

Mean   The average of a group of scores.

Measurement   The process of assigning numbers or categories to performance according to rules and standards (e.g., scoring a test).

Measurement   The process of quantifying or assigning numbers or categories to performance according to rules and standards.

Median   The middle score of when all scores are listed from lowest to highest.

Mode   The score that is obtained by more pupils in a group than any other; there can be more than one mode in group of scores.

N

Negative discrimination   When a test item is answered incorrectly more frequently for high scorers on the test than for low scorers; the item discriminates in a different direction than the total score of the test.

Nonstandardized assessment   An assessment approach intended to assess a single group of pupils, such as a class.

Normal curve   The symmetrical bell-shaped curve.

Norm group   The group of pupils who were tested to produce the norms for a test.

Norm-referenced grading   Determining the quality of a pupil's performance by comparing it to the performance of other pupils.

Norms   A set of scores that describes the performance of a specific group of pupils, usually a national sample at a particular grade level, on a task or test; these scores are used to interpret scores of other pupils who perform the same task or take the same test.

Numerical summarization   Use of numbers to describe performance on an assessment.

O

Objective   Agreement among independent judges, scorers, or observers.

Official assessments   Assessments, such as grading, grouping, placing, and promoting pupils, that teachers are required to carry out because of their official responsibilities.

Options   Choices available to select from when answering a multiple-choice test item.

P

Percentile bands   The range of percentile ranks in which a pupil is expected to fall on repeated testing; a way to indicate the error in scores to avoid overinterpretation of results.

Percentile rank   A standardized test score that describes the percentage of pupils a given pupil scored higher than (e.g., an 89th percentile rank means that a pupil scored higher than 89 percent of the pupils in the norm group).

Performance assessment   Observing and judging a pupil's skill in actually carrying out a physical activity (e.g., giving a speech) or producing a product (e.g., building a birdhouse).

Performance criteria   The aspects of a performance or product that are observed and judged in performance assessment.

Performance standards   The levels of achievement pupils must reach to receive particular grades in a criterion-referenced grading system (e.g., higher than 90 receives an A, between 80 and 90 receives a B, etc.).

Portfolio   A well-defined collection of pupil products or performances that shows pupil achievement of particular skills over time.

Positive discrimination   When a test item is answered correctly more frequently for high scorers on the test than for low scorers; the item discriminates in the same direction of the total score of the test.

Percentage score   A pupil's test or assessment score expressed as a percentage.

Practical knowledge   The beliefs, prior experiences, and strategies that enable a teacher to carry out classroom duties and activities.

Premise   The stem or question part of a matching item.

Procedural knowledge   Knowledge that demonstrates application of multistage processes.

Psychomotor domain   Physical and manipulative activities such as holding a pencil, buttoning buttons, serving a tennis ball, playing the piano, and cutting with scissors.

R

Range   The difference between the highest and lowest test scores in a group; obtained by subtracting the highest test score from the lowest test score.

Rating scale   A written list of performance criteria associated with a particular activity or product on which an observer marks a pupil's performance on each criterion in terms of its quality using a scale that has more than two choices.

Raw score   The number of items correct or the total score a pupil obtained on an assessment.

Reliability   The extent to which an assessment consistently assesses whatever it is assessing; if an assessment is reliable, it will yield the same or nearly the same information on retesting.

Response   The answer choices given for a matching item.

S

Scoring rubric   A rating scale based upon written descriptions of varied levels of achievement in a performance assessment; also called a descriptive rating scale.

Selection item   A test item to which the pupil responds by selecting the answer from choices given; multiple-choice, true-false, and matching items.

Self-fulfilling prophecy   The process in which teachers form perceptions about pupil characteristics, treat pupils as if the perceptions are correct, and pupils respond as if they actually have the characteristics, even though they might not have originally had them; an expectation becomes a reality.

Sizing-up assessments   Assessments used by teachers in the first weeks of school to get to know pupils so that they can be organized into a classroom society with rules, communication, and control.

Specific determiners   Words that give clues to true-false items; *all, always, never,* and *none* indicate false statements, while *some, sometimes,* and *may* indicate true statements.

Standard deviation   A measure of the variability or spread of scores for a group of test takers.

Standardized assessment   An assessment that is administered, scored, and interpreted the same for all pupils taking the test, no matter when and where it is used.

Standards   Statements of what pupils are to know or carry out, usually stated and assessed by a state or district.

Stanine   A standardized test score that describes pupil performance on a 9-point scale. Scores of 1, 2, and 3 are often interpreted as being below average; 4, 5, and 6 as being average; and 7, 8, and 9 as being above average.

Stem   The part of a multiple-choice item that states the question to be answered.

Stereotyping   The act of making a societal generalization about a particular social group (e.g., "Males do better in math than females" "Athletes do poorly in school" or "Asians excel in science").

Subjective   Lack of agreement among judges, scorers, or observers.

Subtests   Sets of items administered and scored as a separate portion of a longer, more comprehensive test.

Summative assessment   The process of collecting, synthesizing, and interpreting information for the purposes of determining pupil learning and assigning grades; assessments made at the end of instruction or teaching.

Supply item   A test item to which the pupil responds by writing or constructing his/her own answer; short answer, completion, essay.

T

Teacher self-assessment   The process of making decisions about one's own teaching performance based on evidence and reflection.

Test   A formal, systematic procedure for obtaining a sample of pupils' behavior; the results of a test are used to make generalizations about how pupils would perform on similar but untested behaviors.

Test battery   A group of subtests, each assessing a different subject area but all normed on the same sample; designed to be administered to the same group of test takers.

Test score distribution   The listing of test scores from lowest to highest; the spread of pupils' scores.

Testwise skills   The test taker's ability to identify flaws in test questions that give away the correct answers; used during tests to outwit poor item writers.

V

Validity   The extent to which assessment information is appropriate for making the desired decision about pupils, instruction, or classroom climate; the degree to which assessment information permits correct interpretations of the desired kind; the most important characteristic of assessment information.

Name Index

Subject Index